A RETURN TO AESTHETICS

Fountain by R. Mutt   Photograph by Alfred Stieglitz

THE EXHIBIT REFUSED BY THE INDEPENDENTS

A RETURN TO AESTHETICS

Autonomy, Indifference, and Postmodernism

Jonathan Loesberg

STANFORD UNIVERSITY PRESS

STANFORD, CALIFORNIA

2005

Stanford University Press
Stanford, California

Frontis image: Marcel Duchamp, *Fountain;* photographed by Alfred Stieglitz and
reproduced in the Blind Man, No. 2, May 1917. Used by permission of the
Philadelphia Museum of Art, The Louise and Walter Arensberg Collection, 1950.

Printed in the United States of America on acid-free, archival-quality paper

Library of Congress Cataloging-in-Publication Data

Loesberg, Jonathan, 1950–
    A return to aesthetics : autonomy, indifference, and postmodernism / Jonathan
Loesberg.
        p.   cm.
    Includes bibliographical references and index.
    ISBN 0-8047-5115-3 (hardcover : alk. paper)
    ISBN 0-8047-5116-1 (pbk. : alk. paper)
    1. Aesthetics.   I. Title.
BH39.L5792 2005
111'.85—dc22

                                                                2005002880

Original Printing 2005

Last figure below indicates year of this printing:

13   12   11   10   09   08   07   06   05   05

To
Gail Grella

Acknowledgments

This book began its life as an accidentally requested article. When Jerry Christensen asked me if I would be interested in writing a review article for *ELH*, he did not have in mind a theoretical article on a French sociologist. Nonetheless, he was more than gracious about what he received and the first half of Chapter 4 was first published in an earlier version in *ELH*. I would like to thank *ELH* for giving me permission to reprint that article here. Less accidentally, Marshall Brown at *MLQ* requested another piece on Bourdieu, which, in a revised form, has become the second part of Chapter 4. I would like to thank him for the request and *MLQ* for the permission to reprint. I would also like to thank *SLI* for permission to reprint a portion of an article that contains some of the material on Duchamp that appears in Chapter 2.

After its beginning at the end, this book and its debts have proceeded in a somewhat more orderly fashion. My colleague Richard Sha has read all of this manuscript as it appeared in its backward way, and I owe much to his comments and encouragement. Carolyn Williams and Yopie Prins have also read parts of the work or earlier versions of it and helped me to shape and think out my arguments. I owe much larger debts to Norma Broude of American University's Art History Department and Jeff Reiman of its Philosophy Department, who both agreed to help me with my encroachments on their academic disciplines in Chapter 2. My defense of postmodernism would have been even less effective than it is were it not for having benefited from considering Jeff Reiman's attacks on postmodernism. Needless to say, I am to blame for whatever remains maladroit in my wanderings through other disciplines, as well as for my employments of my own. I would like, finally, to thank Marc Redfield, who read the book for Stanford and who, despite being a target for some of marginal barbs, in a very generous analysis of it, asked questions and made suggestions for revisions that, to the extent that I have adequately carried them out, have made the book's argument stronger.

Two sabbaticals and a University Senate Research Grant from American University have aided my work. It has also been given the aid of financial support from the American Council of Learned Societies and from the Center for the Critical Analysis of Contemporary Culture at Rutgers University. I would like to thank all these institutions. But I would like especially to thank the Center and its director, George Levine. My year there and the discussions with all the participants made the writing of the chapter on Foucault, and less directly of the whole book, at least attempt to take on some of the ambitions of the theme of the discussions, "Objectivity and the Disciplines."

This book's dedication doesn't begin to exhaust the various debts I owe to Gail Grella.

Contents

Introduction

This book began as an argument against the tendency in literary studies to identify the aesthetic as an ideological support of the modern capitalist state. This was a tendency, rather than a movement, because anti-aesthetics almost became the common belief of all literary theories of note at one point. Believing in a concept of literary value became a cardinal theoretical sin, though many of us indulged on the sly. And "formalism" became a term of abuse, connected with various invidious forms of political befuddlement or conservatism. Thus New Historicists separated off from deconstruction on the basis of their refusal to "privilege" literature and their attention to the element of history, even as deconstructive critics attacked the Romantic aesthetic concept of symbolic embodiment as enabling totalitarian ideology. Perhaps there were different ways of being against aesthetics, but there was a basic shape to the attacks. First, they questioned the concept of aesthetic value, casting doubt on whether objective value existed and connecting the rise of the concept of aesthetic value historically with the rise of the concept of economic value, showing the analogous forms of both. And second, in a more basic attack, anti-aesthetic critics questioned the very criteria by which aesthetics defined what an artwork or an aesthetic experience was. They argued that criteria such as disinterest and autonomous form were themselves class-based or supportive of the class distinctions of the rising middle-class society.[1]

More recently, a string of books has come out defending notions of beauty or aesthetic experience more or less explicitly against this attack.[2] As welcome as these works' theories of the value of aesthetic experience have been, they have not changed the original direction of this book, because, to a large extent, they have not succeeded in responding directly to the force of the strongest attacks on aesthetics. They have all, in different ways, posed forms of aesthetic experience that they offer as valuable without regard to ideology or class or as valuable across classes. Elaine Scarry and Peter de Bolla most nearly return to languages of transcendent value in describing the kinds of experience art gives. Instead of indulging on the sly, they indulge openly and with considerable intelligence. Even Isobel Armstrong, who wants to define a kind of aesthetic effect that would survive radical left attacks on aesthetics while sharing left politics, does articulate psychological responses created by art that are humanly valuable. In this book's third chapter, I will argue the insufficiency of all theories of art based on the positing of a special experience created by the art object, but the problems with these theories as responses to the ideologization of aesthetics is not their weaknesses as art theory. They all, in fact, give interesting turns to the theory that art's value is in the special experience it affords. They do not, I think, adequately respond to the political critiques of aesthetics, however, because those critiques do not have to deny a particular kind of experience afforded by art in order to claim that that experience still serves ideological, extra-aesthetic ends.

When critics note that the aesthetic experience described by a particular writer, Shaftesbury, for instance, accords with the preferences of a specific class, or more generally, that the kinds of experience called aesthetic require, in addition to mere confrontation with an artwork, backgrounds, education, preferences all determined by social class, they do not argue that the experience in question does not exist or that the people who have it do not think of it as particularly valuable. When Bourdieu argues, in *Distinction*, that a taste for autonomous non-utilitarian art is particular to the upper classes, he does not think either that such a taste or that such art do not exist and are mere ideological delusions. Rather, his point is that, although the art and the taste for it do exist, because they represent the value of a specific class, they have no transcendent value. Thus the mere description of a value will not free it from this form of attack. And this will be true even when one tries consciously to be comprehensive, if not universal. Thus Armstrong, looking for a universal value, reasons that "an aesthetic needs to be grounded in experience that happens to everybody. Everybody plays" (58). There are, of course, numbers of things that everybody does. Armstrong chooses "play" because it has long been recognized as having a connection with aesthetic experience. "Play" captures some of the sense of otherness to utility without which we do not have a definition of what makes art special. But once we do capture that otherness, Bourdieu's analysis becomes immediately pertinent. Critics of Bourdieu, as we will see in

Chapter 4, sometimes note that his indication that an aesthetic value or experience plays a role in class distinction does not prove that the value or experience does not exist on its own terms as well. Just because it could be put to use in protecting class distinction, aesthetic pleasure might be real and worth having. But it turns out that the reverse is also true. The description of an experience we might all recognize as specifically aesthetic and think of as valuable does not disprove that that experience does not also have what Bourdieu calls cultural capital. Aesthetic experience may both exist and serve ideological ends. It may be universally valuable though only available to limited numbers as a result of contingent social arrangements. And so the mere fact of competing forms of values aligned with class distinction does mean that the mere description of a kind of aesthetic experience will no longer suffice to establish that experience as definitive of art or as showing art's independence of the ideological.

This book takes a different tack. It does not respond in the first instance to the problem of art's value. Rather it argues directly for the value of such aesthetic criteria as autonomous form, disinterest, and embodiment as they were worked out in the eighteenth and nineteenth centuries, most centrally by Kant, but also by his forebears, such as Shaftesbury, and by his heirs, such as Hegel and Nietzsche. It argues that these concepts were not necessarily connected to the Enlightenment concepts of reason and objective value that such postmodern critics as Foucault and Bourdieu meant to overturn. And indeed, they were necessary to the arguments the postmodernists mounted for that overturning. This return to aesthetics, then, has two distinct parts. First, by revisiting the history of aesthetics, it recuperates the concepts of autonomous form (in the Kantian version of purposiveness without purpose), disinterest (which Kant also labels indifference), and symbolic embodiment. It redefines each of these concepts, but, more importantly, and through that, it argues that aesthetics was not the companion to Enlightenment ideas about reason and objective justice, but was rather the model prior to reason and objectivity from which the Enlightenment attempted to give those concepts value. Because aesthetic structures meant to stand apart from the foundations of reason and value, they become useable by postmodern critics of Enlightenment reason and justice in their own attempt to show those concepts as contingent rather than universal.

The ideological critique of autonomous form has been both philosophical and historical. On the one hand, the concept, in its manifestation as organic form, is criticized as an impossible attempt to give material shape to transcendent design. On the other hand, critics confront the claim of autonomy, particularly in the form of having a value autonomous to economic exchange, with the concurrent rise of aesthetics with capitalist theories of economic exchange and the ways autonomy means constantly to resist that exchange and nevertheless constantly gets captured by it.[3] I do not dispute either of these critiques of the concept of autonomous form as we have received it since the twentieth century, but I do dispute that the concept, as it was developed in the eighteenth century and came to fruition in Kant, meant either to be a definition of the qualities of an art object or to see autonomy in terms of transcendence. In the first chapter, turning from the usual models of economics, I discuss the connection that we have mostly lost sight of but that was constant and central in discussions of aesthetics, the connection between aesthetic apprehension and natural theology. This context gives us both a different history of autonomy in art and a more accurate sense of what Kant meant to achieve in his formulation of it as purposiveness without purpose.

The chapter begins, at the beginning of the nineteenth century, with Coleridge's development of the idea of organic form. That formulation creates the basis for the way the concept of autonomous form emerges in contemporary theory. The Coleridgean criterion of organicism does indeed mean to describe the special feature of an art object, and it describes that feature in terms of an immanental design particular to it and to nature, and thus especially valuable. But Coleridge and his followers arrived at this concept through a pointed misinterpretation of Kant and other German sources, who did not think of the design of nature as, in itself, numinous and whose concept of aesthetic design entailed a certain way in which the mind perceives the world, in the first instance, and not a mysterious quality of art objects. To understand what Kant wanted from aesthetics, we must go back to its concurrent development with theories of natural theology. In these theories, the design of artworks did not reproduce an immanental quality in nature. Instead, their quality as intentionally designed provided the basis for an analogy by which to see the world as so designed. Art shared its form as an object designed according to an end, whose design showed that it was so made by a designer with any book, with watches and all other artificed machines. But art had a special role to play in natural theology. The point of that theory, beyond merely proving by reason the existence of a God, was to give a reasonable basis for assuming the existence of a governor of the world whose moral order looked at least roughly like that of Christianity. This is a somewhat tougher case to make. The raw features of the natural world don't seem to show a moral purpose, at least on their face. Aesthetics had a dual role to play in making the world look moral. First, aesthetic theorists, most prominently Hutcheson and Shaftesbury, argued that general agreement about the quality of artworks indicated an inbuilt aesthetic sensibility and was evidence that human beings had an inbuilt and universal moral sensibility.[4] Second, numbers of theorists used the design by which art achieved its moral effects—the way surprise, for instance, could work effectively to show a moral design where none had seemed to be—to show how the workings of the world were moral even when on the surface they did not appear to be. In both these cases, the value of aesthetics is the way it allows the mind to apprehend, more than it is any pleasure or understanding one is to gain from an artwork, and while the form of artworks is significant in the way it models how to apprehend, and is autonomous insofar as it is a human artifice and not a natural reality (only by standing outside nature could it model how to perceive it), it is in no sense numinous or transcendent.

In the wake of Hume's and Kant's dismantlings of the argument from design, the connection of aesthetic autonomy with a mode of apprehension in Kant became far more pointed. Although, as we will see, Kant did not think that one could use design in the world to prove the existence of any kind of God, much less a moral governor, he did think that living in the world as a moral being depended on being able to construe the world as if it had a morally intended teleology. And further, he thought that the judgment that allowed us to connect the moral rules of reason with our actions in the material world, which are known by the understanding, needed the principle, which allowed us to draw these connections, that the world's materiality was unified purposively. Since his abandonment of natural theology gave him no basis for either of these claims, he grounded a mode of judging he called teleological on the aesthetic judgment (*The Critique of Judgment* concerns as much the teleological judgment as the aesthetic). In effect, the teleological judgment construed natural objects as if they had purposive design, while not, in fact, asserting that they were designed according to a purpose. As Kant quite explicitly realized, this looks like a contradiction in terms (and Kant certainly did not think purposiveness without purpose could be a quality of actual objects, natural or artistic, despite its having been taken this way by contemporary formalism).

Consequently, he defined an aesthetic judgment that perceived objects as purposive while being aware that the purpose whose design it construed there did not exist. This aesthetic apprehension of purposiveness without purpose showed that the teleological judgment was epistemologically coherent. In other words, even more intensely than in eighteenth-century thinkers who actually reasoned from art to nature, in Kant aesthetics was a mode of apprehension. And the purpose of that apprehension was to indicate the coherence of apprehending the natural world as purposive, even though one had no basis for concluding that it was actually designed according to a purpose. By apprehending an object as having purposiveness without purpose, one was both attributing to it a design on its surface and recognizing that that design did not come from any external purpose, and might not even be a feature of the object. Aesthetic form was autonomous, not in the sense that it was transcendent or numinous but in the sense that it was a mental construct that recognized its separateness from the real bases of the object it perceived.

When one connects this Kantian formula with similarly recuperated concepts of disinterest and symbolic embodiment, one has the basis for discussing the importance of these concepts for the postmodern critique of Enlightenment reason as contingent belief and Enlightenment justice as covert ideology. The objections to the concept of disinterest, as unconnected with interests in physical pleasure or as standing apart from interest more broadly construed, or as unimpassioned indifference, go back, as we will see, at least to Nietzsche. More recently, objections to aesthetic disinterest have tracked the broader objections to the concept of ethical and intellectual disinterest. Just as critics have argued that a state in which one stands apart from all interests is epistemologically impossible, so others have argued that an appreciation for art always serves various interests. Again, in Bourdieu's *Distinction*, since an appreciation for art is cultural capital, one's ability to appreciate art directly serves various ideological interests.

The objection to the concept of symbolic embodiment has come mostly from deconstructive critics; it entails both the delusoriness of the concept and its ability to be employed in support of totalitarian states. The ostensible delusoriness of the concept goes directly to the claim that an object's meaning could be completely embodied by its material appearance. If one accepts that meaning always entails reference, then it obviously cannot be absolutely manifest on the surface of an artwork or anything else.

The connection of symbolic embodiment with totalitarianism involves the justification of such a state in the terms of a perfectly organized artwork whose surface arrangement manifested its value.[5]

Although embodiment and indifference may seem like unrelated issues, the book deals with them in a single chapter because the redefinitions of the concepts entail relating them to each other and to the idea of aesthetic apprehension. These redefinitions start with a consideration of Marcel Duchamp's notorious artwork *Fountain*, a urinal mounted upside down. The chapter argues that since this artwork looks exactly like a non-aesthetic object, indeed originally was one, it serves as a counter-example to any theory of art based on the notion that artworks have special features that are part of their material appearance. One must explain the existence of *Fountain* as an aesthetic object first in terms of our ability to apprehend it as such and second, and as a consequence, of our ability to apprehend its appearance as bearing a significance. To define what is happening here, we must put together the concepts of aesthetic apprehension, embodiment, and disinterest in the special ways that Kant discusses them. Kant uses as a synonym for disinterest, "indifference to the existence of the object," which means something rather different than a state of objective neutrality. He thinks that we apprehend certain kinds of objects as beautiful when we see them as manifesting significance in their design. But such manifestations do not occur in reality (thinking that they do is one of the fallacies of misused reason in *The Critique of Pure Reason*). In order to perceive an object in this way, we must concentrate on its surface appearance, without regard to the object's actual causes or to any intended purposes standing behind it. This apprehension is aesthetic indifference, and it sees purposiveness embodied, but without necessarily crediting the reality of that embodiment.[6] In other words, symbolic embodiment does not describe the real features of artworks; it describes how we interpret an object when we construe it as an artwork. And the criterion of indifference describes a stance of reservation or skepticism with regard to the construal of embodiment. The chapter then shows how these ideas of indifference and embodiment shaped the aesthetic theories of Hegel and Schopenhauer, and how Nietzsche made use of the aesthetics he received from this line to mount the first questioning of Enlightenment reason.

To a certain extent, the arguments in these first two chapters should stand by themselves as, in effect, a return to aesthetics, a return to these classic concepts to see them as far more challenging and charged with possibilities than the usual definitions of them make them seem. The chapters attempt to explicate them as worth employing in order to evaluate art on its own terms rather than as a disguised ideology. They also show that their importance within Enlightenment was not to offer an enlightened foundation of the value of art. Rather, they offered Enlightenment philosophy an opportunity to stand apart from its own reasoning, to evaluate it from another perspective. But they have another value, one that should make them more important to the postmodernist critique that has done most to mount the argument that aesthetics is covert ideology. The next two chapters of the book argue the importance of these aesthetic concepts to Foucault's constructions of discursive formations and his view of power, and to Bourdieu's definition of the habitus of aesthetics and the class distinctions created by art and academic discourse. In order to explain that importance, though, I must start with a very broad, but I hope recognizable, generalization of what I take to be the common ground of the postmodern project and how apprehending that project aesthetically will forward its aims.

Very broadly and simplistically, this book understands postmodernism as a project directed at breaking out of the Enlightenment and its heirs in Continental philosophy and political theory. First, postmodernists attempt to call into question Enlightenment reason's ability to ground knowledge, and second they show justice as understood both by Enlightenment theory and by the middle-class democratic state as another version of power rather than neutral space of evaluation outside power. The attempts have had different forms. Derrida, using the model of linguistics, posed an internal contradiction in the arguments, ranging from those made by Plato through those made by Heidegger, by which reason grounded itself. Foucault, among others, questions Enlightenment reason by arguing for its historical contingency and argues strenuously that all concepts of justice are historical results of power conflicts. Bourdieu, of course, argues that the role of culture, from art to academic discourse, is to protect class distinctions. And many feminists have posited a connection between Enlightenment reason and the structures of male thought or notions of justice and patriarchal power.

All of these arguments have faced a relentless and quite repetitious charge of self-contradiction. The ways the argument of contradiction is posed vary, but they come down to claiming that it is a contradiction to argue through reason the limits of reason, to state as a matter of knowledge that there is no such thing as knowledge, to argue, as an ethical critique of modern state power, that there are no ethical norms and that all justice serves power. The repetition of these charges and their effectiveness at least in having elicited an equally repetitious number of answers, coupled with their ineffectualness in that they do not seem to lessen the number of adherents to these modes of thought, should perhaps alert us to what I take to be their essential weakness. One may begin to get at this weakness this way: Posed even in the most extreme way—as I shall argue in Chapter 3—arguments that hold that human beings are incapable of knowing the world at all or that the term *justice* has no real referent because it corresponds to nothing either in the world or in its possible social arrangements, could be true. There is nothing ontologically impossible in the idea that the limitations of human mental abilities might be such that they could not comprehend reality either fully or even accurately in detail. The contradictions regarding the status of a proposition to that effect are more formal than real. Of course, the problem with such extreme relativism is not really that it is self-contradictory but that, like extreme solipsism, it is uninteresting. Once having stated it, one has little more to think about. And virtually no serious thinker who one might label "postmodern" actually corresponds to the journalistic notion of that movement as believing that all knowledge and all morality is just individual belief. Most of them—and certainly Foucault and Bourdieu—as we shall see, have much more refined positions that do allow for knowledge claims and ethical claims. These refinements may free their theories from being formally contradictory, but oddly they recreate the force of the charge of contradiction. While solipsists may be consistent in their claims not to know whether the outside world exists or is an illusion, one would hardly know what to make of such a solipsist then doing research in physics. It's not that it would be logically contradictory, but it certainly would feel like an odd consequence of the epistemology.

It is precisely here that the aesthetic concepts discussed in the first two chapters have a direct role to play. Aesthetic apprehension, construed as a mode of seeing objects in terms of the pattern one sees in their surface appearances and the significances with which one can endow those patterns, gives us a way of understanding the status of postmodern argument not as knowledge claim but as a presentation of a way of apprehending. This perspective, for Foucault and Bourdieu at least, describes in the first instance the structures by which they analyze. As we will see, the status of the discursive formations and of power in Foucault, and the status of the habitus in Bourdieu, both correspond fairly directly to Kant's description of apprehending objects as having purposiveness without purpose. In each case, Foucault and Bourdieu claim explicitly that their readings draw conclusions from a non-structural design in the surface details of a field. This does not mean that formations and habitus are fictions, in the sense of representations of things that never had existence. They are rather ways of arranging details so that we can see a new significance. Such apprehensions neither claim truth nor admit to mere subjectivity. They present an arrangement for a Kantian intersubjective assent: it makes sense, they say, to see the world this way and they offer that making sense to readers for their assent to that sense. If one gives this status to their work, one sees why they have had adherents and antagonists who have not through logic managed to persuade each other to assent to these theories on the one side or to abandon them on the other. The appeal of the work has not been to logic. It is not that they are illogical or affront logic but that their constructions about knowledge claims and justice claims either do or do not accord with the world one thinks one lives in. Consequently, logical arguments cannot really hope to persuade. This does not mean that we are powerless to have a meaningful dialogue about this postmodern critique or how it should ultimately be accepted. But that dialogue may more usefully take place in the mode of literary criticism in the sense of working out what the texts mean and what claims they make according to aesthetic criteria, recognizing that such literary criticism also frequently functions suasively. That, in any case, has been the process by which I read Foucault and Bourdieu here.

There is one important distinction the book draws in its analysis of Foucault and Bourdieu. Foucault handles the aesthetic aspect of his own work quite explicitly. He maintains a distance from his own concepts and works that regularly exasperate his critics; he recognizes the arbitrariness of many of his formulations and he explicitly presents his works as exercises in breaking down our normal modes of apprehending things. Although Foucault, among American literary critics, has played the role of the thinker who called them away from deconstructive aesthetic formalism to higher social responsibility, he worked quite comfortably with the concepts of aesthetic apprehension. Bourdieu, on the other hand, represents more exactly the view of aesthetics as just another way of justifying upper-class elitism. Since the aesthetics this book analyzes is manifestly connected to Enlightenment thought, there is a certain obvious sense in treating it ac-

cordingly. Indeed, much of what Bourdieu says about how aesthetic criteria work in society is persuasive. But, if his extension of the concept to the
workings of academic discourse in a way that includes his own work is capable of the same aesthetic recuperation that I argue for applying to Foucault's work, he surely would not have accepted that recuperation. And, I
argue, although contradiction remains a less telling critique of his work
than others of his critics might think, he denies himself the means of answering it and at times falls into far more tonally disturbing manifestations
of it (particularly, as we will see, in his treatment of Derrida).

And speaking of Derrida, what of deconstruction and aesthetics? Although I have referred to deconstructive attacks on aesthetics in passing in
this introduction, and the chapter on Bourdieu does discuss Derrida by
way of Bourdieu's critique of his aesthetics, nevertheless I focus on Foucault and Bourdieu as the central cases exemplifying the postmodern critique of and dependence upon aesthetics. Consequently, I have left in the
margins the theoretical school that for the American academy, at least, has
been the virtual symbolic embodiment of all theory, all postmodernism,
and all that is wrong with both theory and postmodernism.[7] That seeming
neglect has everything to do with the vexed role deconstructive reading
plays in the first two chapters of this book. There are two stances, generally
speaking, that deconstructive critics have taken to artworks and aesthetics;
they are not contradictory, although they do diverge. On the one hand,
from very early on in their writing, both Derrida and de Man made statements that have famously been taken to privilege literature and make of
deconstruction a new aesthetics. In *Positions (69)* Derrida discussed the role
in his thinking of literary language. And that concept played a central role
in "The Double Session" in *Dissemination*. And de Man made literature's
awareness of its own fictiveness central to his literary thinking from the
first chapter of *Blindness and Insight*.[8] And the sense that literature contains
deconstructive insights within itself, rather than being a body of work that
needs deconstruction, remains a strand in deconstructive criticism and has
manifested itself in the reading of other kinds of artworks as well. In a recent discussion of de Man's writing on aesthetics, for instance, T. J. Clark
argues for Cézanne's painting as exhibiting the materiality with which de
Man critiques aesthetic phenomenality—the belief that meaning can be
sensuously embodied (Cohen et al., *Material Events*, 93–113). On the other
hand, Derrida in *The Truth in Painting* deconstructed Kantian aesthetics
(and the concept of purposiveness without purpose) specifically and aes-

thetics generally as a version of Enlightenment humanism and, as I have noted above, a deconstructive critique of symbolic embodiment and its connection with totalitarian politics has been a feature of current deconstructive thinking.[9]

Since aesthetics has been a field of philosophy that may or may not capture what goes on in artworks, there is no necessary contradiction between seeing artworks as manifesting deconstructive insights while seeing aesthetics as participating in the Enlightenment philosophy deconstruction seeks to undercut. Still, it is one of my central contentions that, as I said above, the concepts of autonomous form, disinterest, and embodiment work to stand apart from Enlightenment reason, to at least keep a certain aesthetic distance from its claims. In the course of the first two chapters, I shall attempt to show more directly the ways in which these aesthetic concepts, while neither deconstructive nor self-deconstructive in any programmatic way, do bracket or look askance at precisely some of the concepts of framing and humanism that Derrida and others use to critique aesthetics. Thus, while the book does group deconstructive critics among the postmodern critics of aesthetics whose attacks it wants to answer, in another way it sees itself as allied with the main thrust of its attitude toward art, extending that attitude toward the concepts of aesthetics and seeing those concepts as capable of reading Enlightenment philosophy in the same way that Derrida and de Man have claimed that literary language reads philosophical language. Indeed, one could go further and say that the reason there is no treatment of deconstruction paralleling the ones of Foucault and Bourdieu is that the perspective the book recommends taking on those two philosophers is not only one deconstruction has long taken on philosophy, but the one it has long argued for most directly. And thus the book's analysis of the version of aesthetics it defends can be its only explication of the role it sees deconstruction as playing.

But it would be disingenuous simply to claim I am allying myself with one aspect of deconstruction against another. While my argument's redefiniton of autonomy, disinterest, and embodiment will show no sympathy for a conservative version of aesthetic value that seeks to align it with value per se against the depredations of postmodernism (indeed I would certainly like to make the aesthetics that articulates these "traditional" concepts an embarrassment to such arguments), its definition of aesthetics as a perspective from which to pose skeptical analyses of Enlightenment foundationalism is surely too timid in its philosophical limitations to claim deconstructive alignment straightforwardly. By posing aesthetics as a perspective that does not undo but suspends questions of truth and grounding, that does not answer those questions one way or another but, at least for a period, makes them seem boring to ask, this argument articulates an aesthetics and a postmodernism seen through its lens that will not fully persuade postmodernism's Enlightenment opponents to recognize the common ground between the Enlightenment and its postmodern critics. And it surely will not satisfy postmodernism's most totalized view of itself as completely outside the orbit of the Enlightenment. And yet if a debate that is becoming stultified can move forward, it will be through recognizing unknown common grounds, and this argument means to offer aesthetics as one of the most valuable areas for such commonalities.

Frequently one hears, partly in the mode of criticizing them for contradiction, that postmodern critics of Enlightenment thought are themselves fully Enlightenment thinkers. Since skepticism, and quite radical skepticism at least in thinkers like Hume, has always been an important strand of the Enlightenment, one can hardly deny this claim, though one does not quite know what to make of it since it merely notes that one cannot escape the limits of a movement that included within itself the most telling attacks of its own foundational gestures. Aesthetics in its own way is a part of this skeptical Enlightenment, though articulated also by its most foundational philosophers. Enlightenment foundationalism generally insisted on the secondariness of art. Kant argues that natural objects, not artworks, are the primary objects of the aesthetic judgment. Hegel thought art a thing of the past. Nietzsche transformed his discussion of the birth of tragedy into a genealogy of morals. But all of them articulated an aesthetic perspective from which their philosophy judged and from which one could judge their philosophy. That perspective has enabled the various postmodern critiques of the Enlightenment. And for their good rather than their ill, I think, it will be from that perspective that they must ultimately be evaluated. The war against the aesthetic as "merely" aesthetic may represent the last real attachment of postmodernism to Enlightenment foundationalism.

Aesthetics and the Argument from Design

At some point in the seventeenth century, God designed the world in such a way that anyone who looked at it in good faith could see clear evidence of both his existence and his moral intentions. Everyone noticed, at least everyone concerned with design, namely theologians and writers on aesthetics. Somewhere toward the end of the eighteenth century or the beginning of the nineteenth century, God evidently gave up the job of designing as a bad business. At least, although philosophers and aesthetic theorists still thought that the order of art offered a good model for talking about the order of nature, they were no longer sure in either case that the internal order of an object needed an external creator of that order to make it explainable. That intellectual history marks the shift from Ralph Cudworth's *True Intellectual System of the Universe* in 1678, Shaftesbury's *Characteristics*, and Bishop Butler's *Analogies* in the eighteenth century (among numbers of other texts); to Hume's *Dialogues Concerning Natural Religion*, published posthumously in 1779, Kant's central discussions of both natural theology and aesthetics in *The Critique of Pure Reason*, in 1781, substantially revised in 1787, and in the *Critique of Judgment*, in 1790.

The connection between aesthetics and theories of natural theology arose because of the issue of the world's moral significance. In the first instance, evidence of design in nature, in the argument from design, only showed that the world must have been designed by a higher intelligence of some kind. But natural theologians in the eighteenth century, as we will see, also wanted to argue that one could deduce from the shape of the world that its designer must be a moral governor on the order of the Christian God. This case was somewhat more difficult to make for two reasons. First, one needed a theory of how a morality that would be independent of the will of God could be known. Only then could nature be judged by an independent standard to accord with that reality. Second, it really was not always self-evident that the world did look moral. Aesthetics responded to both of these problems. First, it provided an example of harmonious form, the pleasure in which was a universal, primary experience and yet was also not quite naturally caused. It thus modeled an explanation for an innate human moral sense that was also a universal sensation. Second, the way in which complex form in art worked out moral explanations for events that were not straightforward allotments of reward and punishment also showed how one could argue that the world was ruled by a moral governor. In other words, aesthetics was the place eighteenth-century theorists turned in order to broach the most problematic of their claims about the order of nature and morality. For that reason, the aesthetics they developed became the most powerful mode, at the end of the century, for responding as well to the undoing of natural theology.

This history might have been articulated a long time ago were it not for Coleridge's revisions of Kant's, Schelling's, and Schlegel's ideas into the concept of organic form, which has been so vital and contentious an idea in twentieth-century Anglo-American literary theory. In the wake of that concept, there seemed little connection between a theology asserting external, mechanistic design and any idea of art that looked like Coleridge's claim of a special internal ordering.[1] The concept of organic form has been central to the New Criticism and to the various attacks against it and against the ideology of aesthetics in recent years. And these attacks have taken as their target not only Coleridge's concept, but through it Kant's theories and other earlier aesthetic positions. For this reason, tracing the history that leads up to organicism takes on a two-sided theoretical significance. First, by separating the concept of organic form from the various aesthetic ideas of form that it transmutes, one can see more clearly both the philosophical and aesthetic problems with that concept and the difference between it and the Kantian arguments often misinterpreted through its lens. Second, separated from that culmination in Anglo-American formalism, the meditations on the problems of design, form, cause, and purpose among British aestheticians of the eighteenth century and Kant's revision of that discourse will emerge less as ideological mystifications in the service of a rising capitalism and more as in fact the form necessary, first, for the questioning of Enlightenment rationality, and second, for contemporary critiques of aesthetics as part of that rationality.

The necessity of aesthetics to that questioning is both historical and logical. Writers like Shaftesbury, Hutcheson, and Kant are not in the first instance literary artists. They migrated toward the topic of aesthetics, toward the definition of beauty, not out of any interest in understanding an activity of their own, as poets such as Schiller and Coleridge did, but because the goal of giving a foundation to a moral system seemed to lead them consistently to art. In effect, the concept of a harmonious form, simultaneously and contradictorily like and unlike a nature whose own order was ambiguous even when most strenuously asserted, seemed necessary not as an adjunct of reason and morality but as an a priori basis for arguing their existence. This connection gives an ambiguous turn to the concept of aesthetic form that will make critiques of it as ideologically driven seem incomplete, not because they are inaccurate but because they do not recognize their own dependence on that concept.[2] For this reason, simultaneous though it was to the ethical bourgeois society's justifications and economic explanations of its rise, aesthetics nevertheless played a slightly askew role. Its own justification could never coincide with what it was designed to justify without the arguments becoming patently circular. And the very toils of the explanatory maneuvers and processes demanded by the ostensibly unaesthetic project of using aesthetics instrumentally in the service of ethics finally detach themselves from the aims of the specific writers. These maneuvers become the process by which subsequent theorists who want to calculate the ideological intents of large social and discursive structures stand apart from that which they analyze. Marking this detachment in the role of form as part of its role in ideological analysis is also central to my argument.

The intent behind proving design can be an extremely conservative project. And writers such as Shaftesbury and Kant surely did mean their aesthetics to support an established order. But focusing on the form of intent, as manifest in aesthetic design, entailed learning to conceive and deploy an analysis of form as sufficient evidence to mark an end or purpose in a structure even while bracketing the question of intent. Seeing the difference between positing a way of apprehending purposiveness in an object without supposing an intended purpose—which will become central to postmodernism—and the objectivist anti-intentionalism of New Criticism and its traditionalism entails seeing the history of aesthetics that stands behind both. In order to understand the postmodern debt to the Kantian definition of autonomous form as purposiveness without purpose, then, we must begin by detaching it from the Coleridgean concept of organic form and see its roots in eighteenth-century natural theology. Starting with contemporary and Coleridgean notions of organic forms, this section will work backward from that concept to the confrontations with design, intent, and form that constitute the real founding ideas of aesthetics and that remain central to our own skeptical attacks on the ideologies in and around literature.

I. Organic Form: From the New Criticism to Coleridge and Kant

As the title for this section indicates, my first aim is to trace the filiations of a concept backward from its theoretical importance to its sources, real and ostensible. Although the idea of organic form has been controversial because of its vital role in contemporary formalism, tracing its history creates a clearer view of the connection between current controversies and the paths that produced the controversial concept. As an example of the importance of organicism in twentieth-century criticism, one may take Cleanth Brooks's essay "Implications of an Organic Theory of Poetry." A consideration of this essay suitably starts the project of defending the concept of autonomous form because it exhibits how the problems that contemporary critics have with it connect so closely with the idea of organic form, with which they identify autonomy. Detaching organicism from autonomy, then, prepares for the recuperation of that latter idea. Brooks's essay uses organic form to address the problem of literature and belief: that the value of literature cannot either easily be connected to or easily detached from one's sense of the truth of the statements contained in a given work. This problem, Brooks argues, derives from a dualistic attitude to the form-content relationship in poetry. If one sees poetry as ornamentally figural statements of propositions that might appear in philosophy, science, or religion, one will, with T. S. Eliot, think that one can only fully appreciate a poem whose beliefs one shares—or at least has sympathy with (Brooks, 54). To escape this position and take poetry out of "ruinous competition with science and philosophy" (Brooks, 55), one could, with I. A. Richards, deny that poetry has anything at all to do with truth and argue that its aim is entirely to achieve emotive effect. But, for Brooks, this leads to a subjectivism that makes criticism impossible: "by locating the values of poetry in certain alleged psychological effects in the reader, Richards severed the connection between the text of the poem and any critical account of it" (Brooks, 56).[3]

The only way Brooks saw to exit from these equally unappealing alternatives was to question the form-content dualism. And hence came the role of organic form, which Brooks also argued was "a description of poetry that would fit the facts." Organic form, in other words, wasn't just a locally useful concept for dealing with the problem of literature and belief. It objectively corresponded to the form of poetry as it is. Form and content are inseparable, Brooks argues, because the relationship of the various parts of a poem is such that one aspect cannot be easily detached from another. It "was organic—not a relation like that of brick with brick or girder with girder, but more nearly like that of cell with cell in a living organism. Such a poem seemed to deny the commonly assumed duality between form and content as these terms are commonly used and, if one wished to do justice to its special kind of unity, to demand another kind of description" (Brooks, 62–63). From here, Brooks could argue toward a version of poetry as providing a truth of coherence whose features were unified complexity and a generalized correspondence to "human responses" and "human nature" (Brooks, 70). Rather than worry about whether Brooks has really solved the problem of belief here or merely veiled it by assuming a set of commonly held beliefs that he groups under the concepts of "human responses" and "human nature," I want to look at the features attributed to the organic interrelationship Brooks asserts.

Brooks's discussion of organicism raises two common aspects of the term that are not always so self-evidently apparent. First, in this passage, organicism is a special kind of relationship opposed to another kind, exemplified by the relation between brick with brick or girder with girder. Living beings, Brooks claims, are organized differently from works of artificial human construction. Second, he claims that organic unity is a "fact," a real aspect of nature. The logical point of the comparison is to see that poetry, a human product, is not organized like most human products—the ones made of girders and bricks—but like living organisms. But only if we in fact know how living organisms are organized, how cell relates with cell, can we use that natural relationship to understand poetic unity. This may seem to be belaboring the obvious, but neither claim is as unproblematic as Brooks seems to think, and those problems point us to the specific history of the term *organic form*. First, for instance, the difference between the two kinds of organization seems more evident on the surface of the analogy than it actually is. If one adds the idea of intention, the distinction will seem to become clearer, perhaps. Buildings are artificial organizations constructed according to human intention. Cells within a body relate as a result of no design but out of the necessities of their own being. This distinction, of course, plays a central role in the New Critical refusal to evaluate a poem in terms of its intention.[4] But without a clearly defined sense of what an organic unity is, rather than what its provenance is or is not, explanations of unity may quickly mix the ostensibly mechanistic with the ostensibly organic. Thus, arguing against evaluating a poem merely in terms of its success at fulfilling its intention, Wimsatt and Beardsley immediately mix the two forms of organization: "Judging a poem is like judging a pudding or a machine. One demands that it work. It is only because an artifact works that we infer the intention of an artificer. 'A poem should not mean but be.' A poem can *be* only through its *meaning*—since its medium is words—yet it *is*, simply *is*, in the sense that we have no excuse for inquiring what part is intended or meant" (Wimsatt, *Verbal Icon*, 4). Note that the poem starts out like a pudding or a machine and ends as a self-justifying being, but in each case it is an example of a thing that works toward an end.[5] Indeed, Brooks himself, only two pages after invoking the concept of organic unity, immediately returns to the concept of mechanic unity: "in the first place, a poem is something made, a construct. A renewed consciousness of a poem as an object—an artifact—and with a renewed respect for craftsmanship, have been salient traits of twentieth-century literary theory" (Brooks, 65). The problem here is that the only real difference in the unities invoked is that one, organic unity is not clearly the product of a designing intention and thus may have the feel of being deeper and more numinous. But if art can reproduce it through an artist's intention, then it will be addressable in terms of other humanly intended orders.

The second problem results from the same unarticulated assumptions. Since it is not self-evident what the special quality of natural form is or even that it really has an internal order to it, talk about the organic unity of a poem may quickly become talk about unity per se. The concept is then open to the criticism of being inherently artificial and falsifying. Thus Murray Krieger, in a recent defense of the concept of organic form, *A Re-*

opening of Closure: Organicism Against Itself, identifies the critics of organicism as arguing against the concept of totalization as repressive: "organi cists, true to their sources in German romanticism, too often project the organic metaphor—once literalized—into the realms of history and metaphysics, and use it to read the character of peoples, powers, and nations. . . . The consequences of such analogies for reactionary twentieth-century ideologies have long been evident enough. . . . Indeed, the use of organicism to aestheticize the political, and hence to politicize the aesthetic, has for some time been a concern of enemies of organicism" (Krieger, 35). Now, a committed organicist might easily argue against such criticism that organic unity cannot be imposed from the outside in this form of repression since its very concept supposes an internal quality that is natural to a state. Indeed, Josef Chytry defended the concept of the aesthetic state in just these terms: "Winckelmann's letters constantly refer to freedom as his life's goal, and in his praise of modern Roman life he reverts frequently to the model of a society given to the study of beauty and a freedom 'where no one commands and no one obeys'" (Chytry, *Aesthetic State,* 27). But Krieger makes no such argument. Instead, he accepts the identification of organic unity with unity per se and argues that organic unity may nevertheless open itself to difference and ambiguity (Krieger, 50–55). Whether or not this is a sufficient defense of aesthetic unity against the attacks of deconstructive skeptics and leftist critics of its repressiveness, it clearly has no specifically "organic" nature to it. The model of something actually in nature has disappeared, leaving Krieger's unity to survive on its own artificial terms.[6]

Both of the problems that Brooks's essay raises about organicism, and that he, Wimsatt, and Beardsley and Krieger struggle with, had emerged even more clearly in Coleridge's articulation of the concept, from which they all more or less draw. To see the connection, one need only quote Coleridge's most explicit and frequently cited statement of the principle:

The form is mechanic when on any given material we impress a predetermined form, not necessarily arising out of the properties of the material—as when to a mass of wet clay we give whatever shape we wish it to retain when hardened—The organic form on the other hand is innate, it shapes as it develops itself from within, and the fullness of its development is one & the same with perfection of its outward Form. Such is the Life, such the form—Nature, the prime Genial Artist, inexhaustible in diverse powers is equally inexhaustible in forms—each Exterior is the physiognomy of the Being within, its true Image reflected & thrown out from the concave mirror. (Coleridge, *Lectures,* 495)[7]

Again we see the distinction between two kinds of forms. And again, the suggestion is that the model for the distinction is a kind of form actually in nature. Moreover he makes clearer in two ways what Brooks more or less assumes in his contrast of girders with cells. First, organic unity comes from within rather than being imposed on from without. Second, and as a consequence, organic form is a more unified presentation of form with content since its physical surface actually embodies its significance; in other words, it is a version of the Coleridgean symbol, which "always partakes of the reality which it renders intelligible; and while it enunciates the whole, abides itself as a living part in that unity of which it is the representative" (Coleridge, *Lay Sermons*, 30).[8]

One should note that returning to the Coleridgean formulation provides an important advantage over considering only twentieth-century discussions of organicism: Coleridge offers examples of precise practical application. Thus, offering a shorter version of the distinction between organic and mechanic form quoted above, Coleridge argues that Shakespeare demonstrates his organicism in his handling of dialogue and characterization (Coleridge, *Lectures*, 359). More generally, as has been frequently remarked, Coleridge uses the concept of organic unity to argue for the essential unity of Shakespeare's plays as against the English critical tendency to see him as a wild and unruly genius. To a certain extent, such practical applications, as well as the connection of organic unity with the immanent symbol, partially alleviate Krieger's problem of identifying organic unity with all unity. If organic unity indeed has the special, immanental quality of the symbol, then many of the problems Krieger is concerned to defend it against will fall away. Such an immanental quality, to the extent that it truly existed, simply could not be applied artificially or repressively.

On the other hand, it raises in an even clearer way the problem of whether such a special unity actually exists and can be pointed to. As earlier critics have noted, there is some problem with insisting on the immanental quality of organic unity while at the same time attributing an example of it to the specific achievement of Shakespeare's genius (Appleyard, *Coleridge's Philosophy*, 113). Indeed, in a manner most critics would class as pointedly un-Coleridgean and mechanistic, Samuel Johnson had earlier made much the same point about Shakespeare's essential unity: "As nothing is essential to the fable, but unity of action, and as the unities of time and place arise evidently from false assumptions, and by circumscribing the extent of the drama, lessen its variety, I cannot think it much to be lamented, that they were not known by him or not observed" (Johnson, *Rasselas*, Poems and Selected Prose, 278). Although Johnson's discussion of Shakespearean organization is almost always in terms of craft and structure, it is clear from the body of his criticism that he cannot mean by unity of action what the French classicists whom he criticizes would mean by it. He is quite aware that Shakespeare's multiplot structures are "crouded with incident" (Johnson, *Rasselas*, Poems and Selected Prose, 281) and have little in common with the kind of unity of action one would find in Racine. His notion of essentiality, though, attributing unity of action to relation to a common purpose, achieves the same defense as Coleridge's, finding a deeper, more essential unity below a seemingly disorganized surface. But, unlike Coleridge, he does not propose an ontologically different form of organization. Thus, lauding Shakespeare's genius in organization, Coleridge, like Brooks, Wimsatt, and Beardsley after him, starts with organicism and ends with concepts entailing intention and craft.

To see the roots of the problem Coleridge and modern defenders of organic form are having, and particularly why definitions of aesthetic unity either fall back into the mechanistic formulations they were meant to avoid or quickly become circular, we need to see the way Coleridge transformed German idealist conceptions of organicism to produce his version.[9] The first distinction to draw is between symbolic immanence and organic unity, concepts that were always distinguished in the German idealist sources from which Coleridge might have drawn. Since Coleridge's ideas of organic form are often compared with Kant's, we may start with Kant's ideas about the symbol.[10] Kant quite explicitly argued that the idea of representing an essence or idea of Reason in a material embodiment with complete adequacy, an embodiment he termed an "ideal," was a fallacy, one of those errors that naturally befall Pure Reason improperly applied:

> Although we cannot concede to these ideals objective reality (existence), they are not therefore to be regarded as figments of the brain; they supply reason with a standard which is indispensable to it, providing it, as they do, with a concept of that which is entirely complete in its kind, and thereby enabling it to estimate and to measure the degree and the defects of the incomplete. But to attempt to realize the ideal in an example, that is, in the field of appearance as, for instance, to depict the character of the perfectly wise man in a romance, is impracticable. There is indeed something absurd, and far from edifying, in such an attempt. (Kant, *Pure Reason*, 486–487)

Ideals, used strictly as concepts of comprehensiveness, may be necessary to thought, but the attempt to realize a specific ideal in a concrete image is impossible. It is indeed, as we will see, the general flaw of the Pure Reason that heads Kant's disproofs of the various arguments for the existence of God. Kant's definition of the symbol thus imbeds its approximate quality within its working: "In the latter case [that of the symbol], to a concept only thinkable by the reason, to which no sensible intuition can be adequate, an intuition is supplied . . . " (Kant, *Judgment*, 197). For Kant, no natural object can adequately embody an idea of reason. All symbols are thus artificed approximations, and the concept of a fully adequate and immanent symbol is thus a fallacy.

Later German idealists certainly differed from Kant in this and did define art in terms of its ability to give material embodiment to transcendental concepts or ideas of human freedom.[11] But whether or not they defined this as symbolism, they thought it the particular achievement of art, not in any sense a form of unity that art might have by modeling itself on a nature that already possessed it. Coleridge may have found the basis for his unification of the two ideas of natural order and symbolic immanence in the definition of organic form that he borrowed from Schlegel, which certainly seems to suggest an internal unity to organic forms as found in nature: "Organical form, again, is innate; contemporaneously with the perfect development of the germ. We everywhere discover such forms in nature" (Schlegel, *Course of Lectures*, 340). But in the context of his book as a whole, even Schlegel does not really believe this unity to be in the material objects of nature. Following Kant more closely than Coleridge, he sees the perception of organic unity to be an organizing concept of the understanding (Schlegel, 244; I will return to this element of Kant in greater detail below). The only society to which he allows a natural experience of symbolic immanence is that of classical Greece (Schlegel, 66). In this, of course, he was following a truism of German aesthetics since Winckelmann, who posited that the Greeks were in special unity with their natural surroundings that led them to actually live ideal beauty in their physical bodies.[12] One sees this idea as well in Hegel's definition of the Greek age as the perfect period for art. But Winckelmann was merely giving figural history to a conceptual ideal that neither he nor his followers saw as currently available. Nature, they all claimed, was different for the Greeks, by which the philosophers among them, at least, of course meant that the Greeks conceived nature differently. In constructing his definition of organic form from Schlegel's statement apart from the various contextual limitations upon it, then, Coleridge gave himself the version of nature he needed for his own claims, but one that his sources saw as inherently contradictory. Nature was precisely that which did not have artistic organization.

This transformation leads to the larger distinction between Coleridge and his sources. Although Kant, Schelling, Hegel, and others all discuss an organic unity in nature, either they make it clear that that unity does not exist in nature or, when they think of organicism as natural, they contrast it with the higher order of art in terms of its insensibility. Thus Kant, in the formula to which Orsini (*Coleridge and German Idealism*, 1/1) and Abrams (*Mirror and the Lamp*, 174) think Coleridge refers, does define natural organization in a way useful for Coleridge: "*an organized product of nature is one in which every part is reciprocally purpose [end] and means.* In it nothing is vain, without purpose, or to be ascribed to a blind mechanism" (Kant, *Judgment*, 222). But there is a new word here, one central to Kant's discussion and indeed to subsequent discussions of natural form as well that Coleridge does not attend to: "purpose." But this word adds a particular problem to the discussion since that which has a purpose is in fact ordered from without according to that purpose and not ordered from within. Later in this section, when we return to Kant and the connection between his development of his aesthetic theory and his disproof of the argument from design, I will discuss in some detail the workings of the concepts of purpose and purposiveness. To mark the difference between Kant and Coleridge, though, we need only its suggestion of externality.

For Kant and Schelling (as well indeed for Schiller, Hegel, and numerous others, but I will here stay with those we know Coleridge read carefully), natural objects, considered apart from human cognition, had to be considered as produced mechanistically. Indeed, only by recognizing fully the complete adequateness of a mechanistic explanation of natural existence could the full implications of purposiveness be addressed. Thus Kant opens his discussion of the teleological judgment by insisting on the necessity of the mechanistic explanation, coupled with the subjective endurance of the concept of purposiveness:

Objective purposiveness, as a principle of the possibility of things of nature, is so far removed from *necessary* connection with the concept of nature that it is much oftener precisely that upon which one relies to prove the contingency of nature and of its form. . . . In other words, nature, considered as mere mechanism, can produce its forms in a thousand different ways without stumbling upon unity in accordance with such a principle. . . . Nevertheless the teleological act of judgment is rightly brought to bear, at least problematically upon the investigation of nature, but only in order to bring it under principles of observation and inquiry according to the *analogy* with the causality of purpose, without any pretense to *explain* it thereby. (Kant, *Judgment*, 206)

Schelling, following Fichte and departing from Kant, insisted that the concepts through which we understand reality had to be real forms, not merely ideals: "How both the objective world accommodates to presentations in us, and presentations in us to the objective world, is unintelligible unless between the two worlds, the ideal and the real, there exists a *pre-determined* harmony" (Schelling, *Transcendental Idealism*, 11).[13] Thus in dealing with purposiveness and mechanism in nature, he argues that the mind's necessary recourse to purposiveness as explanatory marks the presence of that purposiveness in nature, a presence concurrent with nature's mechanism: "Nature, both as a whole, and in its individual products, will have to appear as a work both consciously engendered, and yet simultaneously a product of the blindest mechanism; *nature is purposive, without being purposively explicable*" (Schelling, *Transcendental Idealism*, 12). Schelling shares with Kant, however, the basic claim that nature's purposiveness can only be understood fully if one also sees nature as mechanistic, and if one sees that purposiveness is a conscious comprehension on the part of a perception that is in some sense at war with the object's own mechanistic existence.

If one steps back from the details of these arguments at this point, it will become clear that in the context of their the basic issues, Coleridge's claim of two forms of organization, external mechanism and internal and integral organicism, is, in terms of his German idealist sources, simply incoherent. Both Kant and Schelling mean by mechanism not an external form of design, but empirical, causational necessity, which construes the world as without design, contingently produced by an accidental concatenation of causes. Their use of the words *purpose* and *purposiveness* make clear that the opposite of this mechanism is not an internal order but a design with an end outside that order. Only such a design makes the terms purpose and purposiveness meaningful (I will discuss the problem of why we should use these words with their English suggestions of intentionality in my section on Kant below). Both of them also deny that nature has such an external, intentional cause and so see purposiveness as a construct through which the mind apprehends nature. The nature thus cognized they will at times describe in terms that are available for organic claims, but they never really argue for a complex relationship actually internal to nature. Such a claim would destroy precisely the boundaries that Kant placed on reasoning about empirical apprehensions to preserve reason from Hume's skeptical attacks on it, boundaries that to a great extent, Schelling and Fichte, careful students of Kant, followed.

We can now see the basis for the tribulations befalling the concept of organic form with which this chapter opened. Coleridge takes purposiveness and attributes it to an integral aspect of nature—organicism. He then uses Schiller's opposition between mechanism and organicism as an opposition between organization from without and organization from within—rather than Schiller's actual contrast between perceiving nature as random and perceiving it as organized according to a purpose. Finally, he connects symbolic immanence with organization from within and takes the whole complex as a natural reality upon which art could be modeled. He thus creates a vaguely defined and internally contradictory empirical entity out of a difficult conceptual maneuver in Kant. Brooks and Wimsatt trip over the difference between mechanistic and organic organization only partly because works of art, as intended designs, will never quite fit the description of organic form that they take from Coleridge. More importantly, since the concept of organic form simply elides the difficulty of thinking about form without an external designer, discussions of it will keep moving back and forth between an unanalyzed sense of nature as immanently significant and a discussion of that significance in terms of the usual model of form, intended designs. The application of this internally contradictory model to art, which is by definition opposed to nature at least in terms of its being an artifact of human intention, will only exacerbate the difficulties. To disentangle these difficulties, we need to get back to the original discussions of design—both theological and aesthetic—that preceded them. From this context and Hume's consequent debunking of it, I can then restore the genuine strangeness and resistance of Kant's aesthetics to the development of bourgeois Enlightenment it ostensibly supported and indeed the importance of aesthetics to our contemporary skepticism about organic form.

II. The Order of Art and the Order of Nature

Before proceeding back to statements of the argument from design in the late seventeenth and early eighteenth century, it will help to start with William Paley's *Natural Theology*, an exemplary summing up of design theory written contemporaneously with Coleridge and in the wake of Hume. Paley's first three chapters open with the model incident for the argument from design, a hypothetical walk across a heath in which one first stumbles upon a stone and then upon a watch. The stone, Paley argues, one could imagine as having been there for all time, without any external causation. The watch, however, is a different case: "when we come to inspect the watch, we perceive (what we could not discover in the stone) that its several parts are framed and put together for a purpose, e.g. that they are so formed and adjusted as to produce motion, and that motion so regulated as to point out the hour of the day" (Paley, 5). At the risk of belaboring the obvious, I will note that a number of words that operate with various tensions in the aesthetic discussions we have been addressing suddenly take on a clear logic. A watch has a purpose, to tell time. That purpose defines its design, its order—internal or external. The parts relate to each other with a special complexity because they work to produce the purpose of telling time. And, of course, Paley's point in the comparison follows immediately: "the watch must have had a maker . . . " (Paley, 6).

Paley in the next pages considers a number of counter-arguments that might drive him from supposing that the watch had not been produced by a maker external to it, most of them harking back to Hume. One is worth pausing over: "Nor, fifthly, would it yield his inquiry more satisfaction to be answered, that there existed in things a principle of order, which had disposed the parts of the watch into their present form and situation. He never knew a watch made by the principle of order; nor can he even form to himself an idea of what is meant by a principle of order distinct from the intelligence of the watchmaker" (Paley, 7). Paley here offers a concept of organic form as an internal principle of order. And he declares it incoherent; he cannot even form to himself what is meant by it. Now, of course, that may be because watches are mechanisms, but the inevitable conclusion follows after the handling of a few more suggestions: " . . . every indication of contrivance, every manifestation of design, which existed in the watch, exists in the works of nature; with the difference, on the side of nature, of being greater and more, and that in a degree which exceeds all computation" (Paley, 13).

If the argument from design buys a clear sense of natural design and its source at the expense of a valued literary theory, it nevertheless also offers a clear view of art in return. We know from the workings of art how nature works. Here Paley compares muscles to works of art:

The shape of the organ is susceptible of an incalculable variety, whilst the original property of the muscle, the law and line of its contraction, remains the same, and is simple. Herein the muscular system may be said to bear a perfect resemblance to our works of art. An artist does not alter the native quality of his materials, or their laws of action. He takes these as he finds them. His skill and ingenuity are employed in turning them, such as they are, to his account, by giving to the parts of his machine a form and relation. (Paley, 78–79)

Because artists give us an example of intentional design, their work, like the work of watchmakers, gives us the analogic model for how to read natural design as the work of intentional contrivance. This of course means that we have to think of artworks as machines. But then the word *art*, as Paley was using it, had long covered both what Kant specified as the fine arts and also skilled work directed at achieving an external end through its own instrumentation, such as watch making. And both kinds of art seem more easily explicable in this way, at least on first thought. After all, if it is problematic to think of nature as having an order internal to it without external causation, how much harder to think of art as operating the same way when we know that art is by definition the work of human contrivance?[14]

If contrivance is an evidence of design, though, there is also a logical problem in the use of it to prove an omniscient and omnipotent God. After all, as Paley himself asks, "why resort to contrivance, where power is omnipotent? Contrivance, by its very definition and nature, is the refuge of imperfection. To have recourse to expedients implies difficulty, impediment, restraint, defect of power." (Paley, 26).[15] The logical knot is so neat here that it verges on the kind of false disproof of God's existence that rests on a trick of language: Can God make a stone he cannot lift? Can God design a world without designing it? If God made a world by miraculous fiat, it would look no different from the stone on the heath that shows no evidence of having been created. That appearance would of course be fallacious, since a world created by fiat has still been intentionally created, but the fallacy seems a necessary aspect of a miraculously uncontingent inception.[16] In order to avoid fallacious appearance, though, the creating God could not just choose to show design since the show would thus be separate from the fact of creation, would itself be a creation by fiat and thus fallacious in appearance. The creator would have to leave actual traces of instrumentality. But a world that reveals the instrumentality of its own design disproves the omnipotence of the designer—and of course a designer of a limited power just throws questions about creation and design one step backward. I will return to Paley's answer to this question further below when I discuss the deeper connections between art and natural theology that developed in the middle of the eighteenth century. The question, though, serves well as an introduction to an explanation of how the argument from design took hold at the beginning of the eighteenth century. That explanation begins with a look at the Cambridge Platonists, that group of idealists occasionally taken to be Coleridge's true forebears.

Critics see the importance of the Cambridge Platonists on the aesthetics that followed in the next century in terms of two elements of their beliefs. First their idealism in discussions of morality and art presented an alternative to Lockean empiricism and the Hobbesian politics that followed from it, an influence that made its most significant mark through the work of Shaftesbury.[17] Second their definition of a plastic nature, in resistance to a mechanistic view of the universe, shows an early organicist influence on Coleridge.[18] Discussion of the first influence may be held off until I turn to Shaftesbury. A close look at Ralph Cudworth's articulation of the idea of "plastick nature," in *The True Intellectual System of the Universe*, though, will show why, despite the problem of contrivance, the version of the argument from design that viewed the world as a magnificent machine prevailed. Cudworth's "plastick nature" was, in the first instance, an attempt to deal with the problem of contrivance. Cudworth makes clear that he proposes a power in nature that leads, of its own blind force, to natural ordering, to relieve God of the constant responsibility to contrive:

We insist Largely, upon an *Artificial, Regular* and *Plastick Nature*, devoid of express Knowledge and Understanding, as subordinate to the Deity . . . forasmuch as without such a Nature, either God must be supposed to Doe all things in the world Immediately, and to Form every Gnat and Fly, as it were with his own hands; which seemeth not so Becoming of him, and would render his *Providence*, to Humane Apprehensions, *Laborious* and *Distractious*; or else the whole System of this *Corporeal Universe*, must result only from *Fortuitous Mechanism*, without the *Direction* of any *Mind*. (unnumbered p. 10 of preface)

Although Cudworth, as we will see, insists on the world as ultimately designed by an omnipotent God, he resists making that God active in all creation's laborious details. Far from being design, such an involvement, he later argues, would entail constant, ongoing, direct intention, making the world operate by perpetual miracle (147). Thus, to shield God from the necessity of contriving constantly and the indignity of using his power for the working of such a small thing as material nature in all its messy detail, Cudworth inserts an intermediary, non-intelligent force, plastick nature. And the evidence for this force turns out to be precisely the contrivance that would be not only beneath God's dignity but would contradict his omnipotence: "This Opinion [that God is responsible for all aspects of the ordering process] is further Confuted, by that Slow and Gradual Process that is in the Generation of things, which would seem to be but a Vain and Idle Pomp, or a Trifling formality, if the Agent were Omnipotent" (150).

And this force does indeed take on many of the qualities of organic form. Cudworth, for instance, predicts Schlegel's and Coleridge's distinction in which organic form is internally rather than externally ordered: "Nature is *Art* as it were *Incorporated* and *Imbodied in matter*, which doth not act upon it from without *Mechanically*, but from within *vitally* and *magically*"(155). Moreover, because this force operates from within nature, it is a superior form of human art. Human art, "acting upon Matter from without," is necessarily imperfect while plastick nature, acting on matter from within, "is *Art it self* or *Perfect Art*" (155). In this particularly Coleridgean way, art is said to imitate nature, not through mimesis in its represented content but in that its order is an imitation of the immanent natural order: "wherefore when Art is said to imitate Nature, the meaning thereof is, that Imperfect *Humane Art* imitates that *Perfect Art of Nature*" (155). Still, Cudworth resists identifying this immanence and the unintentional quality of plastick nature straightforwardly with a superiority to art. Rather, he insists that this force's lack of externally intending intelligence makes it inferior to human art:

Wherefore as we did before observe the *Preeminences* of Nature above Humane Art, so we must here take Notice also of the *Imperfections* and *Defects* of it, in which respect it falls short of *Humane Art* . . . and the First of them is this, That though it Act *Artificially* for the *sake of Ends*, yet it self doth neither *Intend those Ends*, nor *Understand the Reason of that it doth*, Nature is not *Master* of that *Consummate Art* and Wisdom according to which it acts, but only a *Servant to it*, and a *Drudging Executioner* of the Dictates of it. (156)

There is almost a contradiction between the claims of perfection and imperfection. Plastick nature is better than human art because, acting from within nature, it has no distance from the matter on which it operates, no space in which the imperfections of human art, operating "at a Distance" (155), may occur. On the other hand, plastick nature, unlike art, does not intend its ends, and thus is the servant of a higher purpose rather than the master of it, as are both the divine artist and the human artist.

The two claims are not contradictory though because they separate the concepts of externality from intention. It is not art's externality per se but its intentionality that makes it superior. If one could imagine a will operating from within nature to design it according to its own intelligent ends, that internal force would indeed be an entirely superior art. Cudworth must deny that supposition, though, since it amounts to hylozoist atheism—the belief that matter is animated by internal, conscious life: "to assert any such *Plastick Nature*, as is Independent upon any higher Intellectual Principle, and so it self the first and highest Principle of Activity in the Universe, this indeed must needs be, either that Hylozoic Atheism, already spoken of, or else another different Form of Atheism, which shall afterwards be described" (109).[19] Since a nature operating according to the mode of a pure organic concept cannot be allowed, Cudworth also proposes an intending will who designs the world according to the purposes of his divine wisdom: "It seems to me in no way mis-becoming of a Theist, to acknowledge such a *Nature* or *Principle* in the Universe, as may act according to *Rule* and *Method* for the *Sake* of *Ends*, and in order to the *Best*, though it self do not understand the reason of what it doth; this being supposed to act dependently upon a higher Intellectual Principle, and to have been first set a work and employed by it" (109). In effect, Cudworth's seemingly internal force turns out to be merely a form of instrumentality, allowing the higher intelligence to operate from outside the world while not getting so close to its details as to endanger its dignity or omnipotence.

In effect, contrivance for Cudworth disallows the straightforward version of the argument from design, calling into question both the dignity and the omnipotence of the contriver. On the other hand, positing a plastick nature proposes thinking of that internal force as without will or intention, and such a force operating alone is by definition imperfect. One cannot attribute the entire design of the world to it without absurdity. Accordingly, a higher intellectual principle, an intending deity, is also a logical necessity and so design can now be attributed, ultimately if not immediately, to that deity and explained accordingly. The problem of contrivance seems to create a space for the concept of an organic form, but the problems of that concept immediately lead to its own modification to the point of disappearance. When Cleanth Brooks, William Wimsatt, and Coleridge all mixed their concepts of organic form with seemingly contradictory mechanistic explanations, they were only reproducing the problem Cudworth had already outlined for them.

In their responses to the problem of contrivance, Paley, from one end

of the eighteenth century, and Cudworth, from the other, model the forms
the argument from design took in that century. By far the most popular
version of it, which led to Paley's classic restatement, argued directly from
the design of the world to the existence of God and accepted the necessity
this argument entailed of committing that deity to all the details of creation. Indeed, many versions of the argument reveled in those details. Thus
John Ray, in *The Wisdom of God Manifested in the Works of Creation*, cata-
logues every pattern he can think of, from the workings of animal bodies
to the arrangements of the stars, as evidences of an intentional creation. So
far from thinking with Cudworth that ordering the life of every fly and
gnat compromised divine dignity, Ray considered such a divine engagement in small detail an absolute necessity. Arguing against the hypothesis
of God as a first mover, Ray notes,

an intelligent Being seems to me requisite to execute the Laws of Motion. For first,
Motion being a fluent thing, and one part of its Duration being absolutely independent upon another, it doth not follow that because any thing moves this moment, it must necessarily continue to do so the next; unless it were actually possess'd of its future motion; but it stands in as much need of an Efficient to preserve
and continue its motion as it did first to produce it. (54–55)

This position carries natural theology to a nearly Humean logical conclusion. Since there is no necessity that links cause to effect, each moment being independent from another, only the intervention of an intelligent being intending the duration of motion could keep the world and all the
things in it moving. If there seems little art in the constant divine intervention into motion that Ray proposes, most writers who adduce design
return to examples of intricate and admirable design, perhaps most frequently the complex features that allow the eye to see.[20] And, as we turn to
more abstracted theories of natural theology, we need to remember that
the testimony of natural theology's strongest opponents reminds us of the
general popularity of Ray's approach. As we will see, both Hume and Kant
recognized its appeal even as they argued against its logic. Moreover, the
reason for this popularity will also lead to the development of aesthetics as
an element in ethico-theological argument. Whatever its extremities, the
argument from design represented an appeal to the evidence of the senses.
And, however idealized art becomes in writers like Shaftesbury and Hutcheson, it too is part of this appeal to the senses.

   Although no eighteenth-century natural theologian abandoned using
design as evidence for the existence of a divine designer, for the most part,

many influential works of natural theology in that period seemed implicitly to have accepted Cudworth's desire to keep God out of the muck of materiality and the dangers of showing contrivance. By taking the greater aim of proving the intellectual and moral attributes of God as evident in nature, they tended to pass over or ignore proofs for God's existence as a designer. Proving that the world indicated a moral governor pushed arguments away from seeing God as a divine artificer, crafting the details of material reality. But that project nevertheless introduced art more deeply into the argument by seeing the world as having the kind of moral significance characteristic of a work with an intentional meaning and moral message. In his highly influential *Analogy of Religion*, Bishop Butler makes quite explicit the comparison between God's moral governance and art as a meaningful whole:

It is most obvious, analogy renders it highly credible, that upon supposition of a moral government, it must be a scheme; for the world, and the whole natural government of it, appears to be so—to be a scheme, system, or constitution, whose parts correspond to each other, and to a whole, as really as any work of art, or as any particular model of a civil constitution and government. (155)

In this chapter, Butler begins with the presumption that the world looks like a moral government or scheme, then offers objections to that supposition and argues that the objections are more strained than the supposition to which they object. Despite this backward form of argument, the structure of Butler's position remains clear enough in this summary passage. Certain kinds of intentionally designed moral systems—works of art, civil constitutions—provide a model to which the world is found to be similar. Although the example of civil government is obvious here, in fact, the example of art is in a sense prior since it exemplifies a relationship of part to whole which, without being by definition designed for moral purpose as a constitution can be said to be, nevertheless evidences in that relationship the fact of moral significance. In other words, Butler defines works of art in terms of an intended meaning that determines their formal structure; they have the form they have in order to convey the meaning they intend. And he argues that this meaning-related formal structure characterizes the shape of material reality, which is, consequently, also readable as conveying a divinely intended meaning.

Samuel Clarke, Butler's less famous predecessor, was more directly concerned to prove divine attributes than to prove the truth of revealed religion. His deduction of God's moral make-up from the features of the world much more clearly defines how to see morality in nature, and that argument ties him even more closely with the order of art. In *A Discourse Concerning the Being and Attributes of God*, Clarke defines morality as "fitness" and "suitableness" in the relations among different things. And he claims that such "fitness" in fact obtains in the world: "by this *Understanding or Knowledge* of the Natural and Necessary Relations of Things, the *Actions likewise* of all Intelligent Beings are constantly Directed, (which *by the way* is the true Ground and Foundation of all Morality)" (114–115). From this claim, Clarke can conclude, "nor can the *natural Attributes* of God be so separated from the *moral*, but that He who denies the latter, may be reduced to a necessity of denying the former likewise" (164). In other words, a certain relationship among things constitutes a moral relationship. This relationship in fact obtains in the material world. Thus once one deduces from material reality certain natural attributes of God, the moral attributes must follow as being part of the relationship of things in nature. This argument, of course, depends upon the notion that the formal features of "fitness" and "suitableness" also count as moral qualities. In effect, aesthetic order, harmonious accord, has been introduced as the basis for making a moral conclusion. We will see Shaftesbury arguing from a taste for art to a moral taste. But he was foreshadowed in that argument by the natural theologians who read the order of the world from the order of art.

Both the justifications of contrivance and the arguments about moral design indicate more than the role of art in natural theology. They also indicate the fundamental ambiguity in the topics that suddenly made art an important concern in the eighteenth century. The rise of aesthetics out of reason's turn to the demands of the body (to speak the language of current criticism) has been a matter of recent comment. Alexander Baumgarten, who coined the term *aesthetics*, was a student of Leibniz and meant to turn Leibniz's system of making everything intelligible through pure rationality on the refractory topic of art by using reason to define art as clear, confused, sensate representation (Baumgarten, *Reflections on Poetry*, 41–42). He thus distinguished art both from unorganized sensate representation and from the distinct and adequate representations of reason.[21] This attempt to make a union out of sensation and reason, or at least to make sensation intelligible through its seemingly most intelligible manifestation, aesthetic response, motivates the eighteenth-century British aestheticians as strongly as Baumgarten, though. We have seen the critical claim that the

Cambridge idealists were more influential than Lockean empiricism on subsequent aesthetics. And yet the empiricism of British aesthetics is also notorious.[22] Indeed, whether as the answer of sensation to the demands of reason (an answer that tends to assert an intelligibility not entirely a matter of sensation) or the colonization of sensation by rationality in order to make its philosophy whole (a colonization that seems always to entrap the colonizers in sensation like the designing deity caught in the muck of materiality), aesthetics constantly works the boundaries of these competing demands. As hard design theory turned toward the claim that contrivance served its own nearly intrinsic purpose, though, thus toward a view of form that was more than the claim of evidence, and moral design turned toward the claim of a natural tendency toward "fitness" in the world, thus toward a claim about material order, the ambiguities of aesthetics suddenly had a central role to play.

The liminality of aesthetics is a key element in the argument that follows since it forces the aesthetics formulated by the British empiricists, and by Kant in their wake, to function in ways well beyond the intentions of its creators. Certainly the argument from design has always had a deeply conservative element in it since it must assume that the world as it is basically works for the best. This position, as we will see, causes trouble for natural theology's defender in Hume's *Dialogues Concerning Natural Religion*, but it certainly never bothered most defenders of the existing order. Still, as we will also see, when aesthetics self-consciously models nature on the order of art, it soon finds that the order of art is more complex then the original analogy presumed, and aesthetics winds up becoming a mode of questioning natural order as much as a way of buttressing it.

Indeed, only these connections with design at its liminal moments really drew aesthetics, as seen by aestheticians rather than theologians, into the orbit of natural theology. In terms of a first view of nature, if the theologians constantly structured the world according to a work of art, writers on art were less sure of this connection. First of all, concerned as they were to delineate the special quality of art, its appeal at once to rational and sensational apprehension, they were not always sure that all of nature had such an appeal. The problem was not the concept of natural design, precisely. But the same writer, who one moment would unproblematically assert a version of the argument from design, in the next moment, when he actually looked at the two kinds of order, would nevertheless proceed to distinguish nature from art. So Addison, in one letter to *The Spectator*, outlines the argument from design in brief—thus incidentally showing how off-handed and comprehensive its dissemination and service had become:

The Body of an Animal is an Object adequate to our Senses. It is a particular System of Providence, that lies in a narrow Compass. The Eye is able to command it, and by successive Enquiries can search into all its Parts. Cou'd the Body of the whole Earth, or indeed the whole Universe, be thus submitted to the Examination of our Senses, were it not too big and disproportioned for our Enquiries, too unwieldy for the Management of the Eye and Hand, there is no Question but it would appear to us as curious and well-contrived a Frame as that of an human Body. We should see the same Concatenation and Subservience, the same Necessity and Usefullness, the same Beauty and Harmony in all and every of its Parts, as we discover in the Body of every single Animal. (Bond, *The Spectator*, IV, 442)

Although Addison sounds no note of doubt about what he would see had he a large enough comprehension, when he compares art to nature, nature looks singularly uncomprehended:

We find the Works of Nature still more pleasant, the more they resemble those of Art: For in this case our Pleasure arises from a double Principle; from the agreeableness of the Objects to the Eye, and from their Similitude to other Objects: We are pleased as well with comparing their Beauties, as well as surveying them, and can represent them to our Minds; either as Copies or Originals. Hence it is that we take Delight . . . in any thing that hath such a Variety or Regularity as may seem the Effect of Design, in what we call the Works of Chance. (Bond, *The Spectator*, III, 549–550)

Here nature in the first instance is made up of "Works of Chance." When they resemble works of art, they please first as if they were designed, but second as copies of actual designs, as "Copies or Originals." The pleasure is the not quite aesthetic one created by the accidental effect of order as well as the actual aesthetic apprehension of order. Now, this contradiction can be explained easily enough by remembering that Addison had argued only that one would see the design of nature if one's view were large enough. Still, the faith of the first passage looks considerably modified when the order of an actual artwork is brought into the picture.

If natural design from the perspective of aesthetics did not look as achieved as it did to theologians, the moral order of the world was even less clear, as the debate over the concept of poetic justice makes clear. As originally formulated, poetic justice demanded that works of art allot punishment and reward proportionately according to the evilness and goodness of the characters in the work.[23] This moral-aesthetic demand has always

been more popular with moralists than with either writers or critics of literature. In the eighteenth century, the most obvious objection to it was
that it would make the writing of tragedy impossible, inasmuch as tragedy
depended on the infliction of pain on morally sympathetic characters.[24]
But critics also objected to the fact that the world didn't obviously work
that way, and if art apportioned its rewards and punishments so program-
matically, it would indicate questionable faith in the actual divine order.
Thus Samuel Richardson, when readers appealed to him to save Clarissa
from death on the principle of poetic justice, inveighed against the principle as doubting divine justice and wanting to replace it with an inappropriately worldly poetic justice (IV, 554). In effect, from piety rather than
skepticism, Richardson doubted that the world offered any justification for
rewarding and punishing characters according to their deserts, and argued
that a literature that worked that way would be arbitrary and lacking in
faith. Addison, less pious than Richardson, was willing to see the good suffer, both to preserve tragedy and because no one is so completely good that
his or her suffering cannot be justified by some recondite sin. But he was
unwilling to see the "vicious" escape punishment, not because that did not
happen but because it offended his moral sensibility enough to become an
offense to his aesthetic sensibility (Bond, *The Spectator*, IV, 465). Despite
his different evaluations, then, he essentially agreed with Richardson about
the world's lack of a very persuasive moral design. Butler, of course, never
denied that the world presented a less than perfect moral design, but he
did assert that it showed a basic system of rewards and punishments not
merely according to actions but according to the characters of people
(*Analogy of Religion*, 80). Authors and literary critics were clearly less sure.

Shaftesbury gave them the ability to be surer by fully integrating natural theology and aesthetic theory. Although he did maintain the traditional claim of natural theology that the rational design of nature implied
a designer and that the world, seen properly, looked as if it had a moral
governor, his central task was to show how one could give a foundation to
moral action without simply appealing to God as having created that
morality. He went about that task by positing a system of interlocking aesthetic and moral harmonies. That system still appealed to art as modeling
meaningful form but it solved the problem of the world's failure to mime
successfully art's moral form by arguing for a much more complex sense of
aesthetic form and a much more complex sense of how its perception enabled moral apprehension. In doing so, he moves our argument fully from
the implications of natural theology for aesthetics to a complete articula-

tion of the kind of aesthetic imagination that an immersion in natural theology produced and the kind of natural theology an aesthetics imagined.
This connection, as we will see, produced a Kantian concept of aesthetic
form that has little to do with organicism.

Turning the attention from the fact of design and its presence or absence in nature to what the awareness of design in art implies also recuperates the connection between aesthetic design, moral design, and the argument that the world shows in its workings that it is the product of a
moral governor. The influence of Shaftesbury on the issue of art's moral
significance is now a common matter of discussion. Most frequently, critics debate whether Shaftesbury, by aligning morality with an aesthetic taste
that had the distinct marks of aristocratic cultivation, was in fact supporting a class-based ethics or instead trying to give that ethics a genuinely
more universal foundation.[25] Few have really investigated on what basis he
makes the claims for connecting morality with taste in the first place. Oscar Kenshur (Levine, *Aesthetics and Ideology*, 57–78) explains well the background of the problem: Hobbes had argued that morality was established
by divine omnipotent will in the first place and by secular monarchy after
that. There was in Hobbes no pre-existing moral code against which the
actions of human beings and their rulers could be measured that would
stand independent of its establishment by force. Cambridge Platonists—
Kenshur instances Ralph Cudworth's *A Discourse Concerning Eternal and
Immutable Morality*, published in 1731 but circulated in manuscript before—argued that for moral dicta to be meaningfully moral, they needed
to stand free not only of human choice but even of divine choice (if a God
were genuinely moral, it would be because he followed rather than created
moral laws). But this left open the prior question of the basis of moral law.
This is an old enough theological problem, no doubt. But the notoriety of
Hobbes's *Leviathian*, the fact that Cudworth's response was directed at it
and that Shaftesbury was clearly influenced by Cudworth, gives it a direct
relevance here.[26] Kenshur notes, in my view rightly, in this vein, that
Shaftesbury's attempt to base a moral sense on an aesthetic one, rather than
constructing an empiricist aesthetics that would support a rising bourgeois
ideology, at least meant to define a genuine human response from which
ethical acts could follow. What causes the ideological skepticism about this
attempt, though, is the evident question it seems to leave unanswered:
what is the basis of aesthetic taste and in what sense is there anything moral
about it? Claiming an internal human aesthetic and moral "sense," as both

Shaftesbury and Hutcheson do, essentially inventing a form of sensation that is not entirely experiential but not innate either, only answers the question if its responses are as universally held as those of other forms of sensation.

Shaftesbury's answer to the question of the moral basis of aesthetic response is in the first instance merely assertive and nearly circular:

> The moral Artist, who can thus imitate the Creator, and is thus knowing in the In-ward Form and Structure of his Fellow-Creature, will hardly, I presume, be un-knowing in *Himselfe*, or at a loss in those Numbers which make the Harmony of a Mind. For *Knavery* is mere *Dissonance* and *Disproportion*. And though Villains may have strong *Tones*, and Natural Capacities of Action; 'tis impossible that true *Judgment* and *Ingenuity* should reside, where *Harmony* and *Honesty* have no being. (I, 207–208)

We have already seen Samuel Clarke identify morality with a fitness in the relationship of things, a position that went some distance toward setting up an aesthetic standard for judging moral claims. If Clarke and Shaftesbury partake of the same argument, though, there is nevertheless a signifi-cant distinction between the two formulations.[27] For Clarke, morality is one type of suitable relationship among others. And the terms "suitable" and "fit" in themselves are already as much quasi-moral as they are quasi-aesthetic. Shaftesbury, in contrast, speaks in terms of "Harmony" and "Disproportion," thus positing purely formal qualities. He then connects these qualities, via formal relationship in human internal life—"the Har-mony of the Mind"—with moral quality. Asserting an identity between moral quality and aesthetic order does give morality a foundation outside itself but only at the cost of throwing the question of what constitutes a foundation one step further back. After all, there is nothing self-evidently ethical about harmony. Moreover, since "Harmony" can look like a class-based taste, the argument at this level certainly does give solid support to Shaftesbury's politically skeptical critics.

In fact, Shaftesbury has a fairly complex sense of how ethical order and formal order relate, one which connects both taste and moral inclina-tion with the problem of awareness. First, he insists that awareness is suffi-cient to create moral inclination: "What Mortal, being once convinc'd of a difference in *inward Character*, and of a Preference due to *one* Kind above *another*, wou'd not be concern'd to make *his own* the best? If *Civility* and *Humanity* be a TASTE; if *Brutality, Insolence, Riot*, be in the same manner a TASTE; who if he cou'd reflect, would not chuse to form himself on the amiable and agreeable Model?" (I, 339). Note here that Shaftesbury does not in fact presume that taste will of its own produce moral action. One may through mere taste desire either to be civil or to be brutal. Nor can one establish out of civilized canons of good taste which tastes are preferable. This passage in fact explicitly calls into question the kinds of assumptions about class-based taste that Shaftesbury often seems to hold. The force that determines the choice between one taste and another is in fact not taste itself but a reflection upon tastes. This, rather than an internal form of sensing that gives one perceptions of taste in the way the eye gives one perceptions of light, seems to be the internal and common sense to which Shaftesbury refers. One who "cou'd reflect" will choose one taste over another. And reflection, much more than taste, is for Shaftesbury a defining quality of at least literary art. Thus, in the essay on "Advice to an Author" (I, 153–364), Shaftesbury in fact advises knowing oneself as a divided self, reflecting on oneself as if on another, as a prime ethical value. Literature has a central role in this value both in its form and in its content. First, in the dramatic technique of soliloquy, it offers a model for going about the process of self-awareness. Second, in a lengthy inserted anecdote in which the protagonist learns to recognize his internal duality, Shaftesbury gives us a narrative exemplification of its value. Finally, and most generally, he claims that literature functions to allow us to see ourselves in it. It does this not only in offering specific techniques of self-awareness such as soliloquy, or specific accounts of it, as the anecdote does, but because representation itself creates, by definition, a kind of mirror.

Shaftesbury is not quite an eighteenth-century Paul de Man, though. Reflection is not intrinsically privileged language or knowledge. Nor, although he speaks of choosing in response to its information, does it merely supply images for a second-level taste to choose from. It acquires its importance from one of the features of harmony as a founding value, which is that every system or harmony, to be fully systematic or harmonious, must also partake of a larger harmony, must be a part in a larger whole:

> NOW in this which we call the UNIVERSE, whatever the Perfection may be of any *particular Systems*; or whatever *single Parts* may have Proportion, Unity or Form within themselves; yet if they are not united all in general, in ONE System, but are in respect of one another as the driven Sands, or Clouds, or breaking Waves; then there being no Coherence in *the Whole*, there can be infer'd no Order, no Proportion, and consequently no Project or Design. (II, 285–286)

The logic here is fairly straightforward. If the universe were made up of discrete, separate systems, whatever the harmony and coherence within these systems, the whole would have no harmony but be merely a concatenation of unities interrelated only chaotically, as are the "driven Sands." This claim also works, at least implicitly in reverse: systems that were not related to each other, as parts of larger wholes, could never be completely harmonious. Chaos would hang about their margins. Accordingly, the value of reflectiveness derives from its relation to the necessities of system and harmony. To be a harmonious system completely, the system must be connected with other systems in a mutually reflective state. Reflectiveness and systematicity thus start to give a basis to each other. One would choose civility rather than brutishness, not perhaps because human beings are naturally benevolent, but because, in reflecting, one catches sight of the systems that also reflect each other—moral inclination, aesthetic sensibility— at the cost of those modes of action that, whatever internal order they might have, are always in dissonance because they are not caught up within the larger system. By the same token, while any given harmony may seem arbitrary and self-imposed, the harmony of all systems starts to look like an intended and significant design. In this way, in making morality and aesthetics ground each other, Shaftesbury posits an internal sense whose information may ultimately be relied on, not because all beings do or ought to share common tastes, but because they share the reflectiveness that will see systemic interrelation. And the special role of aesthetics here is not in a class-given set of tastes but in the reflectiveness on which it depends and which it induces.

So smaller systems imply greater systems and greater systems need to be in place for smaller systems to be truly harmonious. And when he offers his version of the argument from design, Shaftesbury does more than simply imply this reflection between macrocosm and microcosm. In general terms, he follows the pattern we have been seeing in natural theologians whereby the order of art, as a contrived design, becomes the model for reading the order of nature. But his version of the argument takes a slightly different route. Like Addison, he recognizes that the world does not always look patterned. Unlike Ray and Paley, he sees stones as often as watches when he walks on heaths. But he attributes his perception of stones to his lack of knowledge rather than the object's lack of order:

Now in this mighty UNION, if there be such Relations of Parts one to another as are not easily discover'd; if on this account the End and Use of Things does not every-where appear, there is no wonder; since 'tis no more indeed than what must happen of necessity: Nor cou'd supreme Wisdom have otherwise order'd it. For in an Infinity of Things thus relative, a Mind which sees not *infinitely* can see nothing *fully*: and since each Particular has relation to all in general, it can know no perfect or true Relation of any Thing, in a World not perfectly and fully known. (II, 288)

On its own terms, this passage suggests a retreat from the logic of natural theology equal to Addison's argument that the whole design of nature cannot be seen because of human limitation. Shaftesbury more positively asserts design than Addison does. But, by attributing our inability to see it to our limited perspective, he makes design a consequence of faith rather than an evidence of divine creation. But Shaftesbury does see local design as implying comprehensive design and comprehensive design as necessitating local design everywhere. Thus, analogizing the world to a ship under weigh, he argues that a passenger on that ship, having knowledge that it operates toward a general end that he can perceive and also perceiving local elements of the ship operating as instrumental to that end, would assume that parts of the ship whose working he did not understand also served that end. In the same way, the perception of various local orders in the world leads to the conclusion that the world as a whole is ordered (II, 289). In effect, the argument from design operates from the aesthetic concept of interlocking harmonies rather than from a straight progression from the perception of design to the consequence of a designer.

By arguing that interlocking harmonious form offers an aesthetic justification for acting morally, Shaftesbury's theory can also lead to a different way of reading the concept of poetic justice and thus a way of explaining the moral working of the world through aesthetic form. The concept of poetic justice rises both from the perceived connections between the design of art and the possible orders of the world and from an evident disconnection between them. We have seen Richardson complain that to insist on the secular apportionment of punishment and reward to moral action and character was to doubt divine providence. Oddly, Rymer based his argument for poetic justice precisely on that doubt. Putting his argument in the mouths of classical writers on drama, he claims:

Finding also that this *unequal* distribution of rewards and punishments did perplex the *wisest*, and by the *Atheist* was made a scandal to *Divine Providence*. They concluded that a *Poet* must of necessity see *justice* exactly administered, if he intended to please. For, said they, if the World can scarce be satisfi'd with God Almighty, whose holy will and purpose are not to be *comprehended*; a *Poet* (in these matters) shall never be pardon'd, who (they are sure) is not *incomprehensible*; whose *ways* and *walks* may, without impiety be penetrated and examin'd. (Rymer, *The Critical Works of Thomas Rymer*, 22)

The justification for demanding that poets allot rewards and punishments in a comprehensible way is precisely that they can do so and that we understand their intent in terms of their doing so. We, thus, have no reason to withhold a judgment of unjust arrangement in the case of a work of art that did not allot rewards and punishments satisfactorily, though we would have a reason in the case of injustice in the natural world, where judging God's intent would be presumptuous. The real problem with Rymer's demands is not that it is naive in terms of secular ambiguities, or even, Richardson notwithstanding, that it is impious about divine providence. Rather it is both naive and impious about literary design, insisting on a simplicity to which few artists, though numbers of moralists, would assent.

When the world is actually modeled on justice aesthetically designed, though, one can be unsure how to take the explanation. Addison, discussing the mysteries of providence, offers an anecdotal justification that clearly asserts a kind of poetic justice. In the anecdote, Moses discusses with God the "administration of the Universe":

In the midst of this Divine Colloquy [Moses] was commanded to look down on the Plain below. At the foot of the Mountain there issued out a clear Spring of Water, at which a Soldier alighted from his Horse to Drink. He was no sooner gone than a little Boy came to the same Place, and finding a Purse of Gold which the Soldier had dropped, took it up and went away with it. Immediately after this came an Infirm old Man, weary with Age and Travelling, and having quenched his Thirst, sat down to rest himself by the side of the Spring. The Soldier missing his Purse returns to search for it, and demands it of the old Man, who affirms he had not seen it, and appeals to Heaven in witness of his Innocence. The Soldier, not believing his Protestations, kills him. *Moses* fell on his Face with Horror and Amazement, when the Divine Voice thus prevented his Expostulation, "Be not surprised, Moses, nor ask why the Judge of the whole Earth has suffer'd this thing to come to pass; the Child is the Occasion that the Blood of the Old man is spilt; but know, that the old Man whom thou sawest was the Murderer of that Child's Father." (Bond, *The Spectator*, IV, 423)

With the instinct of a narrator rather than a natural theologian, Addison here ends his letter on the ways the mysteries of providence might be understood, drawing no explicit conclusion. From the perspective of a narrative with a surprise ending, this anecdote is a bit primitive but outlines the kinds of satisfactions an ironically switched allotment of justice can create and why this kind of ending is more frequently referred to as "poetic justice" than the ones Rymer requested and Richardson railed against. But one hardly imagines that Bishop Butler would appeal to it as evidence of a moral governor of the world. After all, the boy gets away with theft, and justifying the father's death by saying that it balances his son's theft is hardly more satisfactory. The soldier is still guilty of murder, or at least a somewhat intemperate violence, even if he has been the instrument of a larger justice. Even the old man does not know why he has been killed; thus while a balance of violence has been effected, one may still doubt whether that alone counts as justice.

This is, of course, an extraordinarily flat-footed reading of a tale that is, after all, not that subtle. It makes the elemental mistake of insisting on reading the events from perspective of the participants as if they were real agents of their ends rather than from the perspective of Moses—the embodiment of an audience to the drama—for whose edification the design was created. The mistake has the value, however, of reminding us how artificial and constructed the intended perspective is. Narrative design here offers a possible justification for the workings of human action and divine providence by proposing that surprise resolutions beyond our knowledge may occur. At the empirical level, this justification will only satisfy if we do not question closely what it would mean for a secular judge to act in such a way. As a pure assertion of design first missed and then restored, however, it works so obviously as not to need further comment from Addison. In effect, narrative design does not really propose to justify the actual shape of nature. It merely proposes models for how moral design might work. Seen from the perspective of the connections between aesthetics and natural theology, the eighteenth-century debate over poetic justice looks much more like part of the larger debate of how to use the intentional design of art to read the proposed intentional design of nature. Indeed, it shows us why art and literature, as opposed to things designed with clear instrumental ends, such as watches, had to function as the deeper models of moral design in the world. One couldn't really claim that the moral workings of the world explained its shape as clearly as the end of telling time accounted for the relationship of part to whole in a watch. But one could at least suggest that it had a moral design of the kind one saw in certain kinds of narratives, and, by extension, in artworks generally. The result of the linking was not to insist on a verisimilitude in the represented content of art but to learn to see the world—as a matter of theory in Shaftesbury and as a matter of narrative effect in Addison—in terms of artistic form. The complexity of art and of theories about it here rests not on its "organic," unintended quality but precisely on what its contrivance can tell us about how to read design. In this context, Hume's destruction via precision-instrument analysis of natural theology and Kant's attempt to restore a version of it via a revised aesthetics will, I think, provide a basis for the more recent dissatisfactions with the theory of organic form, as well as the model that the arguments resulting from that dissatisfaction have taken.

III. Purposiveness and Undesign: Hume and Kant

The first readers of Hume's *Dialogues Concerning Natural Religion* probably would not have attributed the quality of precision to his arguments. Cleanthes in the text describes Philo's objections to the argument from design as "the utmost indulgence of your imagination" (*Dialogues,* 169). And Kant, who assented to Hume's basic conclusion about the inadequacy of the argument, also described his analysis as "far-fetched subtleties so elaborately thought out" (*Pure Reason,* 597). Hume's precision, though, lay not in the way he undoes our sense that the world is designed—in fact he barely attacks that perception at all. Rather, he fixes on the logic of claiming to deduce from a designed effect the cause of a designing intelligence whose intention may be read. Although Philo's alternative suppositions to this analogy are often indeed wild and hyperbolic, their point is quite precise: formal pattern cannot logically equal intentional design, and thus no significance can be interpreted from it. Although we frequently speak as if we have digested and surpassed Hume, the skepticism he directs at the analysis of formal pattern remains relevant for most contemporary analyses of literature and literary history—emphatically including this one—that have as their project the reading of ideological or historical relation out of simultaneity of event or formal relationship. In other words, given the connection between natural theology and aesthetic argument, Hume's dismantling of the argument from design will have resonance for more than one kind of design.

Although Philo offers numbers of suppositions for how the world's order may have been produced, his argument against assuming that design presumes an intelligent designer remains basically the one he lays out in part II. Cleanthes proposes that parts relate to wholes in the universe with the artifice characteristic of a contrived machine, that contrived machines we know of are all the effect of design by an intending will, and thus, by analogy, so must the world be (*Dialogues*, 143). To this, Philo responds, "If we see a house, Cleanthes, we conclude, with the greatest certainty, that it had an architect or builder because this is precisely that species of effect which we have experienced to proceed from that species of cause. But surely you will not affirm that the universe bears such a resemblance to a house that we can with the same certainty infer a similar cause, or that the analogy is here entire and perfect" (*Dialogues*, 144). Cleanthes objects that all our experience of order includes the fact that the order has been intentionally designed and so the analogy between the causes he first asserted is very close indeed. And Philo immediately starts proposing examples of undesigned order as well as noting the extreme limits of our experience when it comes to the issue of design in the world (*Dialogues*, 149).

In short, Philo argues not that we do not accurately perceive design but that the analogy between design in the world and human contrivance is not close enough to reach from the cause of one to the cause of the other. The argument, it should be noted, is as counter-intuitive as it is logically forceful. Most of Philo's wild alternative versions of creation, vegetable generation, for instance, or, memorably, insemination by random comet (*Dialogues*, 177), take as their model forms of biological reproduction. To this supposition Paley will later object that imagining a watch that had been designed to reproduce itself naturally would hardly reduce our sense that it must be the result of an intending intelligence. Indeed, it would only enhance our admiration for that intelligence, since the mechanism of biological generation operates as further evidence of a designing intelligence (Paley, *Natural Theology*, 8–9). Philo has answered this question in advance with two arguments. First he argues that the supposition of an intending divine mind still leaves open the question of what caused that mind (*Dialogues*, 161). And second, he says that if we allow that all questioning of origins has to stop somewhere, there is no less reason to be satisfied with vegetable generation or cometary insemination than there is to be satisfied with designing intelligence. Despite the logic of his case, though, Philo's argument cannot overcome the commonsense force of attributing a design to a designer. The conclusion of a designer seems to follow virtually by definition from the apprehension of a design.

In order to get rid of our sense of the power of the argument from design, the most effective argument is to question our assurance that de-

sign in fact exists, but prior to Darwin, this method was never that powerful. Late in the *Dialogues*, Philo tries to question that assurance but abandons the attempt when Cleanthes objects with examples of complex organization—eyes, ears, the usual suspects (*Dialogues*, 186). We are left then
in a rather uncomfortable situation. Philo's logic calls into question quite
effectively the formal strength of the analogy on which Cleanthes's natural
theology rests, but leaves generally untouched Cleanthes's strongest claim:
the perception of design that he argues needs the explanation that only
natural theology seems to provide in a satisfying way. This impasse has two
effects. The first Hume clearly intends: such logical dead ends in Hume always work to question the pretensions of reason itself. They oppose what
seems empirically undeniable with the fallacy of drawing the most obvious
conclusion from that appearance. The second effect, though, results from
the seeming consequences that this impasse has for a formalist view of intentionless design: while seeming to create the need for such a concept,
Hume's discussion of design also shows its deep incoherence. This aspect
of his argument becomes clear as we consider Cleanthes's second assertion
of design. And this moment in the text reconnects even the debunking of
natural theology with aesthetics.

Between Philo's first and his second refutation of Cleanthes's analogy,
Cleanthes reasserts his argument in terms that the narrator of the *Dialogues*
asserts leaves Philo "a little embarrassed" (*Dialogues*, 155).[28] Understanding
Philo's embarrassment and why it does not last reconnect Hume's argument with the aesthetic issues I have been discussing. To undo Philo's objections to an analogy between human design and natural order, Cleanthes
returns to the constant example of natural design, the eye:

> The declared profession of every reasonable sceptic is only to reject abstruse, re-
> mote, and refined arguments; to adhere to common sense and the plain instincts
> of nature; and to assent, wherever any reasons strike him with so full a force that
> he cannot, without the greatest violence, prevent it. Now the arguments for natu-
> ral religion are plainly of this kind; and nothing but the most perverse, obstinate
> metaphysics can reject them. Consider, anatomize the eye, survey its structure and
> contrivance, and tell me, from your own feeling, if the idea of a contriver does not
> immediately flow in upon you with a force like that of sensation. The most obvi-
> ous conclusion surely is in favour of design; and it requires time, reflection, and
> study, to summon up these frivolous though abstruse objections which can sup-
> port infidelity. (*Dialogues*, 154)

In an article that also connects Hume's arguments against natural theology with Kant's aesthetics, Jerry Sobol has argued this passage as a point on the way toward learning to see and talk about formal design in a way that does not insist on an intending designer and that leads toward the Kantian motto of objective formalism, "purposiveness without purpose" (Sobol, "Arguing, Accepting, and Preserving," 274–277). Sobol looks closely at the passage I have just cited, noting how Cleanthes's rhetoric has changed here, how he does not argue logical connection, but appeals to "your own feeling," to Philo's "sensation," and how he asks him to admit a kind of natural assent. These appeals, Sobol argues, quite rightly I think, are quasi-aesthetic, certainly in terms of the eighteenth-century theories of an internal but also empirical sense of moral and beautiful design.

If Sobol shows us how to see this passage in the context of aesthetics, he gets Cleanthes's conclusion and so, I think, its ultimate significance, exactly wrong. Sobol argues that in concluding with an appeal to "the idea of a contriver," Cleanthes has abandoned the image of designed machines inasmuch as "it is 'the idea of a contriver,' that is, design itself, which is to be felt" (Sobol, 277). But "the idea of a contriver" is precisely not the idea of design itself, but the goal of the argument from design, that design always presumes one who designs, one who contrives. Sobol's formalism follows the New Critical antagonism to language about machines, and so when Cleanthes gives up machines and logic for feeling and sensation, Sobol assumes he is giving up argument for aesthetics, theology for intentionless design. Cleanthes's appeal is openly rhetorical here, but he in fact merely reasserts his original argument. The point of the passage is that the eye makes the fact of contrivance, *and so of a contriver*, so empirically obvious, that only a willful metaphysics opposed to common sense could deny it. The post-Coleridgean view of machines as exemplifying a bad because artificially imposed order, one must remember, is one that most in the eighteenth century do not share. The question at hand was whether nature was designed or was merely chaotic. A uniquely aesthetic or organic category of unintended design, "design itself" just did not yet exist.

Obviously, Hume's point differs from an aesthetic theorist's. He wants to put Cleanthes's claims about the messages of our senses in an irresolvable conflict with Philo's reason. His argument, posed before Darwin's empirical explanation of how seeming design could occur contingently, is exactly as paradoxical as his arguments against cause and effect and against the unity of personal identity. After all, if Hume had merely disproven the logic of natural theology, he would have disproven a particular use of reason. Philo's argument, famously, though, is against the pretensions of reason to give intelligible order to reality. Consequently, within the terms of Hume's argument, a mediating position between intended design and chaos, a formalist concept of an intentionless "design itself" is simply incoherent. And yet the two coherent alternatives, either that the world has a contriver or that the world is undesigned, the alternatives constantly offered by prior natural theologians, are shown to be equally unacceptable, the first because it is based on insufficient reason, the second because it affronts our sense of what is before us.[29]

Probably if the issue had been left with an opposition between Philo's logical attack and Cleanthes's appeal to the sight of design before us, the empirical appearance of design would always have held sway over the problems of logic. Hume thus opens a second phase in the argument, one in which Philo's objections to design arise more from the look of material reality and are thus, though far more rhetorically effective, somewhat contradictory in terms of Hume's larger argument. This contradiction—a return in a different register of the contradiction between logically denying design and inescapably seeing it—matters because it indicates why aesthetics must function as a renewed design theory. In its fullest terms, Hume's debunking of design questions all delineations of formal pattern. Few modern cultural or ideological theorists could live with such skepticism, since, though they have no stake in natural theology, they routinely take evidence of function for evidence of design in discussions of historical causation. And Hume's second argument against design shows that he cannot live with it either. This second argument opens when Philo argues that if design implies a designer, that designer's intention should also be able to be interpreted, just as one interprets the meaning of a book or poem. As we have seen, the argument from design was always also about the claim to read the benevolent intention of the deity through the resources of aesthetic interpretation or sensibility. Allowing design, Philo will not allow that the design shows the deity to be particularly moral or even particularly competent. Cleanthes both asserts and admits that in order to move from natural design to divine benevolence, one must also assert the basic goodness of the world. Philo immediately sees that the argument has turned to his advantage (*Dialogues*, 200–201).

We need hardly go over the details of Philo's argument here; it essentially rehearses the problem of evil in the world. One fold of it, though, is worth notice. For the first time in the discussion of human artifice and natural order, Hume proposes using a view of nature to model what an art that followed its order might look like, rather than the reverse. Having noted that if one does not begin with the presumption of a benevolent deity, nature's design flaws are all too obvious, Philo returns to the idea with which the argument started, that a house implies an architect: "Did I show you a house or palace where there was not one apartment convenient or agreeable, where the windows, doors, fires, passages, stairs, and the whole economy of the building were the source of noise, confusion, fatigue, darkness, and the extremes of heat and cold, you would certainly blame the contrivance, without any further examination" (*Dialogues*, 204). We have seen how Addison tries to respond to the problem of injustice in the world by imagining the world as operating like a narrative with a surprise ending. Hume responds to the assertion of moral design with the image of a human contrivance as if built with the inconveniences of nature. In so doing, he shows how central the weak case of moral design was to the stronger case of physical design in natural theology. After all, if the argument from design only indicated a bumbling and incompetent divine artificer, capable of crafting the human eye, but also of having left the most obvious elements of moral reward in a state for which one might blame any human artist, it established no better a case for a Christian God than would the assertion of pure chaos.

Hume's argument against design theory, then, can be divided into two parts whose relationship is finally more rhetorical than logical. In the first part, he attacks the premise in design theory of turning formal relationship and analogy into causal linkage. That eyes see and ears hear only shows that that is what they do, not that that is what they were designed to do. Numbers of causes are sufficient to explain biological organization, no one having any logical priority. At this point, one should note that his argument has a far wider resonance than a mere attack on design. As part of his wider attack on the impostures of reason, as I said at the outset, it questions precisely the mode of making causal connections that is necessary to any basic historical or natural analysis. In other words, if arguing from the eye to an intelligent designer assumes too much, given other possible causes, what would Philo say about arguing from the simultaneity of an aesthetic form and an ideological event to a connection between them, or for that matter arguing from the formal coincidence of elements in natural theology and in eighteenth-century aesthetics to a common project between them. If we accept the strength of Philo's argument, we ought also to share his embarrassment in the face of moments of order, rather than leaping, like a Cleanthes or a Foucault, from a seeming pattern to a divine will or a discursive formation.

Kant's reestablishment of aesthetics as a model for reading natural design, while trying to do justice to the strength of Hume's most skeptical claims, clearly intends to alleviate both Philo's embarrassment and ours in our need to draw empirical conclusions from formal relation. In placing Kant's *Critique of Judgment* in the context first of natural theology and then of Hume's debunking of it, I want to suggest that his concept of harmonious form, purposiveness without purpose, will only make sense if read as a quite conscious attempt both to define a mode of perceiving design without a designer and to stay clear of the obvious fallacy, in the wake of Hume, of presuming such a thing to be an actual feature of objects. As such, Kant's aesthetic judgment, rather than an extension of reason, becomes, as we have seen Terry Eagleton suggesting, a prosthesis for it. But a prosthesis, by definition, marks a lack on the part of its wearer, in this case reason, and thus always exceeds that wearer's original form, even if it fulfills the aims for which it was designed perfectly. Kant's aesthetics, and in particular his revision of the concept of aesthetic harmony—although surely designed to buttress an albeit limited return to pre-Humean concepts of order and regularity in nature—conclude in a view of artificed perception that can only work fully to question designs even as it delineates them, to mark artifice and prosthesis wherever it marks structure and pattern. Kant begins his revision of earlier aesthetics by proposing aesthetic harmony as a mode of interpreting objects, not as a feature of objects. And he constructs that mode out of an awareness of its own internal contradictions without trying either to elide those contradictions or to claim that some higher form contains them. In effect, like the eighteenth-century British aesthetic theorists, whose influence on him is well known, he takes art as a model to understand nature. Unlike them, however, he begins with the recognition that that model cannot explain the essence of nature. It can only explain how we may and must interpret it. Designed art cannot show us how to understand designed nature, since we cannot presume that nature in fact results from design. But how we perceive aesthetic form can tell us what we are doing when we posit natural orders and linkages. Needless to say, this revision also entails extreme revisions in all the concepts he draws from British aesthetics, most particularly that of form.[30] In order to make the case for reading "purposiveness without purpose" as a reaction to the problems of natural theology, we must look at three aspects of Kant's theory: first its roots in the discussion of the argument from design in *The Critique of Pure Reason*; second the tying of aesthetic judgment to the propriety of teleological judgment, or in other words, the judgment of nature as purposive; and third a deciphering of how to make sense of what the phrase means in such a way as to preserve the contradiction in it, of which Kant was explicitly aware.

We have seen Kant characterize Hume's discussion of natural theology as "far-fetched subtleties, so elaborately thought-out" (*Pure Reason*, 597), but to comprehend fully his judgment of Hume's argument, we must also note that he thought Hume justified in applying those subtleties to the claims of the argument from design, because that argument claimed to go beyond an empirical description of the world; thus, though his speculations were far-fetched, "as he rightly held, their object lies entirely outside the limits of natural science, in the domain of pure ideas" (*Pure Reason*, 598). Although Hume would certainly never use such terminology, the passage shows the basic accord between Kant's own quite cursory disproof of the argument from design and Hume's more extended one. The context of that cursory disproof is necessary to understand its logic. As I mentioned above, Kant took all arguments for the existence of God as examples of what he termed the fallacy of the ideal of Pure Reason. That ideal grows out of the impetus to give empirical embodiment to ideas of Pure Reason, which, in reality, apply to no concept of the understanding. All proofs of the existence of an omnipotent God, Kant wanted to show, reduce to versions of this fallacy by reproducing the famous flaw he finds in the ontological argument of taking existence as a predicate. The argument from design—Kant calls it the physico-theological proof—claims to avoid this fallacy because it does not argue from the concept of a perfect being to its existence but from the empirical evidence of the world to that being's causal necessity. Without denying that evidence, Kant nevertheless finds it insufficient to prove anything beyond itself; thus, like Hume, he assents to the appearance of design while disallowing the conclusion natural theology would draw:

On this method of argument, the purposiveness and harmonious adaptation of so much in nature can suffice to prove the contingency of the form merely, not of the matter, that is not of the substance in the world. To prove the latter we should have to demonstrate that the things in the world would not of themselves be capable of such order and harmony, in accordance with universal laws, if they were not *in*

their substance the product of supreme wisdom. But to prove this we should require quite other grounds of proof than those, which are derived from the analogy
with human art. The utmost, therefore, that the argument can prove is an *architect* of the world who is always very much hampered by the adaptability of the material in which he works, not a *creator* of the world to whose idea everything is subject. This, however, is altogether inadequate to the lofty purpose which we have
before our eyes, namely, the proof of an all-sufficient primordial being. To prove
the contingency of matter itself, we should have to resort to a transcendental argument, and this is precisely what we have here set out to avoid. (*Pure Reason*, 522)

Far more than Hume, Kant is willing to admit that the external form of
nature looks designed. But the design of external form can only prove what
the appearance of design in human art proves, a limited designer, a hampered architect, perhaps the builder of Hume's rather inconvenient house.
This figure could not be the supervening God of the world but only a being possessing higher powers than those of humans, one who worked with
the already existing material of the world. In order to prove that matter itself was caused, we would have to move beyond its empirical appearance,
something the empirical evidence of natural theology cannot do. To do so
would be to return to the transcendental fallacy of the ontological argument, essentially taking existence for essence. While avoiding Hume's far-
fetched subtleties, Kant thus still invokes their point: our knowledge of
empirical design and its causes cannot be a proper analogy from which to
conclude about the origin of creation as a whole.

By the end of *The Critique of Pure Reason*, at least with regard to the
status of the argument from design, Kant has left Hume's skepticism relatively untouched.[31] He does allow that one can usefully posit design merely
heuristically, but only in full recognition that one may draw no empirical
conclusions from the use one attains from its application (*Pure Reason*,
560–561). The next stage in Kant's development of the aesthetics of purposiveness occurs with a stronger claim for the necessity of seeing the world
as morally ordered despite the logical inability to claim a designing will.
The Critique of Judgment opens first with a radical circumscription of reason and thus with a consequent requirement for a stronger connection between reason's need to read designed and purposive unity and the understanding's insistence on positing merely contingent physical causality. In
his first section, on the division of philosophy, Kant argues that reason is
limited to articulating *"concepts of freedom,"* which apply to the supersensible, moral realm, while objects of cognition may only be accurately the

subject of the "*natural concepts*" of the understanding (*Judgment*, 7). In other words, while reason posits moral duties, laws, and obligations, it seems to have no empirical function, not even a regulative one. This division leads Kant to argue that the two separated fields of thought must be made to function together through a purposive reading of the world: "The concept of freedom is meant to actualize in the world of sense the purpose proposed by its laws, and consequently nature must be so thought that the conformity to law of its form at least harmonizes with the possibility of the purposes to be effected in it according to laws of freedom. There must, therefore, be a ground of the *unity* of the supersensible, which lies at the basis of nature, with that which the concept of freedom contains." (*Judgment*, 12). Kant affirms this abstract claim much later in the book, when he imagines the possibility of a moral atheist (he specifies Spinoza) and argues that the atheist's commitment to the moral law could not withstand the vision of an amoral world; he would give up his moral purpose as "impossible" in that world. The only alternative would be, as a practical matter, to assume the world as designed by a "*moral* author" (*Judgment*, 303–304), so that he could align his actions with a rational final purpose. In effect, then, moral action presupposes a reading of the world as appearing to be not only designed but morally designed.

It is worth pausing over the coincidence between this argument and Shaftesbury's nearly identical claim. Shaftesbury allows that an atheist could be moral. But, because atheism led to a refusal to assent to a moral order to the world, and only such an order made acting morally ultimately meaningful, he would be less psychologically likely to be able to maintain moral comportment than a believer (*Characteristics*, II, 71). Despite his relentless attack upon dogmatic philosophy, Kant shares what I will in a later chapter call the world-picture of natural theology. He sees human existence as having value only in a world that at least looks ordered. Because he has destroyed the logic that would allow one to see that the world is in fact ordered, he replaces that claim with one of appearance. He will show not that the world is ordered but that it nevertheless appears to be ordered. His aesthetics will give a value to accepting appearance and accepting it as mere appearance. The acceptance of mere appearance as having its own value in turn enables skeptical applications of that aesthetics aimed at undoing the philosophy it was supposed to support. And this double-edged quality to his aesthetics also follows the way the earlier use of aesthetics and its ambiguities to explain the moral order of the world enabled Hume's use of it to attack notions of complex order in the world. The next chapter will turn directly to the ways Kantian aesthetics could, while remaining true to its own form, become Nietzschean aesthetics. And that will prepare the way for showing how postmodern aesthetics, still making use of the resources of Kantian aesthetics, attacked Enlightenment foundations of reason and ethics. But that history starts here with Kant's recognition that his moral order rested on appearance and his project, in his aesthetics, of justifying appearance as appearance rather than finding an essence within.

Arguing that, in order to act morally, we need to think of the world as designed does not, after all, prove that we have any basis for so thinking. By juxtaposing the opening of *The Critique of Judgment* with its later somewhat tenuous argument for a belief in a moral deity, we in effect exacerbate the problem posed in that opening since, on the one hand, our understanding can operate accurately only within its own limits, which disallow the positing of a unifying order to nature, while our moral commitment necessitates such a positing. Kant proposes as a bridge between the understanding and the reason the faculty of judgment, which, he argues, shows us the necessity of presupposing purposiveness.[32] In effect, although Kant allows that we cannot derive any supersensible principles from our knowledge of nature (the mistaken procedure of the argument from design), it is possible to posit natural principles from the necessities of thought. Thus, though we cannot get to a purposed world simply from our moral need of it, we can argue that we are right to analyze as if nature were purposive if those terms were a necessary presupposition of judgment: "The effect in accordance with the concept of freedom is the final purpose which (or its phenomenon in the world of sense) ought to exist, and the condition of the possibility of this is presupposed in nature. . . . The judgment presupposes this *a priori* and without reference to the practical, and thus furnishes the mediating concept between the concepts of nature and that of freedom" (*Judgment*, 32–33). To get to this conclusion that the faculty of judgment presupposes the very principle of reading nature purposively that the moral concepts of freedom demand, we must trace a logic from the needs of judgment to the role of aesthetic judgment in showing the propriety of those needs and the possibility of applying the mode of aesthetic judgment to the demands of teleological judgment. This logic in turn will outline the peculiar definition of aesthetic form that Kant proposes.

Kant begins the process by distinguishing between the determinant and the reflective judgment. Given the concepts of the understanding, the determinant judgment groups various sensations under those concepts (*Judgment*, 15–16). It has no need to generate concepts or laws because it operates with the laws already given it. In contrast, the "reflective judgment, which is obliged to ascend from the particular in nature to the universal, requires on that account a principle that it cannot borrow from experience, because its function is to establish the unity of all empirical principles under higher ones" (*Judgment*, 16). The reflective judgment has to generate higher-level generalities to cover experiences not already sufficiently grouped under already existing concepts or laws. In order to engage in this activity, though, it needs a principle of its own that will regulate its organizing activities. Otherwise those activities would not be truly organizational but simply random groupings. Kant proposes as that general principle the presumption of nature's purposiveness: "the principle of judgment, in respect of the form of things of nature under empirical laws generally, is the *purposiveness of nature* in its variety" (*Judgment*, 17). When at the end of the introduction, Kant connects the concepts of nature and freedom through the judgment's a priori establishment of a principle of natural purposiveness, that principle is not one that the judgment produces but rather the single principle necessary for the judgment to use if it is to operate as a faculty at all. As a highest-level principle of unity, the judgment presupposes that nature has the synthesizing unity of purposiveness.

At this point, we must recall the argument from design and the task I argue that Kant is giving himself of reconstructing its effects without depending on its transcendental presumptions, thus of dealing with nature as designed without presupposing a designer. Many of Kant's critics assume that the point of *The Critique of Judgment* is (or at least ought to be) solely establishing the propriety of aesthetic judgment. By defining natural purposiveness as merely a regulative principle, they then argue that Kant needed merely to show that the aesthetic judgment operated in accord with the structure and limits of that principle. They can then conclude that Kant has properly shown how the aesthetic judgment may claim universal assent without making any empirically verifiable claims about the object of its judgment.[33] In so limiting Kant's project, these critics have missed both Kant's larger claims for aesthetics and the difficulties behind making those claims. After all, the reflective judgment's need for the presupposition of purposiveness hardly, by itself, shows that that presupposition must be taken as necessary in a sense wide enough to act as the connection between the understanding's cognitive knowledge of nature and the reason's articulations of moral obligations. If the judgment has to presuppose purposiveness, that might be merely a Humean predisposition rather than a pre-condition of proper understanding and cognition. Kant both establishes the need to presuppose purposiveness and makes it more ambiguous through his consideration of the difficulties inherent in its very concept.

The formalist reading of Kant, which attends to the aesthetic judgment without considering its role in the teleological judgment, begins by attempting to drain the term *purposiveness* of its problematic element. This criticism constructs a definition of purposiveness that avoids the implications of intent that would make it problematic and would make Kant's quality of purposiveness without purpose contradictory as a description of an actual formal feature of an object. One method for doing this is to follow an alternative translation that renders *zweck* and *zweckmässigkeit* as *end* and *finality*, rather than *purpose* and *purposiveness*.[34] As we will see in a moment, this only apparently solves the problem, since Kant's definitions entail the problem of intention regardless of what English terms one uses.

Two sentences in section X following the first definition of *zweck* make it clear that the word entails all the suggestions of intentionality connoted by the English word *purpose*: "Where then not merely the cognition of an object but the object itself (its form and existence) is thought as an effect only possible by means of the concept of this latter, there we think a purpose. The representation of the effect is here the determining ground of its cause and precedes it" (*Judgment*, 55). If a concept produces an object rather than allowing us to organize sensible appearances into an object we apprehend, and it produces it by representing the effect before it produces it, one can only say that it intends that effect. Indeed, design theory, as far back at least as Cudworth, explicitly posits that intended purpose entails a prior representation of an end as desired that produces an object as a means to that end (*True Intellectual System*, 679). The reason for insisting on this intentionality becomes clear with the definition of *purposiveness* (*zweckmässigkeit*):

An object, or a state of mind, does not necessarily presuppose the representation of a purpose merely because its possibility can be explained and conceived by us only so far as we assume for its ground a causality according to purposes, i.e. in accordance with a will which has regulated it according to the representation of a certain rule. There can be then, purposiveness without purpose, so far as we do not place the causes of this form in a will, but yet can only make the explanation of its possibility intelligible to ourselves by deriving it from a will. (*Judgment*, 55)

Purposiveness, then, Kant argues, is the look of an object that has the form of something that has been designed according to a purpose. So far all this definition entails is the claim that intentionally designed objects have distinctive forms. But Kant then claims that given this feature of the form of objects, one can claim a purposiveness to their form without actually claiming that they are the products of purposes. Thus the judgment could claim to see design in nature, to see it as if designed by a will with moral ends, and could make that claim as one about the form of objects without making the further assertion that one has actually arrived at the proof of the existence of designing will.

Because this definition has so frequently been identified with concepts of organic and aesthetic form as special kinds of self-contained wholes, it is worth replacing it in the context of teleological judgments of nature that it will ultimately serve. If we look again at that watch Paley found on a heath—it takes a philosophical licking, but it keeps on ticking—we will see how fragile Kant's definition is. A watch has the form of purposiveness in the sense that every part of it plays a role in the whole as leading to the function of the whole: telling time. It is not merely an intricate contraption, but an intricate contraption with a purpose. Moreover, the organization cannot be described without reference to that purpose, that it was designed to tell time. If we attribute that kind of form to nature, a form whose definition is that its formal features can only be explained as serving a purpose, an intended function, can we really deny that we are also presuming a purpose at the same time? If we say that the structure of the eye has purposiveness, that it has the form of something designed for seeing, can we then deny that we are also saying that it was designed for that end? Paley would argue that we cannot. Hume would argue that we need to learn to see the eye in different terms, or at least not to make premature presumptions that we are seeing its form rather than a possibly false analogy of it. Kant wants to make the seemingly impossible dual claim that we are right to perceive the form in that way even though we should draw no conclusions from what seems embedded in the very definition of the form.[35]

Kant, moreover, clearly knew the contradiction of what he was trying to define. While he argues in the introduction that the teleological judgment apprehends an objective purposiveness to nature, he also notes later on that one cannot really deny purpose in that situation: "But to represent to oneself a formal *objective* purposiveness without purpose, i.e. the mere form of a *perfection* (without any matter and without the *concept* of that with which it is accordant, even if it were merely the idea of conformity to law in general), is a veritable contradiction" (*Judgment*, 64). That contradiction, though, is necessary to the teleological judgment. When the teleological judgment takes purposiveness as its ordering presupposition, it presumes a natural order readable as if it had been constructed with a purpose and at the same time withholds any claim that it had been so constructed. One can make sense of this presupposition as one that allows us to organize individual items by presuming that there will always be a general law of a high enough order of magnitude under which to classify them, that law being a presupposed purposeful design that orders all of nature. In order to assert such a presupposition as a necessary regulative principle, however, one must first show that it is even a possible regulative principle. The presumption of purposive order synthesizes nature in such a way as to make reason's moral laws meaningful within understanding's cognition of nature. The withholding of the claim that that purposiveness implies a conclusion of purpose protects that presumption from affronting the limits of understanding. It argues the existence of a transcendental ordering principle whose concept the understanding cannot accurately supply, but it does not claim a knowledge it in principle cannot have. But this tightrope walk between seeing a designed nature while not claiming the reality of the design will not work if the concept of objective purposiveness—a purposiveness that may exist at least in the absence of purpose, if not absolutely without it—cannot be made coherent on its own terms. And Kant's definition of the term, with its open acceptance of near contradiction, leaves that necessary coherence doubtful.

At this point, we have reached the vital third stage in the retracing of Kant's argument, which is his definition of aesthetic judgment as apprehending—in its full contradiction—the purposiveness without purpose that the teleological judgment needs as a theoretical possibility. In the introduction, Kant explains the necessary role of the aesthetic judgment—which, as we will see, does not, in the first instance, judge art—and what he must show about it:

In a critique of judgment the part containing the aesthetical judgment is essential, because this alone contains a principle which the judgment places quite *a priori* at the basis of its reflection upon nature, viz. the principle of a formal purposiveness of nature, according to its particular (empirical) laws, for our cognitive faculty, without which the understanding could not find itself in nature. On the other hand no reason *a priori* could be specified—and even the possibility of a reason would not be apparent from the concept of nature as an object of experience whether general or particular—why there should be objective purposes of nature, i.e. things which are only possible as natural purposes; but the judgment, without containing such a principle *a priori* in itself, in given cases (of certain products), in order to make use of the concept of purposes on behalf of reason, would only contain the rule according to which that transcendental principle already has prepared the understanding to apply to nature the concept of a purpose (at least as regards its form). (*Judgment*, 30)

The reflective judgment, as applied to nature alone, cannot justify the principle that it necessarily employs. Only the aesthetic judgment outlines the principle of purposiveness. In the absence of that principle, the teleological judgment would in fact be judging as if there were natural purposes, a principle disallowed by the limits placed on the cognition of nature. In other words, in the absence of the aesthetic judgment's demonstration of the possibility of purposiveness as a principle, the teleological judgment could not posit it, but would in fact be applying a principle of natural purposes, a principle that Kant agrees with Hume in disallowing. The logic here is worth insisting upon since it alone supplies both the role and the definitional structure of Kant's concept of harmonious form. At least in its inception, harmonious form is precisely not a purely formal notion. This form, far from being autonomous, operates as the missing analogon for a reading of nature. It supplies the principle that both art and life lack. As intended art served as the model for reading a designed nature in natural theology, Kant's aesthetical judgment, with its paradoxical stance between claiming purpose and denying it, serves as the model for reading a nature in which one finds the form of design without finding or implying a designer. It is indeed the only possible model for such a mode of reading nature. In the absence of seeing this role for Kantian form, one will, with so many literary critics, either elide the concept into one of organic form—a concept within which Kant himself exhibits the internal contradictions—or with so many philosophical commentators, one will split purposiveness from the concept of intentional purpose, thus producing a more coherent formalism but one that drains the form of apprehension Kant outlines from the context which gives it its point.[36]

In order to see how Kant makes coherent the concept of purposiveness without purpose, we must begin by recognizing that this purposiveness is not a feature of empirical objects. Having allowed that the representation to oneself of sensation is employed in the cognition of an object, and therefore must work in a regular and calculable way, he adds, "But the subjective [element] in a representation, *which cannot be an ingredient of cognition,* is the *pleasure* or *pain* which is bound up with it" (*Judgment,* 26). From this it follows that one's judgment about the beauty of particular objects, a judgment that is connected to a particular kind of pleasure, can never be universal with regard to the status of those objects.

Instead, Kant claims as universal the status of the judging act itself. Thus he distinguishes between two claims to universality in aesthetics:

> If we judge objects merely according to concepts, then all representation of beauty is lost. Thus there can be no rule according to which anyone is to be forced to recognize anything as beautiful. . . . People wish to submit the object to their own eyes, as if the satisfaction in it depended on sensation; and yet, if we then call the object beautiful, we believe that we speak with a universal voice. . . . in the judgment of taste nothing is postulated by such a *universal voice,* in respect of the satisfaction without the intervention of concepts, and thus the *possibility* of an aesthetical judgment that can, at the same time, be regarded as valid for everyone. (*Judgment,* 50)

Paul Guyer helpfully characterizes Kant's claim as one of "intersubjective validity" (*Kant and the Claims of Taste,* 1–2).[37] Our aesthetic taste in the object cannot claim validity since it does not operate through the shared concepts of the understanding. But, once having made the judgment that the object is beautiful, we make it as a universal claim, because the form of the judgment is universal, though not its object. In effect, Kant has taken the paradox he found in Baumgarten—the claim to give intelligible rules to pleasure—and thrown it one step further back. Since judgment itself is not a pleasure but a faculty, it can be shareable as a faculty. But if a sensation is needed to set the judgment off (one does respond to individual objects in the aesthetical judgment), in what sense can the judgment be separated from its object so that the relativity of the one does not reach the universality of the other?

Kant's response to this question connects intricately with his articulation of the aesthetic judgment as a demonstration that purposiveness can be unlinked from purpose. The understanding, according to Kant, operates according to two nearly contradictory principles. First, in accepting its own limits, the understanding must accept that "as far as we can see, it is contingent that the order of nature . . . should actually be conformable to" transcendental ordering laws. But, also, "the discovery of this [order] is also the business of the understanding." Kant then argues that when we then judge order as occurring, we feel a pleasure that is not connected to the actual sensation of the object: "the attainment of that design is bound up with the feeling of pleasure, and since the condition of this attainment is a representation *a priori*—as here a principle for the reflective judgment in general—therefore the feeling of the pleasure is determined by a ground *a priori* and valid for every man, and that merely by reference of the object to the cognitive faculty, the concept of purposiveness here not having the least reference to the faculty of desire" (*Judgment*, 23). The employment of reflective judgment presupposes purposiveness, as we have seen, as an ordering principle. When one sees particular design, which may or may not occur to the understanding, one feels the pleasure of having one's judging principle confirmed. Moreover since that pleasure does not relate to the object but to the judgment's reference of the object to cognition, in other words to the judgment that the object has the design that the understanding seeks, the pleasure can be universally valid since even if the apprehension of design in the case of the specific object is a mistake, Kant claims that the pleasure in the fact of design occurring is an epistemological universal. When one imaginatively apprehends an object as having a purposive design that the concepts of the understanding also confirm, one experiences a harmony of the faculties that Kant characterizes as an a priori pleasure (*Judgment*, 24).

So far the purposiveness occurring, though, is still of the kind that would normally imply purpose. It is a judgment about design in an object (and in this sense only Kant calls it "objective purposiveness"; purposiveness is always a consequence of judgment, and we can never know whether it actually occurs in the object itself). But with the harmony of the faculties, another form of purposiveness occurs:

That apprehension of forms in the imagination can never take place without the reflective judgment, though undesignedly, at least comparing them with its faculty of referring intuitions to concepts. If, now, in this comparison the imagination (as the faculty of *a priori* intuitions) is placed by means of a given representation undesignedly in agreement with the understanding, as the faculty of concepts, and thus a feeling of pleasure is aroused, the object must then be regarded as purposive for the reflective judgment. (*Judgment*, 26)

In other words, the judgment must regard as purposiveness the feeling of pleasure it takes when the purposiveness it apprehends imaginatively seems to match the understanding's apprehension through concepts—the harmony of imagination and understanding—since that pleasure is also a

manifestation of a design, a harmony of the faculties. The object seems designed to give us this pleasure. But this feeling of purposiveness has a certain oddness about it, since, far from standing apart from any conclusion
of purpose, the judgment knows explicitly that that purposiveness *cannot*
be a purpose of the object. The purposiveness itself refers only to the subject's pleasure in the harmony of the faculties, a purposiveness in the subject or what Kant calls "subjective purposiveness." If the object elicits an
internal apprehension of design experienced as pleasure (Kant is quite clear
that pleasure signals the harmony of the faculties rather than being a separable consequence of it and that the judgment of that pleasure and the
pleasure itself are also identical),[38] then, even as the judgment must experience the pleasure as designed, as bound up with a harmony of the faculties, it must also experience the pleasure as undesigned, as explicitly not
part of the concept of the object that sets the process off.[39] The aesthetical
judgment thus apprehends quite literally a purposiveness without purpose,
a purposiveness resulting from the relation between object and faculties
that is not a purpose of the object or of the faculties. It hardly matters
whether this experience is objectively verifiable. As long as it is a universal
part of our faculties, it explains why we experience the aesthetic judgment
as universally valid and, more importantly, it verifies the logical possibility
of attributing purposiveness in the absence of purpose, thus allowing us
then to attribute purposiveness to nature without attributing purpose.

To this point, I have been tracing the logic of Kant's argument entirely from within its own perspective, as if the aesthetics Kant meant to
produce were sufficient to his ends. To a certain extent, my analysis will remain within that traditional perspective, but at this point, it will reach
ends somewhat different from those Kant proposed. Critics who take the
argument for the teleological judgment seriously usually produce a Kant
who, though with considerably greater complexity and refinement, not to
say incredibly large philosophical innovation, nevertheless reproduced a
very Shaftesburian view of the world. Even if we cannot say that that world
was designed by a God, it is essentially ordered, indeed it is ordered in a
morally significant way. Aesthetics, in this view, gives the essence of the
world's order, again as in Shaftesbury or Hutcheson.[40] And indeed, this was
surely, to a great extent, Kant's own view of his project—although one can
overdo such descriptions to the point of forgetting the anti-dogmatic Kant
whom Hume awoke from slumber. To conclude my discussion of Kantian
form, though, I want to address two aspects of his theory that, so to speak,

take it out of the realm of its own purpose to operate with a purposiveness of its own. Kant intended the features of the theory I will discuss, I think, but their implications go further than his aim to refound, in the wake of Hume, a world readable as designed. They produce, indeed, the version of aesthetic form that, I will argue, ideological and historicist analyses deploy instead of dismantling.

The first feature relates to what at first may seem a rather technical, philosophical problem with Kant's theory of aesthetic judgment as occurring with a harmony of the faculties: finding that one's imaginative apprehension of an object's form (depending on how one defines form) coincides with the understanding's concept of the object should not, in Kant, be a particularly unusual event, since it describes what must always happen in the understanding's organization of its sensations if indeed the concepts of the understanding actually do work as necessary categories in the way Kant argues in *The Critique of Pure Reason*.[41] In other words, matching up the sensational appearance of objects with concepts that organize those appearances into intelligible objects is just what the understanding does. If the aesthetic judgment, regarding the Kantian flower and declaring it beautiful, merely sees an order that matches the order the understanding's concept of it applies, it really just sees the flower. It is hard to see, within this definition of the harmony of the faculties, how any perception would not also be a judgment of beauty. This problem can be solved by looking carefully at what Kant means by form and purposiveness in the various moments in the aesthetic judgment. There are, as I noted above, two apprehensions of purposiveness occurring in the judgment that the flower is beautiful. The first declares that the flower looks as if it were designed— the declaration of natural purposiveness that also occurs in the teleological judgment—and takes pleasure in the appearance of design. The second takes that pleasure also as designed for us, even though it knows that that cannot be the case, and this is subjective purposiveness or purposiveness without purpose.

The problem outlined above occurs because the first kind of purposiveness still seems to be essentially part of the apprehension of the particular object. Thus when Kant describes the aesthetic judgment as regarding the form of purposiveness that the flower suggests, without much discussion critics take this to mean that the flower in some sense suggests formal flowerness. But this is to place aesthetic form back onto the object, from which Kant regularly tries to remove it. It is also not quite true to Kant's own description of the aesthetic apprehension. Following his articulation of purposiveness without purpose, in a section entitled "The Judgment of Taste Has Nothing at Its Basis but the Form of Purposiveness of an Object (or Its Mode of Representation)," Kant describes, through negation, what he means by the phrase "the form of purposiveness":

> Therefore it [the determination of an object as beautiful] can be nothing else than the subjective purposiveness in the representation of an object without any purpose (either objective or subjective), and thus it is the mere form of purposiveness in the representation by which an object is *given* to us so far as we are conscious of it, which constitutes the satisfaction that we without a concept judge to be universally communicable. (*Judgment*, 56)

The first part of the passage reasserts the completely subjective quality of the second kind of purposiveness. The second part, however, discussing what is given to us in the object's representation, specifies of this that it is "the mere form of purposiveness" and also identifies that form with the determination of beauty itself. Now, if purposiveness is the look an object has that makes it appear identical to objects designed according to a purpose, it is already a formal feature. So identifying the form of purposiveness with the form of the apprehended object—which already is its purposiveness—would make the phrase either redundant or inaccurate. The form of purposiveness must be the formal quality not of purpose but of the form of purpose, purposiveness itself. It is that formal quality which allows the form of purpose to be an object of apprehension in isolation from purpose rather than an extrapolation from it. And the claim here is that one apprehends this higher form—in effect the form of a form—as a result of an object.

Since the elements of the aesthetic judgment frequently get elided in discussions of Kant, it is worth breaking down quite flat-footedly the steps in the judgment's simultaneous apprehension of the form of purposiveness and its experience of the harmony of the faculties. Seeing a flower, one might apprehend it as exemplary in its flowerness, thus attributing to it a purposiveness: the flower looks as if it were designed to embody an essence or a concept. This purposiveness only seems to accord with the concept through which the understanding perceives the flower. When we see a flower and identify it as such, we do so according to its concepts. If we see it, in addition, as embodying flowerness, we construe it as manifesting its essence. We know this manifestation to be an illusory appearance, not a feature of the flower, since Kant, as we have seen in *The Critique of Pure Reason*, declares such manifestations to be delusory ideals of Pure Reason. In an example to which we will return numerous times (because it is almost the only example of a specific aesthetic judgment given more content than "*x* is beautiful" in *The Critique of Judgment*), Kant describes why one might find the song of a bird beautiful: "the song of birds proclaims gladsomeness and contentment with existence. At least so we so interpret nature, whether it have this design or not" (144–145). The judgment that an object is beautiful occurs when, in addition to identifying it, we perceive it as embodying a recognition of natural order and significance, coupled with the recognition that that embodiment may not be an actual feature of the object, may not be intended by it (the issue of embodiment in Kant will be discussed in the next chapter). At this point, one has seen a purposiveness that one is not sure the object has (in fact one can be pretty sure it does not have it, at least as far as the bird's intent in singing is concerned), rather than purposiveness without purpose. But the judgment experiences a further pleasure because the appearance of meaningful nature coincides with the synthesizing principle of purposiveness that the judgment depends on but can never objectively verify. When the judgment apprehends this linking of the imagined apprehension of significance with the principle, though, the harmony it experiences is not the purposiveness of the flower or the bird but the linkage that that purposiveness causes. The harmony is, thus, a second, internal, form *of* purposiveness, rather than a form identical to purposiveness. It is this purposiveness that must be without purpose.

In this sense, Kant can truly claim that the harmony of the faculties and its consequent apprehension of the form of purposiveness have no connection with the concept of the object. Purposiveness itself may arise from concepts, but its form has no connection in objects since it is exclusively an ordering principle of judgment. In effect, what one apprehends in judging the flower or the birdsong is not flowerness or contentment but a strange and artificial confirmation of the judging process itself. Kant can now identify the two purposivenesses as part of the same determination because each of them is equally a subjective purposiveness, a purposiveness that cannot be related to purpose or any other aspect of the object. One might question empirically how such an apprehension could ever arise from a natural object, but there is surely little problem in distinguishing this from the normal activities of the understanding. Moreover, the purposiveness the aesthetic judgment experiences is so sheltered from any conceivable linking with any actual purpose, that judging an object as conceptually purposive without implying purpose—as the teleological judgment does—seems hardly a problem. The aesthetic judgment is finally a completely reflexive judgment, as well as a reflective judgment, arising from objects but apprehending and analyzing, in the end, only its own processes.

The second feature of Kant's theory I want to look at is also seemingly somewhat marginal: Kant's odd preference for natural beauty over works of art. Marginal as it may be, this ripple in the theory, along with the concept of a form to the formal feature of purposiveness, turns *The Critique of Judgment* away from a theory of beauty or essence in objects and toward a very double-edged way of analyzing how we create and construe relations. The way in which the aesthetic judgment of purposiveness without purpose models the teleological judgment's ability to apprehend purposiveness without concluding purpose also becomes clear when we consider this controversial insistence that aesthetic beauty resides primarily in nature, indeed that there is some question as to whether art can be called beautiful in the sense to which the aesthetic judgment applies.[42] The basic reason for the distinction is clear enough. Part of the a priori beauty resulting from the apprehension of a natural object derives from the fact that the purposiveness is not part of its concept; it is not an intended design but is one that is as it were given to the faculties, and is thus without purpose. Art cannot fit Kant's definition of beauty because it is part of the intention of the artist to create the experience of beauty:

In order to judge of a natural beauty as such, I need not have beforehand a concept of what sort of thing the object is to be; i.e. I need not know its material purposiveness (the purpose), but its mere form pleases by itself in the act of judging it without any knowledge of the purpose. But if the object is given as a product of art and as such is to be declared beautiful, then, because art always supposes a purpose in the cause (and its causality), there must be at bottom in the first instance a concept of what the thing is to be. (*Judgment*, 154)

Art could not be an analogon of natural purposiveness because it was intentionally artificed. For the same reason, it cannot immediately be an object of aesthetic taste. In judging art to be beautiful, we must also always judge it as fulfilling its defining purpose of being beautiful, and that is a judgment about purpose.

Kant of course recognizes the inextricable connection between aesthetics and what he specifies as beautiful art (or fine art).[43] But he expresses that connection in terms of mirroring models that cannot finally be extricated:

In a product of beautiful art, we must become conscious that it is art and not nature; but yet the purposiveness in its form must seem to be as free from all con-

straint of arbitrary rules as if it were a product of mere nature. On this feeling of
freedom in the play of our cognitive faculties, which must at the same time be purposive, rests that pleasure which alone is universally communicable, without being
based on concepts. Nature is beautiful because it looks like art, and art can only be
called beautiful if we are conscious of it as art while yet it looks like nature. . . .
Hence the purposiveness in the product of beautiful art, although it is designed,
must not seem to be designed, i.e. beautiful art must *look* like nature, although we
are conscious of it as art. (*Judgment*, 149)

This passage recognizes that the whole discussion of the beautiful in nature
depends on a field constituted to study a human creation, art. Indeed, we
would never take pleasure in the harmony of the faculties as purposive unless it seemed like the pleasure designed for us by art, even though we
knew it could not be. Thus "nature is beautiful because it looks like art."
But the analysis of beauty Kant has offered shows the logical priority of the
beautiful in nature in creating that apprehension because only it truly offers "purposiveness without purpose," that almost accidental and non-conceptual pleasure that art offers only artificially and despite itself. In creating the model for aesthetic beauty, art always imitated nature, not in the
sense of reproducing its appearance but in the sense of appearing cut off
from all knowledge of its origin as an intentional object. So if nature is
beautiful because it looks like art, at the same time art is beautiful because
it artificially mimes the natural purposiveness without purpose that it cannot actually have. Finally, in the light of this passage, the beautiful in Kant
is so artificial as not to have any true object outside of the aesthetic judgment. Objects of nature do not have the purpose of being beautiful. They
only appear so in the light of a judgment that gets from them certain responses characteristic of those elicited from fine art. But fine art, because it
is intended, can only logically be a second-order beauty, it would seem,
even as it is the conceptual model of the first order. Neither art nor life is
the analogon for nature teleologically judged because neither of them captures or models the contradictions within such a judgment. Abandoning
the conclusion of a divinely designed nature, Kant could no longer read
that nature in terms of a humanly designed art. Only the aesthetic judgment, based on an artifact of a theory built on a moment of self-generat-
ing reflexiveness, can now model the kind of design, neither intended nor
immanent but theoretically constructed, with which Kant replaced that divinely designed nature.

The aesthetic judgment, then, concerns apprehension: it does not attend to objects but to a form it attributes to those objects. Recognizing this

aspect of Kant's aesthetic helps explain what I have meant by saying that the aesthetic concept of autonomous form works to look skeptically at Enlightenment ideas rather than affirming them. In *Truth in Painting*, Derrida wants to deconstruct Kant, as an Enlightenment theorist in part, over the concept of framing. Derrida argues that in raising the issue of frames Kant means to answer the question of "what is a frame?" (63). Frames, of course, divide insides from outsides and so, in answering that question, Kant brings upon himself all the griefs to which the attempt to mark insides from outsides is heir. Taking Kant's examples of ornaments, *parerga* (frames, clothes on statues, colonnades on buildings), Derrida shows all the ways those examples in fact exemplify a concept that will not hold. To the extent that Kant indeed means to define what a frame is, Derrida's critique seems to me unexceptionable. And he is surely right that that definition will come to bear on any formalist theory of art that attempts to define the special form of artworks, since, in order to mount such a definition, one will indeed have to know what is essential to the artwork from what is only a marginal frame or ornament.

But does Kant, in fact, want to answer the question of what a frame is? It is easy to see how one might take in isolation the passage that concerns Derrida as doing that. But if we restore the passage to its place in the larger theory, I think we will see not only that it does not care about that question at all, but that the features Derrida adduces to deconstruct it actually show how unconcerned Kant is with that question. In the section in question, Kant gives examples as to why an aesthetical judgment never concerns the surface charm of an object (a pleasure in a color or sound) but only concerns our apprehension of its design. And he uses for his discussion the example of art objects: "In painting, in sculpture, indeed in all the visual arts, including architecture and horticulture insofar as they are fine arts, *design* is what is essential; in design the basis for any involvement of taste is not what gratifies us in sensation, but merely what we like because of its form" (Pluhar, tr., *Critique of Judgment*, 71).[44] When Kant turns to the issue of frames, then, it is natural to think that he is concerned with something else that might turn our attention from the form of the object. But if we remember that artworks are only secondarily examples of beauty—that because it is part of their purpose to be beautiful, our judgment of them is according to the concept of purpose and therefore not pure—we will be able to take this example as merely showing that when we judge an object as beautiful, we do not look at the features that are part of its material being but at the form we perceive in it. Art exemplifies the distinction Kant wants to draw because it has features that do please in ways that seem aesthetic—the pleasing quality of sounds and colors—but are really only matters of charm, as well as having the design that matters to the aesthetic judgment, whether or not it is a real feature of the object it perceives.

Within this context, Kant's point in bringing up ornaments is not to define what is essential and what a mere frame to the artwork, but to take up an objection to his claim that not charm but perceived design is what matters. After all, we all think that ornaments are beautiful, and surely ornaments call forth the judgment that they are beautiful in response to the pleasing qualities of their physical elements. Isn't that what we mean by the word *ornaments*? But, no, Kant explains:

> Even what we call "ornaments" [*parerga*], i.e. those things which do not belong to the complete representation of the object internally as elements, but only externally as complements, and which augment the satisfaction of taste, do so only by their form; for example, [the frames of pictures or] the draperies of statues or the colonnades of palaces. But if the ornament does not itself consist in beautiful form, and if it's used as a golden frame is used, merely to recommend the painting by its *charm*, it is then called *finery* and injures genuine beauty. (*Judgment*, 62)

The first sentence of this passage does offer a definition of ornament and *parergon* that responds to all the features of framing that Derrida analyzes, but it does so merely to show why one might object that ornaments may please by charming. After all, since they are ornaments, they are only there for that kind of pleasing, aren't they? But Kant responds that one judges frames aesthetically when one judges their form and not their charm. And in this response, he quite noticeably does not consider them as frames at all. In effect, ornaments themselves can be the object of an aesthetic judgment. And when treating them as such objects, Kant pointedly does not refer them to the artworks they ornament. When they work, they do so by their own form, not by their relationship, proper or improper, to any object that they ornament. And when they do not work, when they are merely finery, he does not complain that they damage the beauty of the artwork that they meretriciously recommend, as Derrida argues (*Truth in Painting*, 64), but that they injure "genuine beauty," their own possibly as well as possibly the work's, but "genuine beauty" in the abstract.[45]

Further, this judgment is not a secondary division of bad frames from good frames within the overruling separation of frames as things outside, as Derrida claims (*Truth in Painting*, 64). Rather, Kant judges these ornaments as if they were themselves objects of the aesthetic judgment, not as if they were appended objects to be judged in accordance with their relation, proper or improper, to some object that they frame. So far from answering the question of what a frame is, Kant ignores the ornaments as ornaments or frames, ignores their connection to some other inside, and judges them just as he judged the paintings, sculptures, and so on, in the paragraph above. One might even say that this passage is more noticeable for how little it cares for the formalist question of what frames are than for how it defines frames. In any case, a few pages later, when Kant gives as an example of free beauty "foliage for borders or wall paper" (*Judgment*, 66), he is not contradicting his own prior definition of frames as secondary as a result of some internal inconsistency in formalism (*Truth in Painting*, 98). He is confirming why his aesthetics will not ground the formalism Derrida's deconstruction quite properly critiques. Purposiveness without purpose is so unconcerned with objects that it cannot even be bothered to figure out what frames are. In order to ground the teleological judgment's artificed creation of the kind of moral universe one wants, Kant has created an aesthetic judgment so artificed as to be unable to confirm basic Enlightenment concepts such as framing and form. And Kant had to do that, as we have seen, to create the kind of bridge that responded to his recognition of how wide the chasm was that needed bridging, even if by calling it a chasm he presumed it could be bridged.

The two contradictorily reflexive moments discussed before this consideration of Derrida and Kant (the aesthetic judgment that apprehends in an object the form of purposiveness without any concept, so that it can experience a subjective purposiveness that literally cannot be the purpose of the object which sets the apprehension off; and a definition of beauty that posits art as imitating the nature that first imitated art) almost might be called, then, deconstructions before the letter. In each case, Kant seems explicitly to posit the second-order artificial quality of that which he simultaneously posits as a first-order, definitional ground. And this is, of course, precisely the kind of displacement deconstruction aims to articulate. But these moments also predict the various post-deconstructive theoretical maneuvers that employ deconstructive logical and interpretive strategies to produce an artificed positivity.[46] In effect, Kant clearly wanted a positive end from the aesthetic knots he tied, the reconstruction of a world that looked like the piously designed one Hume had threatened. He wanted to restore the pre-Humean order at least functionally, while not weakening

his case with the dogmatic presumptions that he saw as that order's undoing. And in this sense, it might be said that Kant's aesthetics, like the
British theories earlier in the century, did indeed intend to serve an ideology of order. Certainly, in the end, the world modeled on art in Kant
looked in moral quality much like the religious world of his upbringing. In
the same way, as we have seen, critics can show how Shaftesbury's aesthetic
and moral vision linked up with a certain class vision. But the theory that
created that new positivity always exceeded it as well.

Even if these aesthetic theories merely modeled received and traditional orders, a recognition of the relationship between model and modeled entails a redefinition of the workings of aesthetic form. The enclosed,
Coleridgean organic form, deriving from a vaguely articulated mystification of an order both natural and somehow autonomous, self-contained,
and a matter of the aesthetic object, tells us little about the aesthetic tradition of either British empiricism or German idealism. An aesthetics that
actively purports to model how to read the world hardly intends to function, even in disguise, as an ideologically neutral evaluation of beauty
standing above the fray in order to model ostensibly neutral reason and actually bourgeois property rights. Its constructed qualities, its status as an
artificial product, have been so regularly employed to explain the world as
artifice that one would hardly accuse these theorists of disguising its social
point. Indeed, if the anti-intentionalist versions of organicism had not so
hidden the traces of the historical connection I have been outlining here
between aesthetics and natural theology, given the often noticed connections between moral, religious, and literary discourse, one would think it
could hardly have been missed.

But these writers always used aesthetics to model and read an order
in a world whose origin was in question (even Paley, Clarke, and Ray had
to begin with the presumption of an undesigned world in order to use the
model of art to show it otherwise). Consequently the intention behind that
origin could only be decoded, never directly seen. Their aesthetic theories
thus resulted in a series of self-constituting distortions that pulled them beyond their authors' intentions and made of aesthetics a common method
that was more than any particular use of it. If Shaftesbury wanted a world
of aristocratic tact, what he created was a reflecting system by which that
world could be judged as well as on which it could be based. And the judgment occurred with an aesthetics of justice, narrated by Addison, by which
both the world and its own system might be judged and found wanting.

Shaftesbury, Hutcheson, Kames, and Addison were surely far from desiring such an end. But the determination of a desire against which one may define interpretation as incorrect, or even just antithetic, becomes nearly impossible in Kant. The knots in the system are surely his, tied in full awareness of the problematics of even articulating a system of aesthetics that informs his thinking, from the footnote to the first edition of *The Critique of Pure Reason* that calls aesthetics impossible to the non-conceptual possibility he finally gives it. It will be the work of subsequent chapters on Foucault and Bourdieu to show how this system gets deployed even as it is denied or confronted, as well as how it leads the most aestheticist of critics to be the most virulent enemies of aesthetics. This chapter has merely intended to outline, through the most traditional of intellectual histories, the deeper resources of aesthetic analysis that contemporary critics so regularly both ignore in the theories they read and employ in those they write.

CHAPTER 2

Indifferent Embodiment

Although this book, and particularly these first two chapters, offer rereadings of the history of aesthetics and of some of its key concepts (in the preceding chapter, autonomous form and in this one symbolic embodiment and aesthetic indifference), its argument ultimately is conceptual rather than historical: the value of aesthetics (as opposed to artworks) is that it offers ways of apprehending and interpreting things in the world. Moreover, that mode of apprehending and interpreting has been central and formative for the contemporary literary, philosophic, and sociological theories that have been most significant in the current, widespread rejection of aesthetics as a dangerous or delusory ideology. In the first chapter, I could discuss the origins and the value of autonomous form as a concept without having to justify the claim itself that there was such a thing as an aesthetic perspective. This is because, first, the concept of autonomy is separable from an interpretation of aesthetics as perspective and so justifiable in isolation; and second, whether or not such a perspective exists, it is fairly clear that to understand Kant, one had to understand that that is what he claimed to analyze: the third critique analyzes and justifies a form of judgment not a set of objects classed as art. In attempting to recuperate the concepts of aesthetic indifference (I will be using this term, for reasons we will see, to cover the sometimes more controversial label, disinterest) and symbolic embodiment, I will have to face head-on the issue of whether there is such a thing as aesthetic perspective, since the critics of indifference and symbolic embodiment have attacked them both as claims about perspective and as defining features of art objects.[1]

The following chapter then, will argue three related ideas. First, in a view that was nearly standard in nineteenth-century Continental theory from Kant through Nietzsche, aesthetics is a theory of how to judge objects more than a theory of what artworks are. Second—in a view most clearly articulated and most vigorously contested in figures such as Hegel, Schopenhauer, and Heidegger, but versions of which one finds in Kant and Nietzsche—symbolic embodiment better explains the value of art than notions of special kinds of aesthetic pleasure. But these two concepts would seem to be in necessary contradiction. Claiming that art realizes adequate material presentation of ideas (either transcendental ideas, as, in one version or other, many art theorists since Plato have claimed, or even merely abstract concepts) obviously entails a claim about its object-status, it would seem, not a claim about how we perceive things. Thus the third issue: the concept of aesthetic indifference, employed either knowingly or unknowingly, I will argue, both mediates this contradiction and makes symbolic embodiment not the centerpiece of what often gets criticized as aesthetic ideology,[2] but a definition of how meaning may be constructed around material forms in order to interpret and perceive them with a freedom and skepticism not allowed by non-aesthetic epistemologies. The aesthetic indifference defended here will not be the neutral disinterest connected with an objective claim to have no ulterior motives, a definition that related to a valuing of a pure encounter with an artwork on its own terms, what Hegel called appetitive disinterest (*Aesthetics*, I, 58). Nor will it be the calm dispassionate meditation imagined by Schopenhauer. Rather, I am concerned with what Kant radically labeled an indifference to the existence of the object, a recognition that existing objects were precisely not the targets of aesthetic judgment.

It must be noted that all of the aesthetic theorists cited above are not only German, but quite pointedly participate in, either as adherents to or as opponents of, a discourse in a fairly identifiable tradition (Schaeffer has recently called it the speculative theory of art, a useful coinage). And it is far from the only tradition of aesthetic theory. The eighteenth-century British theorists discussed in the previous chapter were unanimous in seeing art in terms of either a certain kind of experience or of a formal arrangement of experience. And they saw art's value in a certain kind of pleasure or at least a certain kind of valuable psychic state afforded by that arrangement (I will call these theories "experiential formalism" since my critique of them does not extend either to formalism as an interpretive practice or, if the speculative theory of art is taken to be formalism, to that type of it). And although, as we saw, through the concept of organic form, Coleridge aligned symbolic embodiment with formal arrangement, nevertheless defining art in terms of the experience it affords rather than the meaning it embodies has been persistent in Anglo-American theory through the nineteenth and twentieth centuries.[3] I will, in my discussion of Kant's hesitating steps toward a theory of symbolism of which he was deeply skeptical and Hegel's seemingly full embrace of it, try to show why Kant and his successors thought the theories of formal arrangement and experiential effect they inherited from the eighteenth century were insufficient, and why, in response, they posed art as a way of seeing or conveying meaning. But their rejection certainly stems from a certain epistemological service they wanted art to perform, rather than from any necessary problem internal to experiential formalism, and so creates no ineluctable reason for accepting their ideas of aesthetic apprehension, symbolic embodiment, and aesthetic indifference.[4] Merely to articulate these concepts as the outline of an interpretive stance—one constitutive of the late-twentieth-century postmodernism so ostensibly antagonistic to aesthetic ideology— would serve the end of justifying aesthetics heuristically as a stance with a certain local value. But this book has the more ambitious project of using those concepts, along with the first chapter's redefinition of autonomous form, to argue their intellectual necessity to the postmodern theories of Foucault and Bourdieu, and by implication those of their followers. So, in addition to outlining these concepts, I do want to argue why we should prefer them to experiential formalism.

In order to argue for that preference, this chapter will turn to a problem presented to aesthetics by such artworks as Marcel Duchamp's *Fountain*—a urinal mounted upside down—and Andy Warhol's *Brillo Box*. While aesthetic theorists throughout the eighteenth and nineteenth centuries debated what common definition might hold together all objects and only objects that were artworks, what were the features of aesthetic apprehension, what differentiated good from bad art, or what was the value of art to life, no one thought there was any theoretical problem about distinguishing between an artwork and other kinds of objects. Although, for instance, Kant imagines that one might be deceived briefly into taking a human imitation of a bird singing for an actual bird singing, he does not think that the problem of distinguishing could not ultimately be solved by more careful investigation (*Judgment*, 145). And although making its imitation of nature more and more accurate has frequently been taken as the common project of painting roughly through the first half of the nineteenth century, no one thought that the imitation would ever become so perfect as to create a problem about determining whether what one was looking at was a painting of, say, a mountain or an actual mountain.[5] Although its importance was not fully recognized until some fifty years after its inception, since the 1970s *Fountain* has become an icon because it and its heirs have insisted that the question of how to identify an artwork and to tell it apart from a non-artwork that might be perceptually indistinguishable from it, is vital to aesthetics. This problem in modern aesthetics has gone largely unnoticed among literary theorists, or for that matter by the Continental theory that takes itself as carrying out a deconstruction of modernist philosophy.[6] And yet, I will argue, responding to it will show Kantian aesthetics and its articulations most importantly in Hegel and Nietzsche to be not a delusory ideology of materially embodied meaning and neutral, dispassionate observation, but a quite radical theory of what art has to say about our investments in organizing reality into meaningful formations. Duchamp's readymades also propose a model for what it might mean to see postmodern theory in terms of aesthetics. In short, Duchamp's artworks make it impossible to define art in terms of observable formal features or pleasure given thereby. They force a theory of symbolism that, tying symbolism to indifference, is also deeply skeptical of symbolism's ostensible essentialism. Thus, finally, Duchamp's readymades also propose a model for what it might mean to see postmodern theory in terms of aesthetics.

Having established through the discussion of Duchamp and responses to him the value and meaning of the concepts of aesthetic apprehension, symbolic embodiment, and aesthetic indifference, this chapter will turn to working out the details of those concepts through their historical development in Kant and his successors. Though this may seem an odd, achronological ordering of the argument, in fact the opening section on Duchamp serves not as the end of a history discussed first, but as the instance that justifies the more radical definition of those concepts proposed here and their value to aesthetic theory. These definitional and evaluative questions having been addressed, the chapter will go on to its historical task of showing how those concepts have operated in the aesthetics that contemporary theory has simultaneously criticized and employed.

I. Duchamp, Formalism, and Aesthetic Indifference

To discuss the significance of Duchamp's *Fountain*, one must first know the brief history of the actual object, as well as the later history of its critical reception.[7] In 1917, a group of artists, the Society of Independent Artists, a group that included Duchamp, organized an exhibition that was to be unjuried. The only requirement for having one's work exhibited was to pay the one dollar entry fee to the organization and the five-dollar yearly dues. Mallarmé's protest against the 1874 Salon's rejection of canvases by Manet gives theoretical point to the Exhibition of Independent Artists: "Entrusted with the nebulous vote of the painters with the responsibility of choosing, from among the framed pictures offered, those that are really paintings in order to show them to us, the jury has nothing else to say but: this is a painting, or that is not a painting" (quoted in Duve, *Kant After Duchamp*, 264). Mallarmé clearly assumed that the decision of whether something is or is not a painting would be an unambiguous one and all art would have to be included. The Society of Independent Artists, democratic in its ideology, meant to adhere to this requirement of unjuried inclusiveness, an intention Duchamp tested by submitting, under the name of R. Mutt, a urinal mounted upside down and entitled *Fountain*.[8] In what at least seems a breach of the Society's own rules for admission, the board of directors rejected the piece on the grounds that "*Fountain* was not art and it was indecent" (Camfield, "History and Aesthetics," 71). But the committee might have been acting in accordance with Mallarmé's requirement (and thus not really in exception to the society's own rules) if they were actually judging *Fountain* not to be art at all but as one of the objectors to it said, "a joke" (Camfield, "History and Aesthetics," 69; Duve, *Kant After Duchamp*, 91).

Regardless of the reason for rejection, Duchamp, through intermediaries, had the urinal sent to Alfred Steiglitz, who photographed it and exhibited it in his studio for a number of days. The photograph, along with two short articles—an unsigned editorial, "The Richard Mutt Case," and an analysis, "The Buddha of the Bathroom"—were published in a small-circulation art journal, *The Blind Man*. The editorial, written by Beatrice Wood, probably under Duchamp's direction, gave a minimal justification of *Fountain* as an artwork: "Whether Mr. Mutt with his own hands made the fountain or not has no importance. He CHOSE it. He took an ordinary article of life, placed it so that its useful significance disappeared under the new title and point of view—created a new thought for the object" (Camfield, "History and Aesthetic," 76). The analysis offered a fuller appreciation of the "sculpture" as revealing a beautiful shape in the ostensibly functional object (Camfield, "History and Aesthetic," 78–79). After its stay in Steiglitz's studio, the object, *Fountain*, disappeared forever: "All that remains are the replicas made by Sidney Janis in 1950, by Ulf Linde in 1963, and by Arturo Schwarz in 1964, and also, of course, the photograph taken by Alfred Steiglitz in 1917" (Duve, 95–96). An investigation of the photographs of these various versions (reproduced in Camfield, "Aesthetic Object," 134, 157, 160, 162) shows that, despite Duchamp's participation in some of these recreations, no one exactly resembles another (although all are signed on the left rim by R. Mutt and dated 1917 as if the signature rather than the exact features of the urinal testify to the artwork it reproduces).[9] In other words, although the concept *Fountain* has had an extended life in the twentieth century, its existence as an object was very short, and during that entire period its existence as an artwork was contested. Only after it ceased to exist as an object did it become an uncontested artwork.[10]

Both the artwork *Fountain* (in whatever form that artwork exists, since it no longer exists as any single object or even a mechanically reproducible object since no two authorized reproductions have really looked exactly alike, and, thus, whatever the artwork is exceeds its reproducible features) and the narrative of its inception, disappearance, and reappearance, raise a number of aesthetic questions that theorists have been struggling with since at least the middle of the twentieth century and increasingly throughout its final two decades and now into the twenty-first century. The first and most obvious one is, if it is a work of art, what makes it one? To give this question edge, one critic imagines first encountering *Fountain* and trying to determine what makes it like other works of art rather than like other urinals:

This particular urinal has nothing in common with any of the countless things carrying the name of art, except that it is, like them, called art. And nothing distinguishes it from just any ordinary urinal, from non-art, except, once again, its name, *art*. In conclusion, it allows you to administer the striking proof of art's very autonomy, taking the glorious form of a nominalist ontology. (Duve, 13)

One might argue that "*Fountain*" differs significantly from other urinals in that, because Duchamp mounted it upside down and unattached to a flushing device, the urinal became non-functional, and thus perhaps autonomous in the manner of an aesthetic object. But all urinals prior to installation are non-functioning, so the aesthetic significance of this one's non-functionality does not self-evidently occur with the appearance of this object, and so does not differentiate it from other like objects.[11] This problem stands out even more clearly when we consider how, for instance, Hegel can say off-handedly, "Men also take pleasure in leaping and singing and they need the medium of speech, but speaking, jumping, screaming, and singing are not yet, for this reason, poetry, the dance, or music" (*Aesthetics*, II, 632). That Hegel is right only magnifies the problem, since some poetry does look just like speaking, some dance just like jumping, some music just like screaming.

This situation is made more difficult by the particular history of *Fountain*. First, since the object disappeared after 1917, and all reproductions are noticeably approximate, somehow the copious critical discourse about the sculpture has occurred unembarrassed by the absence of an object that it is criticizing. At the very least, the situation gives some support (to which we will turn in detail below) to Kant's claim that, to be disinterested, the judgment of taste must be "indifferent as regards the existence of an object" (Kant, *Judgment*, 43–44), even though the claim is obviously counter-intuitive (in putting paintings in museums so that we can experience them aesthetically, we hardly show ourselves indifferent to their existence).[12] But it is not just that *Fountain* no longer exists. When it did exist, its status as an artwork was hardly a given. The board of the Society of Independent Artists rejected *Fountain* because, they said, it was not a work of art but something else (a joke perhaps). Steiglitz's photograph and his exhibition of the piece insisted on its candidature for the status of artwork, but the debate was hardly resolved merely by his and *The Blind Man*'s endorsement of it as art. That the object disappeared seems to indicate at least that endorsement's failure to persuade a larger audience of its claim. If, with one critic, we can imagine an extra-planetary aesthetician trying to catalogue all human art, we have to note that by the time she or he could have known to include *Fountain* in a catalogue of things human beings called art, she or he would have had either no object to include in the catalogue or a series of candidates for the work, none of which precisely resembled the other (of course, she or he could have included the Steiglitz photograph in the collection, but that would only raise the question of the status of the photograph itself). *Fountain*, then, is not merely an artwork that has ceased to exist, such as a lost statue by Phidias. Nor is it purely conceptual: there was a urinal entitled *Fountain* once. And yet its existence as artwork noticeably fails to coincide with its existence as an object.

If the theories of modernism and formalism had not bound themselves together in a particularly productive way in the middle decades of the twentieth century, it is quite possible that *Fountain* would have remained forgotten. The presentation of a urinal as an artwork has mattered so much since then because of the challenge that presentation offers to theories that define art in terms of its being a special kind of material object. *Fountain*'s challenge to formalist art theory has resulted in two alternatives, an institutional theory of art and an attempt to use the work's significance to reopen the question of whether art has a definable essence. In discussing first the formalism *Fountain* challenges and then the two responses that challenge has elicited, we will be able to see how *Fountain* makes a case for symbolic embodiment and aesthetic indifference as elements of an aesthetic perspective. In the context of modernist formalism, particularly in its manifestation in the art criticism of Clement Greenberg, the achievement of *Fountain* was not merely to show formalism's theoretical insufficiency by being a formally null artwork, but to do that while simultaneously—ambiguously enough—filling many of the demands of the modernist theory of aesthetic value. Although his account of the historical development of abstraction changed, early and late, Greenberg's explanation for the move into abstraction remains the same. Modern art has taken as its end to be as purely art as possible. The path to purity leads to a more and more complete acceptance of the limitations of the artistic medium in which one works. In painting, the primary limitation is the flatness of the canvas and its inherent resistance to the attempt by mimetical painting to create the effect of three dimensions. Avant-garde painting, since the Impressionists, has been, according to Greenberg, a progressively greater acceptance of that flatness. Thus, in 1939, Greenberg writes: "The history of avant-garde painting is that of a progressive surrender to the resistance of its medium; which resistance consists chiefly in the flat picture plane's denial of efforts to 'hole through' it for realistic perspectival space" (Greenberg, *Collected Essays*, I, 34). As if in continuation of this passage, he writes in 1960, "Flatness alone was unique and exclusive to pictorial art. . . . Because flatness was the only condition a painting shared with no other art, Modernist painting oriented itself to flatness as it did to nothing else" (IV, 87).[13] Abstract painting, by eschewing mimetic representation, also abandoned the necessity of trying to represent three-dimensional space and thus presented its own painterliness in a particularly pure way.

But why should painting have changed its project from one of learning to represent three dimensions on a plane to one of openly manifesting the plane? And why was doing this in any sense a particularly good thing? To answer these questions, Greenberg starts with a claim about the value of undistracted attention to one's own sense experiences: "I think a poor life is lived by any one who doesn't regularly take time out to stand and gaze, or sit and listen, or touch, or smell, or brood, without any further end in mind, simply for the satisfaction gotten from that which is gazed at, listened to, touched, smelled, or brooded upon" (IV, 76). Although this claim that art gives us moments of enriched sensual awareness is traditional enough, it gives a particular justification to abstract modernism: Greenberg argues that Western society, because of its insistence on dynamism and movement, offers a particularly strong threat to the values of still attentiveness to the senses. As a result, the West has developed abstraction as an art that especially insists on a purely sensuous response: "only in the West, and only in the last fifty years, have such things as abstract pictures and free-standing pieces of abstract sculpture appeared. What makes the big difference between these and abstract decoration is that they are, exactly, pictures and free-standing sculpture—solo works of art meant to be looked at for their own sake and with full attention, and not as the adjuncts, incidental aspects, or settings of things other than themselves" (IV, 77). Although Greenberg means to justify modern abstraction as especially valuable, this argument justifies all art, and abstraction only as art's purest form.

The clear logical connection between Greenberg's justification of the value of modernist art and his justification of art in general matters because it changes the challenge various artists made to the essentiality of the features of abstraction (which presented itself as art stripped down to its purest form) into a challenge to a more general experiential justification of art. One of the things that had happened to abstract expressionism was the recognition that one could create many of its features without creating any particular formal experience that might be valued according to Greenberg's terms. Even more importantly, one could reproduce those features without creating anything that would normally be described as an artwork.[14] One can see the first of these possibilities in the hypothetical example of a blank, stretched canvas presented as another example of modernist flatness, an example that Greenberg, somewhat uneasily accepts:

Under the testing of modernism more and more of the conventions of the art of painting have shown themselves to be dispensable, unessential. By now it has been established, it would seem, that the irreducible essence of pictorial art consists in but two constitutive conventions or norms: flatness and the delimitation of flatness; and that the observance of merely these two norms is enough to create an object which can be experienced as a picture: thus a stretched or tacked-up canvas already exists as a picture—though not necessarily as a successful one. (IV, 131–132)

Greenberg imagines the blank canvas as fulfilling the features of modernism, thus being a modernist work of art, without actually being a very good work (*successful* must be a loose term for *good* since he has already allowed that the stretched canvas "succeeds" at being art). Because of its sensual barrenness, it could not offer the requisite concentration on sensation, and yet he had to admit that it would be an artwork. And he interpreted Duchamp's achievement, which he recognized as art, in this light, even though he hated it: "Duchamp and his sub-tradition have demonstrated as nothing did before, how omnipresent art can be, all the things it can be without ceasing to be art. For this demonstration we can be grateful. But that doesn't make the demonstration in itself any less boring" (*Homemade Esthetics*, 56–57).

Even taken only this far, the separation that Greenberg recognizes between the formal features requisite to being an artwork and any value or pleasure associated with the experiencing of those features is probably destructive of any experientially formalist definition of art.[15] The blank canvas may not challenge our definition of what art is, but it does challenge explanations of why we take pleasures in artworks. One can see the problem in Wendy Steiner's recent attempt to defend aesthetic pleasure in the face of numbers of recent attacks upon it. She opens *The Scandal of Pleasure* with an account of a formalist defense of Robert Mapplethorpe's photographs at their trial for obscenity. For Steiner, the formalist defense, in the absence of an account of pleasure is obviously insufficient: although Mapplethorpe's photographs certainly highlight formal arrangement of a kind usually found aesthetically pleasing, to note only this element, as if some of the photos didn't also highlight their sexual content, seems obviously artificial. A formalism this obviously split from attention to content becomes somewhat unreal (9–10).[16] But Steiner doesn't seem to recognize that her own alternative explanation will not in fact fare any better: "Experiencing the variety of meanings available in a work of art helps make us tolerant and mentally lithe. Art is a realm of thought experiments that quicken, sharpen and sweeten our being in the world" (8). From this generalization, she can then offer an evaluation of Mapplethorpe's controversial photographs that seems to deal with their content, praising their "fear-lessness in dramatizing his difference from me and from all whose ap-petites have not led their bodies such a chase" (56–57). But in fact, the cri-terion of "experiencing the variety of meanings" and "becoming mentally lithe" (one should note the clear similarity to Greenberg's criteria of learn-ing to pause over one's sensations for their own sake) are detachable from any given material content. Even if we grant that tolerance is intrinsically pleasurable (and there is plenty of evidence that not everyone finds it so; Steiner's moralized description of the value of aesthetic experience presents moral beliefs as experiential givens), there remains the problem that just as a blank canvas could be an exemplary, if pointless, modernist painting, having the formal features of art without any aesthetically pleasing effect, one could imagine photographs reproducing the features of Map-plethorpe's, having the content of the Mapplethorpe photos without being art and thus without leading to the pleasure Steiner describes.[17] Her pro-posed aesthetic pleasure would thus be just as detachable from content as the formalist one she questions at the outset. Once one detaches the formal features of a work of art from those qualities that afford aesthetic pleasure, and that detachment is always possible, formalist justifications, if not for-malist definitions, of art always fail by being at once too general, in that they cover more things than works of art, and not general enough, because they don't cover all works of art.

But Greenberg's stretched canvas, presented as an abstract consider-ation of its own flatness, at least shares some obvious features with easel paintings. It is canvas stretched on a frame. In that it is presented as fin-ished, even the absence of physical paint does not really disqualify it from being an easel painting. And yet we need first to ask how we know it is a painting and not simply a stretched canvas on which the artist has not yet painted anything. And this is the key question presented to us by *Fountain* in the first instance, one that would seem to call into question not merely experiential formalist justifications of art, but experiential formalist defini-tions of art as well. There have been attempts to answer this question and preserve an experiential formalism by offering experiential formalist ac-counts of Duchamp's readymades in general and *Fountain* in particular. The two essays by Camfield cited above for the history of the work intend to argue for a formal beauty in *Fountain* that has to do with its calling our attention to the Buddha-like shape of the urinal and noting its similarity to works by Brancusi. And George Dickie, oddly in the course of articulating the institutional theory of art that seems precisely designed to deal with problematic cases such as Duchamp, argues: "why cannot the ordinary qualities of 'Fountain'—its gleaming white surface, the depth revealed when it reflects images of surrounding objects, its pleasing oval shape—be appreciated. It has qualities similar to those of works by Brancusi and Moore" (*Art and the Aesthetic*, 42). There are numbers of problems with these claims of formal value as an interpretation of Duchamp's sculpture. Most obviously, they don't really seem to respond to what has made it an artwork. In other words, Duchamp's work has not been as important as it has because of the beautiful formal features of the urinal he presented.

This is objecting, though, merely to the likeliness of the formalist interpretation; it is still possible that Duchamp did submit the urinal as *Fountain* with the intention of calling our attention to its beauty as an object.[18] The real problem with this interpretation is that, regardless of Duchamp's intentions, it does not really respond to the artwork *Fountain* at all. The reasons behind this claim show how Duchamp undercuts all experiential formalist definitions. By offering justifications of readymades as showing us the formal beauty already in the objects so presented, formalism preserves itself as a theory, even if it gives up the notion that formalism can any longer differentiate between the values of forms (this, we saw above, was Greenberg's strategy). But it still has to blink certain questions. First of all, does the claim about the formal beauty of *Fountain* extend to all urinals (or at least all urinals of the same precise shape as the one Duchamp entitled and submitted)? If it does, then Duchamp's presentation has not changed the specific, exhibited object, and is not really part of *its* formal beauty. Rather, the selection and presentation notices the formal beauty in a class of functional objects to which this object belongs. But all the objects in the class are clearly all not equally works of art. And so the formalist reading has failed to explain this particular urinal, *Fountain*. If, in view of this problem, a formalist claims that the formal beauty only inheres in the urinal Duchamp entitled and submitted, then, of course, one has yet to explain why the beauty inheres in this version of the object and not in all others. In other words, precisely because readymade artworks are not differentiable from non-artworks in terms of their material appearance, no explanation of that appearance can explain fully both their existence and specificity as artworks (not merely why can a urinal be a work of art but why was this urinal a work of art?).

This situation is made even more critical by the non-existence of

Fountain as an artwork. As I noted above, *Fountain* disappeared after its brief display in Steiglitz's studio. Arguably, at that time, the urinal had not yet become an artwork. It had proposed itself as one, but that proposition was still a matter of debate. It might have remained just a urinal if no one could see it otherwise.[19] And, by the time it had been remounted, discussed in any number of books and articles, widely recognized, it had ceased to exist in the form of the original object. Now of course we know many artworks only by either reputation or reproduction because the originals have been destroyed or lost. But we do not imagine that inexact reproductions, if any reproductions, much less merely reputations, give us those artworks in their entirety. We do not have any way of analyzing, much less evaluating, a Phidias statue that has ceased to exist. *Fountain*, however, remains fully discussible in the absence of the original work. Indeed, it has only been widely discussed in its state of non-existence. Even if formalist explanations felt the need to examine urinals that looked exactly like the one that Duchamp presented, they would still not need the one by Duchamp. Most don't seem even to need copies. The mere concept of a urinal signed by R. Mutt seems to be all that one needs to discuss this artwork. *Fountain*, then, doesn't merely exist as more than its material object (this much can be said of any artwork that has a significance beyond its appearance), it exists without any necessary reference to any particular material object. In this case at least, an experiential formalist reading is not merely insufficient; it is literally irrelevant to whatever makes the artwork an artwork.

In an attempt to deal with experiential formalism's failure to distinguish adequately aesthetic from non-aesthetic objects in terms of their mere appearance, without falling into a claim that art is a matter of perception rather than of objects (a claim I mean deliberately to fall into), George Dickie has offered an institutional theory of art. Dickie argues that an artwork has three features. First it is an artifactual object (one that is something other than natural either by being worked upon or at least, minimally, by being presented by an individual as an artwork). Second, a set of relevant institutions (which, following the title of Danto's first essay outlining his response to the Warhol *Brillo Carton*, Dickie calls the artworld) have conferred the status of art on it (*Art and the Aesthetic*, 1–52). Third, this judgment is based on its having aspects that this artwork or its institutions conventionally agree are aesthetic (147–151). The third criterion resists the claim that the artworld acts subjectively in conferring the status of art while maintaining that the "aspects" on which it bases its decision are conventional. This theory not only deals with artworks such as *Fountain* far better than experiential formalism, but it takes itself as at least partially inspired by the need to deal with such works, or at least Dickie claims that "instances of Dadaist art and similar present-day developments" (among which he explicitly includes Duchamp's readymades) "have served to bring the institutional nature of art to our attention" (44). It solves the problem of *Fountain* by claiming that it is a work of art insofar as that status has been conferred upon it when Duchamp, acting in his capacity as member of the artworld, submitted it as art to an exhibition (though for Dickie, he could also have done the same thing merely by hanging it on his wall).[20]

Although Dickie takes Danto's term *artworld* as a feature of his theory and evidently took Danto as a forerunner of his theory, Danto has criticized the position on the basis that Dickie might explain *how* a work comes to be accepted as art but he obviously does not explain *why* it has come to be so accepted. In the case of *Fountain*, which Dickie designed his theory at least partially to define, while that theory tells us how it is an artwork, it avoids the question of why it is one: "For the Institutional Theory of Art leaves unexplained, even if it can account for why such a work as Duchamp's *Fountain* might have been elevated from a mere thing to an artwork, why that particular urinal should have sustained so impressive a promotion, while other urinals, like it in every obvious respect, should remain in an ontologically degraded category" (*Transfiguration*, 5). In an obvious way, this criticism begs the question: the point of the institutional theory was to avoid questions about why something is an artwork, because it thought such questions resulted in insufficient definitions. It meant to replace such concerns with a definition that looks at what it means to call something an artwork.[21] But Danto does show exactly how Dickie doesn't answer the question Duchamp posed about art but ducks it. Dickie explains how *Fountain* is an artwork precisely by avoiding why it is one, what it means to call it one. For Dickie, the criteria that a work has to be appreciable as art in order for the artworld so to appreciate it means only that it must be appreciated in some way, not that it must be appreciated in some specific way. And he denies that there is any object that it is impossible to appreciate aesthetically (*Art and the Aesthetic*, 41–43).[22]

Having worked through the problems both experiential formalism and an institutional theory of art have in explaining *Fountain*, the next step obviously is to offer an alternative, satisfactory explanation and to argue for its relevance to the three concepts this chapter sets out to defend: symbolic embodiment, aesthetic perspective, and aesthetic indifference. In offering this explanation, then, I will start with Arthur C. Danto's somewhat less melodramatic restatement of Hegel's notorious definition of art as the sensuous embodiment of the Idea (*Aesthetics*, I, 70): "To be a work of art is to be (i) *about* something and (ii) to *embody its meaning*" (*After the End of Art*, 195). One should note immediately that posed this way the definition of symbolic embodiment not only continues to raise the metaphysical and ideological objections to it mentioned at the outset of this chapter, but it also seems to give a view of art that insists on its meaningfulness at the expense of formal appearance, in a way that would be as inappropriate for a discussion of an abstract painting as an experiential formalist analysis is insufficient in the face of Duchamp. And, indeed, while Danto is surely our best interpreter of artworks indiscernible from non-artworks in terms of their appearance, he has not been noticeably sensitive to works that concentrate on their own formal arrangement in ways critics such as Greenberg have analyzed well.[23] I will deal with these criticisms of symbolic embodiment in detail in the next sections of this chapter, which detail the articulation of this concept in Kant, Hegel, and Nietzsche, among others. My point here is to establish the ways Hegel's and Danto's definition solves the aesthetic problem presented by Duchamp and thus the way Duchamp's work suggests responses to the criticisms of that definition. Working out that solution in all its details, however, particularly the way it connects up with theories of aesthetic indifference and aesthetic perspective, will also suggest the more detailed answers to those criticisms.[24]

  With the exception of the few formalist readings of the work, there is of course broad agreement about the basic significance of *Fountain*: it works to challenge our definition of what is art by presenting to us a common object with no features that we usually think of as formally pleasing and by asking us to accept it as art. This rather sketchy interpretation, however, fails to explain why it matters that this commonplace object was a urinal and not a snow shovel or a bicycle wheel or any one of the fifty or so other readymades. That explanation is necessary to fulfill even Danto's reduced definition of embodying a meaning, since if the meaning is in fact embodied, then it must be specific to that material presentation and the presentation cannot simply be one possible sign or example among many. (Indeed, one of the criticisms of readymades, as well as other like forms of art, is that once one understands their meaning, the need for the object ceases to exist and the work becomes only a signified, rather than an embodied meaning.) Once the specificity of the urinal has been explained, a set of other elements, among which the history of its presentation and the history of its reception, will also become part of the embodiment (now no longer entirely a material one), making aesthetic perspective and aesthetic indifference also part of an explanation of the work.

It seems fairly clear that in presenting the urinal, signed and re-versed—thus authored by someone at least in some sense, and also dis-placed from its function according to a standard view that art ought not to have an instrumental purpose—to an ostensibly unjuried art exhibition, Duchamp meant to probe whether the answer to the question of whether or not an object is an artwork would necessarily be self-evident. But the reasons given for the original rejection, that it was not art and that it was indecent, suggest why Duchamp submitted a urinal rather than some other quotidian object. Calling the urinal indecent is both somewhat odd (are urinals indecent even when properly used or only indecent when ex-hibited as art?) and seemingly in moralistic excess of the judgment neces-sary for the rejecting *Fountain* as art. But it recalls Kant's specification that while art may present the ugly in such a way that it becomes beautiful, "there is only one kind of ugliness which cannot be represented in accor-dance with nature without destroying all aesthetical satisfaction, and con-sequently artificial beauty, viz. that which excites *disgust*," and his further specification that "the art of sculpture again, because in its products art is almost interchangeable with nature, excludes from its creations the imme-diate representation of ugly objects" (*Judgment*, 155). Although indecency is not the same as disgust or ugliness, as a sculpture *Fountain* solicits both judgments, and disgust and ugliness could easily be what the original re-jecting judgment intended in the label "indecent." The object's normal use seems to exemplify just the kind of thing Kant was saying was not aesthet-ically appreciable, and, even if we do not automatically assent to a judg-ment that the connection to bodily elimination necessitates revulsion, a urinal's connection with that element of our physicality seems to deny it the ability to be aesthetically appreciated, especially according to the more strict criteria Kant applies to sculpture because of its being more nearly like natural objects. Thus the original judgment could well have been that *Fountain* was not art *because* it was indecent in the sense of being implic-itly disgusting and ugly.[25] The urinal submitted thus is not merely any non-art object but the kind of object that, by virtue of what it is, suppos-edly cannot be art, even if signed and removed from its original function.

Up to this point, I have essentially been reading *Fountain* as one of Danto's transfigured commonplace objects, albeit in somewhat more detail. But I think that there is still another question raised by Duchamp's submission, the answer to which also becomes part of the meaning embodied by the object. And this element of the work will raise the issues of aesthetic indifference, aesthetic perspective, and their connection to symbolic embodiment. That question poses a counter-factual possibility: could *Fountain* have been successfully rejected as art? Most critics seem to assume that the answer to this question is no. As we have seen, Dickie assumes that art status occurs at the moment someone acting as an artist hangs an object on his or her wall or submits it to a museum or exhibition, regardless of the reaction of other members of the artworld. Danto never actually entertains the question since his distinctions between artworks and the nonartworks they look like refer back to the intentions of the artist in proposing or creating the object. The object, then, becomes art at the moment it embodies those intentions by displaying them. But part of Duchamp's intentions manifestly was to have an anti-art object *accepted* as art.[26] Thus the work's significance cannot be completely embodied until it in fact has been accepted, and for this to be the case it must have been logically possible to reject it (that which cannot be rejected cannot in any real sense be accepted). Moreover, if Steiglitz had not chosen to exhibit *Fountain* after it was rejected by the Exhibition of Independent Artists, or even if its disappearance after Steiglitz's exhibit had been total, and if the concept of exhibiting commonplace objects as art had not been reconceived in the 1960s, then in fact the questions asked by *Fountain* would not have even been successfully asked and the rejection of it would have succeeded. Although a Van Gogh painting exists as a painting even if Van Gogh destroys it before it has been seen by anyone other than Van Gogh, precisely because of what Duchamp wanted to do with *Fountain*—have a commonplace object accepted as art—it could not exist as an artwork until it had been accepted as one.[27] For this reason, I said earlier that *Fountain* did not exist as an artwork until thirty years after it had ceased to exist as an object. And because of its particular embodied meaning, one must take these elements of its acceptance as part of the meaning it embodies, even if they cannot have been intended by Duchamp and cannot have been embodied in any actual art object, since the object in question had ceased to exist when the embodiment had successfully occurred.

Fountain, indeed, demonstrates, in an unusually sharp way, Kant's seemingly odd dictum that an aesthetic judgment is indifferent to the existence of its object since the aesthetic judgments made about *Fountain* have virtually occurred in full coincidence with the object's non-existence. The first comments on *Fountain* occurred in response to the presentation of a urinal as an art object. And some of Duchamp's commentators have no doubt seen reproductions of Steiglitz's photo or perhaps one of the authorized reproductions of the work that have occurred since (all different in obvious ways from the original object Duchamp employed to create his artwork). But none of the comments depend in any important way on any knowledge of a specific material object. Even the formal readings discussed above, referring as they do to features shared by any number of urinals if not all of them, have no need, in order to be pertinent as referential remarks about the sculpture, of the particular one Duchamp chose. And most discussions, concerned as they are with either the sameness or difference between this urinal and others that look just like it, obviously don't need the object itself for the discussion to be apt.

Kant, of course, did not have in mind the actual disappearance of the object that occurs here. For Kant, the distinction between satisfactions in the agreeable and the good—both of which are interested—and a judgment of taste is that the first two satisfactions are determined "not just by the presentation of the object but also by the presentation of the subject's connection with the existence of the object" (Pluhar, tr., *Judgment*, 51). In contrast, a judgment of taste "is indifferent to the existence of the object. Nor is contemplation, as such, directed to concepts, for a judgment of taste is not a cognitive judgment" (Pluhar, tr., *Judgment*, 51).[28] In Kant's terms, when we regard an object aesthetically, we consider only its appearance, without regard to concepts that place that appearance in relation to all that surrounds it, knowledge of purpose, and so on. This form of regard is indifferent to an object's existence because it does not attend to any aspect of the object that would distinguish its appearance from an illusory one, regarding only the appearance itself (I will discuss this interpretation of Kant in more detail below). But if Kant imagined aesthetics as concerned with the pure appearance of an object, Duchamp carries that idea to its extreme manifestation; he makes an artwork not out of a singular urinal but by presenting the appearance of a non-specified urinal, in a sense the appearance of a concept, to us for contemplation, the proof of which is that we can continue to contemplate the artwork and the significance of its appearance even when the object has ceased to exist.

Taken together, the Kantian view of aesthetic indifference as pure appearance and Duchamp's hyperbolic display of appearance as coincident with an object's non-existence outline the answer to two common complaints about the concept of symbolic embodiment: first, that it has a tendency to reduce art to its meaning, or at least to divert attention from its appearance to that meaning, and second, that ideologically it takes appearance for essence. The first complaint derives from Danto's first criterion in his definition of a work of art, that it must be about something. Indeed, if a work of art is about something, the something it is about will be important to its being as an artwork, and thus this criterion, at least seemingly, forces us to divide our attention between that which the work is about and the work's appearance. But this criticism does not sufficiently attend to the implications of demanding that an artwork must embody its meaning. Embodying a meaning is not just one form of signifying it among others. Indeed, embodying does not really signify at all. Its claim, whether such a thing is possible or not, is that the meaning occurs entirely, and without remainder, in the surface display, the body that does the embodying. Thus one may explicate the meaning of a work only by recounting *all* of its features. This is its own kind of formalism, I think, but it differs from what I am calling experiential formalism in that this latter attends only to those aspects of appearance that have aesthetically pleasing effect. Experiential formalism claims that these pleasing features are the only aesthetic features of an artwork. But Duchamp's *Fountain* counters that claim. Symbolic embodiment insists on concentrating on appearance but on *all* of appearance in all of its implications and extensions. It may be that no object can be such a perfect embodiment. But, as we will see in Hegel, even this inability to embody adequately can itself become part of the meaning embodied. In the same way, the vagaries of *Fountain*'s fortunes as an artwork, vagaries unforeseeable in all their detail by Duchamp, become part of its embodied meaning.

The decidedly ambiguous relationship between the significance of *Fountain* and its appearance as object also disables aesthetic embodiment, fully understood, from offering the kinds of ideological dangers mentioned above. Those dangers depend on the taking of a delusory metaphysical concept—the possibility of embodying significance in sensuous experience or material reality—as a justification for political constraint or persuasion that functions by passing off the artificed as the real. And no doubt a thin understanding of symbolic embodiment does work in justifications of the aesthetic state outlined in Schiller and critiqued most directly by de Man.[29] But *Fountain* embodies its significance only by going clearly beyond the intentions of its creator and even beyond its own material existence. Even if Duchamp had intended *Fountain* to enact a kind of formal beauty as a Brancusian shape (always a possibility), he nevertheless could not have effected that intention without having the object he presented first go through the kind of interpretation that attends to the identity of its appearance with that of other urinals. The way we would need to resee the object as formally beautiful would depend on noticing as well as working through its preliminary identity. Thus the intention to create formal beauty would have to contain within it the analysis that shows the incompleteness of experiential formalism as a definition of art. And if Duchamp intended *Fountain* to embody the kind of aesthetic challenge I discussed above (the possibility I consider more likely), even so, that embodiment cannot be fully complete without comprehending the alternatives of rejection and acceptance that open up to the kinds of historical vagaries that are in fact part of that meaning but cannot be considered a part of Duchamp's intention. Finally, in this one case, the embodiment occurs with the disappearance of the sensuous object. We will see, in the discussions of Kant and Hegel below, how the whole concept of embodiment within pure appearance (itself a near oxymoronic concept used by Hegel and Nietzsche, in full awareness of the contradiction) undoes the metaphysical claim to symbolic wholeness and transforms the concept of symbolic embodiment even as it introduces and deploys it. Here we have seen how the idea of aesthetic indifference to the existence of the object it regards, an idea necessary for the understanding of *Fountain* as symbolic embodiment, makes embodied meaning an apparitional form and then challenges the idea of adequate *material* embodiment as part of its questioning of the formalist view of art.

One might object in two ways to this argument that *Fountain* accommodates the skeptical attacks on the notion of symbolic embodiment. One might argue first, that my concept of the object in question in this artwork is too simplistic; and second, that by claiming that *Fountain*'s embodiment is non-linguistic, I smuggle in the most numinous definition of embodiment rather than a skeptical version of it. In other words, while the original urinal disappeared, things do have existence as ideational forms and that existence matters as much, if not more, to the embodiment as does any phenomenal object. As I have said, *Fountain*'s conceptual existence raises different problems from the existence of mechanically reproduced works of art, inasmuch as the reproductions are still intended as more or less identical simulacrums of the object, while visibly different urinals can be (or at any rate have been) *Fountain* at any given moment. Still its ideational existence is pretty obviously like that of any work of literature, which does not exist as any particular copy, but whose existence depends on its being copyable. And this ideational existence precisely contests the view that embodiment escapes the woes of referentiality not by being linguistic reference but by being purely meaningful phenomenality.[30] In effect, Derrida's famous observation that the iteration responsible for the vagaries of linguistic meaning is also responsible for the ability to mean at all has as its necessary consequence that iteration will also befall *Fountain*, as long as it exists as a meaningful artwork.[31]

The problem with the first criticism is not that it isn't true but that it is only too true. The iterating grief that fleshy meaning is heir to results from its needing iterability to occur even as iteration allows a wandering from meaning through imperfect simulacra. The problem with iteration in the case of linguistic texts is that the ostensible originating meaning that needs protection from textual wandering is an intention that is available only in textual form. Artwork might escape this particular deconstruction if it refused the role of bearing meaning, but *Fountain*, as embodiment, does have meaning and so should be subject to deconstruction. But unlike other meaningful texts, *Fountain* not only absolutely welcomes reproductions as part of what it is, but it seems to welcome pointedly inexact reproductions. Moreover, it is not an entirely uninteresting question as to whether those remountings are reproductions of the same original or each of them a slightly different, original work, and this not only because they each look slightly different, but because Duchamp authorized each of them in all those differences.[32] And if there were one he didn't authorize, given what he has authorized, what criterion that entails his intention or the work's meaning or existence would make it somehow a lesser version? Now it may be that all artworks are ultimately subject to these wanderings. But can we say that any of these wanderings are in any way beyond the meaning of whatever was the original *Fountain*? Indeed, it is not merely the case that the original object of *Fountain* has disappeared, but all iterations, including even mere concepts of a urinal exhibited as art, are completely sufficient to whatever existence it does have. Every single one of its iterations goes equally well to the question of what it means to present a urinal as an artwork. In other words, if *Fountain*'s tolerance for its own disappearance is part of its working as an artwork, so is its tolerance for all the conceivable wanderings that may occur to its imperfect ideational and reproductive iterations. In such a situation, iteration occurs, but it brings no grief to meaning. And with *Fountain*'s ability to embody its own iterability recurs a meaning of embodiment that is all too numinous to be numinous at all. Because *Fountain*, in a sense "means" all the wanderings of meanings that can befall it (including even the possibility of its being denied the status of meaningful artwork), its embodiment works only because it excludes nothing as a result of all the ways it depends on this oddly disembodied work.

This exceeding of the intentions behind its creation in order to embody its meaning also undoes the aesthetic theory best designed to explain *Fountain*, and the one from whose work the above analysis has most evidently benefited—Arthur Danto's. Working through this problem in Danto's theory will get us to the connection between aesthetic indifference and perspective, as well as the role of indifference as perspective in the workings of embodiment that I am outlining here. Because he has concentrated on artworks whose existence as art raises questions about previous theories of art, artworks that in various ways undercut any claims that one can know what they are by the features of their material appearance, Danto has often been read as a skeptical critic of theories that seek to define art. But, in full realization of all the difficulties raised by his examples, Danto claims to outline art's essence, not to debunk it. He calls into question experiential formalism with the examples of artworks that are physically identical with non-artworks, such as Duchamp's *Fountain* (among quite a number of others, real and imagined), and he rejects Dickie's institutional explanation of such works as begging precisely the questions these works intend to raise: what does it mean to call such objects artworks and what about them makes them artworks? He is left to explain how, if anything could conceivably be appreciated as an artwork, artworks finally differ from other things in terms of what they are. Responding to Cohen's set of examples of what cannot be appreciated, Danto asserts that at least objects that looked like them could be so appreciated even if for different qualities: "Even granting that the thumbtack itself was beneath appreciation, it would not follow that an artwork materially like a mere thumbtack could not be appreciated; and that to which we might respond appreciatively would be the properties of the artwork without necessarily being the properties of the thumbtack" (*Transfiguration*, 93). The properties one would respond to aesthetically would be those of embodied meaning—whatever properties are entailed as a result of taking the thumbtack as an artwork. One would think that in order to make this distinction, since nothing in the material appearance of the hypothetical thumbtack artwork differentiates it from a normal thumbtack (after all, it either once was a thumbtack, or some artist created it to be indistinguishable from other thumbtacks), one would have to invoke a concept of aesthetic perspective, the application of a perspective that apprehended one thumbtack differently from another.

Danto objects, though, to theories of special forms of aesthetic apprehension. Because he wants to offer a theory of artworks, not a theory of apprehension, he must claim that, although one thumbtack may look exactly like another, the one transfigured into an artwork is not merely apprehended differently, but is actually different: "Learning it is a work of art means that it has qualities to attend to which its untransfigured counterpart lacks, and that our aesthetic responses will be different. And this is not institutional, it is ontological" (*Transfiguration*, 99). In order to evidence this claim, Danto argues that seeing an object as an artwork entails an act of interpretation, and that interpretation must attend to the artist's intention. Considering the hypothetical case of a painting consisting of a white canvas with a horizontal line across the middle, by an artist, K, who says the painting is about the first law of gravity: "Not only must you know something about Newton's first law in order to interpret K's painting as you do; you must also believe that K knew something about Newton's first law; otherwise interpretation is simply like seeing faces in clouds. The limits of *your* cloud musings are the limits of *your* knowledge, but we have the artist's limits as special constrain[t]s when interpreting works of art" (130).

Granting for the moment the role of intention in interpreting a work's meaning and the claim that intention does effectively constrain interpretation, one must first ask whether this form of interpretation really is analogous to what we do when we identify an object as a work of art. Danto's image of subjectivist response, seeing faces in clouds, is suggestive here because it comes close to describing precisely what Kant insists we do when we judge things to be either beautiful or sublime. Thus, Kant, as we saw in the last chapter, specifies that when we find a bird's song beautiful, we do so without regard to whether it actually has the significance that we give it: "The song of birds proclaims gladsomeness and contentment with existence. At least so we interpret nature whether it have this design or not" (*Judgment*, 144–145). And he differentiates between regarding the ocean "as implying all kinds of knowledge" and regarding it as sublime: "To call the ocean sublime we must regard it as poets do, merely by what strikes the eye" (110–111). In each of these cases, Kant insists that, in calling at least objects of nature beautiful, what we do precisely is see faces in clouds, endow the appearance of what is before us with meaningful form, without considering constraints of intention—"whether [nature] have this design or not"—or any contextualizing, background knowledge. Knowing the proper identity of an object is a matter of knowledge, and Kant would certainly agree with Danto that identifying an object as an artwork entails judging the purpose behind its creation properly (Kant, of course, did not have before him artworks such as *Fountain* that made that identification more than a matter of observation). But identifying an object as an artwork rather than a natural object was not itself part of the aesthetic judgment in Kant. In his discussion of bird songs, the case of taking a humanly mimicked bird song as a natural one is an epistemological error, not an aesthetic one. The actual aesthetic judgment works precisely in separation from this kind of identification, dealing with appearances without attending to purpose or intention. And this seems more nearly what we do when we regard a urinal as a *Fountain*: we look at it in one way rather than another. If Duchamp intended the urinal to be regarded as a challenge to a certain definition of art, for instance, we would be misunderstanding it if we interpreted it as a Brancusian form. But these are matters of interpreting this specific artwork. Assenting to *Fountain* as an artwork is a matter of apprehending it aesthetically—regardless of Duchamp's intention. And, as we have seen, the significance of *Fountain* captures elements of its history that Duchamp could not have intended.

Danto's objection to this position is that if aesthetic perspective is something we choose to employ or not, without regard to the object of that perspective, then there is no guarantee that when we employ it or not we are doing so correctly.[33] And he is of course right about this. There is nothing in our choice of perspective to tell us when we look at a primed, stretched canvas whether we are seeing a monochromatic modernist painting carried to its logical conclusion or just a canvas that has not yet been painted on, much less to tell us when we are looking at an uninstalled, upside-down urinal and when at a completed readymade. And in certain cases, we will no doubt apply aesthetic perspective incorrectly, although the error here is not an aesthetic one. Knowing the origins of an object and the intentions of its creator are in fact not parts of our aesthetic appreciation of it. One can employ the aesthetic perspective "incorrectly" only in the sense that the object we perceive aesthetically was not in fact presented as such: what is in front of us is just a primed, stretched canvas, not a monochromatic painting. But this error is an epistemological one. Once we accept Kant's idea that aesthetic apprehension allows the possibility of error about the actual purposes, intentions, or concepts of the object (and is indifferent to that possibility), there is no possible aesthetic error to be made in that apprehension. And when aesthetic apprehension is applied with conscious indifference to intention, as we do when judging a bird's song as meaningful when we know (at least as far as the bird is concerned) that we are not accurately recognizing a meaning in the song, there is no error about intention that one can make at all. Indeed, as the interpretation of *Fountain* above argues, going beyond what the author could possibly have intended can sometimes be part of an adequate interpretation.[34]

Finally, it is the very uncertainty brought by the inability to know when aesthetic perspective is in error in its interpretations that protects symbolic embodiment from the ideological dangers inherent in its claims. Since the ability to construe art as symbolic embodiment must come from a perspective, it must always recognize the extent to which it can be a matter of seeing faces in clouds. Resulting from apprehension, rather than being a feature of an object, embodiment can never really be construed as a privileged form of signification. Just as aesthetic indifference undercuts any consequences we might draw from the symbol's existence, the implications of aesthetic perspective undercut any consequences we might draw from any certainty that the appearance we saw in fact embodied the significance we construed. This ambiguity to aesthetic perspective may seem like largely a negative virtue—protecting the interpretation of art as symbolic embodiment from its own excess. But it is precisely the ability to turn aesthetic perspective on non-artworks, that which both Danto and Dickie see as a problem, that this book argues has been its major value for contemporary theory. That value will be the burden of the book's concluding chapters on Bourdieu and Foucault.

By being an artwork undifferentiable from non-aesthetic objects— indeed by having its point depend on that undifferentiable quality— Duchamp's *Fountain*, I have argued, indicates the necessity of defining art not in terms of physical features but in terms of our perspective upon it. My point, of course, is not that Duchamp shows this perspectival theory to be the meaning of all artworks or the claims of all theories. Its perhaps singular situation is that it shows that theories of what art is are incomplete when they do not accommodate its perspectival consequences. In particular, theories of experiential formalism cannot account for artworks such as Duchamp's because those works obviously cannot have material elements special to them as artworks. We must then fall back on a theory of perspective that connects the seeming essentialism of symbolic embodiment with the Kantian skepticism of aesthetic indifference. Having shown how Duchamp demands such a position, the balance of this chapter will show how that position, worked out in various ways by Kant, Hegel, and Nietzsche, was the burden of speculative aesthetics.

II. Disinterest and Indifference in Kant

Disinterest in Kant has always been interpreted as the defining feature of a particular kind of pleasure, one that contrasts with the pleasure we take in the satisfaction of what Hegel calls the "appetitive faculty" (*Aesthetics*, I, 58). According to this view, disinterest grows out of the eighteenth-century British attempt to delineate a pleasure special to aesthetic experience.[35] Because, in this vein, disinterested pleasure is always defined negatively (it is not sensuous pleasure; it is not pleasure in that which is morally good), Derrida characterizes it as "a somewhat arid pleasure . . . a somewhat strict pleasure" (*Truth in Painting*, 43), and after him Bourdieu, in *Distinction*, shows it to be a class-based concept. Indeed, the separateness of this pleasure has led to constant claims to separate aesthetic experience from political interest, and this separation has predictably led to the criticisms of the concept as either quietist or as covertly modeling an impossible notion of neutral reason. While it is quite clear that Kant meant the concept he calls both disinterest and indifference to cover these separations from satisfactions in the sensuously pleasing and satisfactions in the good, his definition is a far more radical one that has no connection with the eighteenth-century concept of an aesthetic pleasure as a form of experience.

So to see the signification of disinterest and indifference in Kant, one must start with the vitally important shift he made from the British aesthetic theorists whose terms he frequently used: in Kant, pleasure, arid or not, is not really a significant consequence of beauty. Although the pleasure produced by the harmony of the faculties sounds similar to pleasure-producing harmony in Shaftesbury or Hutcheson, in fact, even here, as we saw in the last chapter, pleasure is not a purpose of that harmony but alerts us to its having occurred. The harmony has value immediately in seeming to confirm a process of judgment, not because it causes a pleasure. And mediately, again as the prior chapter argued, its value is to give a basis for the teleological judgment. Behind these shifts in the content of an aesthetic experience lies the more important shift explained in the last chapter, whose conceptual consequences this one will explain: for the British empiricists, formal harmony produced pleasure either through divine ordination or because we are just built that way. The world made sense in the way art did but art only produced a model for explaining the implications of the fact that we see formal order in nature. For Kant, the judgment of a certain kind of form, purposiveness, was valuable because it showed us in what way and how far we could make claims about design in nature. Beauty then was not a pleasure-producing form but a perception of a certain kind of ordering. The judgment of beauty had to be distinguished from knowledge as carefully as from pleasure because it was as much a particularly strict and ambiguous kind of near knowledge as it was a strict and arid pleasure.[36]

And thus, despite his continued disbelief in the possibility of symbolic embodiment, Kant articulates a carefully confined theory of symbolism in his aesthetic. We can see this theory first in the very idea of the harmony of the faculties, the content of which is a matching up of the way imagination apprehends form and the way the understanding apprehends intuition through concepts, whose value is an at least seeming affirmation of the form-reading process of judgment. In other words, although the harmony comes with a pleasure, its value is its seeming exemplification of the propriety of judging reflectively. Admittedly this is fairly abstract, and most of Kant's examples of the judgment of taste are thin statements to the effect that "*x* is beautiful," followed by abstract formulations of the meaning of saying "is beautiful." But we do have a couple of more detailed judgments, both of which were cited above. One is the pleasure in the bird's song as proclaiming "gladsomeness and contentment with existence" (*Judgment*, 144). Another is the specification of how the ocean may be judged sublime: "if it is at rest as a clear mirror of water only bounded by the heaven; if it is restless, as an abyss threatening to overwhelm everything" (111). In each of these cases, the judgment imputes to the object judged a certain significance. In the case of the bird's song, the role of interpretation is fairly clear since the bird, in singing, surely does not state its own contentment with existence. Moreover "contentment with existence" is not just any kind of happiness but a claim that the world makes a certain kind of sense, the claim that is the constant content of the judgment that a thing has purposiveness. The bird's song seems purposive, then, because it expresses joy in its place in nature's order. The sublime, in contrast to the beautiful, sees a nature whose magnitude and resistance to the ordering judgment leads to a recourse to ideas of reason in order for the judgment to find a harmony to its experience. Hence the judgment of the ocean as sublime sees either a blank mirror or an abyss. In either case, it does not see the absence of significance but a threatening significance.[37]

These slight hints that the concept of purposiveness, far from being a progenitor of formalism, as is commonly supposed, actually conveys a very confined theory of beauty as symbolic embodiment, starts to become clear in the section on "Beauty as the Symbol of Morality." This section starts by distinguishing from forms of discourse which signify through conventional designation, those forms Kant calls hypotyposis, or the sensible illustration of concepts (either abstract concepts of the understanding or "rational concepts"). This distinction, itself, is worth pausing over since it insists that hypotyposis, under which category *symbols* are classed, is not a form of language and should not be so considered. Hypotyposes are "not mere *characterizations* or designations of concepts by accompanying sensible signs which contain nothing belonging to the intuition of the object and only serve as a means for reproducing the concepts" (197). If we take this distinction seriously, the objection falls away that to think of art as symbolic embodiment is to see as reducing art to a meaning separable from its sensuous appearance. Symbolism as a form of language would do this because the point of characterizations or designations is always to reach the designated referent. Sensible illustration, however, is not really any form of signification. Since it conveys concepts wholly in bodying them forth, those concepts could not be reduced to a meaning differentiable from their appearance.

Having established the distinction, however, by distinguishing between two types of hypotyposis, Kant immediately proceeds to declare the form of it that relates to aesthetics always and of necessity inadequate:

All intuitions which we supply to concepts *a priori* are therefore either *schemata* or *symbols*, of which the former contain direct, the latter indirect, presentations of the concept. The former do this demonstratively; the latter by means of an analogy . . . first applying the concept to the object of a sensible intuition, and then applying the mere rule of the reflection made upon that intuition to a quite different object of which the first is only a symbol. Thus a living body represents a monarchical state if it is governed by national laws, and by a mere machine (like a hand mill) if governed by an individual absolute will; but in both cases *symbolically*. For between a despotic state and a hand mill there is, to be sure, no similarity. (197–198)

If we remember that schemata illustrate pure concepts of the understanding (one illustrates empirical concepts by simple examples), they need not detain us for long. One can give a sensible illustration of a pure concept of the understanding adequately simply because those concepts organize our understanding. Illustrating them will therefore illustrate their workings directly without analogy. The working of the concept in some sensible illustration shows the concept's systematizing operation, which is all there is to the concept in any case.[38] Kant's explanation of the symbol, though, amounts to a skeptical version of the usual kind of definition that compares symbolic reference with conventional linguistic reference in terms of the sensible illustration actually embodying the concept illustrated. For instance, according to Hegel, the lion is a symbol for magnanimity because it in fact possesses that quality (*Aesthetics*, I, 304).[39] And, indeed, Kant goes on to a brief discussion of the buried metaphors in philosophical discourse as indications of buried presumptions, as if he were deconstructing the symbol.

Having offered a highly skeptical definition of the symbol (and, as I noted in the last chapter, this skepticism is quite consistent in Kant, going back at least to his definition of idealism in *The Critique of Pure Reason*), though, Kant then goes on to make a statement which, while traditional enough in aesthetics both before and after, sounds odd here:

Now I maintain the beautiful is the symbol of the morally good; and only because we refer the beautiful to the morally good (we all do so naturally and require all others also to do so as a duty) does our liking for it include a claim to everyone else's assent. . . . The morally good is the *intelligible* that taste has in view, as I indicated in the preceding section; for it is with this intelligible that even our higher cognitive powers harmonize, and without this intelligible contradictions would continually arise from the contrast between the nature of these powers and the claims that taste makes. (Pluhar, tr., *Judgment*, 228–229)[40]

This passage has been quite important to critics who think that beauty's moral content gives it its significant universal validity and in turn validates Kant's claim to connect the realms of nature and freedom through the aesthetic judgment (as Guyer, *Claims of Taste*, 373, notes).[41] One of the problems with this claim is that while Kant does say that a taste for the beautiful in nature at any rate may be the mark of a person's having a moral character because having that taste indicates a certain attitude that is conducive to being moral (*Judgment*, 41), he does not actually argue that the beautiful has a moral content the recognition of which is necessary to connect the realms of freedom with the realms of nature. Nor could he make that claim, since his definition of the symbol presupposes that the illustration of morality that beauty gives is considerably less than perfect.

If we put this claim back in the context both of the few judgments of taste we see in the *Critique* and of that work's overriding concern with seeing the beautiful as manifesting a sense of purpose in nature that we cannot actually ascribe to nature, the meaning of saying that beauty symbolizes the morally good becomes clearer. Kant lays out clearly in his introduction, and reintroduces in his solution to the antinomy of taste, the two conflicting claims that the aesthetic judgment must mediate: (1) There is an unbridgeable gulf between the supersensible laws of freedom and the sensible laws of nature given to the understanding. This gulf includes the impossibility of ascribing purpose to nature. (2) Despite the fact that one cannot ascribe purpose to nature, the concept that nature operates purposively is a transcendental principle of judgment. In order for judgment not to be based on a fallacy, and, as we have seen, in order for it to be psychologically possible as opposed to merely rational to act morally in the world, then, it must be at least coherent to act as if nature were purposive. We have seen how the aesthetic judgment in terms of the harmony of the faculties intends to demonstrate this coherence. Its first step, however, is always the satisfaction that the spectacle of significance in nature, either the bird song's gladsomeness or the ocean's abyss, provides. Beauty symbolizes the morally good by presenting specific appearances of purposiveness as illustrations of a larger purposiveness in nature. Still, nature's purpose cannot be illustrated adequately because it is a transcendental principle and thus not capable of sensuous embodiment. The inadequacy of the symbol, the surprising burden of a section that means to offer symbolization as explaining the moral significance of the aesthetic, protects the beautiful from becoming a fallacious idealism. One never really has grounds to believe in any given embodiment of nature's moral purpose as fully accurate. Nevertheless the activity of so seeing nature in general is something like a psychological ground for acting morally.

It is in this context that I wish to place the Kantian concept of disinterest or indifference. And what this context shows, I think, is that aesthetic indifference does not primarily distinguish the kind of pleasure the aesthetic entails, but rather qualifies our investment in the symbolic embodiment we judge to occur when we experience an object as beautiful. The first thing to be noticed about Kant's definition of this term is that contrary to the standard definition of *disinterest* in English, which denotes not the absence of interest but a more specific freedom from selfish motive or self-concern in one's judgment, Kant in fact means precisely a negation of all interest, not a position of neutrality.[42] All of his specifications detail kinds of interest that do not exist in the case of the aesthetic judgment, most prominently, of course, interest in the sensuously pleasurable and interest in the good. Kant certainly does mean to include such interests and pleasures in his negation, but a look at his examples of interested judgments in his opening discussion of the term indicates a broader concern:

If anyone asks me if I find that palace beautiful which I see before me, I may answer: I do not like things of that kind which are made merely to be stared at. Or I can answer like that Iroquois Sachem, who was pleased in Paris by nothing more than by the cook shops. Or again, after the manner of Rousseau, I may rebuke the vanity of the great who waste the sweat of the people on such superfluous things. (*Judgment,* 38–39)

The second and third cases do fairly unproblematically exemplify kinds of judgment that, because they are concerned with other interests and other pleasures, do not qualify as aesthetic. The example of the Iroquois Sachem, because it manages to be simultaneously ethnocentric and slightly tangent (it is hard to imagine responding to the question "Is this palace beautiful?" with the answer "I like Parisian restaurants," since one liking hardly precludes the other), seems to be the one that sticks in many critics' minds. As we will see in a later chapter, both Derrida and Bourdieu, in criticizing the term, fasten on the distinction between the aesthetic and the sensuously pleasurable. The case of the Rousseau-like philosopher also demonstrates a negation of an interest, since his judgment about the palace concerns the moral shortcomings in its having been built (vanity and exploitation).

The first example, though, deserves some consideration. Although there may be a moral judgment implicit in the phrase "made merely to be stared at," not only is that implication not an obvious one, but it makes the third example, involving the Rousseauvian moralist, redundant since both would demonstrate judgments based on an inappropriate interest in the good. Without that implication, however, this example could quite easily be read as the kind of formal aesthetic judgment that critics usually think that Kant's theory espouses. By "made merely to be stared at," this critic might be judging that the ornamentality or the grandeur of the palace exceeds the formal necessities of the palace as a whole, thus eliciting mere staring, an appreciation fixed on those parts, rather than the whole. Indeed, as we have seen, in judging the beauty of ornaments Kant makes just this kind of judgment: "But if the ornament does not itself consist in beautiful form, and if it is used as a golden frame is used, merely to recommend the painting by its *charm*, it is then called *finery* and injures genuine beauty" (*Judgment*, 62). Although the criticism of charm connects the golden frame with an inappropriate appeal to sensuous pleasure, the injury it does to genuine beauty can only be explained by the inappropriate attention it calls to itself. In effect, we could take the first example of a supposedly inappropriate interest as a fully Kantian judgment about a disproportionate relation between part and whole. But there is one more implication in the phrase "made merely to be stared at" that ties this judgment with that of the moralist and with that of someone on a desert island who, if he had a sufficiently comfortable hut, wouldn't give himself the trouble of wishing for such a palace. In each of these cases, the unaesthetic judgment entails a judgment about the purposes behind the object's existence, its reasons for being. The moralist imputes the palace's existence to the self-display that assuages "the vanity of the great." In a like manner, the first critic, without making a moral judgment, still judges that the purpose of the building is merely to elicit stares. And the desert-island construction worker, not looking for the approval of others, has no motive beyond comfort to satisfy. In other words, these cases exemplify the flaw of judging the palace within the context of what brought it into existence and what that context tells us about its being as an object.

Kant, in summing up his own objection to these three judgments, makes clear how this common concern with the purposes and motives behind the palace disables the judgments from being aesthetic:

We wish only to know if this mere representation of the object is accompanied in me with satisfaction, however indifferent I may be as regards the existence of the object of this representation. We easily see that, in saying it is *beautiful* and in showing that I have taste, I am concerned, not with that in which I depend on the existence of the object, but with that which I make out of this representation in myself. (*Judgment*, 39)

Again, the word translated as "representation" here is *Vorstellung*—in this context, a presentation to the senses. As I noted in the discussion of Duchamp, Kant here claims that the aesthetic judgment concerns what Plato calls an object's appearances, and Plato considers an object's appearance as merely a representation of its form. Kant thus reverses a line of thought dating back to Plotinus's response to Plato (and incidentally starts one that carries through at least to Nietzsche). Plato, of course, had argued that because art represents objects present to the senses, which themselves represent universal forms, it merely represents a representation. In response, Plotinus had claimed that art in fact aimed at representing these universal forms and represented sensuous objects only incidentally in this process. Kant, in effect, accepts Plato's claim at least about our aesthetic judgment: it concerns itself with the pure appearance of an object, without reference to purpose or motive behind it, without reference even to the concepts that allow us to construe it as an existing object (these concepts perform some of the functions that the forms do in Plato, since they gather experiences into coherent categories). Even though we must of course employ those concepts even just to know that the palace is a palace, we do not refer to these concepts in judging its aesthetic quality and are thus indifferent to its existence as a palace.

At this point, we must make some distinctions because of slight shifts in terms that occur between Kant's epistemology and his aesthetics. In Kant's construction of the understanding, an appearance of an object is all we ever know of it and the concepts of the understanding enable us even to recognize which appearance we are sensing. A *Vorstellung* is not a representation of a form, as is an appearance in Plato, or a surface beneath which we can meaningfully plumb. It is all that is present to us. Under these descriptions, we may be indifferent to an object's existence, but we can't ignore its concepts without losing the ability to recognize it at all. Kant clearly has in mind here something like seeing the surface appearance of a thing without attending to its meaning, its causes, or its actual place in the natural world. Hearing a bird's song or seeing the palace or the ocean, we must identify it as a bird's song, a palace, or the ocean to get the effect of seeing purposiveness, and so we cannot see any of those objects without *any* regard for their concepts. But in attributing gladsomeness to the song, we surely are also not drawing conclusions about its natural causes, about any real meaning it might have, about what the bird or even a more primary creator might intend. In this sense, we attend to its surface appearance, to which we attribute meaning, rather than to the conditions of its existence. And caring, as we do, for the attributed significance rather than for the actual causes of the song, in this sense, we are indifferent to its existence. And it is also in this sense that Kant starts the discussion in nineteenth-century aesthetics of aesthetic presentation as the presentation of appearance for its own sake.

We can now deal with a common objection to Kant's argument: many critics object that we are not in fact indifferent to an object's existence when we appreciate its beauty since the appreciation must depend on the existence. These critics note that we keep paintings that we value in museums, for instance, or on the walls of our houses, precisely because we are not indifferent to their existence. But paintings, as we have seen, are not the primary objects of the aesthetic judgment because, since they are created with the intention to appeal to our aesthetic judgment, when we judge them beautiful, we do so precisely with regard to the purposes behind their creation. For this reason, we do not regard them as mere appearances and are not indifferent to their existence. But in the case of the bird's song, our sense of it as expressing contentment with its existence in fact does not regard whether that is the song's design. It is indifferent to it precisely as the actual bird's song. It judges only the pure appearance of the sound, apprehended as music. As Danto would complain, this is like seeing faces in clouds, and it as little cares for the bird's existence as the spectator of the clouds cares for theirs.

But unlike Danto, Kant sees this indifference to the reality beneath an object's appearance not as a problem with his theory but as definitive of an aesthetic judgment. We can now see the connection between aesthetic indifference and Kant's peculiar version of symbolic embodiment. For Kant, all symbolic expressions of abstract concepts are inexact analogies, merely a kind of shorthand. The beautiful symbolized the moral by at least seeming to offer a spectacle of some part of nature as significant that embodied a way of seeing all of nature as significant, thus conforming to the law of judgment that necessitates that significance and enables us to act as moral agents in the sensible world. But from a strictly epistemological perspective, one might ask what real service this symbolism provides if it comes to us with the proviso that it is really only an analogy and that the significance it sees might be only a seeming one. And even if such hesitant connections between meaning and sensible expression could do the work Kant wants them to do, in what sense can a symbolic embodiment ever really occur when it is really only an analogue rather than an actual sensuous manifestation bearing a significance on its surface? The demand that the aesthetic judgment be indifferent to the object's existence answers these objections by specifying what it means to say that a thing bears its meaning on its surface. If all of the significance of something reveals itself entirely on that thing's surface, and if the surface is only significance without remainder, it follows that the significance of the thing *is* its appearance, that that appearance, without reference to essence or ideal form or even organizing concepts of understanding, is all significance and, more importantly, is all the significance there is. To the extent that aesthetics, in particular, concerns not objects but only their appearance, as the criterion of indifference to existence asserts, then only beautiful objects can really work as symbolic embodiments because only they fix on appearance in complete disregard to anything else, on the object's appearance both as merely appearance and as purely appearance. And beautiful objects work as symbolic embodiments precisely because they rest the quality of "purely" on the quality of "merely," accepting that a complete sensible embodiment of significance may well be the same as no significance at all, but *mere* appearance. And that acceptance can only occur with an indifference to questions beyond that appearance, an indifference to the object's existence.

Before we conclude this discussion of Kant's indifference as a concept skeptical of meaning rather than ratifying neutral objectivity, though, we must take a final pass through Derrida's deconstruction of Kant precisely on this issue. If aesthetic indifference seems to authorize a choice in how to perceive things, nevertheless, at times, there seems to be a limit on that choice, which does seem to point back to Kant's aesthetics as a theory of objects. As both Derrida (*Truth in Painting*, 104–107) and Marc Redfield (*Phantom Formations*, 16–17) note, when Kant distinguishes between free and dependent beauty, with the aesthetic judgment being pure only when it concerns free beauty, he exemplifies the difference in terms of objects, not perspectives. And the distinctions he draws seem to carry a certain essentialist weight. We see free beauty in certain kinds of natural objects:

Flowers are free natural beauties. Hardly anyone but a botanist knows what sort of a thing a flower ought to be; and even he, though recognizing in the flower the reproductive organ of the plant, has no regard to this natural purpose if he is passing judgment on the flower by taste. . . . Many birds (such as the parrot, the humming bird, the bird of paradise) and many sea shells are beauties in themselves, which do not belong to any object determined in respect of its purpose by concepts, but please freely in themselves." (*Judgment*, 65–66)

In contrast to these natural objects (and certain kinds of ornaments), Kant adds another list of things that can only be seen as adherent beauty: "But human beauty (i.e. of a man, a woman, or a child), the beauty of a horse, or a building (be it church, palace, arsenal, or summer house), presupposes a concept of the purpose which determines what the thing is to be, and consequently a concept of its perfection; it is therefore adherent beauty" (66). One does not have to go through too much interpretive heavy lifting to get to the essential difference here (although perhaps because Derrida's reading is already bearing much of the weight for us). The flower, explicitly, has (almost) no internal purpose, and so opens itself to being read without reference to its purpose. Buildings, particularly the ones Kant instances, do serve purposes. And we see horses in terms of how they serve us; their purpose is their purpose for us. Human beings are, of course, according to one of the versions of the categorical imperative, by implication here, and explicitly only a few pages later, entities that have their ends in themselves: "The only being which has the purpose of its existence in itself is *man*" (69; also quoted to this effect in Redfield, *Phantom Formations*, 16). Human beings, thus, cannot be detached from their purposes.

Within the formal terms of Kant's argument in *The Critique of Judgment*, this distinction follows naturally in the same way that his claim that beauty in the fine arts is secondary to beauty in nature does from the concentration on those objects whose purposiveness does not belong to them because we do not perceive their purpose. Still Derrida is surely right that the distinction also has everything to do with the occluded central place of human beings in the theory (*Truth in Painting*, 108–109). Human beings can only have adherent beauty because, in contrast to the building and the horse (one made by humans, the other an animal whose purpose too evidently is to serve humans), only human beings, having their purpose intrinsic to their being, having their end in themselves, are capable of being an ideal of beauty: "This *man* is, then, alone of all objects in the world, susceptible of an ideal of *beauty*, as it is only *humanity* in his person, as an intelligence that is susceptible of the ideal of *perfection*" (*Judgment*, 70). Human beings thus do not fit within Kant's theory of aesthetic because the theory is there to make the world beautiful for them and according to the ideal they embody. As Derrida puts it:

Man, equipped with a reason, an understanding, an imagination and a sensibility, is that X from which, with a view to which, the opposition is taken in view: the opposition of the pure and the ideal, the errant and the adherent . . . the without-end and the not-without-end, that is also the opposition of non-sense and sense. The subject of that opposition is man and he is the only subject of this *Critique* of judgment. (*Truth in Painting*, 111)

Nothing I have been saying about Kant's theories of purposiveness and indifference should be taken to deny this centralizing of the human subject as the purpose, so to speak, of the theory. In the last chapter, I argued that the aesthetic judgment served to justify the teleological judgment, whose point was to make it tenable to read the world as having a moral purpose suitable for human beings as moral agents to live in. And that is surely to make the theory serve human beings.

But I have also been arguing that to reach this teleological judgment without affronting his sense of its lack of basis in nature, Kant defined an aesthetics of judgment that targeted solely a kind of judgment, without defining what kinds of objects it could be applied to. If Duchamp's *Fountain*, showing the importance of perspective to the definition of art, also showed the force of Kant's theory that aesthetics was a perspective, if a urinal can be taken for art, then it should be the case that there would be no limitation on what could be seen as beautiful, what could be seen in the absence of its purposes, regardless of what purposes it had, so that it could be endowed with a purposiveness without purpose. In the following section, I will be arguing that the internal necessities of Kant's definition of aesthetics, as developed in Hegel, Schopenhauer, and Nietzsche, always forced a bracketing of Enlightenment reason and subjectivity, even in the case of philosophers—perhaps Hegel, certainly Schopenhauer—who clearly meant aesthetics to support those ideas. Similarly, I could argue that Kant's theory of judgment should allow a pure aesthetic judgment of buildings, horses, and humans regardless of what Kant in fact says here.

In this case, however, I do not need to propose a logic to aesthetics that would even deconstruct the ends to which philosophers put it, because Kant in fact does not say that we *cannot* regard objects with adherent purposes in any other way. His first example of the flower is of something that could be judged, at least by botanists, according to its purposes (even though Kant says no one does this). Of the three examples of things that "presuppose" concepts of purpose, buildings, horses, and humans, Kant shows us, elsewhere in the *Critique*, judgments of two of them in the absence of their purposes. The building, in the particular example of the palace, of course opens the section on disinterest, which we have already discussed. To see the palace as beautiful, we had to be able to see it in isolation from the purposes for which it was built, which that section quite clearly supposes we can do. More pointedly, human beings, too, can be dehumanized. Having said that to see the ocean as sublime we must see it merely as it strikes the eye, Kant continues, "The like is to be said of the sublime and beautiful in the human figure. We must not regard as the determining grounds of our judgment the concepts of the purposes which all our limbs serve, and we must not allow this coincidence to *influence* our aesthetical judgment" (*Judgment*, 111).[43] Even in the section in which he isolates buildings, horses, and humans as things we cannot judge with a pure aesthetic judgment, he clearly means to say that we cannot so judge them if we judge them according to their purposes. Those purposes are hard but not impossible to ignore, and he does imagine us ignoring them:

A judgment of taste, then, in respect of an object with a definite internal purpose, can only be pure if either the person judging has no concept of this purpose or else abstracts from it in his judgment. Such a person, although forming an accurate judgment of taste in judging of the object as free beauty, would yet by another who considers the beauty in it only as a dependent attribute (who looks to the purpose of the object) be blamed and accused of false taste, although both are right in their own way—the one in reference to what he has before his eyes, the other in reference to what he has in his thought. (*Judgment*, 67)

The logic by which Derrida's deconstruction explains why human beings should be sectioned off from being the subject of a pure aesthetic judgment, I think, indicates the importance of the fact that they are not so protected. I have worked out the line of argument that moves Kant toward defining the aesthetic judgment in terms of its perspective and not in terms of the status of the object it perceives. Since the teleological judgment, which does justify the world for human beings, in order not to affront the limits Kant places on the understanding, must judge in a way that approaches contradiction (nature has the form of purposiveness, even though we do not conclude from that that it has a purpose), the aesthetic judgment shows such a way of judging to be possible by showing how to judge by appearance in isolation from purpose—even when judging things whose purposes we know. This line of argument leads to a judgment that must be able to see even human beings apart from their purposes, even that intrinsic purpose that defines their humanity. It demands a judgment that can turn human beings into disarticulated body parts. And even though this ability may be taken as tasteless by those who cannot view humans apart from their internal purposes (tastelessness is such a small sin among the many of which anti-humanists stand accused), its tastelessness is oddly a purer judgment. The ability of aesthetics to do its service to humanity depends on its ability to see humanity as lacking that which calls forth its service. That ability does not really deconstruct its own Enlightenment purposes. It just rests indifferent to them, able at times to hold them in suspension, see around them, propose an embodiment, and propose that embodiment as just a perspective, a pure appearance, with all the conflicting meanings that pure appearance entails.

III. Sensuous Embodiment, Indifference, and Hegel's Historicism

In Kant's articulation, then, symbolic embodiment can never be available for the kind of ideological deployment that makes critics so suspicious of it. In the above discussion of Duchamp, we saw that our claim to see a symbol in an object must be accompanied by a skepticism about the success of the object's embodiment as a result of the uncertainties of aesthetic perspective. By turning epistemological uncertainty into aesthetic indifference, however, Kant goes a step further. Since, from the perspective of aesthetic indifference to the object's existence, embodiment can only be mere appearance, any ideology that claimed to manifest its validity sensuously would have simultaneously to claim that its validity was mere appearance, without a foundation in existence. It seems unlikely that an ideology would try to employ this Kantian version of the concept. It is far more likely that one could interpret ideologies from this kind of aesthetic perspective to drain them of authority and validity, to see them as mere appearance, and in my final discussions of Foucault and Bourdieu, this is what we see will happen. But at this point, one might object that, after all, Kant often seems to stand alone in the German aesthetic tradition in his skepticism about symbolic embodiment. In fact, though Kant was the most explicit in his skepticism about symbolism, he was by no means alone in seeing symbolic embodiment as occurring, so to speak, only as an apparition.[44] Hegel's definition of art seems the most wholly dependent on what we now think of as the Romantic ideology of the symbol, and his definitions of embodiment seem without irony. Still, far more insistently than Kant, as we will see, he tied symbolism to appearance and thus also constructed an aesthetics more likely to undo ideologies than to undergird them.

Hegel's *Aesthetics* (at least until Danto's idiosyncratic revivification of its historicism in *The End of Art*) has surely been one of the least read and most undervalued works in the tradition of nineteenth-century thought on art and aesthetics. Partly the book's all too literally stunning length has surely contributed to its lack of readership (although since that length occurs as a result of a close engagement with numbers of artworks in all genres and all periods, one wonders why more art and literary critics have not shown more interest). But perhaps more important has been the central content of its two claims: first, that beauty is the sensuous embodiment of the idea, and second, that art is a secondary form of thought that has been historically surpassed. We already have seen critical objections to the idea of embodiment, and Hegel's definition of it seems pointedly absolute. Indeed, for Hegel, a perfect embodiment cannot even be symbolic since symbolism is still a kind of linguistic designation—"the symbol is *prima facie* a sign" (I, 304)—and so, "in order to remain a symbol it must not be made entirely adequate to that meaning" (I, 305). Claiming for art, during its highest period, an embodiment so complete that it is entirely sensible manifestation, Hegel at the same time encloses this perfection within the past. Thus he at once makes art too perfect and at the same time philosophically surpassed.[45]

But if Hegel makes both these claims, and at various points in the opening pages of the *Aesthetics*, he certainly seems to, then each of them must shade the other. In other words, if sensuous embodiment has been philosophically surpassed, then its status as a "perfect" form of art (not to say a superior form of discourse because of the complete adequacy of signifier to signified) must be defined so as to recognize its much less than perfect limitations. But in reverse, if philosophy ultimately surpasses the stage of sensuous embodiment, one must question the state to which that surpassing leads us. Embodiment may be considered a merely ornamental illustration of abstract thought if, in fact, in a Kantian definition, it is never really perfect. But a perfect adequacy between sensible manifestation and manifested concept, in which the whole concept were completely visible on the surface of the whole sensuous appearance, without remainder on either side, would of necessity communicate completely, without chance of misinterpretation or miscommunication. Any other form of communication, whether surpassing or surpassed, would be a falling off from such a complete sensuous embodiment of the concept. Indeed, this section will argue, Hegel's *Aesthetics* has as its point a conscious working out of this contradiction into a theory of embodiment that is considerably more ambiguous than is generally allowed, linked with a historicism that defines philosophical surpassing in terms that make it function as aesthetic indifference.

Hegel starts by insisting that his aesthetics constitutes an objectification of Kant's subjective aesthetic unification between "universal and particular," between "concept and object" (I, 60). But he then shows how that objectification still makes aesthetics a self-questioning awareness, as Kant's subjectification also makes it, rather than an actual harmonious union. Hegel thus establishes how the concepts of embodiment and indifference always work, whether taken subjectively or objectively, as an interrogating perspective, one that, as a later section of this chapter will explain, leads to Nietzschean perspectivism as well as, ultimately, to postmodern theory. The course of this analysis of Hegel's reformulating of embodiment and indifference, then, first takes up his definition of embodiment and how it necessitates the problematic concept of surpassing. It concludes by showing how, in Hegel, aesthetic indifference manifests itself not in what Hegel understands to be Kant's concept of disinterest, but in his own historicism, which prepares the way for aesthetics as perspectivism.

Hegel makes explicit the turn, which occurs only implicitly in Kant, from defining art as pleasure in formal arrangement to defining it as sensuous embodiment, and he does so precisely by showing the insufficiency of definitions of art as a form of pleasure. He begins the *Aesthetics* by posing two objections to treating art "scientifically," or as a fit subject for philosophy, and his responses to these objections lead both to his definition of art as embodiment and to his consignment of it to the past. The two objections to such treatment are as follows. First, to the extent that art is a form of pleasure-giving ornament, either it is too trivial to demand philosophic treatment or, if the pleasure serve some higher end (for instance mediating the demands of reason and duty), the art itself does not thereby become philosophically treatable, because it matters still only as a means (I, 4).[46] Second, even if it could be shown that fine art "in general is a proper object of philosophical reflection, it is yet no appropriate topic for *strictly* scientific treatment" (I, 5). Hegel explains that the beauty of art presents itself to "*sense*, feeling, intuition, imagination" (I, 5), while scientific thought brings details under the order of abstract formulations and concepts. Thus, while art may make vivid a concept, the scientific analysis of art would merely reverse the process: "While art does brighten and vivify the unilluminated and withered dryness of the Concept, does reconcile its abstractions and its conflict with reality, does enrich the Concept with reality, a *purely* intellectual treatment [of art] removes this means of enrichment, destroys it, and carries the Concept back to its simplicity without reality and to its shadowy abstractions" (I, 6).

In answering the first objection, Hegel retraces our steps in moving from the definition of art in terms of a pleasure produced by formal arrangement to a theory of embodied significance. Hegel calls "art" that "which is *free* alike in its ends and its means." Art, Hegel claims, can only be free in its ends and means when it does the work of all thought: "when it is simply one way of bringing to our minds and expressing the *Divine.*" And he then defines, famously, the special way art does this:

In works of art the nations have deposited their richest inner intuitions and ideas, and art is often the key, and in many nations the sole key, to understanding their philosophy and religion. Art shares this vocation with religion and philosophy, but in a special way, namely by displaying even the highest [reality] sensuously, bringing it thereby nearer to the senses, to feeling and to nature's mode of appearance. (I, 7–8)[47]

I have traced so closely the argument that leads to this famous declaration of art as sensuous embodiment to show how nearly it predicted the logic by which Duchamp undid twentieth-century formalism as an adequate theory of art. Duchamp showed how an object could be an artwork without having any formally distinguishing features that would give pleasure in a way that its non-artwork counterpart would not. Although Hegel certainly did not imagine such extreme cases, he did recognize the conceptual split between an object and the pleasure it gives, and so turned to an attempt to define a non-material essence to the art object.

But this definition of artistic embodiment would seem to raise all the objections to symbolic embodiment that Kant's skeptical version skirted. Indeed it will claim an embodiment so complete in art at its height, during the classical period in ancient Greece, that its sculpture made visible all of that culture's theological understanding. Hegel's response to the second objection to the scientific treatment of art, however, fairly quickly leads to a drastic modifying of what sensuous embodiment in art means. That objection was that a scientific treatment, in its analysis of art, would split the sensuous surface from the concept, thus undoing that which made the object analyzed special as art. And in fact, it is hard to imagine how any kind of analysis, either scientific or philosophical, could avoid doing this since, if that analysis works from the surface to some meaning or significance indicated by that surface, it then follows that the significance arrived at did not exist entirely on the object's surface and the analysis in fact had separated one from the other. Indeed, any interpretation or analysis of an artwork that works under a theory of embodiment must hold some skeptical or constrained version of that embodiment—either knowingly or not—since the fact of interpretation automatically undoes a full claim to embodiment.[48] And, of course, Hegel cannot answer this objection in any easy way since he fairly immediately links his definition of sensuous embodiment with his notorious statement that, since, for well or ill, the modern spirit can no longer be satisfied with thinking sensuously, so to speak, "art, considered in its highest vocation, is and remains for us a thing of the past" (I, 11). And he immediately follows this temporal distancing of art with an affirmation of philosophy's analytic separation of it into its conceptual and sensuous elements: "What is now aroused in us by works of art is not just immediate enjoyment but our judgement also, since we subject to our intellectual consideration (i) the content of art, and (ii) the work of art's means of presentation, and the appropriateness of both to one another. The *philosophy* of art is therefore a greater need in our day than it was in days when art by itself as art yielded full satisfaction" (I, 11).

I will detail below the way Hegel's historical circumscription of art functions as a bridge between Kantian indifference and Nietzschean perspectivism. I want to continue to look at Hegel's answer to the second objection against analyzing art scientifically, however, because working through its implications will show how Hegel's absolutism about sensuous embodiment as an aesthetic reality—the objectivism in his theory that he opposes to Kant's subjectivism—produces out of itself a radical doubleness in all of his claims. Indeed, this doubleness vies with Nietzsche's aesthetic ironies and necessitates Hegel's production of a theory of history within an aesthetics. In fact, in answering the second objection, Hegel does not discuss directly how to maintain the integrity of sensuous embodiment against the divisions of analysis (as we have seen, he could not do so), but instead picks up an issue that had not been directly mentioned in that objection: "So far as concerns the unworthiness of the *element* of art in general, namely its pure appearance and *deceptions*, this objection would of course have its justification if pure appearance could be claimed as something wrong. But appearance is essential to essence. Truth would not be truth if it did not show itself and appear" (I, 8). This, of course, is Hegel's key revision of Plato's claim that only Ideal forms are unitary and true; for

Hegel, that only is fully true in which the ideal form receives a concrete embodiment (this is stated explicitly at I, 143). But for the moment, let us stay with the restatement of the second objection as one against art as appearance. Since the central sensuous element in art is, in terms Hegel shares with Kant and Plato, art's connection with appearance, there is some ground to this shift. But the second objection was actually an objection to applying science to art because science would lose precisely the value of art, its sensuous embodiment of concepts. Here Hegel claims that the problem is that appearance, as deception, is unworthy of scientific treatment, not that scientific treatment etiolates the value of art.

In his response to this objection, however, Hegel not only answers the actual objection he first offered, as well as this rephrasing of it, but he offers a definition of pure appearance that leads to all the various ambiguities of his theory of embodiment and the reconstruction of aesthetic indifference as historical difference. Hegel notes that appearance is deceptive only to the extent that it presents itself as actual, and the appearance that presents itself as actual is not art but the phenomena and the inner world of our own experiences (I, 8). Precisely because art presents itself as pure appearance, then, it does not offer this deceptive suggestion that it is sufficient in its materiality: "In comparison with the appearance of immediate existence and of historiography, the pure appearance of art has the advantage that it points through and beyond itself, and itself hints at something spiritual of which it is to give us an idea, whereas immediate appearance does not present itself as deceptive but rather as the real and the true, although its truth is in fact contaminated and concealed by the immediacy of sense" (I, 9). Art, then, as in Kant, is pure appearance, but pure appearance—as opposed to immediate empirical appearance—does not deceive because it presents to us as part of its appearance its own incompleteness. Presenting itself as mere appearance, through the revelation of its "mereness," art points through and beyond itself. Nietzsche, as we will see, will ring changes on this paradox, but Hegel already establishes it: "pure appearance" presents itself as needing interpretation precisely in the adequacy of its self-presentation to its import. And this adequacy can only result from artifice, since appearance is never, by definition, in and of itself adequate to any import, import being by definition something in addition to appearance. The objection then that a scientific analysis of art divides the concept from the sense that is its essence as sensuous embodiment misses the point that sensuous embodiment must always, as part of itself, call forth the analysis that divides it in order for it to complete itself. For example, if a classic Greek actually perceived his statuary as manifesting, without remainder or loss, the entirety of his culture, he would not be seeing the statues as art because he would perceive them as meaningful appearance rather than pure or mere appearance. Only the scientific perspective of the philosophy of art restores the artificiality to a statue's embodiment and thus recognizes its participation in art's more general recognition of itself as "mere" appearance.

So art is a complete sensuous embodiment transcending interpretation, but is so only to the extent that it is recognized as artifice and thus interpreted as "mere appearance." The solution to this problem, I will argue, involves the establishment of the perspective of aesthetic indifference as a standpoint outside art's history, from which one offers an historicist explanation of art. In effect, a total sensuous embodiment of a concept turns out to be as epistemologically impossible in Hegel as it is in Kant, as impossible as Hegel's critics, thinking they are arguing against his concept of the symbol, claim it to be. But Hegel is aware of the problem, and so he captures the varieties of differences between sensuous embodiment and meaning within separate historical periods, allotting to each period a special, definitive form of difference in their art. As a result of these allotments, Hegel can further argue that the form of flaw in embodiment specific to each period in fact embodies that period's form of art. Moreover, the differences between sense and meaning, the flaws in embodiment, are themselves defined and distributed according to a pre-ordained set of possible relations, so Hegel can claim that his history is free of empirical fluctuations and caprices. The history itself has the formal closure of an aesthetic presentation. As a consequence of this aesthetically organized history, one can see the way Hegel's historicism operates conceptually in three ways: first, the way its various stages and forms are extrapolated out of the formal possibilities in the way matter and concept may relate; second, in the way that all inadequacies of artistic representation may be read as adequate in terms of historical appropriateness, a relationship that in turn makes the final philosophical appropriation of art, through analysis, become its own form of adequate explanation; and finally and (given the historical detail of Hegel's theory) astonishingly, an explicit indifference to the empirical accuracy, in certain areas, of his theory as an account of the historical manifestations and appearances of art forms.

Hegel's introduction of the three historical periods of art establishes their formal nature explicitly; he defines those periods in terms of the logical possibilities in the relations between sense and significance: " . . . through the unfolding and then the reconciliation of the particularizations of the Idea, and, through this development, artistic beauty acquires a *totality of particular stages and forms* . . . we must see how beauty as a whole decomposes into its particular determinations" (I, 75). Before going through these particular determinations, we should note that Hegel declares the combination of all of them to be necessary for art, as a whole, in all its material manifestations, to embody its own Idea. A particular artwork, to embody significance, as we have said before in discussing Duchamp, must have all its features involved in the signification without either excess or lack, and the features must display that signification on their face. But, for Hegel, art in its totality embodies the Idea of beauty, not specific artworks. If art in its totality is to do this, however, then art as a whole must somehow also embody all its own specific manifestations. Consequently, each of the logically possible forms of relation between sense and significance must be part of art. Beauty not only acquires but also requires a totality of particular stages and forms.

And indeed Hegel lays out the stages of art in the first instance as a set of almost synchronous, structural transformations. "Art begins when the Idea, still in its indeterminacy and obscurity, or in bad and untrue determinacy, is made the content of artistic shapes. . . . The first form of art is therefore rather a *mere search* for portrayal than a capacity for true presentation; the Idea has not found its form even in itself" (I, 76). Since at this point, the Idea itself is grasped only vaguely, it follows of necessity that its embodiment can be only vague and imperfect. Hence this is the Symbolic period, since symbol in Hegel is still a form of reference rather than embodiment, though a reference that works through concrete illustration. In the next stage, "the classical art-form clears up this double defect; it is the free and adequate embodiment of the Idea in the shape peculiarly appropriate to the Idea itself in its essential nature" (I, 77). Although one would think this would be the end of art since it looks to have achieved totality, in fact, its lack of awareness of itself as art entails a lack within the art. Thus Hegel limits the totality in this second transformation by specifying that the Idea can be embodied totally only because it is known insufficiently: " . . . classical art presents the complete unification of spiritual and sensuous existence as the *correspondence* of the two. But in this blending of the two, spirit is not in fact represented in its *true nature*" (I, 79). Accordingly, the attainment of a fuller awareness of the Idea leads to a loss of adequate sensuous embodiment, in preparation for a higher correspon-

dence outside art: "The romantic form of art cancels the undivided unity
of classical art because it has won a content which goes beyond and above
the classical form of art and its mode of expression" (I, 79).

All of these formal possibilities of art are of course identified as historical periods as well. Even in this section, the classical period is explicitly
limited to pre-Christian, Greek art, and "classical" is here a period as well
as an evaluation. Romantic art, as well, is explicitly identified with Christian art from the medieval period through near-contemporaneous realist
fiction (although to the extent that the *Aesthetics* begins after the end of art,
Hegel's Romantic period is coming to its close just as Romanticism, normally so-called, is beginning to flourish). And although the symbolic period is given the title of a referential relation rather than an historical period, Hegel attaches it to ancient Egyptian, Persian, Indian, and
pre-classical, Old Testament art and artifacts.

One could fully understand the formations of art Hegel is laying out
without reference to any historical periods. The descriptions of the various
ways in which the mind grasps the Idea and embodies that comprehension
might almost be a phenomenology expressed via historical metaphor. Critics frequently read the historical references in *Phenomenology of Mind* in
this way, of course. But the history is not just a metaphor here; Hegel insists on it throughout this work, far more than he does in the *Phenomenology of Mind*, because these particular stages must be historical periods for
the aesthetic theory to work here. They could not exist side by side spatially
since from that synchronous perspective, the differences both between and
within them could not be reconfigured as embodiments of a specific historical period's form of art. They would constitute only disruptions between sense and significance. Nor can they be part of a history that contains us. If we were within that history in a period in which sense and
significance did not match entirely, then art would not work for us. But if
we were in the period in which relations were perfect, there would be no
way out of that period and none of the awareness necessary not only for
philosophy, but as we have seen, for art as a whole. But from a perspective
outside that history, we can see both the divisions of art's parts and the totality comprised of the entire history.

We have seen how Hegel's famous claim of an end to art corresponds
to the scientific dissociation of art's elements. In this context, we can see
how the whole statement can be taken perspectivally:

In all these respects art, considered in its highest vocation, is and remains for us a
thing of the past. Thereby it has lost for us genuine truth and life, and has rather

been transferred into our *ideas* instead of maintaining its earlier necessity in reality and occupying its higher place. What is now aroused in us by works of art is
not just immediate enjoyment but our judgement also. (I, 11).

De Man has argued that one should take Hegel's definition of art's pastness
to say that art is a matter of memory (*Aesthetic Ideology*, 103). If by this he
meant that Hegel did not mean to say that art was temporally past "for us,"
he surely merited the complaint this interpretation has drawn.[49] But de
Man's interpretation and the usual one need not be seen as contradictory.
The passage above insists that it concerns what art is "for us," and what art
arouses is "in us," ending by juxtaposing our enjoyment with our judgment. Art can be fully art only when we see it at a distance, when analysis
judges art's embodiment. That distance cannot be merely an epistemological indifference or disinterest as it was in Kant if Hegel's absolute form of
embodiment is to be total. Consequently he claims an historical distance,
a real one perhaps, but one which nevertheless functions as a perspective,
in the sense of a stance chosen in order to see a thing in a certain way.
From our position outside this history, we can view art after all with a
Kantian indifference to its own purpose, "genuine truth and life," and subject it to "our judgement."

   Noting that indifference may be a perspective—a position chosen to
see a thing from a certain angle—gives us, as one might say, a different
perspective on it. Both supporters and critics of the concept of disinterest
tend to see it as a stripping away of beliefs and irrelevancies, to see an object or idea objectively, without pre-suppositions. But aesthetic indifference
is less a stripping off than a putting on. To look at an object as it appears,
indifferent to its causes, purposes, and normal functions in the world, is
highly artificial, a perspective that one adopts, puts on. Kant's use of the
term "disinterest" in a way that recalls the criterion he demands for a motive to be moral has perhaps led to critical elision of the artifice of indifference in his aesthetics. But the role Hegel's historicism plays in performing
the task of indifference in his aesthetics highlights that artifice, especially
in light of the other strange claims and twists it has added to his view of
art: his insistence on art's pastness, his giving it something like a coherent
project whose completion declares an end, even when artworks continue to
get produced, his insistence that the formal possibilities of the project create the realities of the history far more than the empirical vagaries of particular artworks—in other words, his insistence on a coherent narrative of
history that allows him to see art whole in the face of any actual history.

   If the absoluteness of Hegel's definition of sensuous embodiment

forces the transformation of aesthetic indifference into an assertion of historical pastness, it also creates, as it logically must, a very paradoxical view
of what counts as a perfect sensuous embodiment of the Idea, one both capacious to the point of being unmeaning and, at the same time, so constrained as to be an empty category. By the same logic that demanded that
art embody, in structurally defined historical periods, all the logical possibilities that the relations of sense to concept are capable of taking, it would
follow that any given relation must be a perfect embodiment from within
some historical viewpoint. And indeed Hegel declares that successful embodiment is not really a matter of how perfect the particular artwork is but
rather one of how the embodiment connects to the state of the mind's
grasp of the Idea. Thus, as he is about to introduce his explanation of the
Symbolic period of art and the ensuing history he will lay out, Hegel distinguishes between two forms of adequate embodiment:

> Thus if in this Part we encounter art-forms at first which are still inadequate in
> comparison with the true Ideal, this is not the sort of case in which people ordi-
> narily speak of unsuccessful works of art which either express nothing or lack the
> capacity to achieve what they are supposed to represent; on the contrary, the spe-
> cific shape which every content of the Idea gives to itself in the particular forms of
> art is always adequate to that content, and the deficiency or consummation lies
> only in the relatively untrue or true determinateness in which and as which the
> Idea is explicit to itself. (I, 300)

Hegel can claim that all aesthetic embodiments are adequate—even
though every stage of his history depends on whether that stage's art form
embodies adequately or not—by postulating that inadequate embodiment
will always be the result of the historical form of the Idea to be embodied:
the only perfect embodiment of an imperfectly embodiable Idea, either an
Idea too unindividuated to be sensuously embodied or an Idea too ad-
vanced toward independent thought to be available for adequate sensuous
embodiment, would have to be an imperfect embodiment. Thus the seemingly astonishing claim that every specific shape that the Idea takes in artworks "is always adequate to that content." If in Kant, symbolic embodiment was, via its skepticism about it own adequacy, too indifferent to
operate as an ideology, in Hegel, via its absolutism carried to logical extremes, it is too comprehensive to endorse a choice of any particular ideology. All manifestations of thought are sensuous embodiments so the fact of
being one, in and of itself, hardly forms a basis for choice.

    All manifestations—or perhaps none. The perfect form of art for

Hegel is of course the art of classical Greece and particularly its sculpture. Indeed, one could argue that Hegel ought to have claimed that all art ended roughly around 300 B.C.E., inasmuch as after the decline of the classical Ideal, art ceased to be sufficient to its own subject and became the inadequate expression of the Idea in a state of development beyond the capabilities of merely sensuous embodiment. And to the extent that Hegel was aware that artworks continued to be created after his own declared end of art, but that "art no longer affords that satisfaction of spiritual needs which earlier ages and nations sought in it" (I, 10), that statement also could apply, by his own theory, to art after the end of the classical age. Greek art may perfectly embody the Idea sensuously, of course, only because of the still imperfect state through which Greek culture understands that Idea: " . . . classical art comprehends free spirituality as determinate individuality and envisages it directly in its bodily appearance" (I, 435). Consequently, a sculpted body can embody this vision. The problem here, though, is not the imperfection of the Idea in and of itself. If the only problem with Greek art were its content, nothing about the art itself would drive it from its own adequacy, and one would have to say that that adequacy was perfect in its own terms and merely at the mercy of an extra-aesthetic, cultural development. But, again, because to be a perfect embodiment, art as a whole must also be a total embodiment of the cultural knowledge of the Idea, embodying even the inadequacies and dissolutions of that culture's knowledge and development, even the Greek ideal must contain its dissolution within itself and thus also its own imperfection.

The claim that the dissolution of Greek art is already implicit in the very limitations that allow it to embody its apprehension of the Idea has as its consequence that classical art is no more a completely adequate embodiment than the Symbolic one was unsuccessful. Adequation, of course, leaves no room for an internally enforced dissolution. If the Idea is completely and adequately manifest in its sensuous embodiment, then it would have to leave nothing to be desired that would force a movement beyond that embodiment, at least in terms of the artwork before us (disruption can always befall even internal perfection from without). But because art as a whole must always comprehend its own history in order to be as a whole the embodiment all its specific manifestations seek, the logic that forces us to see imperfect embodiments as perfect manifestations of a certain historically constrained knowledge will also see the one ostensibly perfect embodiment as still inadequate so that the further history may also be internally driven.

In effect, the very absoluteness with which Hegel insists on sensuous embodiment as both total and objective drives Kant's skeptic indifference into its workings as part of the logic of embodiment conceived so comprehensively. Absoluteness also forces the depiction of this whole history as one constructed by the apprehension of the philosophic judgment, which stands outside the history and defines it. By this I do not mean, obviously, that Hegel construes the history he writes as fictional. But he does see it as constructed by a philosophical analysis sufficiently forceful not to be, so to speak, led astray by deceptive empirical facts: "Yet in answering the question of where art has begun alike in conception and in reality, we must throughout exclude both the empirical facts of history and also the external reflections, conjectures and natural ideas that are so easily and variously propounded about it" (II, 630). Hegel justifies a history that does not attend to empirical facts by finding as simplistic the idea of looking for the essence of a thing in its chronological origin, since empirical beginnings, from the perspective of "philosophical thinking," are "entirely accidental" (II, 630). The proper mode of constructing a philosophic history of art, in contrast, "is to establish the beginning of art by so deriving it from the Concept or essential nature of art itself that we can see that the first task of art consists in giving shape to what is objective in itself, i.e. the physical world of nature" (II, 631). Thus art begins in architecture, regardless of whatever empirical art objects might have occurred earlier or later. In the light of Hegel's view that empirical circumstance is irrelevant to a history properly construed from the Concept of art, his claim of an end to that history seems much less odd. Having worked out theoretically art's essence and the stages that essence takes, Hegel deduces the history as a logical consequence and thus is indifferent to accidents that do not properly belong to that history. Just as sensuous embodiment brings appearance before us in a purity that forces us to recognize its apparitional quality, its historical manifestations, in ambiguously mixed adequacies and inadequacies, can be properly apprehended only through a philosophical stance outside that history that is indifferent to the history itself as other than the apparitional manifestation of the philosophic concept constructing it.

So in Hegel, history, displaying art and all its aspects in its visible temporal stages, sensuously embodies art's concept. But it does so only by being an appearance constructed by a philosophic perspective. And that does not contradict its being an essential history since, as we have seen, according to Hegel, only a pure appearance, a mere appearance, recognizes itself as an apparition needing to be read through to an essence. Art sensuously embodies the Idea only by containing within itself the disruptions to that embodiment that enforce an historical unfolding, and by displaying those disruptions and inadequacies across the temporal spectacle of history's appearances. And Hegel's aesthetics narrates this historical unfolding always from the perspective of a philosophy that, by having moved beyond art, is also indifferent to it, except to articulate (thus interpret and disrupt) its embodied significance.

To argue Kant's skepticism about symbolic embodiment and thus the role of that skepticism in his view of the interplay of embodiment and indifference, although it disputes a common reading of Kant as forebear to twentieth-century organicism and its experiential formalism, is at least to follow a recognized skepticism in Kant's thinking about ideals. But Hegel's aesthetics wears a certain Romantic absolutism about the possibility of embodying significance on its face, so to speak. Does this reading then propose a hitherto unrecognized deconstructive turn to Hegel's aesthetics? Or is it simply a deconstruction of Hegel?

Well, the opening of this chapter argued that art's "essence" entailed embodying a subject by reducing it to a disappearing and ambiguous appearance: a non-existent urinal embodied the essence of art split from its formalist illusions about meaning. And this embodied appearance would only appear from a perspective indifferent to the motives, intentions, and purposes that normally give appearances their significances. The balance of this chapter will argue that, from the perspective of aesthetics, there is no difference between a deconstructive reading of aesthetics and a reading of aesthetics as deconstructive. Whatever one might think of Hegel, Schopenhauer is surely the most essentialist of idealists. And yet what follows will outline his view of art as preparing the way for Nietzsche's well-recognized view of aesthetics as undoing all views of the world as significant. In Schopenhauer, art manifests the hidden meaning of phenomena, their very will, and results in a subjective resignation of one's own will—Schopenhauer's explicit version of indifference. And yet, as we will see, Schopenhauer's essentialism enables Nietzsche's joyful reduction of the world to its appearances. The aesthetics that comes out of Kant will always depend both on an essentialism and on its own undoing of that essentialism, regardless of the essentialism or the skepticism of the philosopher, and it is precisely that deconstructive balance that will enable the postmodern employment of it worked out in this book's concluding chapters.

IV. The Indifferent Embodiments of Appearance: Schopenhauer and Nietzsche

One encounters Schopenhauer in books on aesthetics (to the extent that he comes up not merely in reference to Nietzsche's divergence from him), largely as representing a quaint, Neoplatonic, astonishingly pessimistic idealism. And, from the perspective of a large overview of *The World as Will and Representation*, there is little to complain about in this view. Schopenhauer's theory of the will as an essence driving our bodies and the matter of the world, despite our consciousness rather than through it, and his view of art as offering first an embodied image of that will and thereby a consoling mode of resigning ourselves to it, have largely served as an example of all that can go wrong with idealism and aesthetics.[50] However, by looking only slightly more closely at the hinges and transitions that bring us from a world as representation to a world as will, and to the role art has to play in what in most ways is a pointedly *anaesthetic* metaphysics, one can see the conflict in Schopenhauer's view of art as both will-less appearance and as the imaging of the will that allows us finally to deal with will's threatening essence. We can then see how that conflicting view prepares the way for Nietzsche to make manifest the complex and skeptical view of art as embodiment more or less implicit in Kant and Hegel.

The strange operation of aesthetics in Schopenhauer's philosophy begins with the strange structure of the work, which one can only describe as predicting more or less that of Julio Cortazar's *Hopscotch*, in which one first is given a novel and then given a series of chapters to interpolate into the novel while rereading it.[51] One might think that Schopenhauer did not create this artificed construction by design. He wrote a second volume commenting on his first many years later, and since the later comments are keyed to the earlier chapters, not only can the second volume not be read alone, but at some level or another, it forces one to reread the first volume. But even the first volume runs through each of its worlds, representation and will, twice, with parts III and IV adding elements respectively to parts I and II, as if various units of the work, first part I, then parts I and II, then all of volume I, could at any point have stood alone (and volume I was, of course, at first intended to have stood alone). This organization facilitates the treatment in isolation of Schopenhauer's aesthetics in part III and in chapters in volume II that treat the same topics as part III, but that isolation can make their workings seem more simplistic than they are. Consequently, simplistically enough, I want to summarize the arguments about representation and will that lead up to the treatment of aesthetics as a higher form of representation.

Schopenhauer's metaphysics, then, starts with a solution to the status of objects of perception that recalls Berkeley's idealism read through Kant's *Critique of Pure Reason* (Schopenhauer himself gives this genealogy a number of times, for instance, *World as Will*, I, xxiii; I, 3; and II, 3). He solves the dispute between dogmatists, who insist that every perception of an object has a cause in an externally existing thing-in-itself, and the skeptics, who assume that by denying the existence of this thing-in-itself, they are denying the existence of the object and thus the reality of the perception: "Both these views are open to the correction, firstly, that object and representation are the same thing . . . and that the demand for the existence of the object outside the representation of the subject and also for a real being of the actual thing distinct from its action, has no meaning at all and is a contradiction" (*World as Will*, I, 14). Like Berkeley, Schopenhauer claims that all we know of objects is our perception of them. But, unlike Berkeley, he also claimed that that representation of objects within the subject is the reality of those objects. Object and representation are identical. Since perceptions in the mind have an obvious transience to them that would tend to dissolve the reality of objects, Berkeley famously stabilized his world in the mind of God. Schopenhauer stabilizes it within the knowing subject: "The world is entirely representation, and as such requires the knowing subject as the supporter of its existence" (I, 30). Although one might wonder what gave the subject its stability, as both Hume before him and John Stuart Mill contemporaneously did, Schopenhauer is untroubled by the radical solipsism this idealism threatens, going so far as to argue that to the extent that representation just is the reality of the world, then it must follow that the world came into existence only with the first knowing animal capable of perceiving it (I, 30). He alludes to an escape to this solipsism in his recognition, to come, of the will as the thing-in-itself that gives the world its externality. But he also claims that that recognition is unnecessary for the internal coherence of his epistemology. And, indeed, he might have left matters here, never adding the world as will, without creating any internal problems for the system so far.

Schopenhauer introduces the world of will by adding one twist to the subject's representation of objects to itself. One of the objects that the subject perceives is itself, both in its bodily existence as an object and in its mental activity of reflection. Individuals perceive their bodies in two ways though. First, they perceive their bodies as other objects in the natural world, as representations. But here the perception as representation is not sufficient. If we perceived our bodies only this way, we would see them only as objects following natural laws, with no internal life:

All this, however, is not the case; on the contrary, the answer to the riddle is given to the subject of knowledge appearing as individual and this answer is given in the word Will. This and this alone gives him the key to his own phenomenon, reveals to him the significance and shows him the inner mechanism of his being, his actions, his movements. To the subject of knowing, who appears as an individual only through his identity with the body, this body is given in two entirely different ways. It is given in intelligent perception as representation, as an object among objects, liable to the laws of these objects. But it is also given in quite a different way, namely as what is known immediately to everyone, and is denoted by the word *will*. (I, 100)

One should note here that the will of which one becomes conscious is not the will of the conscious intelligence, giving itself ends based on which it directs its body to act. If that were the case, one's awareness of one's body under a double aspect would not be relevant. If will meant conscious ordination, the body could still be construed as a natural object being acted on in a special way in accordance with a particular natural law. Rather, one becomes aware of one's body as acting with a will of its own that has nothing to do with one's aspect as a knowing intelligence. One becomes aware of the body's "inner mechanism," of its will rather than one's own. The body expresses its will in all its appetitive desires and processes, eating, digesting, sleeping, procreating, and so on. Having attributed to the body an organizing principle to its non-intelligent, appetitive functions, an internal will, the subject can then see that all the objects of the world, hitherto seen only as phenomenal representations, in fact express in all their actions the internal will which is the essence of all things.

But because of the separation between the two parts of the argument so far, the integrity of the second part remains under two stresses, each of which leads to the return to the world of representation under the aspect of art. The first of these is that since the subject merely extrapolates from his own sense of his body to the world, he might in fact refuse to do so and insist that the world is merely the phenomena represented to the perception. In the very fury with which Schopenhauer denies this option, he also admits its possibility within the logic of his own first part:

Suppose this [false reduction of original natural forces to each other] were feasible, then of course everything would be explained and cleared up, and in fact would be reduced in the last resort to an arithmetical problem. . . . But all content of the phenomenon would have vanished, and mere form would remain. . . . But this will not do; phantasies, sophistications, castles in the air, have been brought into being in this way, but not science. (I, 123)

In fact, of course, Schopenhauer has insisted in part I on the identity of representation to reality being sufficient for perception. If the perception of the body does not absolutely necessitate the acceptance of the will, then a threat that without the will we will only have representation will hardly be any more compelling.

Although he shouts down the possibility of not accepting the will here, he effectively entertains it in his explanation of the second stress, which leads to the discussion of aesthetic representation. Although the subject's knowledge, in its separation from the bodily will, first recognizes the will, that knowledge is of only one specific manifestation of the will, its objectification in one's own body. Following the Platonic logic by which any specific, material version of an Idea is by definition also not a perfect manifestation of that Idea, which because it comprehends all individual versions cannot appear fully as any particular version, Schopenhauer argues that it follows that a subject in its own individuality can never really know Ideas and essences: " . . . in so far as the subject knows as an *individual*, the Ideas will also lie quite outside the sphere of knowledge as such. Therefore, if the Ideas are to become object of knowledge, this can happen only by abolishing individuality in the knowing subject" (I, 169). Having claimed that one must not fall back into accepting the phenomena as representations, Schopenhauer now insists that, in one's individuality, one has no other recourse, really. It is not enough to be aware of one's body under a double aspect to know the will as the Idea behind phenomena. One must also lose one's own individuality, or it will remain a manifestation of the will, rather than a recognition of it. Thus we are led to representation in art, in a theory that indeed insists on aesthetic embodiment as revelation of truth and perspective as angelic, appetitive indifference, in a way that best matches the aesthetics criticized so vigorously by various schools of twentieth-century postmodernism. And we will also see how even this aesthetics, because of the workings of aesthetics itself, contains the presumptions that will lead to its own return, in Nietzsche, to a more comprehensive recognition of its own perspectivism.

Schopenhauer offers us the possibility of seeing the will through art through a two-stage process that leads us from aesthetic disinterest to the aesthetic embodiment of essence. In the first stage, we negate our own individuality through a contemplation of the appearance of an object:

[We] devote the whole power of our mind to perception, sink ourselves completely therein, and let our whole consciousness be filled by the calm contemplation of the natural object actually present, whether it be a landscape, a tree, a rock, a crag, a building, or anything else. We *lose* ourselves entirely in this object, to use a pregnant expression; in other words, we forget our individuality, our will, and continue to exist only as pure subject. (I, 178)

Although this passage imagines us looking at a natural object with a particular perspective, Schopenhauer makes clear that this perspective—which he classes as a particularly disinterested knowledge—is identified with aesthetic presentation.[52] And as a result of losing ourselves in the object, we cease to be an individual, and thus, in the second stage, see the representation before us as the representation of an essence: "First of all, a knowing individual raises himself in the manner described to the pure subject of knowing, and at the same time raises the contemplated object to the Idea; the *world as representation* then stands out whole and pure, and the complete objectification of the will takes place" (I, 179).

At this point, however, it is worth recalling where we are in the argumentative structure of *The World as Will and Representation*. Having shown us the world as will, Schopenhauer nevertheless was unable to establish that the view drawn from our observation of our bodily appetites, actions, and desires in fact could establish the will as essence. Parts I and II thus establish two, free-floating, alternative views of the world—as representation and as will. Part III and its raising of the subject of aesthetics, wherein we actually see the will as essence, nevertheless returns us to the world as representation. And this return is absolutely necessary to put the first two parts together and to prepare for the essential moral of the fourth. Since we now see the will represented to us in the phenomena, the two views of the world are unified in a knowing subject who is not subject to the delusions that the will employs to its ends. Moreover, since we can see the will in the consciousness that is the one thing in the world that also stands apart from it, since the will is now mirrored in perception (I, 266), we can now employ our own consciousness against the demands of the will. Instead of an alternative, partial view of reality evolved to allow us to act according to the will, perception of the world as representation has become a separate space in which to see the will and choose to withdraw from it. This suggestion that we negate the will, of course, constitutes Schopenhauer's central moral doctrine and the basis for the responses to him, first, as a life-denying philosopher, and now therefore as a faintly ridiculous one. And the difference between aesthetic representation and the perceptual representation outlined in part I, the difference that allows aesthetics to serve its central structural and moral purpose, entails a resting in the representation without any further analysis of it, an acceptance of representation, whole and pure. This view of aesthetic presentation returns us to Kant's and Hegel's view of art as putting before us mere appearance as pure appearance. Schopenhauer assents to this view of aesthetic apprehension all but explicitly when he describes how the artwork allows the apprehension of Ideas through its silencing of the will:

Thus the *work of art* so greatly facilitates the apprehension of the Ideas in which aesthetic enjoyment consists; and this is due not merely to the fact that art presents things more clearly and characteristically by emphasizing the essential and eliminating the inessential, but just as much to the fact that the absolute silence of the will, required for the purely objective apprehension of the true nature of things, is attained with the greatest certainty. Such silence is attained by the perceived object itself lying entirely outside the province of things capable of reference to the will, in that it is nothing actual but a mere picture or image. (II, 370)

The first part of this passage recalls the standard Neoplatonist claim that art represents Ideas by representing only imagined essentials rather imitating the inessentials of material reality. But Schopenhauer sees the more important aesthetic achievement as the silencing of the will, which art effects by presenting itself to us as "mere picture or image." Indeed, to the extent that one could say that the one essential thing to accomplish in Schopenhauer is the silencing of the will, one could turn the second half of this passage back on the first: art emphasizes the essential and eliminates the inessential by silencing the will and showing us "mere picture." Thus this most essentialist of aesthetic theorists returns us to Kant's most anti-essentialist view of indifference as seeing appearance without concepts, external form without explanatory purpose. The same contradiction we saw Hegel working through, the one that occurs when aesthetics identifies art's essence as its display of itself as mere appearance, recurs here. Art displays the image of essence—will, in Schopenhauer—only when, by presenting itself as mere appearance for our will-less contemplation, it allows us, in silencing our will, to see an essence in that mere appearance.

One might have objected, in my readings of Kant and Hegel, that their definitions of beauty or art as mere appearance is less anti-essentialist than it seems since appearance without remainder becomes, in effect, essence embodied in appearance, the surface of appearance showing all there is. I think the reading of Hegel shows that an awareness of this problem tends always to make the essentialism that results from an aesthetic concept of mere appearance disrupt itself. Schopenhauer shows the disruption to be intrinsic to aesthetics. If mere appearance can conceptually reproduce pure embodiment, it also turns out that pure embodiment ends up presenting itself as mere appearance, thus questioning whether it is an embodiment at all. In turning to Nietzsche, we will see how he takes the aesthetic concept of pure appearance to employ it in a corrosive reading of the metaphysical desire to know essence. But we will also see how he takes the ideas of indifferent appearance and embodiment from both Hegel and Schopenhauer in order to achieve this end. And Nietzsche's aesthetics finally will prepare us for the postmodern employment of the concepts of purposiveness, indifference, and embodiment articulated in this first half of this book.

One can see how Nietzsche extracted from Kant, Hegel, and Schopenhauer the aesthetics that always questioned their metaphysics by charting the movement from his one book devoted to aesthetics, *The Birth of Tragedy*, to the later rereadings of it, with their partial disavowals and partial affirmations. As Alexander Nehamas has explained, Nietzsche, in *The Birth of Tragedy*, did believe that there was an ultimate truth to life, one that language could not reach. But this truth was "that the ultimate nature of the world is to have no orderly structure: in itself the world is chaos, with no laws, no reason, and no purpose" (Nehamas, *Nietzsche*, 42–43).[53] Tragedy, in contrast to Schopenhauer's view, does not resign us to life's blind movement but teaches us to participate in it with pleasure. In his later work, Nietzsche of course gives up the idea that there is an essence, even a negative essence, behind appearance. Thus in *Ecce Homo* he says of *Birth of Tragedy*:

Taken up with some degree of neutrality, *The Birth of Tragedy* looks quite untimely: one would never dream that it was begun amid the thunder of the battle of Wörth. . . . One might sooner believe that the essay was fifty years older. It is indifferent toward politics—"unGerman," to use the language of the present time—it smells offensively Hegelian and the cadaverous perfume of Schopenhauer sticks only to a few formulas. An "idea"—the antithesis of the Dionysian and the Apollinian—translated into the realm of metaphysics; history itself as the development of this "idea"; in tragedy this antithesis is sublimated into a unity; and in this perspective things that had never before faced each other are suddenly juxtaposed, used to illuminate each other, and comprehended. (*Genealogy and Ecce Homo*, 270–271)

One should begin by noting that the perfume of Schopenhauer, even if it sticks only to a few formulas, is at least stronger in *Birth of Tragedy* than Hegel's offensive smell. Not only does Nietzsche quote him approvingly on music (*Birth*, 101–103), but the very categories of Apollinian and Dionysian, the first being illusion, image, and representation, the second being will and drive, have a Schopenhauerian resonance—indeed, Nietzsche cites Schopenhauer as he defines the Apollinian and Dionysian (*Birth*, 36, 38). The formula whereby tragedy captures Dionysian will within Apollinian image and brings it before its audience as a spectacle also clearly follows Schopenhauer. Hegel's smell comes not from the metaphysics of this but from the move whereby history becomes the development of an idea that an art form, tragedy, sublimates into a unity. But finally, Nietzsche does not really disavow the view of Dionysianism and Apollinianism, or the view of tragedy as their unification. He disavows a belief that the aesthetic content of the book can be unified into a metaphysics that explains history, calling that aesthetic "a perspective." Moreover, as a perspective, even this offensive smell and cadaverous perfume have the Nietzschean virtues of being untimely and un-German. *Birth of Tragedy* then lays out a view of art as giving us the essence of existence. But this essence has the features of a chaotic and deceptive appearance in which we participate rather than being an entrapping will from which we withdraw. The later Nietzsche maintains the aesthetic perspective outlined in this book, but maintains it as a perspective. In contrast to Kant, Hegel, and Schopenhauer, he regards even his aesthetics from an aesthetic perspective. But that perspective remains fairly largely the one they have defined.

The difference between defining an aesthetic perspective and further defining it through simultaneously assenting to the perspectival position from which one does the defining should not be minimized. Between the two stages in Nietzsche's philosophy proposed by Nehemas, Jean-Marie Schaeffer posits a middle, positivist period in which Nietzsche reduced religion, metaphysics, morality, and art to the status of delusion by way of psychological or anthropological genealogy as the perspective of a disabused truth (*Art in the Modern Age*, 222). Thus the comprehensive perspectivism of his final stage amounts to a recovery of aesthetics, not simply a change in the way it is taken. And this skeptical perspectivism, not an ongoing version of an aestheticism of myth—as Allan Megill would have it (*Prophets*, 99–102)—is the real content of his final aestheticism and the ground of his connections with the speculative theory he inherits and of his simultaneous reduction of it.

Although, as in both Hegel and Schopenhauer, the value of art in *The Birth of Tragedy* remains its ability to make essence available to us in appearance, to give a material embodiment of a chaotic essence, even here, Nietzsche's more intense aestheticism tends to bring to the surface the implications, which I have been working out, of viewing art as signifying appearance. Thus, for instance, Nietzsche extends Hegel's version of classic aesthetic embodiment into a claim that only aesthetic embodiment is effective, thereby suggesting an aesthetic perspective that either demystifies Hegel's metaphysics or simply makes its aesthetic bases apparent. Having explicated Greek knowledge of "the horror of existence," Nietzsche outlines how this knowledge may be turned to joy:

The same impulse which calls art into being, as the complement and consummation of existence, seducing one to a continuation of life, was also the cause of the Olympian world which the Hellenic "will" made use of as a transfiguring mirror. Thus do the gods justify the life of man: they themselves live it—the only satisfactory theodicy! Existence under the bright sunshine of such gods is regarded as desirable in itself, and the real pain of Homeric men is caused by parting from it, especially by early parting: so that now, reversing the wisdom of Silenus, we might say of the Greeks that "to die soon is worst of all for them, the next worst—to die at all." (*Birth*, 43)

Nietzsche reproduces here Hegel's picture of Greek art as perfect embodiment because of its ability to show all of its knowledge of the divine in a material appearance. The Greeks see the gods live their lives in the transfiguring mirror that calls their art into being. But he then extends the meaning of the embodiment by calling it "the only satisfactory theodicy." Nietzsche's claim has an obvious strength: only a god who willingly lives only and entirely a human life can give the fullest justification of human life: such a divine affirmation of a value in life leaves no remainder to it that would need consolation or justification outside itself. All of life would be divinely worthy. But this is to claim that aesthetic appearance must be complete as appearance in order to work completely. One must be able to take joy in all of the material and only the material, apprehended nevertheless as merely apparent, to accept the theodicy. There can be no gesturing toward some significance or essence beyond that appearance.[54] And this affirmation leads to what can only be taken as a somewhat ambiguous reversal of Silenus's wisdom that the best would never to have been born, the second best to die soon. Although that wisdom may be a dire pessimism, it has at least the value that the second best will always occur, death coming soon enough to all humans. The reversal of this advice, however, while it may manifest far more joy in life, must always signify the dissatisfaction it denies since while the worst may be avoided, the next worse is unavoidable. This ambiguity lies at the core of *The Birth of Tragedy*, which wants to see aesthetics as an ultimate value and also wants to see that ultimate value as bestowing a meaning on life that is its essence.

In the same manner, Nietzsche's core early definition of aesthetic perspective contains an ambiguity that owes to his inability to shed completely Schopenhauer's cadaverous perfume. In the passage that contains one of the book's most famous claims, Nietzsche proposes how art shows us essence:

The entire comedy of art is neither performed for our betterment or education nor are we the true authors of this art world. On the contrary, we may assume that we are merely images and artistic projections for the true author, and that we have our highest dignity in our significance as works of art—for it is only as an *aesthetic phenomenon* that existence and the world are eternally *justified*—while of course our consciousness of our significance hardly differs from that which the soldiers painted on the canvas have of the battle represented on it. (*Birth*, 52)

Nietzsche carries out to an extreme extent the metaphor of seeing life as a work of art. He places us as a represented character in the work, knowing nothing of its origin, or its unreality. We are simply caught within the work as representations unaware of the apparitional quality of our existence. The world may be justified only as an aesthetic phenomenon in the sense that, since only such phenomena contain no justification outside themselves, only they have value just in their appearance. But as aesthetic images, we cannot be aware of that justification. By placing us in the work of art, Nietzsche denies us the perspective from which we could get value from appreciating ourselves as aesthetic apparitions.

And so Nietzsche imagines an almost textbook version of double consciousness:

Thus all our knowledge of art is basically quite illusory, because as knowing beings we are not one and identical with that being which, as the sole author and specta-

tor of this comedy of art, prepares a perpetual entertainment for itself. Only insofar as the genius in the act of artistic creation coalesces with this primordial artist
of the world, does he know anything of the eternal essence of art; for in this state
he is, in a marvelous manner, like the weird image of the fairy tale which can turn
its eyes at will and behold itself; he is at once subject and object, at once poet, ac-
tor, and spectator. (*Birth*, 52)

The separation between will and image in Schopenhauer here recurs in the
double perspective of the artist who has will and purpose and the figure in
the painting who is merely an image. To perceive the world as an aesthetic
phenomenon—and an aesthetic phenomenon unperceived as such can
hardly justify anything—we must stand outside it from the perspective of
its creator. But from that perspective, the world would not be self-justifying (the point of perceiving it as an aesthetic phenomenon) but justified as
fulfilling the ends that we had as creator, even if the end were simply to
create an artwork, since, as of course Kant insisted, an artwork is not necessarily quite the same thing as an aesthetic phenomenon. For our existence and the world to be justified, we must imagine ourselves as a character in the painting with no end or knowledge outside that painting, no
teleology beyond the painting that would explain our role in it, even as we
recognize that our position in imagining does stand outside the painting.
Thus we make ourselves the spectator of a work we are in, and that we create in perceiving ourselves as in it. Nietzsche's preference for an aesthetics
constructed from the perspective of the artist is already here, but its point
is not primarily to achieve the orgiastic creativity of the artist but to use
that perspective to construct a philosophy that reads existence as aesthetic.[55]

 But, also here, Nietzsche defines the world the way Kant, Hegel, and
Schopenhauer define art. It is "mere" appearance and justified by being
only appearance with no significance imposed from without. Also like
them, he takes its state as "mere" appearance as containing a significance,
indeed like Schopenhauer an essence, which justifies it. He takes their definition of art and/or beauty and consciously uses it to cover all features of
the category of the extra-aesthetic, termed existence, the world, or life. In
doing so, he shows clearly the way the artwork, defined as symbolic embodiment because perceived, with aesthetic indifference, as pure appearance, always held within it a perspective on the world that would drain it
of all illusion of extraneous significance rather than illuminate it with its
invisible essence. But he also shows why, posed this way, the idea of em-

bodiment always reproduces the romantic desire for meaning that it ostensibly questions, since pure appearance construed as essence is essence nevertheless. In this context, Nietzsche's famous definition of the task of *Birth of Tragedy*, from the later perspective of the "Attempt at a Self-Criticism," becomes more dangerously multi-edged: "The task which this audacious book dared to tackle for the first time: *to look at science in the perspective of the artist, but at art in that of life* (*Birth*, 19). The first half of this task is easy enough to construe as the usual undercutting of science as just another art in the sense of just another artificed perspective. If the sentence were to continue in this mode, though, it would have had to have wanted to see life in the perspective of art. To see art from the perspective of life amounts, one would think, to the task of all the multitude of moralist art critics who see the value of art in terms of the directions it gives us for living our lives. But in seeing life as an aesthetic phenomenon and being justified as such, in effect Nietzsche does recapitulate the moralist's position, since he uses art to find life's meaning. To drain that moralist position of the appeal to something beyond art, which would for Nietzsche undercut the point of justifying existence from an aesthetic perspective, he must turn the concentration of that task from art per se to the *perspective* of art and the artist, a perspective always recognized as one perspective among others.

Critics, either in praise or blame, generally take Nietzsche's perspectivism to relativize values and interpretations.[56] If Nietzsche really thinks his perspective is just one among others, all of them equal in value, what would be its particular value? What we will see, I hope, in the balance of this reading, is that just as his perspectivism makes his aesthetics both the most consistent and the most consistently anti-absolutist of the ones I have been outlining in this chapter, his aesthetics gives the specific value to his perspectivism that the perspectivism taken by itself does not have. The workings and the problem of perspective in Nietzsche manifests itself most clearly in *The Genealogy of Morals*, precisely because the conclusions Nietzsche draws about morality from his perspectivism are so clearly antithetical. One of Nietzsche's edged, ironic analogies is a good starting point:

That lambs dislike great birds of prey does not seem strange: only it gives no ground for reproaching these birds of prey for bearing off little lambs. And if the lambs say among themselves: "these birds of prey are evil; and whoever is least like a bird of prey, but rather its opposite, a lamb—would he not be good?" there is no reason to find fault with this institution of an ideal, except perhaps that the birds of prey might view it a little ironically and say: "*we* don't dislike them at all, these good little lambs; we even love them: nothing more tasty than a tender lamb." (*Genealogy and Ecce Homo*, 45)

The situation seems to set up two mutually exclusive viewpoints, each of which Nietzsche declares justified from within its own perspective. In order to see the problematic application of this analogy to Nietzsche's ethics, however, we need to note two features of this supposedly mutually exclusive situation. First of all, it is not mutually exclusive as it stands. While the birds of prey cannot entertain the lamb view of things and still continue on as birds of prey, the lambs can quite well entertain the perspective of the birds. They know full well how much the birds like them and in exactly what way, and they never claimed otherwise. They claim the birds to be evil for acting on their particular love, and as far as the analogy goes, their position has the strength of accommodating that of the birds. Second, the positions become mutually exclusive only from the third perspective of the ironist here, who endows the birds with an allusion to *caritas* in their appetites, which is not their own. The pun on loving lambs and loving the taste of lamb gives their desires the illusion of being another internally consistent ethics.

For the analogy to really depict mutually exclusive forces, Nietzsche must make of the birds and the lambs forces without choice, analogous to the aesthetic representations in the *Birth of Tragedy*'s painting. Thus he denies a separation between will and act: "Popular morality . . . separates strength from expressions of strength, as if there were a neutral substratum behind the strong man, which was *free* to express strength or not to do so. But there is no such substratum; there is no 'being' behind doing, effecting, becoming"(*Genealogy and Ecce Homo*, 45). In particular, this mistake gives the consoling force of miming an ethical statement to the *ressentiment* of the lambs, and its fallacy exculpates the birds of prey: "No wonder if the submerged, darkly glowering emotions of vengefulness and hatred exploit this belief for their own ends and in fact maintain no belief more ardently than the belief that *the strong man is free* to be weak and the bird of prey to be a lamb—for thus they gain the right to make the bird of prey *accountable* for being a bird of prey" (*Genealogy and Ecce Homo*, 45). The position of the lambs in the above analogy is now not one of greater comprehension. Rather, they commit a metaphysical error that they persist in because it serves their ends, just as the strength of the birds, expressed in the pun given to them by the ironist, serves theirs.[57] But of course, from the perspective of a thoroughgoing perspectivism, one should not classify the belief of the lambs as an error but as a weapon of war, no different than the "love" of the birds for their prey. The very language of internality by which the lambs have a vengefulness and a hatred that exploits a belief would be inappropriate if, like the birds, they express their way of defending themselves rather than acting on a belief that they could will not to act upon.

And, in effect, Nietzsche's attitude to the priests and slaves of *ressentiment* is far more mixed than is generally recognized. He lauds the perspectival values of the "noble" people who judge in terms of good and bad, judging what they do as good because it comes from them. But he recognizes that, for better or worse, the slave morality has been triumphant and thus has shown the value of a kind of strength: "Let us stick to the facts: the people have won—or the 'slaves' or 'the mob' or 'the herd' or whatever you like to call them" (*Genealogy and Ecce Homo*, 36). This sentence not only recognizes the victory of the lambs, but also turns Nietzsche's own rhetorical analysis against himself. In the light of that victory, the labels he uses for them, "slaves" or "mob" or "herd," seem precisely the mode by which the lambs attribute guilty internality to the birds of prey. And one regularly finds in the early discussion of the development of Christian morality as slave morality a recognition that it has supplied him with the weapons of his attack upon it, even in moments of his greatest scorn for its sickness:

While the noble man lives in trust and openness with himself . . . the man of *ressentiment* is neither upright nor naïve nor honest and straightforward with himself. His soul *squints*; his spirit loves hiding places, secret paths and back doors, everything covert entices him as *his* world, *his* security, *his* refreshment; he understands how to keep silent, how not to forget, how to wait, how to be provisionally self-deprecating and humble. A race of such men of *ressentiment* is bound to become eventually *cleverer* than any noble race; it will also honor cleverness to a far greater degree. (*Genealogy and Ecce Homo*, 38)

The passage insists famously on the psychology behind the morality of good and evil as a sickness. It would be easy enough to note again that the language describing the sickness owes everything to a sense of being behind action, however, to an analysis of the "real" motive behind a certain stance. But the last sentence's attribution of cleverness to "men of *ressentiment*" is more important, given Nietzsche's attribution of cleverness to himself, in *Ecce Homo*, written only a year or two later, as one of his significant qualities.

A pure perspectivism, so to speak, would then be unable to take sides between the lambs and the birds that prey on them. In the sense in which "perspectivism" always implies a partial perspective, always entails a taking of sides, the position that refuses to take sides would be without perspective. This position, without perspective, is the disinterest and resignation attributed to Kant and Schopenhauer that we Nietzsche scorns. In *Genealogy of Morals*, he attributes this position to "men of knowledge" who "have gradually come to mistrust believers of all kinds" (148). He connects these modern philosophers with the ascetic priests of *ressentiment* in terms of their *"faith in truth"* (150), even as he realizes their difference in that their will to truth must lead them to try to question all perspectives, even their own: "The will to truth requires a critique—let us define our own task—the value of truth must for once be experimentally *called into question*" (153). One might connect this position with Nietzsche's—and he does call it his own task—but this will to truth does not allow Nietzsche to take on a perspective, only to be skeptical of perspectives. Thus he opposes art to the science of this position: *"Art*—to say it in advance, for I shall some day return to this subject at greater length—art, in which precisely the *lie* is sanctified and the *will to deception* has a good conscience, is much more fundamentally opposed to the ascetic ideal than is science" (153–154). Art opposes itself to the ascetic ideal in taking a perspective guiltlessly. One might say that a perspective that does not accept its position as perspective is deceptive, but art even accommodates that: because it sanctifies lies, it allows deception in good conscience. If we connect Nietzsche's position as the genealogist of the morality of good and evil with that of aesthetic apprehension, indifferent to the truth of the appearance created, then the position by which he undercuts the position of morality as just the perspective of the lambs does not disable the sympathy with the "noble" ethics of good and bad, even though that sympathy must grow out of a recognition of that position as a perspective. His point is not to be outside perspective, but to offer perspective.

By moving from aesthetics through ethics back to an aesthetic ethics, Nietzsche has taken the aesthetics of Kant, Hegel, and even Schopenhauer despite himself and made of it not a particular position from which to look at objects and concepts differently (because indifferently), but the only perspective that recognizes perspective as a limit. One cannot argue that the perspective is self-contradictory since it claims not to be seeing truth but only appearance. The refusal to claim truth for itself will not make it self-undercutting either, since an art that is defined as pure appearance—a definition by Nietzsche's time that is completely conventional—can only present its meanings by recognizing that it is only appearance. Nietzsche has taken the aesthetics of Kant and Hegel, in which the definition of art as symbolic or sensuous embodiment depends on the claim that it is also a mere appearance that one sees as art only by a stance of indifference; he has caught the way that that position catches even Schopenhauer, who surely does not consciously share any of Kant's or Hegel's skepticism about art's "truth"; and he simultaneously defines that aesthetics as a perspective and that perspective as the only way to live happily in the world. From the standpoint of truth, saying that every position is merely one more perspective always leads to the question of the status of the perspective from which the statement comes: is it a perspective or a truth about all perspectives? But from the standpoint of aesthetic apprehension, saying that every position is "mere perspective," "mere appearance," has no such outcome. The statement may easily be both an aesthetic apprehension and one more perspective among many, since aesthetics, as we have seen, begins in a perspectival choice (the ability to see a urinal as art, Kant's indifference, Hegel's historicist indifference). The ability of aesthetics to make contradiction irrelevant by accepting perspectival appearance would extend even to the Nietzschean aesthetic of viewing things simultaneously as an artist and as a figure in a work of art, simultaneously as the ironist who sees both the complaint of the lambs and the exultation of the birds of prey and as party to the hunter's view.

V. Indifferent Perspective, Genealogy, and Aesthetic Historicism

In this short section, I will conclude these two long chapters by outlining the connection between the theories of autonomous form and indifferent embodiment that they argue for and the Foucaultian and Bourdieuvian theories I will claim they support in the final chapters. I will trace here that connection's appearance in Nietzschean genealogy. That genealogy that Foucault will claim as a significant influence Nietzsche defends explicitly in terms of the aesthetics we have been working out here. We saw, in the first chapter, Kant argue for the propriety of apprehending objects without regard to their causes, purposes, or intentions in terms of a form of purposiveness that one always recognized might be imposed but that was justified by its value to the general faculty of judgment. In this chapter, we have seen how he further explicated the value of that perspective in terms of a symbolic embodiment of a moral view of nature. The terms of the understanding found that moral view of nature unprovable. To alleviate the contradiction between valuing something and also thinking it to be more wish than fact, he held that embodiment with a skeptical indifference that, as it apprehended embodiment, also apprehended it as pure appearance. Nietzsche extended that idea of apprehending embodiment as aesthetic appearance, taking its significance therefore as only self-justifying, into a perspectival aesthetics. And that perspectival aesthetics results in enabling a genealogy of morals that will connect Hegel's historicism to Foucault's via aesthetics, as we can see in Nietzsche's explanation of the meaning of punishment.

Nietzsche begins his discussion of punishment by separating its origins and its purposes so that he may detach us from what one might think is its obvious explanation: "that punishment was devised for punishing" (*Genealogy of Morals and Ecce Homo*, 77). He does this not by denying that we may use punishing to punish, but by denying that it is the only way to view it:

> There is for historiography of any kind no more important proposition than the one it took such effort to establish but which really *ought to be* established by now: the cause of the origin of a thing and its eventual utility, its actual employment and place in a system of purposes, lie worlds apart; whatever exists, having somehow come into being, is again and again reinterpreted to new ends, taken over, transformed, and redirected by some power superior to it; all events in the organic world are a subduing, a *becoming master,* and all subduing and becoming master involves a fresh interpretation, an adaptation through which any previous "meaning" and "purpose" are necessarily obscured or even obliterated. (*Genealogy of Morals and Ecce Homo*, 77)

The gesture Nietzsche makes here is, in a larger sense, the founding one in *Genealogy of Morals*, which opens by disputing the moral theories of "English psychologists" by insisting that they do not recognize the origin of moral judgments. And in both the opening and here this gesture faces two obvious problems. First, logically, reducing either the value or truth of something to the motives behind its origination is a classic case of the genetic fallacy, which mistakes a thing's value for the validity of the motive that produced it.[58] Put simply, no matter how judgments of good and evil or good and bad came about, or how punishment originated, their values and meanings must be determined by their current contexts and uses, not by a forgotten origin. More importantly, although Nietzsche claims to undercut the arguments of the psychologists and of the belief that punishment is for punishing by appealing to an origin, by "the *historical spirit*," even the most confirmed Nietzschean must notice that history is thin on the ground in this book. There are narratives of origin but these narratives lack any evidence of their historicity.

Nietzsche answers both these objections, though, implicitly in the second half of the paragraph. In order for things to have purposes or meanings different from those with which they began, they must be "reinterpreted," "transformed," "redirected." From this perspective, the origin one proposes, rather than being irrelevant to the "purpose" or "meaning" an object currently has, comes to be seen as an alternative purpose or meaning. If it is not an explanatory origin, it is at least an alternative interpretation of equal interest. This would leave us no reason to choose posited origin over present cause, though, were it not for the consequence Nietzsche draws from the fact of reinterpretation: " . . . purposes and utilities are only *signs* that a will to power has become master of something less powerful and imposed upon it the character of a function" (77). The point of Nietzsche's genealogy is not to find an actual origin against which to measure an object, practice, or function, but to pose the fact of development away from origin as a way apprehending it in contrast to what we "know" to have caused it, so we may see what about it our knowledge hides. Not an actual alternative, but mere alterity is what matters here.

And he achieves this alterity by looking at an object while ignoring its current purpose, finding what designs and meanings he can from its pure appearance. The aesthetic nature of the remainder that genealogy produces after it has turned its regard from purpose emerges as Nietzsche returns to the subject of punishment, in a passage one might think was lifted from Foucault's *Discipline and Punish*:

To return to our subject, namely *punishment*, one must distinguish two aspects: on the one hand, that in it which is relatively *enduring*, the custom, the act, the "drama," a certain strict sequence of procedures; on the other, that which is *fluid*, the meaning, the purpose, the expectation associated with the performance of such procedures. In accordance with the previously developed major point of historical method, it is assumed without further ado that the procedure itself will be something older, earlier than its employment in punishment, that the latter is *projected* and interpreted *into* the procedure. (79)

Although Nietzsche still insists on assuming that the procedures chronologically predate the varieties of meanings, the argument of his genealogy necessitates only the logical priority of procedures, upon which a variety of purposes, meanings, and functions may be imposed. We do not have to press upon that assumption a demand for chronological priority. A set of practices seen without regard to purposes can now be seen as act or drama in order to call into question whether these purposes constitute society's actual goal in punishing. The aesthetic nature of Nietzsche's regard here, not only in Kantian but in Hegelian mode, should by now be evident. If not purposiveness, he at least identifies a strict sequence of procedures without purpose. This sequence he can identify as a result of a genealogical perspective that functions with fair correspondence to the historicist perspective that allowed Hegel to posit art as both sensuous embodiment and as pure appearance. And as in Hegel, once the historicist perspective that allows us to see this apparitional embodiment is in place, the actual empirical history becomes irrelevant. Such a genealogy can hardly pose itself as a truth that will replace the ideological deception of current explanation. As perspective, both aesthetic and historicist, however, it allows us to see current explanation also as perspective, and one we may look around. We are now ready to see how this aesthetic historicism shapes Foucault's genealogies.

CHAPTER 3

Foucault's Aesthetics

Foucault's interest in art and literature is no secret. He has written on both fairly extensively. Comments on the style in which his books are written (especially *Histoire de la folie* and *The Order of Things*) have been fairly frequent.[1] And, of course, in his last years, he started to put considerable stress on the concept of making an art of one's own life. Still, critics usually construe the late period as representing a distinct change in numbers of his views (I will discuss this issue farther down in this chapter), and in dealing with his books, as histories of science, as theories of knowledge, power, and resistance, neither allies nor attackers have considered that art affected his ideas or the artfulness of his style as other than ornament or obstruction.[2] More importantly for my focus, in his reception by American literary critics, his methods and arguments have frequently been taken as a curative to the formalism and quietism that, depending on the critic's viewpoint, either Derrida or his American literary followers have espoused.[3] With no particular view of how to make art work centrally in Foucault's theories of history and power, critics have mostly ignored his obvious tendencies toward interpreting paintings and literary works as part of his arguments, his marked writing style, his interest, evident not only in numbers of essays but centrally in *The Order of Things*, in literary language and particularly its manifestation in twentieth-century French modernism. They have taken all of these things as subsidiary to a larger political and historical project. And this is the case even though the manifest literariness of many of his maneuvers and modes of interpretation have made literary critics more receptive to his thinking than to the theories of many French post-structuralists with similar ideas but a less clear interest in literature (Foucault's ideas about the history of science are famously and vitally formed by the ideas of Georges Canguilhem and Gaston Bachelard, yet many of their works are not even translated into English).

As with Foucault, so with postmodernism. But before broaching aesthetics and postmodernism, I need to narrow that second term at least a little, covering as it does such a multitude of sins. In using this term, I have no interest in the rebellion among artists against mid-century abstract modernism, or in more recent literary narrative experimentation, or indeed in many strands of current American philosophical and literary anti-foundationalism (Rorty's and Fish's different forms of pragmatism, those American feminists who do not concern themselves with Continental theories, for instance). I mean particularly that movement that began in France in the 1960s to look skeptically first at the foundational projects of phenomenology and structuralism, and then through that at Enlightenment philosophy and political thought.[4] And I wish, moreover, in dealing with Foucault, to concentrate on two linked strands of that movement. First, postmodernism, through a number of different routes, has questioned the philosophical project, dated variously from Descartes or Kant through Husserl and Heidegger, to found the natural and human sciences on a clearly articulated, regulated form of reason, a foundation that begins with a properly defined state of consciousness. Second, numbers of postmodernists, many of them the same ones, have questioned the justice or ethics of the bourgeois or liberal democratic state, and its ostensible recognition of human rights and liberty, by arguing that that state operates through inexplicit but effective hegemonies, ideologies, or institutions that constrain subjects quite effectively even through the establishment of those rights and liberties.[5]

Although this definition is still extremely comprehensive, it has certain features that go directly to my discussions of Foucault and Bourdieu. First Foucault has engaged in both the activities above and Bourdieu importantly in the second. Perhaps more importantly, almost all thinkers who analyze Continental Enlightenment philosophy and political thought from this perspective have in common at least the accusations they face. Those who question Enlightenment reason are accused of using reason against itself in a contradictory way, while those who question the justice of the liberal, democratic state are accused of also denying all ethical standards in a way that questions the validity of their own ethical position. Finally, the status of aesthetics in this postmodernism pertains to Foucault quite directly but in a way that I think is adequately representative. On the one hand, there is a sense that Derrida, Foucault, the Tel Quel group, those in general who follow Nietzsche's critique of philosophy since Kant, operate within the Nietzschean sense of a Dionysian, irrationalist art and question truth from this perspective of art.[6] On the other hand, paradoxically, many of these same critical positions have also served within American ideological criticism to argue that aesthetics is just another ideological excuse for class domination or distinction (endnotes in prior chapters have already documented the various strands of this attack on aesthetics), and certainly that was the explicit point of Bourdieu's writing on aesthetics. This laundry list of qualities and critiques has a focused pertinence for my analysis of Foucault because I intend to argue for the centrality of a certain aesthetics to both his theories and to the way he meant his books to be construed, one that, far from making his positions "merely" aesthetic, will show how the concepts of aesthetics outlined in the prior chapters will make sense of his project as a whole and free him from the various forms of contradiction of which he stands accused.

Placing notions of autonomous form, aesthetic indifference, and symbolic embodiment at the center of Foucault's thought, as enabling a critique of Enlightenment foundationalism from within its own resources, has at least a partial justification in the fact that aesthetics already played that role in Kant and the nineteenth-century philosophies that followed, and thus enabled Nietzsche's critique of them from within their own aesthetics, as the prior chapters have argued. Indeed, after Kant, virtually no Continental philosopher failed to give significant attention to aesthetics (this in pointed contrast to Anglo-American empirical and analytical philosophy). The centrality of art in post-Kantian German philosophy at least through Heidegger has been discussed before, of course, but mostly as an odd feature of that philosophy rather than a response to Kant's own sense of the need for a third *Critique*.[7] And yet Kant makes quite explicit his belief that aesthetics was the lynchpin that enabled his moral theory—in which the free individual regulates his actions through reason—to operate in the natural world, the comprehension of which begins with one's recognition of the fairly extreme limits on human understanding. Thus, he opens *The Critique of Judgment* by claiming that, since the first *Critique* argues centrally that the dictates of reason, when applied to the natural world, lead to all the problems of the dogmatic philosophies that preceded him, and yet the moral imperative is a dictate of the pure practical reason, on the terms of the first two critiques, it is not clear how one can in fact meaningfully act morally in the material world. This creates the book's opening problem: "Now even if an immeasurable gulf is fixed between the sensible realm of the concept of nature and the supersensible realm of the concept of freedom, so that no transition is possible from the first to the second (by means of the theoretical use of reason), just as if they were two different worlds of which the first could have no influence upon the second, yet the second is *meant* to influence the first" (*Judgment*, 12).

I have gone over the bridge between the understanding and reason Kant means to create through a transition from the aesthetic to the teleological judgment in the first chapter. I will go over its features quickly here because I want to stress the generally unrecognized way in which Kant operates with what Nietzsche would call a justification of existence as an aesthetic phenomenon (*Birth*, 52). In short, Kant claims that the judgment, an ability to capture specifics under general principles, also has the ability to extract principles out of details. It can, out of the elements of the material world, extract moral principles under which it can then deduce moral action. But, for two reasons, the judgment can only coherently so operate if it construes nature as operating according to a purpose. The first and logically necessary one creates the basis for much of the aesthetics articulated in the prior two chapters. In order to draw conclusions about action in the natural world, the judgment needs as a principle that nature operates coherently, indeed purposively: "The purposiveness of nature is therefore a particular concept *a priori*, which has its origin solely in the reflective judgment" (*Judgment*, 17). Purposiveness entails more than mere mechanistic regularity. It construes the world as having the appearance of being made for a purpose, as seeming to have a meaning or a significance, and this even though, as we have seen, Kant explicitly denies, in *The Critique of Pure Reason*, the argument from design. In the third *Critique*, he argues that aesthetic pleasure, which occurs at moments in which we see natural objects as purposive, as meaningful, even when we know we have no basis for drawing that conclusion, entails construing them as having purposiveness without purpose. Our ability to see objects in this way shows that construing an object as having purposiveness while not claiming that it has a purpose is a coherent way of judging. On that basis, the judgment can construe the world as operating as if designed without claiming that it was in fact designed and so Kant can show that the principle on which judgment regulates moral action is coherent as a principle of judgment, though not as a concept of the understanding.

Although this argument makes the judgment logically possible, it does not really show us why we need a principle more than mechanistic regularity in order to make judgments about the world and act in it according to moral principles. The reason, in a little noted passage in the section on the teleological judgment, as I discussed in the first chapter, is Kant's claim that one could not in fact continue to act morally in a world that one thought gave no basis for that action. Kant imagines a morally upright atheist, and claims that the experience of a world operating according to no principle, allowing evil to thrive and ending in universal death, would make the purpose of pursuing moral laws "impossible." Such a person would have to "assume the being of a *moral* author of the world, that is, a God" (*Judgment,* 303–304). This argument, which would have seemed nearly self-evident in the eighteenth-century world of natural theology that Kant did so much to overthrow, may seem to us banal and dogmatic. But we should not, for that, ignore its centrality to Kant's sense of what he was doing. Having shown that one could not prove either the existence of God or the ordering of the world according to a reason that posited its own dictates as an ordering principle, he effectively reestablished a basis for looking at the world as having the appearance of being so ordered. If it was coherent to construe natural objects as having purposiveness without purpose, as the aesthetic judgment showed was the case, then construing the world as purposive without actually knowing that it had a purpose, as the teleological judgment does, is at least intellectually coherent. If the world was not quite justified as an aesthetic phenomenon, it was made coherent as one. The articulation of the aesthetic principles of autonomous form, indifference, and embodiment in the last two chapters, I think, enables extending this Enlightenment turn to aesthetics as a foundation, if not of truth, of value, not merely through the next generation of German Romantics (who made it much more explicit), but to the works of Hegel and those who followed upon him, who regularly struggled to articulate in what way, given their sense of the world seen as art, philosophy was different from art.[8]

My point here is not to deconstruct Kantian philosophy and its Continental heirs as aesthetic phenomena, and I have avoided such claims in my discussion of their aesthetics up to now because it would be redundant and, more importantly for my argument here, because I do not really think that this turn disables a project's claim upon our assent, even in Enlightenment terms.[9] Kant's anomalous insistence on seeing the world through the lens of a natural theology that he also thought was dogmatic suggests that value judgments can almost never be justified all the way down. For that reason, it is a mistake to ask of Foucault for completely grounded justifications of his values. Foucault's allies frequently describe his project as an extended argument in favor of freedom or liberation from various constraints, and he has been famously faulted because, in arguing the omnipresence of power, he seems to deny the possibility of freedom that so obviously funds his analyses.[10] But what if one asked, as no one does now but as one might have prior to the eighteenth century, why freedom is a value? The argument would quickly turn to a world-picture similar in form if not in content to the one Kant offers in his defense of teleological judgment. Such world-pictures look "merely" narrative or "merely" aesthetic when we no longer assent to the values they can embody but not argue for. But they are, I would argue, something like a requirement for having values, and they show up in philosophy often to provide as much as it can of value foundations. World-pictures are not false because they are unprovable; they are just unproven. They are aesthetic presentations, pictures of meaning, not proofs of it.

If all philosophies of values depend on such world-pictures, then, of course, so do Foucault's. But I want to argue that aesthetics played a central role both in the content of his world-picture and in the construction of it in three key ways. First, not merely in his last works but throughout, his most basic value is a sense of what would make a good life—in form, though, not in content, almost in the traditional Socratic sense—and that sense is not only aesthetic in that it presents what Nehamas would call an art of living but also aesthetic in the sense that it entails an art of self-construction.[11] In other words, aesthetic values are the ones his world-picture endorses as well as the mode by which it is constructed. Second, his view of history, his structuring of discursive formations, his definition of power, indeed his definition of his approach as at all points anti-interpretive and unstructural, may all best be understood as versions of purposiveness without purpose. And finally, without meaning his works to be untrue, he does not deny that they present their truths fictively, in effect that they embody meanings as much as they argue for them. In all of these cases, I do not want to argue that Foucault evaded arguments by falling back on to the "merely" aesthetic, but that his philosophic positions assume much of their sense through this aesthetic understanding and presentation.

To the extent that he exemplifies a postmodern attack on Enlightenment reason and politics, he persuades by allowing us to see what it means to think through problems in that way. Nor should this be taken as an evasion or a weakening of the argument. Certain arguments can only be presented this way. If, for instance, one wanted to argue for an extreme form of epistemological relativism (as I do not think Foucault does), the logical contradictions at the level of articulating the theory might well be inescapable. And such arguments regularly fall into the temptation of using definitions of "truth," "knowledge," "belief," and so on, that are only too obviously special pleading or self-contradictory. And yet, it might be the case that human beings can no more know the world accurately than, say, worms can hear. A logical contradiction in thought and language manifests limits in our ability to articulate, not limits in the world. In a like manner Derrida can be taken to mean, at points Nietzsche at least seems to argue, and Heraclitus surely did think that reality is literally non-identical with itself, that it so constantly changes that no coherent thought about it is possible. Again, although it is impossible to think in a fully logical way about such a situation, our inability to think about it through logic does not prove that the world could not actually be such that things in it had no identity with themselves. And one would have to be too much a philosopher and not enough of one, too much a literary critic and not enough a reader of literature, not to follow Nietzsche with at least some fascination when he tries to show what it would mean to think about such a world. I do not think either Foucault or Bourdieu are such extreme cases, and indeed, few postmodernists are. And I mean to show how accusations of Foucault's contradictoriness usually result from refusing to see precisely what he is saying, the picture of the world he is trying to paint. But depicting a world in which Enlightenment reason and value are arbitrary limits rather than foundations is necessary to its project of questioning those foundations. Thus the misreadings of Foucault do not derive merely from ignorance, willed or not. Rather, they show an inability to credit the world he pictures. In the same way, his influence, and the influence of postmodern skepticism generally, has precisely to do with the way that skepticism offers a concept of how to live in the world that makes more sense to many of us than does Kant's willed teleology. When postmodernists, then, as we will see when we turn to Bourdieu, argue the ideological bases of Enlightenment definitions of art, even if they are accurate as far as their analysis goes, they do so through the resources of those definitions.

I. Being Without End

Foucault's basic sense of what it meant to be in the world, the way that sense was embodied in his world-picture, and the role of the aesthetic concepts of indifference and autonomous form in that picture, remain consistent throughout his writing. One can see that consistency when one juxtaposes two aspects of his thought not usually considered as much connected with each other: his discussion in *The Order of Things* of the death of man and his late espousal of an aesthetics of existence. The first of these ideas is usually taken as the essence of an anti-humanist philosophy of a world without agency or point.[12] One sees the second position in the late, ostensibly more humanist Foucault, who starts to see himself as a philosopher within the Enlightenment tradition and to break away from his earlier, more extreme positions.[13] And yet there is a very clear line from one position to the other: Foucault's theory of the death of man, which might more accurately be called the death of human being in the world as an object of knowledge, leads to a vision of human being as function without purpose. That vision creates the possibility of breaking free of oneself, of never having a self or a mode of being that would constrain one's action, of becoming other than what one is. The late statements about an aesthetic of the self look directly toward these earlier ideas: the late aesthetic is a possibility that the earlier ideas allow, a value that they enable. Nor do the calls for aesthetic self-construction really withdraw any element of those earlier positions that one might find objectionable. There is about this sense of being in the world neither an early nor a late Foucault, an anti-Kantian nor a newly reconverted Kantian, but a consistent opposition to a notion of a world with ends and a consequent espousal of what it means to live in one without them. Finally, as we will see, this picture also structures his basic stance, the articulation of a position of extreme distance, of a perspective that is defined only by its own alienness from all other perspectives. Oddly, this alienness rejoins Foucault with a form of objectivity that he is blamed for falling short of even as he is blamed for holding it in a too extreme manner—because he holds it as a manner of aesthetic indifference.

To see how Foucault's position on the death of man connects with his desire for aesthetic self-construction, we have to begin with a redefinition of what he meant by that death. According to the standard view, Foucault sees man as an invention of the modern period. Beginning with Kant, moderns invented man as both the subject and object of knowledge. That invention for the first time called into question representation as a mental act and centered on human being as defining itself as the subject that constitutes the world and its objects.[14] This view is not incorrect, but it stresses the wrong part of what Foucault calls "the empirico-transcendental doublet." Foucault's analysis of this idea is famously obscure and often depends on assumed readings of Kant, Husserl, and Heidegger. But despite the project all these philosophers have of either establishing or questioning a foundational consciousness, it is man as object of knowledge far more than as knowing subject that Foucault means to show as an historical invention. If one does not begin with the presumption that, like other post-structuralists, his target is post-Kantian definitions of consciousness, a reading of the section that defines the doublet clarifies his attack on man as an object of knowledge. The opening statement would seem to make this target clear enough: "Man in the analytic of finitude, is a strange empirico-transcendental doublet, since he is a being such that knowledge will be attained in him of what renders all knowledge possible" (*Order of Things*, 318). Descartes' cogito, according to Foucault, did not turn upon its own consciousness to define it as an object of potential knowledge. Its moment of self-consciousness merely tried to establish what form of perception could be taken as reliable. By trying to determine what aspects of the mind were necessary pre-conditions of perception or of thinking, Kant made the mind the first object of knowledge and thereby made all further objects of knowledge dependent on the definition of that first object.

For the mind to become its own object of knowledge, it can no longer be transparent in its workings. There must be something there to be an object. Hence, Foucault defines something he calls the "unthought":

If man is, indeed, in the world, the locus of an empirico-transcendental doublet, if he is that paradoxical figure in which the empirical contents of knowledge necessarily release, of themselves, the conditions that have made them possible, then man cannot posit himself in the immediate and transparent sovereignty of a *cogito*; nor, on the other hand, can he inhabit the objective inertia of something that, by rights, does not and never can give way to self-consciousness. (*Order of Things*, 322)[15]

Foucault does not primarily care to contest the establishment of the Enlightenment self-awareness that presumes to ground all knowledge. Instead, he contests the necessity of that consciousness to turn itself into an object that may be known, that may be studied and defined by the fields of the human sciences. A purely observing mind could not have the content to be knowledge. It would be a transparent sovereignty. A pure object could be studied but would not be an aspect of human consciousness, would neither lead to it nor open itself to it. Thus, Foucault claims, "it is now a question not of truth, but of being" (323). The mind might know an external truth. "Man" comes into existence for Foucault with the introduction of being as something that can be known and defined. Being becomes an object of knowledge, but it can only do so by changing the nature of mind since mind cannot be external to being. At this point, human being can become an object of study, even a field of study, the human sciences, and it can be given limits, ends, and purposes.[16]

To this idea of humanity as having an end which may be known, even in the manner of a knowingly held myth, Foucault opposes, in an interview given only one year after the appearance of *The Order of Things*, the concept of a human being as simply an entity that functions. At this moment in the interview the outlines emerge of a long argument between Foucault and those who cannot accept this idea. For the interviewer, simple functioning is a fetishism; one must justify functioning and humanism does that (*Dits*, I, 646, 647). For Foucault, any proposed end to function would be a form of constraint or regulation:

Humanity is a species endowed with a nervous system such that it can, up to a certain point, regulate its own functioning. It is clear that this possibility of regulation incites continually the idea that humanity must have an end. . . . We say to ourselves: since we have an end, we must regulate our functioning; whereas, in reality, it is only on the basis of this possibility of regulation that ideologies, philosophies, metaphysics, religions can emerge. (*Dits*, I, 647)

For the interviewer, in asserting mere functioning, Foucault is being either willfully obtuse or nihilist. There must be some basis on which to choose how one should function. Foucault does not deny choice. Part of functioning for human beings is the ability to regulate functioning. But he sees any end or value coming from the outside as an artificial constraint, an ideology, philosophy, metaphysics, or religion. And these are all myths. He concludes, even at this early date, with a positive definition of the philosopher that accords well with the ostensibly new acceptance of the term in his later work: "The role of the philosopher, who is the one who says 'this is what is happening,' consists, perhaps today in demonstrating that humanity begins to discover that it can function without myths" (*Dits*, I, 648).[17] One sees, in this interchange, juxtaposed with the section of *Order of Things* on which it comments, something like Foucault's revaluation of all values, both the logical trouble it causes and the vision it serves. Foucault does not object to all truths, but to that claim to knowledge of human being which would in a sense pin it like an insect to a taxonimized board. An acceptance of functioning without end would perhaps take away any basis for choosing one end over another, but, at the same time, it would provide unlimited choice to any individual as to how to regulate his or her functioning.

For the moment bracketing any possible ethical or moral constraints on the individual choosing functioning, or indeed even the question of whether one can meaningfully conceive an individual in this kind of complete isolation (these questions cannot be confronted until I turn to the discussion of Foucault's notions of power and the disciplinary society), one might argue that any contradiction here between valuing choice and denying a value on which to base one's choice is really only verbal. Although, in one sense, Foucault does have a "value" that would be a constraining end, the "value" of having unconstrained free choice over how to function, this contradiction comes from our ability to capture what Foucault wants under the single concept of "value," not from a contradiction between the situation he espouses and the one he imposes. A world with no natural values that would constrain choice is hardly a logically impossible one. And arguing that the only way to live coherently in such a world entails an acceptance of function without any ends external to it is not really in conflict with that picture. As I said above, many contradictions might be ironed out this way, but, although I will make hay of this mode of analysis in time, I want here to restore the contradiction to its original grassy state because that state gets us to the deeper philosophical and imaginative problem of Foucault's world-picture. One can approach this problem by noting one of the rare moments in which Foucault reverses rather than extends a Nietzschean epigram. Nietzsche subtitled his autobiography "How One Becomes What One Is," extending a long-standing argument that self-overcoming entailed embracing change and becoming over essence and being. Foucault, in an interview published after his death, pushes that epigram over an edge that raises the question of whether the position can be a coherent one: "The principal interest of life and work is that which allows you to become someone different from what you were at the starting-point" (*Dits*, II, 1596). What Foucault desires is constantly to become what he is not. And to the extent that he thinks that that is something he might do and also something that he might fail at doing, something that gives his work interest, he seems to have a notion that there is a someone who one is whom one might fail to move away from. But then, if his principal in-

terest is to move away from that being, if he succeeds, hasn't he, by fulfilling that interest, become what he is?

If this contradiction may be recuperated as verbal, I do not think the
path will be an easy one, as we may see by comparing Foucault's attempted
inversion of Nietzsche with Nietzsche's attempt to take any element of goal
or meaning away from becoming by basing becoming on his idea of recurrence. Nietzsche's version of a cosmology that explained the meaning and
value of life, the picture of his that is most analogous to Kant's claim that we
must imagine the universe as ordered, and to Foucault's of human being as
function without end, is his assertion that all things recur eternally. The first
appearance of this idea makes clear that its purpose is to outline a value
rather than make an ontological claim. After criticizing Socrates for his dying words—"I owe Asclepious a rooster"—as defining life as a disease that
death cures (*The Gay Science*, 272), Nietzsche hypothesizes a demon who
prophesies to the reader, "'This life as you now live it and have lived it, you
will have to live once more and innumerable times more; and there will be
nothing new in it, but every pain and every joy and every thought and every
sigh and everything unutterably small or great in your life will return to
you, all in the same succession and sequence'" (*Gay Science*, 273).[18] To experience life truly as intrinsically valuable, rather than as a disease needing a
cure, as needing no external value to justify it, for Nietzsche, one would
have to welcome this prophecy with joy rather than recoil in horror. In what
is at this point just a thought experiment, Nietzsche means with recurrence
to describe life as without justifying meaning, without an end outside itself.
Only by being able to accept each moment of life without looking to something outside it can one be said to value life and not to see it as a disease
needing curing. For him, Kant's cosmology is another event in European
nihilism, the belief that life is not its own value. Even Nietzsche's "proof" of
eternal recurrence shows what he has in mind with it:

If the world had a goal, it must have been reached. If it were in any way capable of
a pausing and becoming fixed, of "being," if in the whole course of its becoming
it possessed even for a moment this capability of "being," then all becoming would
long since have come to an end. . . . The old habit of associating a goal with every
event and a guiding, creative God with the world, is so powerful that it requires an
effort for a thinker not to fall into thinking of the very aimlessness of the world as
intended. This notion—that the world intentionally avoids a goal and even knows
artifices for keeping itself from entering into a circular course—must occur to all
those who would like to force on the world the ability for *eternal novelty*, i.e., on a
finite, definite, unchangeable force of constant size, such as the world is, the
miraculous power of infinite novelty in its forms and states. (*Will to Power*, 546)

This statement indicates the connection of eternal recurrence with eternal becoming. The world could only change constantly if it had as a purpose, as a part of its essence, the intention or design not to change. Without such a purpose, leading to the constant invention of novelty, recurrence would be inevitable. Although the argument for recurrence here does sound like a statement about the reality of the world, for Nietzsche its point is always the new values its acceptance leads to. Thus he says in a fragmentary note: "Means of *enduring it*: the revaluation of all values" (*Will to Power*, 545).

But Nietzsche smuggles back purpose and goal into his idea of the one preferred response to the prophecy of recurrence. The strong response, in which one exults in the opportunity to live one's life over, whether it is just another recurring event in the life one will live over again or not, does stand apart from other recurring events as the one that describes how such a life may have value. If not the essence of endless becoming's infinite re-currence, it is at least the meaning of the passage in which the demon prophesies. The basic problem is that Nietzsche still has a concept of some-thing like authenticity that gives exultation in recurrence a value. Through it, one is able to become who one is. In contrast to Kant's world, in which purposiveness allows us to project purpose without claiming its reality, Nietzsche depicts a world with neither purposiveness nor purpose. As a re-sult, though, he returns to an even more reified notion of being.

In the passage in which Foucault discusses functioning, that concept works as becoming does in Nietzsche. It designates operation, hence move-ment and change without goal. His idea of becoming different from what one is insists on this movement. It evades the question of what one "is" by specifying that his goal is to become different from what he is "at the start-ing-point," this being no more who he is than what he might be at any other point. But, if this advances in the Nietzschean path away from pre-supposing any essence, it does so only by accepting the Kantian aesthetic maneuver of projecting purposiveness in terms of a value onto the activity of becoming. And, in the sentence immediately following his claim that only becoming different has interest, Foucault makes explicit the value in that activity: "That which gives value to writing or to a love relationship also gives value to life. The game isn't worth the candle except to the extent that one does not know how it will end" (*Dits*, II, 1596).

But, as I argued earlier, Kant defined aesthetic purposiveness as an imposition of the mind, not as a trait of some objects as opposed to others. Although Foucault wants to insist on change and difference in becoming, he is still Nietzschean in his recognition that he is ascribing a value rather than claiming a cosmology or an ontology, and they both, in this, follow rather than critique Kant's aesthetic. From this perspective, Foucault's ostensibly late turn toward an aesthetic of the self becomes entirely consistent with his earliest project of undoing what he took to be the human science's claim to know being. The questions to which he responds when he asks rhetorically in an interview why life can't be a work of art indicates the connection between his early idea of function without purpose and his late aesthetic of the self. The interviewer, clearly at this moment somewhat skeptical, notes that the idea of making one's life a work of art is popular among various groups in Berkeley, thus suggesting that Foucault is supporting a culturally shallow dandyism. Foucault resists the opportunity to separate this idea from dandyism and differentiates what he is espousing from Berkeley activities because "I am afraid that, in most of these examples, most people think that if they do as they do, if they live as they live, it's because they know the truth of desire, of life, of nature, of the body, etc." Seemingly not having gotten the distinction he wants, the interviewer asks how this conception of making one's life in the absence of knowing universal laws differs from Sartrean existentialism. Foucault again responds not in terms of some less "self-indulgent" version of what he says, but in terms of the absence of an end to the self-crafting: "From a theoretical point of view, I think that Sartre sets aside the idea of self as something we are given, but, because of the notion of moral authenticity, he falls back on the idea that one must be oneself and truly oneself. In my opinion, the only practical and acceptable consequence of what Sartre has said is to tie his theoretical discovery with creative practice and not to moral authenticity" (*Dits*, II, 1211). In each response, Foucault distinguishes the aesthetics of the self for which he argues in terms of its having no end other than the mere creativity of operating changes on the self. Although aesthetics suggests a more directed activity than mere functioning, in terms of the description he gives of it, both functioning and the value of self-creating are the same.

To recuperate the contradiction between arguing that there is only function without any constraining value and seeing a value to function, then, one has to turn to the picture of a world in which there is no knowledge of being, in which man is a dead concept. Kant wants a world that gives meaning to moral action by being, at least in appearance, one with moral ends. Nietzsche sees a world with no justification beyond its own existence and wants to see a way of taking joy in living in such a world. Thus its existence would become a real justification. Foucault wants to extirpate being so completely that human being could not be a subject of knowledge; thus he sees that being only as an entity that functions. Like Nietzsche, though, in order to avoid positing an external value (an act Nietzsche thinks of as nihilist and Foucault thinks of as accepting constraint), he must assert a value to exulting in function as Nietzsche insists that we need to learn to exult in mere existence. We are free to function rather than being condemned to it. Hence we have the opportunity to craft our lives.

This value to crafting one's life may be taken as a response to the questions Foucault's critics raised about the evaluative basis on which he critiqued power. The question of how sufficient or consistent it is must wait until I address those theories directly. Here I would like to note that, while Foucault follows Kant and Nietzsche in proposing as a fundamental value to his work something like a proposed picture of what it means to live in the world rather than a deontology, the aesthetics of this activity is doubled by the fact that the value he puts before us is itself an aesthetic one. He imagines a kind of life as having value, and the value he proposes for that life is itself an aesthetic one. As might be expected, this position satisfied few of his critics, who saw in it an elite dandyism; disappointed some of his erstwhile allies, who agreed with that critique; and found support only from allies who denied his dandyism. But Foucault did nothing to avoid that charge himself, noting that the Renaissance and turn-of-the-century dandyism were other periods that held the view that the self could be worked on aesthetically (*Dits*, II, 1221).[19] The problem with dandyism is that it is supposed to be self-indulgent, without necessary attention to social and political injustice and constraint. Construed as a turn in a late Foucault, then, this aesthetics of the self would also be a turn from the political engagement that American followers especially wanted, in a Foucault who would stand as an alternative to the ostensible quietism of Derridean relativism.

The charge of self-indulgence, the belief that dandyism is bad because self-indulgent, comes down to the belief that an aesthetic value must be somehow hollow, "merely" aesthetic. This belief in turn rests on the definition of beauty as harmonious appearance, appearance being by definition hollow of meaning and value. The last chapter argued that only a definition of art as embodied meaning, coupled with a recognition that such embodiments are illusory, only apparent, this recognition being the Kantian indifference to the existence of the object, which is what he meant by disinterest, was adequate to accommodate the forms art has taken in the twentieth century. When Kant demanded that moral action necessitated seeing the world as if authored by a moral governor, he openly demanded seeing the world as apparently embodied meaning. No one charges this aesthetic presentation as dandyism because it evidently embodies an extra-aesthetic moral meaning. But Foucault's presentation, of self-crafting as a meaning-giving activity in the context of human being viewed only as functioning, differs from Kant only in its post-Nietzschean refusal to recognize externally imposed goals or values on existence, not in some ostensible departure from moral concern. This was true of actual turn-of-the-century dandyism, as well, but that argument has been made elsewhere frequently enough. Foucault's sense of being in the world as justified, if at all, only on intrinsic terms is neither novel nor more nihilist than any post-Enlightenment recognition of such a world. It differs in Foucault's more radical insistence that a definition of humanity as empirically knowable must in such world entail both delusion and constraint. If it fails to tie that claim to some bedrock ontology, its "failure" is also a traditional, indeed a necessary one, since aesthetic presentations of value occur regularly when one cannot justify the value any other way.

Foucault's aesthetic stance both toward the content of his research and toward his view of the world has one last aspect that enhances critics' response that he is not quite intellectually responsible—the aesthetic disinterest that one finds so usually tied to ideas of objectivity. Critics frequently comment upon and distrust Foucault's cultivation of a stance of ironic distance toward his subject matter and toward the status of his work. Indeed, the way in which his critics describe this stance is particularly interesting since they seem to be detailing qualities that one would think they would value. Here, for instance, Habermas describes a personal impression: "I can only relate what impressed me: the tension, one that eludes familiar categories, between the almost serene scientific reserve of the scholar striving for objectivity on the one hand, and the political vitality of the vulnerable, subjectively excitable, morally sensitive intellectual on the other" (*The New Conservatism*, 173–174). While one must allow Habermas his impressions, one may also note that the tension resides only in a certain impressionism. He surely does not think there is a tension between objectivity and political vitality. Only by characterizing that vitality as "subjectively excitable," can he make of Foucault's temperament the kind of self-contradiction he finds in his work. But the temperament he saw in

Foucault is also the temperament others find in the work, and to equally surprising effect. Charles Taylor, in a quite astonishing moment, connects Foucault's ostensible relativism with an impossible objectivity:

Foucault's monolithic relativism only seems plausible if one takes the outsider's perspective, the view from Sirius; or perhaps imagines oneself a soul in Plato's myth of Er. Do I want to be born a Sung dynasty Chinese, or a subject of Hammurabi of Babylon, or a twentieth-century American? Without a prior identity, I couldn't begin to choose. They incarnate incommensurable goods (at least prior to some deep comparative study, and conceivably even after this). But this is not my/our situation. We have already *become* something. ("Foucault on Freedom," 99)

One might think, after the first three words, that one had suddenly dropped in on a critique of some objectivist theory of knowledge, perhaps John Rawls's description of the original position, from which people, without knowing their sex, class, economic situation, and so on, construct a just society. Taylor's critique of Foucault has more the tenor of some skeptical critiques of Rawls. One hardly expects criticism of Foucault for underemphasizing our irrevocable placement within history.

Habermas and Taylor respond not precisely to an objectivist disinterest, but to the manner in which Foucault declares his distance. Foucault stresses an irony and laughter that seem not to feel the moral burden of objectivity. Here, for instance, is his invocation of Borges at the beginning of *The Order of Things*:

This book first arose out of a passage in Borges, out of the laughter that shattered, as I read the passage, all the familiar landmarks of my thought—*our* thought, the thought that bears the stamp of our age and our geography—breaking up all the ordered surfaces and all the planes with which we are accustomed to tame the wild profusion of existing things, and continuing long afterwards to disturb and threaten with collapse our age-old distinction between the Same and the Other. This passage quotes a "certain Chinese encyclopedia" in which it is written that "animals are divided into: (a) belonging to the Emperor, (b), embalmed, (c), tame, (d) suckling pigs, (e) sirens, (f) fabulous, (g) stray dogs, (h) included in the present classification, (i) frenzied, (j) innumerable, (k) drawn with a very fine camel-hair brush, (l) *et cetera*, (m) having just broken the water pitcher, (n) that from a long way off look like flies". In the wonderment of this taxonomy, the thing we apprehend in one great leap, the thing that, by means of the fable, is demonstrated as the exotic charm of another system of thought, is the limitation of our own, the stark impossibility of thinking *that*. (xv)

Showing us the unthought taxonomies by which we order our knowledge may be a perfectly appropriate game of wit for a Borgesian fable. Here, though, attempting to think that way, thus recognizing the limitations of our own system, begins the project of calling into question the foundations of knowledge. Thus, if it is an objectivity, it must be an irresponsible one, more of an inhuman laughter than a properly humane, scholarly practice. What makes it irresponsible is again what makes it aesthetic. It is distance in the manner of the artificially assumed, Kantian indifference to the object's existence, an objectivity that matches all too well with Foucault's pre-existent desire to see modernity as only one possible formation. And yet it remains a virtually paradigmatic objectivity, a perceptual stance that begins in trying to presume nothing, or more accurately, in trying to rid oneself of any presumption one already has. The problem with postmodern relativism, at least as Foucault embodies it here, is not that it is subjectively excitable. Rather, it is all too objective; it recognizes the roots of its objectivity in aesthetics and thus accepts (or imposes) a status of artwork on the knowledge and politics it analyzes. This declaration of Borgesian distance, as we will see, not only introduces but also deeply informs the structure and point of *Order of Things*, just as a similar declaration informs *Discipline and Punish*. In effect, in different ways, it informs and unifies the projects that get labeled archaeology and genealogy.

Before turning to that analysis, though, I want to end this section with a moment in which its various themes combine, giving a sense both of the coherence of Foucault's intellectual project and of the reasons for the way it has exasperated some people. At the end of the introduction to *Archaeology of Knowledge*, Foucault gives voice to a critic who asks whether Foucault really intends the methodology he is about to outline: "Aren't you sure of what you're saying? Are you going to change yet again, shift your position according to the questions that are put to you, and say that the objections are not really directed at the place from which you are speaking?" The worry of this fictional critic turns out to be well founded, since, while *Archaeology* quite consciously extracts, rather than describing, a system from his former books, it also ceases to describe or control his work, as a system, as soon as it is written. And Foucault, in effect, having posed himself this question, answers yes. He writes, he says, to create a labyrinth in which to lose himself, in which his discourse will be forced into unexpected directions. And he concludes, "More than only me, doubtless, write in order no longer to have a face. Don't ask me who I am and don't tell me to remain the same. That is the morality of the Public Records office; it keeps track of our papers. It can at least leave us free when we write" (*Ar-

chaeology, 17, translation modified).[20] One sees here, in his desire to be free of the stabilities of identity governed by public records, the way in which he sees knowledge of human being as constraint. One sees the desire, in his search for a labyrinth in which he and his writing will lose themselves and be changed, the goal of becoming different from who one is. And finally one sees that hyper-objectivity that entails losing one's face, both one's identity and the place from which one would normally see things. I have split these elements up here, but they are part of a certain kind of unity. That unity is not, I think, the unity of an oeuvre, much less an art of living or an extrapolation of some biographical identity that gets expressed in the writing. I intend it as the judgment of a design that claims only to see a pattern in features, like Kant's purposiveness without purpose, not to delineate intention, meaning, or purpose. My justification for what might be construed as self-indulgence will be that the effect that Foucault gets from this procedure in his archaeologies and genealogies allows me to hope for similar results.

II. Aesthetics and Seeing the Limits of Knowledge and Justice

To the extent that, as I have argued, even Enlightenment values and aims find support, at a certain level, in an aesthetically structured world-picture, there would be nothing special to the postmodern interrogation of Enlightenment reason and the modern state in also having recourse to such a picture. Even an argument that such recourse represented an undercutting of Enlightenment aims to ground thought in reason, coupled with a better, more postmodern self-awareness in its recognition of this limit, common to all thought, would not get very far in allowing any further consequences, either philosophical or political.[21] The aesthetic values Foucault's aesthetic picture founds, however, create a very different situation. Foucault's world-picture is hardly novel. Indeed, most modern philosophers, objectivists or not, would certainly start with the proposition that the world does not have intrinsic meaning or purpose and would claim that that insight is part of the Enlightenment, Kant's resistance to it and Hegel's absolute contradiction of it notwithstanding. But Foucault does not see aesthetics as a form of admitting epistemological failure, a thing to which one has recourse when reason ceases to be able to plumb any farther down. He exemplifies the postmodern questioning of Enlightenment by using its aesthetics to show what the world would look like if knowledge constrained actions rather than describing objective limits, and the liberties of the middle-class state all rested on forms of accepted discipline. While using the techniques of this aesthetic to depict post-Kantian knowledge and the modern state to show how to see the one as historically located and the other as caught within the power-constraints from which it claims to free us, one can only offer a perspective rather than a position of knowledge. But to accept its status as perspective, as we will see, only creates a contradiction in making knowledge claims if one takes Foucault as having given his method of articulating that perspective either empirical or epistemological grounding, a grounding for which his work has no need. Such an acceptance can further have a liberating force by redefining what it means to be within power. In each case, it does what postmodernism has to do to effect its interrogation; it makes its reason work within an aesthetic depiction, and makes its project coherent through both the methods and reservations of the concepts of purposiveness without purpose, aesthetic indifference, and embodied meaning. To show the role of these concepts in Foucault's work, this section will look first at Foucault's initial ambition to articulate a genuine alternative to reason, an excluded experience, variously identified with madness and with modernist literature. He fairly quickly and famously abandons the idea that he can articulate a genuine voice of madness, but he seems much slower to abandon the idea that modernist literature embodies a stance of difference from which to evaluate Enlightenment claims to knowledge, and to the extent that he ever does abandon it, he does so only by reappropriating the stance of distance, of both difference and indifference, that it allows in defining discursive formations and power, formations that, consciously or not, explicitly deploy notions of structure without purpose as explanations of how they work.

In his review of the first edition of *Histoire de la folie*—originally entitled *Folie et déraison*—Jacques Derrida famously criticized Foucault for thinking he could write a history of madness itself, an account of the actual experience of madness, even "letting madness speak for itself" (*Writing and Difference*, 33).[22] Although some critics have claimed that Foucault did not mean this claim seriously, the statement of it seems to be the theme of the original preface, and even his strictures about how the task may be accomplished do not withdraw the book's sense that there is a genuine experience of madness whose content could be posed against reason's attempt to silence and imprison it.[23] The opening of the preface, for instance, having quoted Dostoievski to the effect that one cannot persuade oneself of one's good sense by confining one's neighbor, continues:

We must write the history of this other trick of madness—of this other trick whereby men, in the sovereign gesture of reason that confines their neighbor, communicate and are recognized across the merciless language of non-madness; we must rediscover the moment of this conjuration, before it had been definitively established in the reign of truth, before it had been reanimated by the lyricism of protest. We must try to return, in history, to the zero degree of the history of madness, where it is an undifferentiated experience, an experience not yet separated from separation itself. (*Dits*, I, 187)

Although Foucault does recognize that it would be impossible to encounter this state directly anymore, he still outlines a structural study of the "historical ensemble—ideas, institutions, legal and policing measures, scientific concepts—that holds captive a madness whose primitive state may never be restored in itself" (*Dits*, I, 192). In other words, by writing the history of the structures that surround madness, he will at least be able to locate where its original state is held captive, thus opposing that state to the institutions that hold it captive. Although Foucault responded with some asperity to Derrida's critique of his reading of Descartes as exemplary of this expulsion of madness—thus leading to a line of trying to read this dispute as one initiating a conflict significant for the arguments between American Derrideans and American Foucaultian New Historicists—in withdrawing the preface and retracting the claim to articulate an actual subjective experience of madness, he essentially granted Derrida's main point.[24]

If he retracted the original preface and its claim to voice madness, so to speak, he nevertheless left unchanged the text of the book and its discussion of literature's insight into that state. Having wanted to return to the moment in which undifferentiated madness was not yet separated from separation itself, he finds a moment of first separation in the way madness is treated in literature:

Despite many interferences that are yet visible, the separation is already made; between the two forms of the experience of madness, the distance will never stop lengthening. Figures of cosmic vision and movements of moral reflection, the *tragic* element and the *critical* element, henceforth will go, always being separated further, opening in the profound unity of madness a gap that will never more be covered over. On the one hand, there will be a Ship of Fools, loaded with faces twisted in frenzy that will, little by little, sink into the night of the world, amid landscapes that speak the strange alchemy of knowledges, the hollow threats of animality and the end of time. On the other hand, there will be a Ship of Fools that constructs for the wise an exemplary and didactic Odyssey of human flaws. (*Histoire*, 45)

The next few pages make clear that to call these elements tragic and critical is not to employ a loose metaphor. The two stances are articulated through forms of art and literature—the tragic experience in "Bosch, Brueghel, Thierry Bouts, Dürer" (*Histoire*, 45), the critical experience in Erasmus (46). Moreover, it is not simply separation that damages the original experience of madness. Foucault mourns the tragic element that is separated out. If never voiced directly, this tragic element does seem to be the excluded experience of madness that Foucault wants to delineate. Both the fact of separation and the suppression of one of the separated elements become the work of silencing madness: thus perhaps the odd locution in the preface of going back to an experience not yet separated from separation itself. Finally, this tragic element of madness still leaves its traces for Foucault in art and literature, even in the nineteenth century: "It is [the tragic consciousness of madness] that has awakened the last words of Nietzsche, the last visions of Van Gogh" (47).

Perhaps Foucault thought that he could reconstitute *Histoire de la folie* as a study of the way reason manifests its own limits in the various irrational ways in which it pronounces its difference from madness—a giving voice to reason's moments of unreasoned assertion rather than a giving voice to madness—merely by eliminating the original preface. Though Foucault's evaluation of the alterity that literature embodied changed (he ceased to think it gave access to an actual experience of madness), his sense that literature did offer a perspective of alterity did not change; this may be why he thinks the structure of the book's argument survives the abandonment of a claim that he thought had been its original ground.[25] The status of *Histoire de la folie* as a history has been more seriously damaged by the criticism of historians than perhaps any other of Foucault's books. At the same time, that criticism has never quite undone its effect on those who have read it, not least because the book reads, particularly in its complete version, as a philosophical-literary meditation with extensive historical footnotes.[26] The translated abridgement cuts out the ways in which the book regularly introduces its descriptions of a period's ideas about madness with analyses of literary texts or of philosophical texts in terms of their metaphors or formal structures. It also cuts the book's frequent claims that it means to break from the historical stance that begins with the assumption that madness is a unified subject, and that knowledge has progressively disengaged from myth and superstition (see for instance, *Histoire*, 111). The abridgement and its English translation thus eliminate much of the book's literary effect. Foucault sees that literary effect as manifesting the historical and structural status of reason's need to define itself by confining madness, because the literary perspective seems to hold onto an implicit claim on our attention after the epistemological claim of offering a new definition of madness has been abandoned.

As late as *Order of Things*, Foucault maintained that literature, especially modern literature, has a particular status in being able to step outside the modern discursive formation of the human sciences. He seems at the end of the book, in a passage on modern literature, to claim again that it articulates an experience of madness, but, read carefully, the passage indicates what he wants from modern literature, which is not quite an evidence of an experience:

And, as if this experiencing of the forms of finitude in language were insupportable, or inadequate (perhaps its very inadequacy was insupportable), it is within madness that it manifested itself—the figure of finitude thus positing itself in language (as that which unveils itself within it), but also before it, preceding it, as that fathomless mute, unsignifying region where language can find its freedom. And it is indeed in this space thus revealed that literature, first with surrealism (though still in a very much disguised form), then, more and more purely, with Kafka, Bataille, and Blanchot, posited itself as experience. (*Order of Things*, 383–384)

Language—specifically in literature, as the context makes clear—shows us the forms of finitude, thus the forms standing behind the human sciences' mode of knowing, which identified human finitude as a knowable topic. Within the modern discursive formation, which rested on the presumption of knowable finitude, the experience of its forms would be insupportable. Thus the experience, in the first instance, seems to manifest itself in madness (Foucault hasn't yet abandoned this theme). But the appositive for this manifestation quickly throws us back upon language: the figure of finitude posits itself in language. And this form of linguistic positing quickly becomes literary: it is a space revealed in literature. As they did in *Histoire de la folie*, the perspective of literary language and a certain analysis of literature enable Foucault to point to the formal limits of a discursive formation that claims the status of unmediated knowledge without quite positing an actual, pre-linguistic experience that would fall outside those limits.

Histoire de la folie may be so easily reconceived as an archaeology of reason confining madness, and *Order of Things* may so easily accommodate Foucault's earliest interest in literature as an expression of alterity, because, although his project and its increasing interest in something that looks like a history of science, or at least a sociology of knowledge, has changed, its dependence on concepts of aesthetics continues to fund a notion of literary value that gives the continued meditation on literature its currency. Various critics, as we have seen, ascribe to Foucault an aestheticism that, as Nietzsche's, sees in art a connection with a Dionysian, ecstatic realm that would be an alternative to rationality and discourses of truth. Just as in the last chapter we saw Nietzsche give up the idea that Dionysian chaos embodied the real truth of the world, but preserve aesthetics as a way of talking about a world without an essence, even an essence of void and chaos, so Foucault, giving up madness as a special experience, finds in his idea of archaeology something that works exactly like purposiveness without purpose and affords the aesthetic distance his later works seek, a distance his reading of literature now incorporates. The outlining of this interpretation of archaeology as an aesthetics, in addition to showing how deeply aesthetics is embedded in Foucault's critique of post-Enlightenment knowledge, will also show in what ways that archaeology can and cannot be taken to be contradictory. That outline starts with contrasts between archaeology and interpretive explanation on the one hand, and archaeology and structuralism on the other.[27]

Foucault fairly consistently distinguished what he was doing from what would commonly be called interpretation, in the sense in which to interpret is to find, beneath the surface appearance of a text or set of events, what it actually means. In an interview that appeared the year after the publication of *Order of Things*, responding to a question about his method, he first defines the traditional method of treating texts up to that point, which was to find what was truly said underneath what was actually said, "to find the author's true thought, that which he had said without saying it, wanted to say without having arrived at it, wanted to hide and nevertheless allowed to appear." He then defined a new method:

In the place of reconstituting the immanent secret, it takes hold of the text as an ensemble of elements (words, metaphors, literary forms, set of narratives) between which one can make appear connections that are absolutely new, to the extent that they are not in the control of the author's project and are not rendered possible by the work itself, such as it is. The formal relations one discovers thus have not been present in the mind of anyone; they do not constitute the latent content of statements, their indiscreet secret; they are a construction, but an exact construction insofar as the relations thus described may be actually assigned to the materials treated. (*Dits*, I, 620)

And in *Archaeology of Knowledge* Foucault makes this claim about the relation archaeology finds among statements in a discourse in pretty much the same terms, this time explicitly contrasting his method with interpretation:

> But in no way would [the relations between statements in a discourse] constitute a sort of secret discourse, animating the manifest discourse from within; it is not therefore an interpretation of the facts of the statement that might reveal them, but the analysis of their coexistence, their succession, their mutual functioning, their reciprocal determination, and their independent or correlative transformations. (*Archaeology*, 29).

In effect, Foucault points to patterns among statements, relations among them, without tying those patterns to the intentions of an author or even to any unifying historical cause lying beneath or behind them. This raises the question of how and in what sense he can claim that the connections he describes are exact, are actually in the treated material.

Structuralism offers one coherent answer to this question. In analyzing a given sentence, in addition to explaining what an author might have meant in uttering the sentence, one could describe the various structures and conventions of language, from deep grammars to the surface relations among parts of speech, that allow the sentence to be meaningful at all. Since it is clear that these structures and conventions do have some form of existence, even though it is not a material one, one can distinguish between merely tracing patterns among words and describing the structures that actually do obtain. It may be difficult or even impossible to determine a method for distinguishing between real and apparent structures, since one does not have an intention or a cause to which to appeal, but inasmuch as, in order to convey meaning, language depends on things in addition to the intentions of any particular speaker, there will be real structures. And there will be at least one feature necessary to such descriptions that will determine that one is describing real structures. If language patterns were arbitrary and shifting, they would not be able to function at all as the necessary pre-conditions for language to mean, since their changeable nature would make them unfit for operating as stable pre-conditions. Consequently, structural relations must be logically interrelated, with coherent categorical and taxonomic breakdowns. And any extension of structuralism beyond linguistics, in order to claim the analytical strength of structural linguistics, will have to follow at least this criterion.

Although Foucault's famous antipathy to being labeled a structuralist began only some years after he wrote *Order of Things* (he wrote the intemperate remarks about the "tiny minds" of those who persist in calling him that, which appear in the foreword to the English edition, only in 1970), it does have a basis in an important distinction between his discursive formations and linguistic structures. To see that distinction, though, and how it will lead us to an aesthetic model of understanding discursive formations, we need to start with the common ground between Foucault and structuralism, which for a while he recognized comfortably enough. As early as the introduction to the first version of *Birth of the Clinic*, he opposed to interpretive commentary the "structural analysis" of medicine he was undertaking here (xvii).[28] And as late as 1968, even after he had stated what he took to be the significant difference between his work and structuralism, he was willing to postulate in what way one could construe him as a structuralist:

Let us say that structuralism explores, above all, an unconscious. At this moment, structuralists are trying to cast light on the unconscious structures of language, of the literary work, of knowledge. In the second place, I think one could say that what they study essentially are forms, systems; that is to say that they try to bring to the surface the logical correlations that may exist between a large number of elements belonging to a language, to an ideology (as in the analyses of Althusser), to a society (as in Lévi-Strauss), or in different fields of knowledge; this is what I myself have worked at. (*Dits*, I, 681)

One could say, following this description, that Foucault's archaeology claimed to bring forth an historical unconscious by showing the logical correlations among the different elements in a field of knowledge.

Even as he was willing to consider himself aligned with structuralism, though, he recognized that, because he dealt with the historical contingency involved in the appearance of systems of knowledge, the patterns he uncovered had to lack systematic interconnection: "One cannot say that I do structuralism, since, at bottom, I do not concentrate on either meaning or on the conditions according to which meaning appears, but on the conditions according to which meaning is modified or interrupted, the conditions according to which meaning disappears to allow something else to appear" (*Dits*, I, 631). This difference is vital, since it implies that that which Foucault describes can have neither the status of rules nor the criterion of logical correlation. Meaning may appear according to a system, but systematic interruptions and modifications would not be interruptions and modifications at all but structural transformations, which are the conditions according to which meaning appears. Moreover, in describing the appearance of statements in a discursive formation, he must be concerned, at least at the level of evidence, as much with the question of why some statements do not appear as with why others do, since the whole point of seeing knowledge as constructed within a system is to see its construction in terms of what it excludes as well as what it includes: "The question posed by language analysis of some discursive fact or other is always: according to what rules has a particular statement been made, and consequently according to what rules could other similar statements be made? The description of the events of discourse poses a quite different question: how is it that one particular statement appeared rather than another?" (*Archaeology*, 27).

We are faced then with a descriptive system that cannot claim to trace meaning back to the reality of an origination in consciousness, as does an interpretation. Nor can it refer a pattern to an organizing structure whose reality is indicated by the way in which it can logically describe the appearance of an infinite number of events with the rules it adduces, as does structuralism. Foucault insists on both the positivity and the regularity of the rules he adduces as standing behind statements. But their contingency and specificity calls into question both these features: "We are now dealing with a complex volume, in which heterogeneous regions are differentiated or deployed, in accordance with specific rules and practices that cannot be superposed" (*Archaeology*, 128). But if each region has its own rules and practices (as might be expected in the description of contingent historical event), and if the rules and practices are themselves so different that one system will not bear comparison with another—they "cannot be superposed"—then it will be hard to determine whether the regularity one delineates is actually there as a rule or is simply an accidental occurrence. It would be as if, in describing a game, one were not able to differentiate between a rule and a possible move that the rule allows and that may occur more or less frequently.

Foucault puts a couple of consequent limits on the claims he can make for determining archives, and although admitting these limits may sound like modesty, the admission would be devastating if he did have the ambition of describing genuinely positive regularities:

It is obvious that the archive of a society, a culture, or a civilization cannot be described exhaustively; or even, no doubt, the archive of a whole period. On the other hand, it is not possible for us to describe our own archive, since it is from within these rules that we speak, since it is that which gives to what we can say—and to itself, the object of our discourse—its modes of appearance, its forms of existence and coexistence, its system of accumulation, historicity, and disappearance. The archive cannot be described in its totality; and in its presence it is unavoidable. (*Archaeology*, 130)

Both of these limitations are perfectly consistent with archives having ontological existence. They could be there even if we could not be aware of them at all, much less only aware of them in the limited and partial way Foucault posits. They are not consistent with any claim to know the archives, though, even to know them only in part. For a moment, let us return to an analogy with linguistic structuralism. Any claim to delineate a linguistic structure that did not accompany at least the theoretical ambition to outline a structural totality would not describe a structure at all but only a randomly perceived regularity. Further, the completion of a structural theory, or indeed any explanation of even one part of a structure that went deeper down than the grammatical rules specific to a single language—which are obviously not pre-conditions for meaning, since meaning occurs in more than that single language—would have to be applicable to our own language in order for it to be meaningfully applicable at all. By claiming to know only local archives and archives not our own, Foucault tacitly admits that the rules for determining the place of a statement within an archive may not be rules at all but simply descriptions of what happens within a set of statements that happen to belong to the same discursive formation. Indeed, he cannot even be sure that the statements he groups together are part of an objectively existing discursive formation or just a concatenation of statements he has grouped together, as he effectively admits when he hypothesizes a critic asking what privilege he claims, in *The Order of Things*, for the grouping of natural history, economics, and general grammar. Foucault answers, "Privilege, none; it is only one of the describable groups; if, in fact, one took General Grammar, and tried to define its relations with the historical disciplines and textual criticism, one would certainly see the emergence of a quite different system of relations" (*Archaeology*, 159).

It is important to establish just how far this objection to Foucault's archaeology goes, because I think it goes less far in one sense and much farther in another than critics who propose something like it generally think. First, it does not prove that archives and discursive formations do not exist or even that the specific ones Foucault describes do not exist. It does prove that he has no firm way to establish their existence. He can only offer a picture whose persuasiveness is only its own formal coherence and likelihood (a weak enough case, taken from one perspective, but I will return to this in a moment). Because the discursive formations may exist, and because being within a discursive formation and being an accurate account of something are not mutually exclusive, Habermas's criticism of presentism, or the problem of being trapped in a radical historicism, fails as a disproof of archaeology or of the history it allows (*Philosophical Discourse*, 278). Even if one construed Foucault's archaeology as positing a strong relativism, in which the status of all propositions of all sciences were called into question by the fact that consistency with the rules of a discursive formation was a necessary and sufficient condition for the formulation of a proposition, this would not make discursive formations ontologically impossible. Even articulations of such formations could be accurate, though one could not base their accuracy on any system that would extract accuracy from entrapment within historical formation.

And Foucault's theory is not relativist in this strong sense. It neither commits one to the presumption that knowledge does not exist, nor even to an argument that one could never know that some specific items of knowledge are in fact knowledge. The fact that discursive formations determine which statements can exist and which cannot makes them necessary but hardly sufficient conditions for knowledge statements to come into existence. They limit the kinds of things we can know and those limits may be more or less expansive, but their background role in enabling and excluding various categories of statements does not exclude specific allowed statements from being accurate and being held because they are accurate. Foucault's archaeology does not even limit our ability to establish some forms of grounding criteria for distinguishing true from false statements within particular sciences. For instance, let us posit with *Order of Things* that organicism is a determining condition of the modern discursive formation that in actuality holds together biology, economics, and linguistics. Let us further posit, with Foucault, that this organicism, as it enables the idea that human being can become a field of knowledge, is, as he would say, merely a fold in history, doomed to disappear like a face in the sand at the edge of the ocean. And, finally, let us posit that Darwinian evolution as the transformation of species according to biological laws inherent in a life-process, rather than according to a pre-existing taxonomy, could not have come into being without the emergence of the modern period and its organicism. These positions represent the strongest claims Foucault makes for his discursive formations and their appearance and disappearance. And yet they do not show that Darwinian evolution does not in fact describe accurately the way transformation of species occurs. They do not show that the theory has no evidential grounds outside of the discursive formation of organicism and that its truth will not survive the modern period on its own terms. And, in fact, Foucault asserted numbers of times that the positive existence of discursive formations does not call into question the scientificity of any particular science (see, for instance, *Archaeology*, 181).[29] The relation Foucault claims between power and knowledge works in exactly the same way, so when I turn to Foucault's theory of power, we may pass over the question of relativism with regard to it fairly quickly (the accusation of cryptonormativism, however, works rather differently and will need its own discussion).

The real contradiction in Foucault's archaeology is not in his ostensible postmodern relativism but in something like a confusion in the picture he gives us of his stances. On the one hand, relativist or not, the narrative of *Order of Things* and the methodological explanations of *Archaeology of Knowledge* do seem to propose an historicism that, if it does not claim that separate historical periods are entirely closed off from the knowledge of all other periods, is still fairly radical in the implications of the closure it insists upon between differing discursive formations. Although one can clear him logically of easy charges of relativism, the theory of discursive formations does draw a picture of historical conditions limiting knowledge claims and calling into question even more pointedly the human sciences that arose in the wake of the Enlightenment. As Dickens's Mrs. Gradgrind might say, there is relativism somewhere in the room, even if we cannot be sure that it is his. At the same time, as we have seen, Foucault cultivates a tone of extreme distance. Although he posits that one cannot exit one's own discursive formation, his analysis of the death of man certainly seems to suggest that he has exited the period of organicism that produced human being as a subject of knowledge, even as he can only declare the end of that period to be near. And Nietzsche, in the reading of him suggested by *Order of Things*, seems to have stepped outside this formation while it was in full flourish. Indeed, Foucault's expressed desire to "write the history of the present" (*Discipline*, 31) surely carries the suggestion that he means to step outside the present, to treat it as if it were already history. And although one might argue that *Discipline and Punish* represents a shift from Foucault's archaeological to his genealogical period, the ambition to treat the present as if it were a past one could see whole pretty clearly structures the treatment of the human sciences in *Order of Things*. And, regardless of whether there is a logical contradiction here or whether it could be logically recuperated, there does seem something clearly incommensurable about drawing a picture of a historicism with no exit and at the same time writing from a Hegelian perspective of absolute spirit that sees the present in its totality.

The recuperation of this contradiction takes us back finally to my claim for the importance of aesthetics in understanding how to take Foucault's archaeology. We may start by taking more literally Deleuze's statement about Foucault's archaeology: "Foucault presents a theatre of statements, or a sculpture made from articulable elements, 'monuments' and not 'documents'" (*Foucault*, 54). If we take seriously the notion that we should see the archives as theater or sculpture, this would entail that Foucault sees them as designating a purposiveness without reference to purpose, the apprehension of a meaningful form, about which one reserves judgment as to whether the meaning is actually there or the form is just a randomly perceived pattern with insignificant natural causes. The aesthetic element of the response inheres both in the apprehension of material appearance as meaningful and in the recognition that that meaningfulness may be mere appearance. I want to argue, first, that there is ample justification in Foucault for taking his formations in this way; second, that it connects his "historicism" with his tonal distance by taking that distance as a constructed aesthetic indifference, and then that this aesthetic construction of Foucault in fact makes sense of what he has been trying to do from *Histoire de la folie* through *Order of Things*. This explanation will then prepare a similar aesthetic explanation of Foucault's theory of power.

We may start by quoting the whole sentence in which Foucault makes the famous claim about writing the history of the present: "I would like to write the history of this prison with all the political investments of the body that it gathers together in its closed architecture. Will this be a pure anachronism? No, if one means by that writing the history of the past in the terms of the present. Yes, if one means writing the history of the present" (*Discipline*, 30–31).[30] Foucault does not think he is judging the past with the conceptual terms of the present because he does not think he is writing about the past at all. He is writing about the contemporary prison as if he were writing its history. To make sense of this claim, we must take the history of the prison outlined in the book as an aesthetic spectacle whose significance is its embodiment of an alternative view of the purpose of prisons (one might say their "real" purpose, except that since the history is accepted as anachronistically directed at the current situation, one must bracket that judgment as at least not verified by the history offered). This passage fairly clearly claims that the importance of history in Foucault is not its historicity but the distance it affords that allows the historical view of the present.

Nor do I think this is a position that Foucault moved to in moving away from discussing discursive formations after *Archaeology of Knowledge*. It would be more accurate to say that that book hardened the concept of discursive formations into empirical positivities as it gave a methodological explanation of the three books that preceded it. Even in that book, as we will see, the ultimate position is one of a distance that calls into question the status of the formations. But in *Order of Things*, Foucault's real interest in creating a perspective through the concept of the formations is clearer. For one thing, the book's opening, with Borges, establishes the impossibility of actually thinking within the space of an absolutely alien taxonomy:

The monstrous quality that runs through Borges's enumeration consists, on the contrary, in the fact that the common ground on which such meetings are possible has itself been destroyed. What is impossible is not the propinquity of things listed, but the very site on which their propinquity would be possible. . . . Where else could they be juxtaposed except in the non-space of language? Yet, though language can spread them before us, it can do so only in an unthinkable space. (*Order of Things*, xvi–xvii)

Foucault offers the text by Borges as quite explicitly the inspiration for seeing the seemingly strange concatenations of superstition and observation of past ages not as primitive approaches to modern clear knowledge but as systems of thought of which we have lost the coherence. But if it is impossible to think the taxonomy of a lost system, if we must think through our own taxonomies and discursive formations, then although we could posit the alienness of a past system, we could hardly quite describe it.

Unsurprisingly, then, when Foucault notes the irrevocable passing of the Renaissance, he attributes our ability to recover how it thought to literature. He first states that the Renaissance was the last age "in which the signification of signs did not exist because it was absorbed into the Sovereignty of the Like."[31] Claiming that nothing any longer at all resembles this situation, he then offers an exception: "Nothing, except perhaps literature . . . 'literature', as it was constituted and so designated on the threshold of the modern age, manifests, at a time when it was least expected, the re-appearance of the living being of language" (*Order of Things*, 43). Similitude may be gone as a knowledge formation, but it remains in a literature thought of as "the living being of language." Thus we can see the past knowledge as part of a system by using a literary concept as the model for the system. Indeed, although I have not seen it remarked on, all of Foucault's period labels refer to a mode of linguistic or aesthetic designation: certainly similitude and representation but, if organicism is to be taken as the ruling concept of the modern period, that one as well. In effect, the orders of things the book designates are forms of literary reference. To say that the discursive formations are posed as aesthetic forms does not deny them any reality, but it does deny them real historicist intent.[32]

But what would be the point of taking Foucault's archaeology in this way? Why would he propose such a complicated edifice as an aesthetic construct? Construing the archival analysis as the construction of a perspective rather than the unearthing of an archaeological positivity recuperates possible contradictions in Foucault at the expense of recuperating all the historicism out of his ideas. To answer that question, we must first return to Foucault's counter-Enlightenment worldview, discussed in the first section, and then place that in the context of a large-scale view of the narrative purposes of the histories he writes. In common with the Continental postmodern interrogation of the Enlightenment's establishment of reason on the basis of a properly considered form of consciousness, Foucault means to enclose reason and Enlightened consciousness back within the unstable world of psychology and history, to relabel them as just other forms of limited perspectives. In contrast to more purely metaphysical critiques that followed Nietzsche and Heidegger in questioning the methods or assumptions with which reason sought to ground itself, though, he wants to depict the Enlightenment move toward reason as a historical process, one whose unreasoned motivations history allows us to see around. The reason for this difference is that, in contrast to Derrida, for instance, who wants to undo what might be thought of as modern philosophy's overweening ambition to found all knowledge in a transcendental act of consciousness, Foucault cares more about the way that consciousness enables human being to become a matter of empirical knowledge and the way that knowledge constrains possibilities of self-fashioning. Accordingly, even in his work from *Histoire de la folie* through *Archaeology of Knowledge*, Foucault was never really concerned either with the history of science or with the sociology of all knowledge. He calmly allowed mathematics a special status as a system of thought that founds its own scientificity outside history (*Archaeology*, 188), and implicitly accepted the status of physiology, chemistry, and microbiology as sciences, while recognizing that the fields he studied had not always crossed this threshold (*Archaeology*, 181). And much later, he stipulated that if one wanted to know the relations between power and knowledge, one could not start, at least, with physics and chemistry, because that would place the bar of explanation too high. In terms of scientific knowledge, Foucault cannot be considered a relativist at all, unless having no very worked out position is equal to holding a relativist position. He really is indifferent to science except as he sees it as functioning as power and constraint. He does not want to unmask science as mere ideology (see the discussion of knowledge and ideology, which allows something to be both ideology and knowledge in *Archaeology*, 184–186). He wants to show how it constrains even when true.

The constraint of knowledge is the constant theme of his narratives. Wanting to loosen the grip that he thinks knowledge claims have on human self-definition, he wants to show how they work within history. This entailed the writing of historical narratives that reconstrued moments usually written as change toward progressively greater knowledge as shifts toward merely different categorizations of knowledge that allowed different forms of constraining definition. This narrative direction preceded its formalization into an archaeology and survived Foucault's explicit use of archaeology as a method. In *Histoire de la folie*, for instance, Foucault faulted the usual historical narrative, whereby the study of madness was humanized and became a science in the nineteenth century. Instead, he offered a reconstruction of the shift between the classical age and the modern as entailing new categorizations and definitions of madness. And these looked no less arbitrary than those that preceded them; creating asylums, modern psychology merely reconfigured where confinement would take place. In *Birth of the Clinic*, Foucault's least polemically charged work, he still opposed a narrative whereby medicine became anatomical as it became more scientific. In its place, he describes a move from observations of the surface of the body as the place where signs of disease were revealed, to observations of internal organs, as a view of organic disease replaced the earlier taxonomy and led to a revival of anatomical research. We have seen how *Order of Things* replaces a description of discovery in the fields of economics, linguistics, and natural sciences at the beginning of the nineteenth century with a narrative of a shift from representation to organicism that led to the rise of the human sciences. *Discipline and Punish* famously opposes the view that the end of torture as punishment was a progress in humanization. It proposes instead a shift from the notion in a monarchical state that punishment declared the king's power over the body of the criminal to the concept, in the disciplinary state, that punishment reformed the criminal by confining him even more tightly into a situation that oversaw and regularized all his movements. Finally, *History of Sexuality: An Introduction* also notoriously opposed to a narrative of liberation from sexual repression in the twentieth century the description of the rise, from the eighteenth century, of a science of sexuality that both defined and confined human being by defining the body's pleasures as the psyche's desires.[33] These books may have large methodological differences among them, but they tell the same story of the rise of the human sciences as the development of a new system of constraint. It is the definition of that narrative that the methodology serves.

From *Histoire de la folie* through *Archaeology of Knowledge*, one sees an increasing attempt to formalize this narrative picture into a coherent capturing of knowledge within history. First, Foucault abandons the notion of an alternative epistemology in madness; then he abandons the structuralism of *Birth of the Clinic*. Finally, in *Order of Things*, he offers an explicit concept of a history of contingent systems that would capture the knowledge they codified within the histories of their emergence. Even at the height of this move toward a formalization of what he was doing into a historical methodology, though, Foucault never shifted his real interest. He always wanted to articulate a historical picture that would let him step outside of the human sciences and see them as contingent historical events far more than he wanted to step outside of knowledge as a philosophical concept. In *Archaeology*, for instance, discussing the unities of discourses and explaining the reason for privileging his discussion of the human sciences, Foucault also indicates the reason that drives his largest argument:

Lastly, how can we be sure that we will not be left in the grip of insufficiently reflected upon unities and systems concerning the speaking subject, the subject of

the discourse, or the author of the text, in short, all of the anthropological categories. Unless, perhaps, we consider all the statements out of which these categories are constituted—all the statements that have chosen the subject of discourse
(their own subject) as their "object" and have undertaken to deploy it as their field
of knowledge?

This explains the *de facto* privilege that I have accorded to those discourses
that, to put it very schematically, define the "sciences of man." (*Archaeology*, 30,
translation modified)

Foucault immediately goes on to call this privilege a provisional one. And
the passage, at one level, surely means to offer another explanation for why
Foucault limits himself in his history of knowledge to fields of uncertain
scientificity. Still, the picture of the researcher in the grip of unreflected
upon unities puts before us that form of constraint through human knowledge that Foucault designs the archaeology to allow us to see.

I have said that the postmodern critique of Enlightenment epistemology intends to depict that epistemology's reason as ungrounded, that
that picture of the world is a logically possible one but that it cannot be established solely with the reason it means to destabilize. It depends on the
presentation of a picture of what such a world looks like. That picture can
only be presented by giving us the means to see askew the world the Enlightenment presents. Foucault's instrument for turning Enlightenment
epistemology askew is the archaeology that reconstructs its advances in
knowledge as recategorizations of what kinds of information will constitute
knowledge. In suggesting that, whether explicitly or not, Foucault construes discursive formations as designs perceived by attributing purposiveness without purpose to them, I do not mean to suggest that he invents
them out of whole cloth or that they are arbitrary and that one would do
as well as another. Kant thought that people would construe a bird's song
as expressing contentment with nature, even though they wouldn't care
whether the bird intended that meaning (and would probably know it did
not), because that apprehension of the song accorded with a certain view of
the world as benevolently meaningful and might even be, within limits,
authorized by that worldview. In the same way, Foucault's formations are
justified by the worldview they present rather than by exemplifying some
sound epistemological foundation that distinguishes them from other,
flawed history. The perspective Foucault takes toward them, the moment
of uneasy distance allowed by Borges's impossible taxonomy, is at once the
perspective that allows them to emerge into perception, the perspective

whose skepticism at what they represent allows them not to function as a new foundation and the perspective whose skepticism about Enlightenment knowledge of human being the formations also embody. In effect, they operate precisely as do the indifferent embodiments discussed in the last chapter.

Critics of Foucault almost universally see a shift occurring, between *Archaeology of Knowledge* and *Discipline and Punish*, from the archaeological method to a new genealogical mode, one that would escape the epistemological problems of the archaeology.[34] The shift itself is inescapable in the sense that Foucault ceases to talk about knowledge formations and begins to be concerned more directly with power. This shift in concern no longer made of central interest the archaeology as a methodological statement about freeing perception from the constraints of Enlightenment knowledge of human being. But there is less a real methodological shift occurring here than a shift in what aspect of the Enlightenment now functions as Foucault's primary target. His definitions of what he means by genealogy are dispersed and, though coherent, hardly amount to proposing a considered method of analysis. Largely, he seems to want to follow Nietzsche in giving institutions and ideas a new and destabilizing context by proposing for them a redefined history, and as we have seen the archaeology was already one mode of doing that. But there is an important shift in topic in Foucault's later work. If Foucault's real point, as I have argued, was to free human activity from the constraints knowledge put on it, one would have to say that the reception of *Order of Things* and *Archaeology of Knowledge*, the questions about what kind of history he was writing, about whether one could have knowledge sufficient to ground political action, and so on, would have seemed to him, as many of the interviews from this period indicate, to have missed his point. The turn directly toward power really just clarifies Foucault's continuing concern with the Enlightenment as a form of constraint by making its focus not Enlightenment knowledge but the analysis of the bourgeois state and its institutions as new forms of constraint rather than as liberations from the monarchical state.

The concept of aesthetic form plays a particularly vital role in understanding Foucault's theory of power and the narratives that theory constructs in *Discipline and Punish* and *History of Sexuality* because it clears up many of the misunderstandings that the misconstructions of that theory have caused. Foucault explicitly posits a picture of the world in which power is inescapable, unlocalizable, and frequently working both covertly

through juridical forms that ostensibly embody justice and through constructions of human being that seem like fields of knowledge. In both
cases, in our participation in a state that organizes our bodies and behav-
iors and in our acceptance that our beings are determined by our sexual
identity, we are under the control of a disciplinary system that seems omnipresent because it inheres neither in a state nor in a psychological drive.
Marx, of course, thought that the juridical forms of the bourgeois state actually protected the economic domination of the bourgeois class rather
than embodying justice. But, at least under most readings, he did have a
norm from which to make this claim, a posited state of unalienated working-class consciousness that connected up with the basic realities of how
economic production worked; there is available in his argument both a
goal to work toward and an unmystified consciousness that would see that
goal. Nietzsche, on the other hand, did see a will to power as a basic element of consciousness from which there was no exit, and this denied him
a theory of justice. But he was not looking for such a theory. He sought,
rather, a way of apprehending a value to life that he did not see as based on
any justification or consolation that went beyond the act of living. Since
his will to power was a psychological drive, by not trying to justify it one
could choose coherently to live in accord with its drives.[35] Thus, both these
formative views of the genealogy of power can offer consequent choices.

Foucault, in contrast to both, seems to see power as fundamental, in
the manner of a psychological drive, yet external and constraining in the
manner of a state arrangement. On the one hand, he insists that we must
decentralize our notion of power, claiming famously that "in political
thought and analysis, we still have not cut off the head of the king" (*History of Sexuality*, 88–89). On the other hand, this power that is all around
us is also external to us and affects the way we think at every level:

The question is often posed as to how, before and after the Revolution a new foundation was given to the right to punish. And no doubt the answer is to be found
in the theory of the contract. But it is perhaps more important to ask the reverse
question: how were people made to accept the power to punish, or quite simply,
when punished, tolerate being so. The theory of the contract can only answer this
question by the fiction of a juridical subject giving to others the power to exercise
over him the right that he himself possesses over them. It is highly probable that
the great carceral continuum, which provides a communication between the
power of discipline and the power of law, and extends without interruption from
the smallest coercions to the longest penal detention, constituted the technical and
real, immediately material counterpart of that chimerical granting of the right to
punish. (*Discipline and Punish*, 303)

Because of a "carceral continuum," we allow ourselves to be coerced and punished. Though the state makes use of this willingness, it does not cause it or exhaust its reach, which starts with the smallest coercions. If Foucault has cut off the head of the king, he seems to have replaced it with an invisible, multi-headed beast. The usual view of power in Foucault, evoked by passages such as the one above, is that, although it is invisible and not attached to any single person, class, or institution, it is nevertheless a unified, coherent, external, constraining force that controls all aspects of our existence without our awareness.

It is precisely this view that I want to contest; it has led to accusations that Foucault denies all human agency. Even when he says explicitly that inherent in every power relation is the possibility to resist it (*History of Sexuality*, 95), given this larger picture of power, this seems only to mean that, while resistance is possible, it is merely a part of the larger workings of power's control of us. Espousing a lack of agency would not itself be logically disabling, though. It might be the fact that the conditions of our existence preclude our having meaningful ability to effect change. Since Foucault not only regularly says that we can resist local expressions of power, and since the point of his late works seems pretty clearly to get us to resist it, however, critics have also found his position incoherent. The most articulated version of this charge is Habermas's charge of cryptonormativism (*Philosophical Discourse of Modernity*, 282), which finds Foucault guilty of arguing that there are no norms, only power, and simultaneously of positing norms to ground the resistance to it that he calls for.[36] Nor, to the extent that Foucault holds the position about power described above and also espouses resistance, can his position be recuperated, in the manner of his position about the history of knowledge, either by appealing to an ontological possibility of this picture beyond the contradictions of language or by arguing that, just as his contextualism of knowledge does not imply that there is no knowledge, the omnipresence of power does not entail the absence of ethically preferable positions. It might be coherent to depict a world in which there was no outside to power, even conceptually. But it is not clear how, in such a world, one could coherently espouse any basis beyond mere preference or psychological satisfaction for choosing to exert power against power to achieve one aim rather than another. Equally, if one takes it that the omnipresence of power, with no external norms available, in fact means, by definition, the presence of unjustified coercion—without norms, what would create justification?—then one obviously cannot argue the coexistence of justice and power in the manner of arguing the coexistence of a discursive formation and accurate knowledge.

It is at least clear from reading his interviews that Foucault, far from denying agency, thought his attitude toward power enabled meaningful action more than did theories that demanded the ability to mount total resistance. Because he did not think that power emanated from a single place, he did not believe that the only successful resistance had to be total. Indeed, he thought that the belief that only a resistance completely untouched by all institutional co-option was a real one was a recipe for denying successful opposition to some specific oppression that one could change:

> As soon as something succeeds and is realized, they cry that it has been co-opted by the established regime! In short, they put themselves in a position never to be co-opted, which is to say they will always be checked. . . . In contrast, the struggle against quotidian power has the goal of succeeding. They believe truly in winning. If they think that the construction of an airport or a power station at such and such a place is bad, they block it right to the end. They do not refuse to content themselves with success like the extreme left, which says: "Our movement has advanced two steps but the revolution has lost one." Success is success. (*Dits*, II, 529–530)

Clearly Foucault did not think that because resistance was part of the system of power, it was therefore co-opted by it. It would be more accurate to say that he thought that resistance was effective precisely because it was part of that system. After all, what would a resistance that was in no relation to power be able to achieve? The fact that he believed successful resistance possible only at a local level does not reduce its effectiveness, since power itself only exists at specific sites of struggle. One cannot overturn a unified essence of power because such an essence simply does not exist. Of course, the possibility of effective resistance does not show that there is a basis for engaging in it beyond personal preference, that resistance will lead to some better state of things. In other words, the fact that one can do something does not provide a norm that tells one that it should be done.

The answer to this question begins in the recognition that power is not an invisible essence. The basis for this reading is the desire to make sense of the coherence and system to Foucault's sense of disciplinary power, given his refusal to see power as coming from a single site, source, or intention. But in Foucault, there is no Power as such, just specific actions that occur among people: "The exercise of power is not simply a relation between 'partners,' individual or collective; it is a mode of action of some things on others. This means, of course, that there is no such thing as the power or as power that would exist globally, in a solid or diffused state, concentrated or distributed; power exists only as something exercised by some upon others" (*Dits*, II, 1055). He goes on to insist that power derives neither from the consent of the governed nor from violence. It is the relation of free people acting upon each other. For Foucault, power is everywhere because it is the field in which we move, like the space around us. Power is a necessary constraint on people in the way the properties of space are. We can do any number of things in space, but we do so always within its laws. One can no more get outside power than outside space because it does not exist as a thing to get outside. It is where we are. On the other hand, just as we build things that fly by obeying natural laws, the fact of power is a condition, not a direct constraint of particular actions.

Within such a conception of power, neither a psychological drive for domination nor the constraint exercised by the state, but a description of the ways people relate to each other to achieve certain ends, it makes no more sense to want a norm standing outside of power than it does to want a place to move in that stands outside of space. But by the same token, power is not in an absolute opposition to justice. It is not a state to be remedied. In a more or less direct response to Habermas's theories, he says:

The idea that there could be a state of communication that would be such that the games of truth could circulate without obstacles, without constraints and without coercive effects seems to be utopian. It is precisely not to see that power relations are not something bad in themselves from which one must free oneself. I believe that there cannot be societies without power relations, if one understands them as strategies by which individuals try to direct, to determine the conduct of others. The problem, then, is not to try to dissolve them in the utopia of perfectly transparent communication, but to give oneself the rules of law, the techniques of administration and also the morality, the *ethos*, the practice of self, that would permit us to play the game of power with the minimum possible of domination. (*Dits*, II, 1546)

It may be that in the opposition between power and its sub-category, domination, Foucault reestablishes in other terms, and indeed not at all cryptically, an opposition between just relations and coerced relations. The choice, however, is always among various and changing possibilities of relations. Foucault objects to concepts of justice as outside power because he does not think there can be a unitary, transparent mode of relationship any more than relations of power are unitary, not because he thinks there are no bases at all for choosing some relations over others. One could still object that the concept of domination as an undesirable sub-category of power itself covertly imports universal norms. But that question starts to look merely formal next to what I think is the real problem in the connection between these statements in interviews and the view of power given in the books they respond to.

That problem is that power in those books seems not diffusive and local at all. It is not simply a description of the various ways people relate in a society, as the laws of gravity are a description of the ways bodies move in space. It is only too coherent, uni-directional, and threatening. The passage from *Discipline and Punish*, cited above, makes only too explicit that if power is the nominal label for a variously manifested force of relationships among people, nevertheless, power in the modern state does operate toward a describable and threatening end and does seem omnipresent. In order to understand how these two views of power (as the word for various relations and as the description of a very deliberate, pervasive aim of disciplining and controlling) cohere, one needs again to step back from arguments over details of Foucault's theory and look at the picture of modern society he meant to create. To begin with, he shares neither the Marxist position that the bourgeois liberal state is merely the protection of bourgeois power through the ideological creation of principles of "justice" that facilitate that protection, nor the view, with which he is often connected, that the liberal state is a system of internalized coercions that are the cost of the individual freedoms that that state promises and even endows. We have already seen his distinction from the first position. The distinction with the second starts with the fact that Foucault almost never discusses liberalism and its theory, and in the one place where he does, he sees it as a response to the modern state, an attempt to put limits on governmentality that fails only because, in order to achieve its ends, it must become part of a political life that is governmentality under another name:

Rather, therefore, than a more or less coherent doctrine, rather than a politics pursuing a certain number of more or less definite goals, I would be tempted to see in liberalism a form of critical reflection on the practice of government. . . . The question of liberalism, understood as a question of "governing too much," has been one of the constant dimensions of this recent phenomenon in Europe, which appeared, seemingly, first in England: that is to say, "political life." It is even one of its constituent elements to the extent that political life exists when governmental practice is limited in its possible excess by the fact that it is the object of a public debate over its "good or bad," over its "too much or too little." (*Dits*, II, 824–825)[37]

For Foucault, disciplinary power is not the secret instrument of the liberal state. It is rather the outgrowth of a new knowledge of human being as it is put to use by various groups in various ways. The rise of disciplinary power is one with the rise of human being as an object of knowledge, although Foucault now places the beginning of this process farther back in time. In the seventeenth and eighteenth centuries, government became focused not on overseeing the distribution of feudal power, which was for Foucault, the basis of the concept of sovereignty (*Dits*, II, 185), but on controlling the state of its population, which was now discovered as central to the social health:

It was discovered that population was that over which power was exercised. And population meant what? It did not mean simply a numerous group of humans, but living beings, crossed through, commanded, ruled by processes, by biological laws. A population had a birth-rate, a rate of mortality, an age curve, an age pyramid, a morbidity, a state of health. A population could perish or could, on the contrary, flourish. (*Dits*, II, 1012)

In effect, in discovering population, society was finding the laws of human being—rates of birth, forms of health and morbidity—as the subject of management. Controlling the health and state of a population, though, meant that power had to be more far-reaching, more subtle, more dispersed. Thus discipline, manifested by various groups in various ways, to produce positive ends, begins to replace juridical power: "Power became materialist. It ceased to be juridical. It had to deal with real things, which were bodies, life" (*Dits*, II, 1013). For Foucault, the mistake of the movement for sexual liberation or individual liberation in the nineteenth century was not that liberation itself was a delusion. It was to base itself on the concept of life that was the foundation of disciplinary power in the first place: "Moreover, against this power that was still new in the nineteenth century, the forces that resisted relied for support on the very thing that it invested, that is, on life and man as a living being" (*History of Sexuality*, 144).

In effect, Foucault binds together the two elements of the postmodern critique of the Enlightenment foundations of knowledge and political liberty. Enlightenment knowledge, as a knowledge of human being, constrained the possibilities of functioning beyond the limits of subjectivity as knowledge defined its limits. Moreover, consequent on the knowledge of human being was the power to adjust it in the best way possible for social functioning, of whose ends that knowledge informed us. And just as the distance provided by construing an archive of discursive formations that turned modern knowledge into a category of thinking as well as a collection of accurate statements gave a freedom from the knowledge of human being, construing powers as coherent but not sovereign and unitary gives the possibility of identifying something sufficiently coherent to resist while in fact making it something one can resist without the necessity of transcendental norms that would necessitate the form of knowledge Foucault meant to resist in the first place.

These necessities determine the extremely paradoxical description of power Foucault gives in his discussion of it in *History of Sexuality*. There he first describes power as both omnipresent and yet merely a word given to hold together numbers of different effects: "Power is everywhere; not because it embraces everything, but because it comes from everywhere. . . . One needs to be nominalistic, no doubt: power is not an institution, and not a structure; neither is it a certain strength we are endowed with; it is the name that one attributes to a complex strategical situation in a particular society" (93). Just in case one does not find sufficiently contradictory the notion of something that is only a name and yet a name for a real "situation," Foucault insists that this situation has ends but does not derive either from causes or the will of a subject:

> Power relations are both intentional and nonsubjective. If in fact they are intelligible, this is not because they are the effect of another instance that "explains" them, but rather because they are imbued, through and through, with calculation: there is no power that is exercised without a series of aims and objectives. But this does not mean that it results from the choice or decision of an individual subject. (94–95)

These quotations come from a series of assertions that are offered as propositions that one begins with rather than conclusions one draws from evidence. And one can only make sense of them in that way. They align with Kant's purposiveness without purpose both in the paradoxicality of the order that they assert and in their recuperation of that paradox, in that they are proposed as a way of looking at things rather than a quality of objects that have been shown to possess them. But taken in that way, they give force and coherence to the "histories" Foucault offers in *Discipline and Punish* and *History of Sexuality*.

It is easy to see the element of *Discipline and Punish* that insists on the omnipresent imprisoning quality of disciplinary power, barely distinguished in that book from carceral power.[38] But the scornful tone Foucault uses to describe the workings of the disciplinary society pretty clearly implies that his point is to incite resistance. Here he describes the techniques of discipline:

These were always meticulous, often tiny techniques, but they had their importance: because they defined a certain mode of detailed political infestation of the body, a "new micro-physics" of power; and because, since the seventeenth century, they had constantly reached out to ever broader domains, as if they tended to cover the entire social body. Small bits of trickery endowed with a great power of diffusion, subtle arrangements, apparently innocent, but profoundly suspicious, mechanisms that obeyed economies too shameful to be acknowledged, or pursued petty forms of coercion—it was nevertheless they that brought about the mutation of the punitive system, at the threshold of the contemporary period. (139; translation modified)

In the face of such descriptions, it is insufficient to discuss Foucault's conception of power in terms of its inescapability. This passage does not describe an enemy too powerful to be opposed but a force of deceit simply waiting to be exposed. One need only understand the ruses and pettiness of quotidian discipline as shameful acts of coercion, one might think, to begin to believe that one could well confront them. And if *Discipline and Punish* solicits that confrontation, *History of Sexuality* shows how possible it is.

Because *History of Sexuality* attacks the "repressive hypothesis" and thus questions the ideology of sexual liberation, it is almost universally taken as the depiction of a power/knowledge one cannot escape. The book makes clear the connection between the early theory of discursive formation, the connection between knowledge and constraint, and the ways these things lead to power: "And finally, the essential aim will not be to determine whether these discursive productions and these effects of power lead one to formulate the truth about sex, or on the contrary falsehoods designed to conceal that truth, but rather to bring out the 'will to knowledge' that serves as both their support and instrument" (11–12). Discursive productions and effects of power are nearly synonymous and both derive from a will to knowledge (this was the title of the book in French). And these connections might lead further to the response that Foucault means in his depiction of the rise of sexuality as a field of knowledge and constraint to outline an inescapable power. But this reading seems to me to miss the obvious comedy of the book, the way Foucault depicts knowledge of sexuality as an absurdity whose power and success are equally absurd. Rather than it being too large to conceive of or confront, it is all too easy to understand and one can confront it at almost any point.

One may miss the comedy in English because of a perhaps necessary solemnization of some of its passages in translation. In reading the opening to the section translated as "The Deployment of Sexuality," a few notes on the French will make the passage almost Disneyesque. First, the word translated throughout as "deployment"—*dispositif*—more literally means apparatus or mechanism. Second, *le sexe*, which is translated properly enough as "sex," also has as a far more usual meaning in French than in English, of genitals. Third, *bijoux de famille* has the same slang connotation in French as "family jewels" in English. And the Diderot fable about "jewels" is about a magic ring that makes people's "jewels," their genitals, speak. Here is the opening:

> The aim of this series of studies? To transcribe into history the fable of *Les Bijoux indiscrets*.

> Among its many emblems, our society wears that of the talking sex. The sex which one catches unawares and questions, and which, restrained and loquacious at the same time, endlessly replies. One day a certain mechanism, which was so fairy-like that it could make itself invisible, captured this sex and, in a game that combined pleasure and compulsion, and consent with inquisition, made it tell the truth about itself and others as well. (*History of Sexuality*, 77)[39]

In trying to discover the secret of sexuality, for Foucault, we are questioning our genitals and imagining that they will answer, a strange activity that it would at least seem we could abandon. Throughout the book, Foucault depicts what he argues is our attempt to define ourselves through our sexual desires as quaint as much as constraining. It is even more quaint in that, in denying that the ethic of sexual repression in the nineteenth century was a way of controlling destructive energy and making the working classes more amenable to regulated labor, he suggests that the middle class, oddly, chose the ethic as a self-imposition: "it seems that the apparatus of sexuality was not established as a principle of limitation of the pleasures of others by what have traditionally been called the 'ruling classes.' Rather it appears to me that they first tried it on themselves" (122).[40] It would be false to suggest that Foucault thinks that we have merely to stop thinking that we live in a Diderot fable, or a strangely pornographic Disney cartoon in which talking genitals speak deep truths, to free ourselves from the strange notion that we are defined by desires. Since the roots of the notion go back to Christian confession, its hold on us is hardly negligible. But surely the point of this comedy is that resistance to this fantastic form of discipline is hardly impossible.

One could easily have a critique of the disciplinary and the carceral of *Discipline and Punish* and of the disciplinary knowledge of sexuality from the perspective of a position—even merely a conceptual one—free from power, thus avoiding the problems of critiquing from an absence of norms (or opening oneself to the inference of suggesting a powerlessness to resist). Similarly, one could undercut specific claims to knowledge of the human sciences without trying to capture all knowledge under controlling categories of discourse. In each case, though, the critique would not achieve what Foucault wanted. He did not care about demystifying delusory claims to knowledge or undoing power masquerading as knowledge. He wanted to free human agency from the constraints that the claim to define human being (even accurate claims) would create, and at the same time, to maintain for human being the power of self-transformation, which entails accepting power as an inescapable element of life in the world.[41] Foucault's participation in the postmodern attack on the Enlightenment basing knowledge on reason and state power on an essential or original position of freedom may ultimately share a large common ground with Enlightenment liberalism. Like that liberalism, its ultimate aim is individual freedom rather than a justly restructured state, of which it is always suspicious. But its postmodern perspective is necessary to the form of living in a world without teleology—either an end that is known or a utopia one would achieve. And that is the world it intends to depict.[42] Through its construction of discursive formations and power, it gives us the artificial perspective from which to see that world twice over and explicitly after the model of something construed as having purposiveness without purpose.

III. History, Fiction, and Aesthetic Presentation

But what is the difference between arguing that Foucault's claims about discursive formations and power are aesthetically derived and seeing them as *merely* aesthetic, in the sense of a meaningless game? One may pose the question from two different directions, though they will come to the same place. First, what does it do to Foucault's concept of power to see it in terms of the kind of perceived form that Kant called purposiveness without purpose? Kant quite explicitly did not think this contradiction could actually be a property of objects; we see this way only when we are indifferent to the existence of objects. Thus, if we imagine power as an object in the world whose coherence Foucault describes, Charles Taylor's objections seem pertinent: "Purposiveness without purpose requires a certain kind of explanation to be intelligible. The undesigned systematicity has to be related to the purposeful action of agents in a way that we can understand" (Taylor, "Foucault on Freedom," 87). What does it mean to call power "intentional" but "non-subjective," since intention is a property only of subjects? Kant recuperated his contradiction in terms of its being a mode of judgment necessary to thought, and he abandoned the notion that he could use the criterion to say concrete things about objects in the world.[43] But for Foucault to recuperate his concept in the same way, he would have to say about power what Kant says about bird's songs, that they might not actually have the meaning we construe them to have. Alternatively, if his concept of power is to have force, one would think it would have to derive from a cause or an intended end.

The second direction from which to raise the problem is Foucault's willingness, repeated more than once, to label his writing as fiction. These statements first exacerbate but then, I think, finally explain the position. The fullest and most interesting of these statements responds to the suggestion in an interview that *The History of Sexuality* has the quality of fiction:

As to the problem of fiction, it is for me a very important one; I well recognize that I have never written anything but fictions. I don't want, for all that, that it would be outside of the truth. It seems to me possible to make fiction work within truth, to induce truth effects with a fictive discourse, and to work in such a way that the discourse of truth incites, produces something which did not exist before; it therefore "fictions." One "fictions" history, beginning with a political reality that makes it true; one "fictions" a politics that did not exist before beginning with a historical truth. (*Dits*, II, 236)[44]

On the one hand, that fiction and truth are not mutually contradictory is hardly an original discovery. Using narrative representations of events recognized as not having taken place to exemplify or symbolize an abstract truth hardly counts as a postmodern innovation. And, of course, fictions also do frequently narrate events that have taken place.[45] The problem, though, is that if one accepts Foucault's books as historical fiction, in which we take the discursive formations and disciplinary power as fictive representations, it is hard to know how to construe the truth status of even the political consequences he wants to draw from those representations. If there is no modern formation of organicism that allows the creation of the human sciences, then in what sense can we free ourselves from them by learning to see them as enabled by a contingent category of history? If disciplinary power is a fiction, then how does it constrain us with the discourse of sexuality? The admission of fictiveness seems to give a sharper edge to Taylor's claims about seeing power as having purposiveness without purpose.

But Foucault actually makes a slightly different claim about how his fictions work. In addition to inducing truth effects with fiction, he argues that one can use the discourse of truth to create new things, which he describes as producing and fictioning. Thus a political reality could be used to fiction (in the sense of both produce and invent) a history, and it would make that history true. In the same way, a history could fiction, produce, or invent a politics. In other words, the present reality of a situation would give truth to the history one asserts as having stood behind it, and the historical perspective one describes would create a political possibility that did not seem available before. These statements accord well with Foucault's desire to write the history of the present, to give us the sense of seeing our own categories of thought to be as unlikely as a Borgesian taxonomy. But we are still left with the question of what it means to call a "history" true merely because it could lead up to a political reality, or in what sense we can create a new political possibility based on a history that would be true in such a way.

To answer this question and the larger one with which this section started—what value do Foucault's arguments have if they are based on aesthetic form—we must return to the prior chapter's discussion of symbolic embodiment and Duchamp's *Fountain*, that artwork that looks just like a urinal. All we need of that discussion, though, is that the object Duchamp sent to be exhibited was an actual urinal and, although different urinals have served as the same artwork, none of them were false or illusory ones—nor could they have been for the work to have had the import it did. In other words, there is no necessary contradiction between the aesthetic presentation of an object and that object existing, even in the mode in which it is presented. It simply brackets the claim that the meaning we attach to the presentation is one we know to inhere in the object. When Kant gives as an example of beauty our sense that a bird's song expresses contentment with existence, regardless of whether the song actually originates from contentment or not, his point is that our judgment of beauty makes no claim about the actual status of the import we give to the object,

194   *Foucault's Aesthetics*

nor a claim about whether it does or does not have that import. In the case of Duchamp, the urinal's import as an artwork exceeds its purpose as a urinal—and thus exemplifies a Kantian beautiful object—but also depends on it. If we take Foucault's use of the word *fiction* to be more or less synonymous with aesthetic presentation—and the claims of the passage make the meaning of false representation impossible—we can start to make sense of Foucault's claims that he uses fictions to produce truth as well as using truths to produce fictions that then become truths, in the sense of things that now have existence though they did not have existence before.

Taking Foucault's histories of discursive formations and of disciplinary power as aesthetic presentations—in the manner, if not of *Fountain* or a Warhol Campbell's Soup can, perhaps of one of the fictions of Borges that look like literary criticism or even a transcription of *Don Quixote*—neither confirms nor denies the accuracy of the presentations as historical descriptions, but changes the way we interpret them.[46] The presentation of the relationship between fields of knowledge in terms of the continuities among and the discontinuities between discursive formations embodies a view of knowledge—at least in the human sciences—as historical constructions, from which perspective we can separate ourselves from the ends set for us by contemporary human sciences. Whether the formations Foucault outlines correspond to actual past formations, or whether the readings of events he offers in explication of these formations correspond to events in the past in detail, their reading of the past takes on the justification they have in terms of the persuasiveness of the readings they allow of contemporary thought. Thus, many readers of Foucault seem willing to accept the theory of discursive formations without worrying about the status of the actual formations *Order of Things* identifies as having characterized the Renaissance and the classical age. The fact that Foucault cannot give a good account of how disciplinary power has acquired its coherence and purposive constraint, similarly, will not be disabling for those for whom his description of a disseminated but coherent power explains the forms of constraint inherent in certain fields of knowledge and in certain social institutions. In both cases, there is a connection between the status of the history and that of the political position, whereby the persuasiveness of one gives at least interest to the other. This is why the histories have been so resistant, for many, to the serious criticism they have received in terms of their historical detail, and why the descriptions of power seem telling even though they do not give a worked-out account of how to distinguish between power that dominates and power that does not.

Taking Foucault's works as aesthetic presentations does not deny that they have the status of accurate accounts. As I have said, the fact that we cannot claim that our knowledge about the world is historically constructed without falling into certain formal contradictions does not in fact disprove that the world looks that way and that such kinds of statements describe it. Similarly, while taking all human relationships as inescapably constructed by power will create for the consequences we draw from that, in terms of how we want to manage those relationships, the same kinds of formal contradictions, if the world looked like that, the kinds of choices Foucault outlines would be no less desirable merely because we would have trouble accounting for their foundational base. Obviously, this construction of the works does eliminate any status of the histories as evidence for the epistemological positions Foucault outlines. But descriptions of a world that does not provide transcendental justifications of knowledge or power-free norms of value will, by definition, never have the value of an evidence that stands apart from construction or interpretation. Foucault often describes his books as experiments, as paths to the next book. In particular, he says about *History of Sexuality*:

This book is without demonstrative function. It is there as a prelude, to explore the keyboard and sketch out a little the themes and see how people are going to react, or what are going to be the criticisms, or where the misunderstandings will be, or where people will get angry: it is to make the subsequent volumes, in a way, open to those reactions that I have written this first volume. (*Dits*, II, 236)

Although the books are not all preludes, I think Foucault would say that they are without demonstrative function, and that the way in which his work has developed has been to account for what he has done and the reactions the works have evoked in developing a next step (this is perhaps why so many of his interviews, introductions, and passages in works describe the part all of his past works have had in leading up to the present ones, and why we should not take those descriptions as histories and be disturbed that they are not all identical with each other, but take them as ways of construing the project of the work they lead up to). Nor does it seem to me to diminish the work to take it in this way, though it may diminish some of the methodological claims that have been founded upon it. Given the picture of being in the world that Foucault wants to give us, formal philosophy and its foundational ambitions were closed to him, and an aesthetic presentation's limitation of being unable to function as evidence would not be a large drawback.

There is one further lesson to be drawn from the example of Foucault. I have intended this reading not as a deconstruction of his claims but as an account of them. And, indeed, Foucault's own deep and sympathetic interest in the contemporaneous French literature that paralleled post-structuralist philosophy, as well as his statements about the historicity and fictiveness of his own work, seem to me to make this account more likely than many of his more politically and philosophically attuned commentators might allow.[47] One can readily understand why a postmodernism that wanted to contain the Enlightenment by seeing it as an historical event, an ideological maneuver, or an unjustified philosophical hyperbole would want to include Enlightenment aesthetics within the orbit of this containment. And the readings of aesthetics as covert ideology, my arguments with which I have registered in the notes to the first two chapters of this book, for the most part certainly participate in the project defined as postmodern at the opening of this chapter. But it has also been the argument of those chapters that in order to make a place for aesthetics, both the natural theology of eighteenth-century England and post-Kantian Continental philosophy had to articulate an aesthetics that already created the forms by which that philosophy could be interrogated. I would argue that Foucault did not merely use those forms, but showed their necessity for the kind of interrogation his work exemplifies. To complete that argument, my next chapter will show the importance of that aesthetics to the postmodern sociologist who has done most to argue the ideological effects of autonomous form and aesthetic disinterest, Pierre Bourdieu.

CHAPTER 4

Bourdieu's Aesthetics

I. The Sociology of Aesthetics

Pierre Bourdieu's theoretical project begins—not precisely chrono-logically, but with an intrinsic logic—as the attempt to formulate a method of sociological and anthropological analysis that mediates between simply reproducing the perceptions of the culture studied and a scientific codification of those perceptions that gives them objective shape, but not a shape that corresponds to anything in that culture.[1] Driven by the exigen-cies of that project, Bourdieu turned to defining a series of concepts and concerns that has recently revivified among literary critics and theorists an interest in the sociology of literature. In particular, most centrally in *Distinction: A Social Critique of the Judgment of Taste*, he has offered a power-ful explication of "taste," in all its meanings from choices in art through choices in dress, furniture, and the like, to taste in food, both as a unified subject matter and as a method for producing and reproducing power dif-ferences among social classes. In *Language and Symbolic Power*, he has fo-cused the same analysis on the subject of language, claiming that meaning, both linguistic and literary, depends on the same activities of power and social differentiation.[2] And a series of articles on Flaubert in particular and aesthetics in general again discussed aesthetics and aestheticism in nine-teenth-century France in terms of the same sociological analysis.

All of these works explicitly contest formalist theories of culture, lan-guage, aesthetics, and literature with an analysis that argues the main force of these discourses as creating and maintaining hierarchies of power and domination. Bourdieu himself talks of this analysis as fundamentally transgressive, remarking in the English-language preface to *Distinction* that "although the book transgresses one of the fundamental taboos of the intellectual world, in relating intellectual products and producers to their social conditions of existence—and also, no doubt, *because* it does so—it cannot entirely ignore or defy the laws of academic or intellectual propriety which condemn as barbarous any attempt to treat culture, that present incarnation of the sacred, as an object of science" (xiii). This claim of transgressing was already absurd when Bourdieu made it; his project has been a central one in literary studies for some time. And it corresponds to the postmodern project of even longer date, discussed in the last chapter, which aimed at finding fundamental values of Western society to be ideologically motivated. His science of culture means to show the roots of cultural forms and values in the work of preserving class distinctions. But the claim of his analyses upon our attention was never the novelty of thinking that literature, canon formation, culture, and language have some connection to the manifestation of social power, but the methods he gave for articulating that connection more clearly. Bourdieu, in other words, said with theoretical detail and precision something that literary critics have been looking for a way of saying for some time.

In working out the connections among the various aspects of Bourdieu's theories in this chapter, I do not really want to dispute this central sociological claim in the service of some reformulated formalism. Rather, I want to look at its dependence upon another aspect of the title of this section, not the sociological analysis of aesthetics, but the kind of sociological analysis that aesthetics produces. Without trying to trump Bourdieu by showing that he reproduces the aesthetics he ostensibly contests, I will argue that at crucial moments, at the moments in which he most pointedly moves from the anthropological to the literary and in which he most clearly leads to the uses literary critics have made of him, he uses the aesthetics he simultaneously analyzes. This dependence shows not some formalist problem of infinite reflection, but that the politics that critics want from Bourdieu's analysis of culture can be outlined by them fully only through an analysis of the sociology that determines the turn to such discourse—an analysis that like Bourdieu's is simultaneously aesthetic and sociological.

Both Bourdieu's argument about how culture works and the mode of analysis he applies to culture and aesthetics to make that argument have their roots in the theory of practice that he opposes to anthropological structuralism. To understand the basis of Bourdieu's cultural concerns, then, we must first understand the goal of that theory. He begins by proposing three modes of knowledge of the social world, which exist in a dialectical relationship with each other. The first form, which he variously calls primary or phenomenological, "sets out to make explicit the truth of primary experience of the social world, i.e. all that is inscribed in the relationship of *familiarity* with the familiar environment, the unquestioning apprehension of the social world which, by definition, does not reflect on itself and excludes the question of the conditions of its own possibility" (*Outline*, 3). This mode of knowing is the experience that participants of a particular social world have of it. It is neither available to an observer, since he does not know as a participant, nor describable by a participant without his ceasing to experience it as a participant: "one cannot really *live* the belief associated with profoundly different conditions of existence, that is, with other games and other stakes, still less give others the means of reliving it by the sheer power of discourse" (*Logic of Practice*, 68). Effectively, this primary knowledge creates the subject for research and discourse, but it has no other relationship to theoretical or anthropological knowledge, either as goal or as method.

Bourdieu sees the structuralism that he spends most of his theory criticizing as providing a necessary beginning to anthropological knowledge; it is "a necessary moment in all research," because of "the break with primary experience and the construction of objective relations which it accomplishes" (*Outline*, 72). Structuralism, which Bourdieu also calls objectivism, accomplishes this break by abandoning the impossible task of reproducing primary experience for a description of the connections and relations among the practices it observes without experiencing: "The philosophical glosses which, for a time, surrounded structuralism have neglected and concealed what really constituted its essential novelty—the introduction into the social sciences of the structural method or, more simply, of the relational mode of thought which, by breaking with the substantialist mode of thought, leads one to characterize each element by the relationships which unite it with all others in a system" (*Logic of Practice*, 4). And Bourdieu never abandons the task of describing relations. His dissatisfaction with structuralism pertains to the status of the relations and structures it posits.

Essentially, for Bourdieu, structuralism falters because it produces the structures it uses to explain experiences and practices with an attention to logical relationship that has no connection with the rules that actually produce practice. The relations structuralism proposes come from outside practice: "The 'grouping of factual material' performed by the diagram is in itself an act of construction, indeed an act of interpretation . . . the difficulty was made all the greater by the fact that interpretation cannot put forward any other proof of its truth than its capacity to account for the totality of the facts in a completely coherent way" (*Logic of Practice*, 10–11). In effect, diagrams and logical structures provide coherence to a mass of primary experiences but nothing shows that the coherence determines how the practices occur. They are external superimpositions, designed to comprehend, but with nothing that shows the comprehension to be other than an interpretive construct.

But Bourdieu argues objectivism's arbitrariness from more than the mere fact of its structures' externality. The structures and diagrams proposed derive from a logic that in principle has no connection to the practices they structure:

> In contrast to logic, a mode of thought that works by making explicit the work of thought, practice excludes all formal concerns. Reflexive attention to action itself, when it occurs (almost invariably only when the automatisms have broken down), remains subordinate to the pursuit of the result and to the search (not necessarily perceived in this way) for maximum effectiveness of the effort expended. So it has nothing in common with the aim of explaining how the result has been achieved, still less of seeking to understand (for understanding's sake) the logic of practice, which flouts logical logic. (*Logic of Practice*, 91)

Because an agent engaging in a practice has no interest in a formal explanation of that practice, but merely in "maximum effectiveness of the effort expended," any formal explanation cannot correspond to anything within the practice that produces it or determines its shape. Even a subconscious design or motivation still could not correspond to the kinds of formal diagrams structuralism proposes, because the rules that govern practice simply do not follow formal logic, "logical logic."[3] This logical impasse is familiar in post-structural attack on the unverifiability of original moments of consciousness and the arbitrariness of the structural turn to external codes. On the one hand, one cannot describe primary experience and still convey the feeling that makes it primary. On the other, the descriptions one can offer lack accuracy precisely because, lacking the feeling of primariness, they do not correspond to primary experience.[4]

Refusing to abandon structuralism's turn to relation and connection, then, Bourdieu must define a mode of describing these relations and rules that neither imposes them from the outside nor turns from the actual working of practice toward a formalism imposed by its own logic. He wants to create a description that accepts its separateness from primary experience, that provides objective explanations, but whose explanations in fact explain the rules that govern a practice as it is undertaken.

One should note here the parallels between Bourdieu's critique of structuralism and Foucault's. Although he never becomes as antagonistic to this method of analysis as Foucault did, Bourdieu has the same basic attraction to and problem with the structural project. On the one hand, he recognizes that he wants to articulate structures that explain events (here primary experiences) rather than merely detail the experiences themselves, whose phenomenological primariness he could never re-create in any case. On the other hand, he sees the forms of relationship offered by the structuralism of his discipline, at least, as having an order created by a logic internal to its own demands for system rather than an order that arises from the primary experiences themselves in all their contingency. This parallel will lead him, like Foucault, to a definition of the structure of practice that accords well with Kant's outline of aesthetic form. Unlike Foucault, however, Bourdieu insists on the scientificity of what he does and so represses the aesthetic basis of his analysis of culture and finally of aesthetics.

Practice, he argues, follows no formal rules of logic, flouts logical logic, but it does have certain kinds of systemic regularities that agents follow, even if unconsciously. Bourdieu's theory of a *Logic of Practice* describes what such regularities look like, how one generates them, how they differ from the rules of structuralism. One can get an idea of the difference between the regularities of structuralism and the practical logic that his theory tries to articulate when Bourdieu sums up the differences between structuralism's theories of kinship and marriage and his own:

This takes us a long way from the pure—infinitely impoverished—realm of the "rules of marriage" and "the elementary structures of kinship." Having defined the system of principles from which the agents are able to produce (and understand) regulated, regular matrimonial practices, we could use statistical analysis of the relevant information to establish the weight of the corresponding structural or individual variables. In fact, the important thing is that the agents' practice becomes intelligible as soon as one is able to construct the system of principles that they put into practice when they immediately identify the socio-logically matchable individuals in a given state of the matrimonial market; or, more precisely, when, for a particular man, they designate for example the few women within practical kin ship who are in a sense promised to him, and those whom he might at a stretch be permitted to marry. (*Logic of Practice*, 199)

In other words, when one knows how an agent knows who he might marry and how he might make his choices, one can describe the system of principles he uses unaware that they guide his practice. This sounds more different from structuralism than perhaps it actually is, however. The principles Bourdieu proposes involve the homologies, symmetries, and transferences familiar to readers of structural diagrams, either anthropological or literary critical. Bourdieu certainly describes his subjects with greater specificity and refers more to particular situations. The externality of structuralism, though, results not from its abstractness but from its formalism. And specificity of reference does not reduce the formalism of principles.

The real difference between Bourdieu's logic and structuralism's lies in the concepts and methods Bourdieu develops that allow him to produce the regularities he defines. These ideas and practices have not only been those that have exercised primary influence on literary critics, but they also are permeated, I will argue, by aesthetic modes of interpretation and evaluation. Further, in this light, Bourdieu's turn from marriage and kinship structures to the topics of culture and aesthetics becomes comprehensible not merely as a contingency in his intellectual development but as an absolutely logical development in his practice. If he can produce a sociology of aesthetics, if he can comprehend aesthetics within a sociological explanation, then the aesthetics that permeates his key anthropological concepts and ideas will be contained within the sociology of that larger practice. First then, I will detail the aesthetic elements in Bourdieu's concepts of the habitus and of symbolic capital. In each case, I will also argue the potential destructiveness for the task of analyzing the sociology of aesthetics in the dependence of these concepts on aesthetics. I will then show how the project of containing culture and aesthetics within a larger sociology recuperates the aesthetics of his practice but also finally comes to rest in a process that enacts both sociological and aesthetic analysis simultaneously. Finally, I think, an analysis of Bourdieu's project thus shows that one can see the politics of aesthetics only by accepting the aesthetic quality of that project. That analysis entails the prolonged look at the way Bourdieu tries to separate himself from Derrida over their readings of Kant, even as he reproduces Derrida's reading, just as Derrida's reading of Kant's aesthetics, which intends to deconstruct it, itself uses the resources of Kant for its deconstruction. In each case, a political end produces a declared opposition that nevertheless employs the aesthetics it ostensibly opposes.

Bourdieu's definition of the habitus practically designs the concept for use by literary and cultural critics. Like Foucault's discursive formation or Jameson's structurally articulatible political unconscious, it proposes structures that determine individual action, thus allowing the political analysis of language, works of art, and cultural institutions, without necessary reference to the beliefs or awarenesses of specific individuals caught up in those larger structures. As with the opposition between his logic of practice and structuralism's logic, though, Bourdieu insists on the specific, unformal element of the habitus:

The conditions associated with a particular class of conditions of existence produce *habitus*, systems of durable, transposable dispositions, structured structures predisposed to function as structuring structures, that is, as principles which generate and organize practices and representations that can be objectively adapted to their outcomes without presupposing a conscious aiming at ends or an express mastery of the operations necessary in order to attain them. Objectively "regulated" and "regular" without being in any way the product of obedience to rules, they can be collectively orchestrated without being the product of the organizing action of a conductor. (*Logic of Practice*, 53)

The habitus is thus a system that generates action but does not correspond to any definable rules. The actions it produces have regularity, but the regularity has no external shape; thus the activity has orchestration but no conductor. Because the habitus regulates very specific, practical choices of individual agents, and because it corresponds much more closely to the specificity of the historical or social situations it analyzes than do more overarching concepts such as discursive formation, it has a clear attraction to historicist literary critics or literary critics of ideology and culture. The habitus seems to describe just the kind of concrete detail that frequently elicits literary or cultural interest. Thus Toril Moi praises Bourdieu precisely for the potential specificity of his explanations: "Bourdieu's originality is to be found in his development of what one might call a *microtheory* of social power. Where Gramsci will give us a general theory of the impositions of hegemony, Bourdieu will show exactly *how* one can analyze teachers' comments on student papers, rules for examinations and students' choices of different subjects in order to trace the specific and practical construction and implementation of a hegemonic ideology" (Moi, "Appropriating Bourdieu," 1019).

But literary critics may be comfortable employing the concept of the habitus for historical and sociological analysis, as much because its working is thoroughly familiar as because of the greater specificity of analysis it allows. The habitus in fact constructs the field in which practice occurs and is read as Foucault constructs discursive formations—through the concept of purposiveness without purpose:

In other words, if one fails to recognize any form of action other than rational action or mechanical reaction, it is impossible to understand the logic of all the actions, that are reasonable, without being the product of a reasoned design, still less of rational calculation; informed by a kind of objective finality without being consciously organized in relation to an explicitly constituted end; intelligible and coherent without springing from an intention of coherence and a deliberate decision; adjusted to the future without being the product of a project or a plan. (*Logic of Practice*, 51)

"Finality" and "end" are, as we saw in Chapter 1, alternative renderings of the German words that get translated more frequently as "purposiveness" and "purpose." They are also the common French translations (see translators' footnotes to Derrida, *Truth in Painting*, 51, 68). Thus "informed by a kind of objective finality without being consciously organized in relation to an explicitly constituted end" comes fairly close to Kant's definition of beauty as "the form of *purposiveness* of an object, so far as this is perceived in it *without any representation of a purpose*" (Kant, *Judgment*, 73). And the final clause above virtually paraphrases Kant's application of the aesthetic judgment to the perception of nature as having a teleology that is neither mechanical nor intended, but simply part of its internal constitution (Kant, *Judgment*, 205–207). The habitus, creating of practice an orchestrated activity without a conductor, makes of it an aesthetic object, readable by the same interpretive methods. Indeed, the logic of practice as constructed by the habitus, finally, distinguishes itself from the rules of structuralism far more explicitly than in Foucault, in terms of the artistry of its patterning:

The coherence without apparent intention and the unity without an immediately visible unifying principle of all the cultural realities that are informed by a quasi-natural logic (is this not what makes the "eternal charm of Greek art" that Marx refers to?) are the product of the age-old application of the same schemes of action and perception which, never having been constituted as explicit principles, can only produce an unwilled necessity which is therefore necessarily imperfect but also a little miraculous, and very close in this respect to a work of art. (*Logic of Practice*, 13)

Bourdieu's difficulty in precisely describing the rules for interpreting the logic of practice, or for adducing a habitus, finally comes down to the aesthetic patterning of the practice by the habitus. One does not recognize such patterns scientifically. Indeed, as a matter of the Kantian aesthetic theory Bourdieu appropriates, one cannot claim that these patterns inhere with certainty in the object at all. Bourdieu thus reads the habitus through an even more objectivist aesthetic formalism that thinks of aesthetics as describing objects rather than apprehensions.

Despite the difficulty of describing the concept of the habitus precisely, it functions centrally in Bourdieu's argument that Kant's concept of aesthetic disinterestedness functions, sociologically, as mode of distinguishing dominating from dominated classes.[5] And this significance makes its own aesthetic patterning at least somewhat ironic. The core argument of *Distinction* against Kant is twofold. First one finds Kant's criterion of disinterestedness only in the aesthetic ideas of the elite: "When one sets about reconstructing its logic, the popular 'aesthetic' appears as the negative opposite of the Kantian aesthetic . . . the popular ethos implicitly answers each proposition of the 'Analytic of the Beautiful' with a thesis contradicting it" (*Distinction*, 41). But, second, the popular aesthetic, which affirms the importance of art appealing to pleasure and moral interest, does not merely oppose an elite aesthetic. That elite aesthetic uses the internal difference that disinterest creates between art and everything else to create a social distinction: "It should not be thought that the relationship of distinction (which may or may not imply the conscious intention of distinguishing oneself from common people) is only an incidental component in the aesthetic disposition. The pure gaze implies a break with the ordinary attitude towards the world which, as such, is a social break" (*Distinction*, 31). In other words, regardless of the intention of the individual, the elite experience of perceptual disinterest, as taught by Kantian aesthetics, creates the experience of social distinction. But a theoretical difference between two aesthetics (the difference being one's affirmation of difference, the other's denial of it) could only function as an experience of social difference for those who believed in difference if the theories that each class held were not theories at all but practices determined by habitus (Bourdieu uses the word both as a singular and as a plural).

And indeed, the habitus works in *Distinction* to allow us to misinterpret learned and acquired aesthetic tastes as natural to us and therefore as creating natural distinctions. The habitus confuses the learned with the natural as part of the way it works, without regard to aesthetics particularly: "The habitus is necessity internalized and converted into a disposition that generates meaningful practices and meaning-giving perceptions; it is a general transposable disposition which carries out a systematic, universal application—beyond the limits of what has been directly learnt—of the necessity inherent in the learning conditions" (*Distinction*, 170). In effect, the habitus allows us both to think that we have chosen what is necessary to us and to think that what we have learned is actually natural to us. When this transformation determines our modes of living in the general area of taste as well as the specific area of aesthetic taste, it allows us to misinterpret acquired tastes as primary, experiential preferences: "Even in the classroom, the dominant definition of the legitimate way of appropriating culture and works of art favours those who have had early access to legitimate culture, in a cultured household, outside of scholastic disciplines, since even within the educational system it devalues scholarly knowledge and interpretation as 'scholastic' or even 'pedantic' in favour of direct experience and simple delight" (*Distinction*, 2). Thus the political effect that arises from the way the habitus constructs the aesthetic: early experience of "legitimate culture" occurs in the dominating classes and with it the sense of the aesthetic as a natural pleasure. Consequently one can distinguish one class from another in terms of its greater possession of this more elite natural pleasure.

The aesthetic shape of the habitus has a devastating implication for this argument, though, if one takes it seriously. Bourdieu has been arguing that the Kantian aesthetic of disinterest is, on the one hand, simply a taste of the elite and on the other, a social tool of domination, and that a taste inherent in a single class gets transformed into a tool that distinguishes classes because of the way the habitus makes over the learned into the natural. But if the habitus in general works according to the rules of the aesthetic, having purposiveness without purpose and the coherence and unity of works of art (and Kant defines all of this integral shaping as the way that artistic perception is separate from pleasure or moral judgment and therefore disinterested), then the preference of the dominating classes for a Kantian experience of the aesthetic is not a simple class preference constructed by the habitus. The Kantian aesthetic enables one to recognize the larger shaping forces of society, to write the work that seemingly questions that aesthetic. At the moment of placing the aesthetic as a political force, he employs its most characteristic distinguishing acts of construing objects. One critic has argued that Bourdieu's is a "project which from the outset has necessitated an unequivocal negation of all idealist conceptions of art" (Codd, "Making Distinctions," 151). This negation does not seem to have stopped him, however, from having artistic conceptions at the outset.

Perhaps even more important to the literary critical deployment of Bourdieu's theories is his concept of symbolic capital and the related idea of symbolic power.[6] Like the concept of the habitus, this idea has clear value for sociological analyses of literary works and history. One may circumvent the debate over whether economic or historical explanations of literary works and forms ever succeed in comprehending their subjects or whether there will always be something in excess of the economic, the sociological, or the historic, which constitutes the literary, by redescribing that excess, in its very aesthetic purity, as embodying a symbolic capital, distributing a symbolic power. According to one definition, symbolic capital does not operate in a particularly literary way—unlike the habitus and despite its label. Symbols—linguistic, literary, and cultural—simply get exchanged in a way analogous to economic exchange. Their worth depends on economic value or some other manifestation of material base. Working with Bourdieu's early explanation in *Outline of a Theory of Practice*, for instance, one article distinguishes, in this way, between the working of symbolic power and capital and what Bourdieu calls the "economism" of Marxism:

The classical Marxist tradition emphasizes the political functions of symbolic systems, and explains the connections between these systems in the interests of the dominant class, and the problem of false consciousness in the dominated classes. From Bourdieu's perspective this approach tends to reduce power relations to relations of communication. The real political function which he sees symbolic systems as fulfilling is their attempt to legitimate domination by the imposition of the "correct" and "legitimate" definition of the social world. (Mahar et al., "Basic Theoretical Position," 5)

Here, classical Marxists describe symbolic systems essentially in terms of their propaganda value, while Bourdieu sees them as more powerfully creating a social space in which the interests of the dominant class get legitimated for everyone. Still these systems finally function to legitimate some power structure that lies beneath their symbolism and gives it its power.

They exist in a homologous or an analogous relation to the power—still essentially economic—that they legitimate.

Bourdieu frequently does use the concept in this way, and to great effect. Arguing that language has a symbolic power in excess of its power to communicate, for instance, Bourdieu contends that "utterances are not only (save in exceptional circumstances) signs to be understood and deciphered; they are also *signs of wealth*, intended to be evaluated and appreciated, and *signs of authority*, intended to be believed and obeyed" (*Language and Symbolic Power*, 66). And he further contends that language's communicative power frequently depends upon the authority and wealth it also signifies. Discussing the dependence of felicity in J. L. Austin's theory of performative speech on institutions of social power and hierarchy, he remarks, "Only a hopeless soldier (or a 'pure' linguist) could imagine that it was possible to give his captain an order. The performative utterance implies 'an overt claim to possess such or such power', a claim that is more or less recognized and therefore more or less sanctioned socially" (75).

As long as behind the symbolic power of symbolic capital there is some real power (usually in some definable relation to real capital), this method works quite well and provides suggestive explanations of certain kinds of cultural and stylistic effects. Bourdieu's explanation of the political significance of Heidegger's style avoids the usual discussions of the connection between his philosophy and his Nazism by noting that Heidegger's importance to the field of philosophy, in the first instance, related to a seemingly absolute split between what a text said and its simplest meaning. This split may have discouraged any consideration of political significance of what was said, but its form enacted another kind of political effect:

For academic logocentrism, whose limit is set by the verbal fetishism of Heideggerian philosophy—the philo-logical philosophy *par excellence*—it is good form which makes good sense. The truth of the relation between philosophical aristocratism (the supreme form of academic aristocratism) and any other type of aristocratism—including the authentically aristocratic aristocratism of the Junkers and their spokespersons—is expressed in the imposition of form and the prohibition against any kind of "reductionism", that is, against any destruction of form aimed at *restoring discourse to its simplest expression* and, in so doing, to the social conditions of its production. (*Language and Symbolic Power*, 151)

Heidegger's style, by its refusal of social relevance, its insistence on an integral form as its value, validates a professional class of philosophers, whose privilege in understanding Heidegger is analogous, in its philosophical aristocratism, to an "authentically aristocratic aristocratism." Bourdieu even goes on to explain the role of this academic aristocratism of philosophy for its practitioners in terms of their class background: "The petit-bourgeois elitism of this 'cream' of the professorial body constituted by philosophy professors (who have often come from the lower strata of the petite bourgeoisie and who, by their academic prowess, have conquered the peaks of the hierarchy of humanist disciplines to reach the topmost ivory tower of the educational system, high above the world and any worldly power) could hardly fail to resonate harmoniously with Heidegger's thought" (157–158). In effect, Heidegger's style receives symbolic power from its ability to validate the professionalism of academic philosophy. And that validation has value because it marks the academic arrival of its practitioners into an elite (even if only an academic elite) class that they, as petite-bourgeoisie, have striven to occupy. Symbolic power, defined this way, must always be referred to some more "authentic" power.

Except to the extent that any analogical concept operates through figurative transfer, the concept of symbolic capital is not yet particularly literary or aesthetic—no more so at any rate than any other analogy. Its explanatory power, in fact, rests on its separation from the literary, its establishment of a ground beneath the linguistic or the stylistic that gives them value and power. By the same token, though, and for that reason, this version of symbolic capital does not manage to resolve the aesthetic into the social or the historical. All that Bourdieu says about the social significances of the linguistic, the literary, the stylistic, could be true, and their value could still be constituted by some pure aesthetic content. Thus a reviewer ends a fairly favorable account of *Distinction* with the following complaint: "The assertion that aesthetic discrimination rests upon principles of social inclusion and exclusion in no way logically discounts the possibility of justifying universal norms of aesthetic appreciation" (Giddens, "Politics of Taste," 304).[7]

Perhaps more importantly, this definition of symbolic capital cannot explain the working of culture or art when they cease to align themselves directly with economic or power benefits for which they can no longer thus be cashed in. Because Bourdieu wants precisely to explain that which seems to indicate the pure aesthetic, he is drawn to explain its definition sociologically in terms of symbolic power. But these explanations soon lead to a covert re-creation of an intrinsic aesthetic value. For instance, Bourdieu explains the aesthetic disposition of disinterest generally in terms of its dependence upon a space freed from economic need; thus experiencing aesthetic disinterest will coincide with having the economic means to do so. But he also realizes that the aesthetic thus exists in a certain opposition to the concept at least of economic power. So a purer engagement in aesthetics becomes a way of claiming a freedom from an economic domination that is part of one's field:

> It is not surprising that bourgeois adolescents, who are both economically privileged and (temporarily) excluded from the reality of economic power, sometimes express their distance from the bourgeois world which they cannot really appropriate by a refusal of complicity whose most refined expression is a propensity towards aesthetics and aestheticism. In this respect they share common ground with the women of the bourgeoisie, who, being partially excluded from economic activity, find fulfillment in stage-managing the décor of bourgeois existence, when they are not seeking refuge or revenge in aesthetics. (*Distinction*, 55)

His explanation for the resistance of artists to comprehension even by upper-class patrons (228–229) and for the split, at the upper registers of the dominant class, between those with relatively high cultural capital and relatively low economic capital—teachers for instance—and those with relatively higher economic capital and relatively lower cultural capital—members of the professions—follows the same pattern (283–295). In each case, the cultural becomes an intrinsic value in terms of its opposition to economic domination.

But where does the symbolic power of cultural capital come from in this situation? Originally, the ability of culture to distinguish was expressed by distinguishing the economically privileged, who had the leisure for obtaining cultural capital. But since cultural capital's distinction can no longer be cashed in for economic privilege or political power (its value now belongs to relatively dominated groups: adolescents, women, teachers), that capital must inhere in the pure power either of the aesthetic or the pure power of distinction (which comes to the same thing if, as we have seen, the aesthetic is defined by the internal distinguishing power of disinterest). If Bourdieu ascribes to a thorough relativizing of cultural and aesthetic tastes, he can no longer explain the odd effects that occur when aesthetics becomes an activity that resists economic benefit (and the very theoretical comprehensiveness of his sociological aims forces his attention to these moments). But if, on the other hand, he allows even the act of distinction that aesthetics enables to become a value that cannot be cashed in, he seems to have simply a new version of an intrinsic aesthetics.[8]

Bourdieu's later definitions of symbolic capital in effect solve this problem, in its workings with regard to aesthetics, by making symbolic transfer itself the grounding act of value (of which economic transfer is merely another version). Once one does not have to cash in symbolic capital to see its value, an analysis of aesthetics that analogizes its activities to the workings of economic capital becomes sufficient indication of its sociological effect. To escape economism as the ground of symbolic capitalism, Bourdieu argues the greater extension of uneconomic practices of exchange, making symbolic capital the larger category, of which economic capital is one version. He argues that "economism is a form of ethnocentrism" (*Logic of Practice*, 112) because it treats all economies, even pre-capitalist ones, as if they were explicable in terms of capitalist economics. But such economic explanations often simply cannot comprehend how some exchanges work: "In the work of reproducing established relations—feasts, ceremonies, exchange of gifts, visits or courtesies and, above all, marriages—which is no less vital to the existence of the group than the reproduction of the economic bases of its existence, the labour required to conceal the function of the exchanges is as important as the labour needed to perform this function" (*Logic of Practice*, 112). A labor that conceals the function of an exchange cannot of course be exchanged without the concealment being reified and thus undone. In such exchanges, the value can only occur if the basic economic exchange involving labor cannot occur. In order to create the value, a seemingly extraneous act of labor must occur, one that the value cannot be reduced to but must depend on. Accordingly, Bourdieu can argue the priority of symbolic capital to economic capital in these terms:

In an economy which is defined by the refusal to recognize the "objective" truth of "economic" practices, that is, the law of "naked self-interest" and egoistic calculation, even "economic" capital cannot act unless it succeeds in being recognized through a conversion that can render unrecognizable the true principle of its efficacy. Symbolic capital is this denied capital, recognized as legitimate, that is, misrecognized as capital. (*Logic of Practice*, 118)

Symbolic capital is, then, not merely a symbol for economic capital but the capital that exists when economic interests are denied or negated. This negation can occur in a pre-capitalist economy. But it can also occur in a capitalist economy when agents resist economic interests. Finally, capital per se amounts to the value that motivates any conversion, whether economic exchange or the disguise of economic exchange. One might argue that disguise is always a form of exchange, but this would be true only if exchange were always a form of disguise. From this perspective, then, capital just is symbolic.

Although this version of symbolic capital may remove any standpoint outside the misrecognized symbolic exchange from which to mount a straightforward political critique, it also removes the problem that, in certain circumstances, one cannot cash in the symbolic or cultural capital of an aesthetic position to ground its value in some outside power.[9] After all, what need has one to cash in a symbol if the symbolic capital creates the relations of power and value in exchange rather than merely representing them? By accepting metaphoric transfer fully at the conceptual level of his theory, then, Bourdieu resolves the problems in his sociological analysis of the practice of aesthetics.

One can see this resolution at work most clearly in his discussions of Flaubert and the development of the concept of a pure art. Bourdieu posits three groups of writers in what he calls "the literary field" of mid-nineteenth-century France. The first of these, "the advocates of social art," demanded that literature fulfill a social or political function. For them, the value of art cashes in fairly easily in terms of the value of the political position it espouses. The second group, "the representatives of 'bourgeois art'," wrote "in a genre that presupposed immediate communication between author and public and assured these writers not only significant material benefits . . . but also all the tokens of success in the bourgeois world" ("Flaubert's Point of View," 550). This group presents even fewer sociological problems because their art cashes in for cash. The third group, however, might seem to re-create the problems of evaluating an aesthetic that resists the forces that might give it sociological value:

The writers located outside these two opposing positions gradually invented what was called "art for art's sake." Rather than a position ready for the taking, it was a *position to make*. Although it existed potentially within the space of existing positions, its occupants had to invent, against the established positions and against their occupants, everything that distinguished their position from all the others. They had to invent the social personage without precedent—the modern artist, full-time professional, dedicated to his work, indifferent to the exigencies of politics as to the injunctions of morality, and recognizing no jurisdiction other than the specific norm of art. ("Flaubert's Point of View," 551)

Bourdieu also describes the ways the occupants of this group created internal sanctions and rewards, analogous to other social sanctions and rewards but determined by a negating resistance to them.[10]

The questions asked above, about a similar analysis, in *Distinction*, of the role of aesthetics for marginalized groups within the dominating class, do not quite evaporate in the light of the more central position given to symbolic capital, but they become local and historically specific rather than theoretical. We might still wonder why artists gave up the calculable social rewards available to bourgeois writers for the less evident rewards of prestige within a socially marginal group, or why the larger society proceeded to grant respect to that group by endowing their negations of surrounding social values with various kinds of institutional verifications of their status as a profession. But these are empirical questions about how an event occurred. In terms of what this group of artists does, their actions do not amount to exchange and creation of capital in terms of some incalculable analogy to economic capital and exchange. Rather, the activities the group engages in just constitute the value-creating activities of exchange and disguised exchange that found all capital. It may be that, in creating this socially definable group, artists must also create an object to which their immediate relation is one of disinterest, but if the purpose of that relation is to allow one to enter into a larger system of exchanges, then a full description of aesthetic activity has to comprehend various sociological interests.

Again, Bourdieu validates his sociological analysis of culture and aesthetics by accepting a certain aesthetic status for the tools of his analysis. His field reversal, whereby symbolic capital, instead of being a specialized metaphorical version of economic capital, becomes the general category of which economic capital is a subset, reenacts an almost archetypal deconstructive maneuver with the categories of literary and philosophical language.[11] Above, the aesthetic status of the habitus suggests that the aesthetic sensibilities of the elite class correspond in a confirming way to the ground from which the sociological analysis is performed. Here, the affirmation of a constituting symbolism to exchange, which creates value in the first instance, though it shows the interest in the symbolic investments that created the aestheticized art object, does so by creating a grounding space which, while not precisely interest free, cannot be calculated in terms of any form of external interest. Again, to place art and culture sociologically Bourdieu has first aestheticized his sociology.

I do not mean, in the above analysis of the aesthetic bases of the habitus and of symbolic capital, to suggest an aesthetic reading of Bourdieu's sociology in order to capture it in some more generalized formalism. The rupture with that formalism occurs with what I take to be Bourdieu's most completely aesthetic, theoretical maneuver, the self-reflective turn in his theory that both changed the content of his research from anthropological case studies to studies of the morés of academics and changed the concern of his theories more relentlessly toward cultural and aesthetic topics. In a move that directly parallels the claim in deconstructive literary criticism to privilege its position by a claim of greater self-awareness, Bourdieu asserts a sociological self-awareness as freeing him from the imprisonment within academic culture that his sociology of that culture constructs.

Both of Bourdieu's most explicitly theoretical books, *Outline of a Theory of Practice* and *The Logic of Practice*, present themselves as reflections upon past versions of their own theories and of Bourdieu's researches. They do so because they insist that the route from objectivism to an understanding of the logic of practice goes through a reflection upon one's own practice. *Outline* opens with the claim that an anthropologist can only exit objectivism by first realizing how his own role as anthropologist both enables and necessitates that stance (*Outline*, 1–2). In other words, the first practice the anthropologist must understand in order to truly understand practice is his own. The later *Logic of Practice* generalizes this situation into a philosophical rule:

> This critical reflection on the limits of theoretical understanding is not intended to discredit theoretical knowledge in one or another of its forms and, as is often attempted, to set in its place a more or less idealized practical knowledge; but rather to give it a solid basis by freeing it from the distortions arising from the epistemological and social conditions of its production. It has nothing in common with the aim of rehabilitation, which has misled most discourse on practice; it aims simply to bring to light the theory of practice which theoretical knowledge implicitly applies. (*Logic of Practice*, 27)

Neither merely negative, moving from reflection to skepticism, nor naively positive, moving from reflection on skepticism to a recuperated positive knowledge, Bourdieu's reflection reproduces his theory of practice by extrapolating the theory from its own practice. Thus Bourdieu insists on reflecting on his own role as researcher and on thinking that that reflection will describe both the practice of such a role and the theory of how to elucidate such practices.

What the reflection has to say about the sociology of its own practice begins, for Bourdieu, in the consideration of the system that produces that practice—the French educational system. Quite early in his career, as part of thinking about his own role as a French observer of social practices in the one-time French colony of Algeria, Bourdieu turned his focus to the educational system that was the field of his own practice. This research led to two conclusions, one about the system, one about what might be called the habitus of the students and professors within it. First, Bourdieu found that even within the French educational system, ostensibly rigorously structured along meritocratic lines, social origin consistently predicted educational success: "Social origin is doubtless the one whose influence bears most strongly on the student world, more strongly, at any rate, than sex or age, and certainly more than any clearly perceived factor, such as religious affiliation" (Bourdieu and Passeron, *The Inheritors*, 8). This conclusion should not surprise anyone who has discussed the make-up of the student body in the United States educational system. Bourdieu, though, unlike many critics in the United States, while not objecting to programs that equalized access across social classes, does not think such programs will particularly change anything: "The mechanisms which ensure the elimination of working-class and lower-middle-class children would operate almost as efficiently (but more discreetly) in a situation in which a systematic policy of providing scholarships or grants made subjects from all social classes formally equal vis-à-vis education" (Bourdieu and Passeron, *The Inheritors*, 27).

What mechanisms work so surely that direct action on access to the system would be ineffectual? To answer this question, one has to turn to Bourdieu's second conclusion regarding the less empirically calculable issue of what cultural and intellectual practices produce success in the academic world. Here Bourdieu argues that the instrumentality that defines the roles of both the students and the professors, combined with the impossibility of recognizing that instrumentality and still performing the activities that enable its working, produce the particular practices in the educational field. In other words, in one obvious sense, "to be a student is to prepare oneself by study for an occupational future" (Bourdieu and Passeron, *The Inheritors*, 56). But if students acted as if this were the case, "the professor's occupational task would then become merely an aspect of an occupational project of which he is no longer the master and whose full significance lies beyond him" (58). The result is a double mystification: first students see their own principle activity as a kind of self-creation that can be enacted only by rejecting anything that might constrain that creation by suggesting that choice is not absolutely free: "the aspiration to create and choose oneself does not impose a determinate behavior, but only a symbolic use of behavior intended to signify that this behavior has been chosen" (38). In addition to denying the students' own instrumentality, this mystification "enables the teachers to see themselves as masters communicating a total culture by personal gift" (58). Thus students and professors each deny each other's and their own instrumentality by creating practices that distinguish themselves from the surrounding society in terms of an intrinsic concern with creation and culture.

Three aspects of this conclusion are worth noting. First, in one sense, the cultural and intellectual practices of students and professors do not, in fact, result directly from the class-distinguishing effects of the educational system. Even if the system were actually meritocratic, the role of students would still be instrumental, directed at fitting them for their future occupations, and professors would still be, in reality, auxiliary to that role. Thus the double mystification of those roles that constitutes the academic field would occur. But second, the content of that mystification leads directly to the conclusions of *Distinction*. The way in which students and professors distinguish themselves from their social roles creates a sense of culture that seconds the class-differentiating activities of the educational system as a whole. Because the content of academic intellectual mystification does not result directly from the full sociological role of education, though, does not simply function as an ideological mask of that role, an academic intellectual may, through reflection on his own practices, see their sociological effects even while he reproduces them. In effect, precisely the intellectual field Bourdieu describes in *The Inheritors* and *Distinction* produces the research and the intellectual practices that led to those books, as Bourdieu himself well realizes.

Bourdieu's implication in the activities he places sociologically may question the political freedom of his analysis. One critic remarks that *Distinction*

would only be likely to be read by people situated in the top left corner [the dominated fraction of the dominating class, which is relatively richer in cultural capital than in economic capital]—as a life-style token, like the music of Boulez, of the possession of the kind of high cultural capital associated with university professors. . . . Because *La Distinction* could not possibly enable non-readers to reflect on the class disposition which ensured that they were non-readers, it could not fail to be a book about non-readers for readers. (Robbins, *Work of Pierre Bourdieu*, 28–29, note 4)

But also, because both writer and any reader, coming from the habitus of the university, will enact the distinguishing practices that separate them from non-readers, regardless of their intent to see those practices skeptically, they will still reproduce them. But paradoxically, by accepting that aesthetic presumptions govern one's own practices, one may describe the sociological working of those presumptions fully precisely because the aesthetic practice differs enough from the sociological ends to enable one to see them even as one produces them. If we do not demand transcendental grounds for our sociology, the fact of the reflection will not automatically disable the specific sociological conclusions. Indeed, as we have seen, that reflection may be necessary to those conclusions.

The situation of Bourdieu's sociology of aesthetics, then, looks something like this. Bourdieu describes a habitus—a cultural or aesthetic field—that deliberately splits itself from social influence or effect, but within which professional interests operate in a sociologically describable way. Within that field exist art objects whose aestheticization also deliberately drains them of immediate social interest. But the immediate freedom of that object from interest creates its professional interest for those who operate within the field. His sociology describes in this way both the political role of Heidegger's style—if we do not cash it in for the empirically questionable analysis of its particular value for the petite bourgeoisie—and the role of art for art's sake for Flaubert. That the tools of analysis—the habitus and symbolic capital—are themselves aestheticized concepts, though, seems to suggest an ultimate ground for aesthetic disinterest. To accept as aestheticized the reflection in the analysis that produces this sociology, however, is to recuperate the sociological force of the analysis: by analyzing the sociological roots and effects of disinterested analysis, even the analysis doing the examining, one can attach the sociology back to the analysis that examines even as one accepts the necessity of its claims to an aesthetic disinterest. This recuperation only works, however, when coupled with the acceptance outlined here, as we can see at moments in which Bourdieu tries to separate himself radically from the form of analysis he deploys.

It will be the burden of my final section on Bourdieu's critique of Derrida's deconstruction of Kant to indicate the failure of this separation. But my argument about Bourdieu's sociology of aesthetics has, it seems to me at this point, two implications. First its specific practices—definitions of habitus, specifications of symbolic capital and symbolic power—will not result in readings of literature or literary history that will have performed some decisive break with aesthetic evaluations, though such readings may have any number of other local values. But, second, its analysis of the sociology of academic practices, particularly in its most self-aware moments, has much to say about the cultural wars literary professors are currently fighting with ourselves, and more recently with our own *Nouvel Observateurs*. *Distinction* offers a skeptical glance at culture that certainly offers support, for instance, for the most skeptical readings of traditional canons and literary evaluations. But the cost of casting that glance is that its first skepticism must always be about the presumptions of the field that constructs the ability to cast it. Traditional canons and readings occupy *that* field in a close embrace with the analyses that attack them. Only by abandoning the desire to exit that field into a realm from which a pure political attack may be launched, and by doing so as considerably more than a matter momentary rhetoric carrying with it no larger implications, may one coherently obtain the political implications many have wanted from Bourdieu.

II. Bourdieu's Derrida's Kant: The Aesthetics of Refusing Aesthetics

In the closing pages of *Distinction*, a sociological analysis of the way in which class membership constitutes both physiological and aesthetic taste, and an argument that the two kinds of taste are coextensive, Bourdieu returns to a confrontation with Kant's *Critique of Judgment*, the exemplar of the pure, philosophical aesthetics that his sociology means to counter. As he recognizes, the return is necessary since without it his argument and its close attention to social detail and such possibly marginal topics as taste in food, fashion, and furniture may seem simply to run parallel to more abstract discussions of aesthetics:

> And if we must now allow the "return of the repressed", having produced the truth of the taste against which, by an immense repression, the whole of legitimate aesthetics has been constructed, this is . . . in order to prevent the absence of direct confrontation from allowing the two discourses to coexist peacefully as parallel alternatives, in two carefully separated universes of thought and discourse. (*Distinction*, 485–486)

Bourdieu ends with an extremely harsh critique of Derrida's deconstruction of Kantian aesthetics. This is surprising, since, by Bourdieu's own description of the deconstruction, Derrida's argument differs very little from Bourdieu's except that it remains in form a philosophical analysis rather than a sociological survey. The exception is no small detail: Bourdieu wants centrally to argue that such an analysis, regardless of its explicit purpose, reproduces the abstraction of Kantian disinterest that allows aesthetics to function as a mode of class distinction. Still, since the criticism of Derrida's ostensible Kantianism takes the form of a rather abstract complaint at the end of a rather abstract philosophical analysis of Kant, one wonders why Bourdieu would end his plea for material detail with a philosophical analysis of a philosophical analysis. Why must he dispense with Derrida in order to put Kant in his place? And what does this tell us about the place of Kantian disinterest in Bourdieu's own attack on it?

I mean to answer these questions by ratifying Bourdieu's critique of Derrida and then turning it back on him, in the end suggesting that a Kantian aesthetic disinterest is necessary to both the poststructural and the sociological skepticism about classic aesthetics. But by taking this tack to discuss Bourdieu, I raise a deeper version of these issues: what finally will be the relevance of this analysis of aesthetic form in postmodern ideological critique? Bourdieu offers five hundred densely researched pages on the material manifestations of aesthetic claims and distinctions, and as a discussion of its limitations, I respond with a return to Kant at three removes—through Bourdieu's version of Derrida's version of disinterest. Surely this is the kind of evasion Foucault had in mind when he famously accused Derrida of producing "a historically well-determined little pedagogy" (*Dits*, I, 1113–1136). I want to answer the criticism at its most general level, that aesthetics, by evading the material, enacts not disinterest but merely elitism and that philosophical and academic analysis reproduces that well-determined little evasion.[12] In this response, though, I do not want to return to the notions of disinterested formalism that buttressed a disguised humanism that both Bourdieu and Derrida attack. As I have throughout this book, I want to show that their attacks and the analytic and political benefits we desire from them, depend on a form of Kantian disinterest they both repress and reproduce.

To grasp the basis for both his reference to and his rejection of Derrida, one must start with his rejection of Kant. *Distinction* outlines a quite complex structure of class groups and consequent aesthetic attitudes, but in the two moments in which Bourdieu addresses Kant directly, he contrasts his theories only with popular tastes, that is the tastes roughly of the working class, the most economically and culturally dominated segment of society. Thus, in the beginning of the book, Bourdieu titles the popular taste "An Anti-Kantian 'Aesthetic'" and remarks: "It is no accident that, when one sets about reconstructing its logic, the popular 'aesthetic' appears as the negative opposite of the Kantian aesthetic, and that the popular ethos implicitly answers each proposition of the 'Analytic of the Beautiful' with a thesis contradicting it" (*Distinction*, 41). He follows by contrasting Kant's distinction between aesthetic pleasure and pleasure that is merely physically gratifying or dependent on physical charm with the working class's explicit praise of that which is physically gratifying or pleasing. He then contrasts Kant's universalism with a working-class sense of relative value, and contrasts Kant's ostensible formalism with a working-class utilitarian evaluation of art (*Distinction*, 41–42). At the end of the book, he shows Kant returning the working-class favor, defining his aesthetic in terms of a repulsion from popular values: "Kant's principle of pure taste is nothing other than a refusal, a disgust—a disgust for objects which impose enjoyment and a disgust for the crude, vulgar taste which revels in this imposed enjoyment" (*Distinction*, 488).

This suddenly compressed distinction, ignoring the connection between Kantian taste and all the other various class tastes Bourdieu details, derives from the fact that only the popular taste, in Bourdieu's system, exists in complete contrast not only to Kantian aesthetics but to all other forms of dominant tastes and preferences. Both the dominant class (wealthy industrialists, senior executives, etc.) and the dominated segment of the dominant class (university teachers, adolescents and women, artistic producers, etc.) share basic aesthetic values Bourdieu roots in Kant. Indeed the aestheticism of the dominant class's dominated segment takes its power as resistance from a more educated possession and articulation of the Kantian values they share with their class's dominating segment (*Distinction*, 55, 287, 291). And Bourdieu defines the petit bourgeoisie in terms of an alienation from self that arises from its attempts to enact cultural preferences foreign to its class-based upbringing and experiences (*Distinction*, 319–323). But these attempts implicitly recognize the aesthetic and taste values of the Kantian upper classes. Only the working classes, in Bourdieu's system of connecting class with aesthetic taste, represent a complete rejection of this system of tastes.

Indeed working-class tastes and preferences, instead of being marks of their domination, might merely represent an alternative aesthetic theory, in the manner of the most elitist academic aesthetic relativism, were it not for two positive marks of its dominated quality.[13] First, at least the material preferences of the working classes, their tastes in food and possessions, are in part determined by what Bourdieu labels "the Choice of the Necessary":

The fundamental proposition that the habitus is a virtue made of necessity is never more clearly illustrated than in the case of the working classes, since necessity includes for them all that is usually meant by the word, that is, an inescapable deprivation of necessary goods. Necessity imposes a taste for necessity which implies a form of adaptation to and consequently acceptance of the necessary, a resignation to the inevitable. (*Distinction*, 372)

In other words, we know the working-class taste to be a mark of their domination because they tend to reject what they in fact cannot have and to choose what is economically feasible for them to want. Even as far as material necessity, the correspondence between preference and want is not perfect, though, which leads to one of those fascinating insights in Bourdieu that at once confirm and challenge his theories:

When one moves from the manual workers to the industrial and commercial employers, through foremen, craftsmen and small shopkeepers, economic constraints tend to relax without any fundamental change in the pattern of spending . . . the food consumed is increasingly rich (both in cost and in calories) and increasingly heavy (game, foie gras). By contrast, the taste of the professionals or senior executives defines the popular taste by negation, as the taste for the heavy, the fat and the coarse, by tending towards the light, the refined and the delicate. . . . The taste for rare, aristocratic foods points to a traditional cuisine, rich in expensive or rare products (fresh vegetables, meat). (*Distinction*, 185)

Foie gras may be more expensive than fresh vegetables but it exists on a continuum with calorically rich and heavy foods that begins with beans and starch, for which the working classes develop the taste of necessity, while vegetables are "lighter" and also rarer than the basic popular diet. While this insight shows how the categories of necessity may become the choices of popular luxury, it also calls into question whether necessity in fact determines the choice. This question becomes more pointed as one moves to less material preferences. Since various aspects of the dominant culture are economically inexpensive, such as museums, high culture films and books (allowing the less wealthy but better educated dominated segment of the dominant class access to them), the popular distaste for them is not economically necessary at all. It may be explained by their lack of what Bourdieu calls educational capital, but it may simply be an alternative taste, possessed by the working classes by chance rather than forced on them by some disability tied directly to class distinction. The second mark identifying working-class tastes as dominated rather than merely relative, though, is precisely the Kantian disgust for it. One might think that Kant-

ian disinterest would extend to a neutrality toward tastes for physical gratification that, as such, while not being pure aesthetic tastes, would be without other valence. But Bourdieu argues that Kant finds such pleasures degraded: "In Kant's text, disgust discovers with horror the common
animality on which and against which moral distinction is constructed:
'We regard as coarse and low the habits of thought of those who have no
feeling for beautiful nature . . . and who devote themselves to the mere en-
joyments of sense found in eating and drinking'" (*Distinction*, 489). One
might also add, since it occurs with the very definition of disinterest,
Kant's rather lugubrious joke about "that Iroquois Sachem, who was
pleased in Paris by nothing more than by the cook shops" (*Judgment*, 38).
Whether or not Kant's remarks reflect a class judgment on his part or a
more thoughtless elitism, they surely do allow the contemporary elite
marking of working-class tastes as barbarous. Thus Kant allows the marking of different class tastes in Bourdieu's system as dominating and dominated rather than merely different, even as the ungrounded nature of that
Kantian evaluation simultaneously allows a position from which to see his
aesthetics as using taste to create merely artificial distinction.[14] The attack
on Kant thus works to make Bourdieu's sociological analysis operate as an
anti-Kantian theory rather than merely a parallel discourse.

From this perspective, however, in turning to Bourdieu's discussion
of Derrida, one must first ask, "Why Derrida?" That question actually occurs in more than one way. First, as we will see, in "Economimesis" particularly, Derrida's deconstruction of Kant has much in common not only
with the general basis of Bourdieu's critique but even with the theme of
disgust he raises and the passages he discusses. But even if we accept the
grounds of Bourdieu's criticism of Derrida, regardless of the similarities between the two positions, there is a second version of the question that we
need to address. Since the weakness of Derrida's critique from Bourdieu's
perspective is its refusal to escape the protocols of philosophic analysis set
up by Kant even as it deconstructs his theories, one wonders in what sense
the critique of Derrida adds anything to the prior critique of Kant. The
discussion of Kant, as we have seen, gave traction to the claim that taste
distinctions operated as part of class domination and also made that sociological analysis aesthetically pertinent. But once Kant, as the exemplar of
what both Bourdieu and Derrida agree in thinking of as classic aesthetics,
has been determined to work toward class-based distinctions, why is it necessary to demonstrate that a contemporary Kantian's theories will work the

same way?[15] To answer this question, we will have to see how Bourdieu's criticisms of Derrida may be applied to himself, and to see the Kantianism within both Derrida and Bourdieu, which Bourdieu seems to hope to expel by trying to expel Derrida from his own text. It is as if Bourdieu has transferred the Kantian disgust with working-class taste (a disgust in excess of disinterest and yet marking it off as class based) to a disgust with Derrida that should also be in excess of what his theory demands and that is thus equally indicative of its linkages with what it would vomit up. This mirroring of disgust becomes particularly pointed given its importance as a theme to both Derrida and Bourdieu. The violence of Bourdieu's rejection of Derrida marks the attempt to separate his analysis from the class-based academic analysis he also means to critique. To the extent that the attempt fails, his analysis of class and culture are threatened again with the problem of separating his analysis from the elite academic discourse within which he will not assent to remaining. Bourdieu's treatment of Derrida is, as he admits, extremely compressed, only four to five pages, of which the entire summary of Derrida's argument and his dissent from it—the direct treatment of Derrida—takes up the first two:

> Derrida does indeed see that what is involved is the opposition between legitimate "pleasure" and "enjoyment" or, in terms of objects, between the agreeable arts which seduce by the "charm" of their sensuous content and the Fine Arts which offer pleasure without enjoyment. He also sees, without explicitly connecting it with the previous opposition, the antithesis between the gross tastes of those who "are content to enjoy the simple sensations of the senses, at table or over a bottle"— "consumptive orality" seen as "interested taste"—and pure taste. He indicates that disgust is perhaps the true origin of pure taste, inasmuch as it "abolishes representative distance" and, driving one irresistibly towards consumption, annihilates the freedom that is asserted in suspending immediate attachment to the sensuous and in neutralizing the affect, that is, "disinterestedness", a lack of interest as to the existence or non-existence of the thing represented. And one can, no doubt, though Derrida avoids doing so explicitly, relate all the foregoing oppositions, which concern the consumer's relation to the work of art, to the last of the oppositions picked up, the one which Kant establishes, at the level of production, between "free art", involving free will, and "mercenary art", which exchanges the value of its labour for a wage. (*Distinction*, 494)

If one wanted to mount a defense of Derrida, one might note a number of things here. For instance, although a prior footnote, and indeed Bourdieu's entire attack on Derrida, refer only to *Truth in Painting*, this passage directly describes "Economimesis." The theme of the distinction between the pleasures of fine art and other gratifications is common to both works but far more explicit in "Economimesis." The discussions of disgust and of free and mercenary art occur only in "Economimesis," which concentrates on the aesthetic quality of disinterest in Kant. Indeed the quotations are from that earlier essay. The section on Kant in *Truth in Painting*, "Parergon," has more to do with seemingly formal themes, the difference between ornament and essence, and Kant's definition of purposiveness without purpose.

To be sure, Derrida's two essays refer to each other explicitly more or less as if they are parts of a single project. Moreover, since Derrida's themes are more formal, at least superficially, in "Parergon," and since Bourdieu clearly wants to recognize openly the common elements between his analysis and Derrida's, the latter work's discussions of margins and "pure cuts" are less amenable without analysis to assimilation with a sociological project than are the themes of "Economimesis." Still, since Bourdieu's critiques are limited to the aspects of formal play in "Parergon," not merely the play of typography but the claim to be treating the *Critique of Judgment* as a work of art, with complete disinterest even in its existence, one may question whether those formalist flaws apply to the more material themes of the earlier essay, or whether, if they do, the formal play might not also be analyzed back into the political analysis, the lack of which Bourdieu criticizes: "Failing to be, at the same time, social breaks which truly renounce the gratifications associated with membership, the most audacious intellectual breaks of pure reading still help to preserve the stock of consecrated texts from becoming dead letters, mere archive material, fit at best for the history of ideas or the sociology of knowledge" (*Distinction*, 496). But this problem is augmented by the occlusions even in the positive summary quoted above. Bourdieu suggests that the political implications of Derrida's discussion are unrealized because Derrida does not connect the themes explicitly toward that end. But, whatever the weaknesses of its analytical connections, the primary argument of "Economimesis," as its title indicates, is that Kant's seemingly disinterested aesthetics participates in an Enlightenment humanist economy. Derrida opens with the claim that "a politics, therefore, although it never occupies the center of the stage, acts upon this discourse. It ought to be possible to read it. Politics and political economy, to be sure, are implicated in every discourse on art and on the beautiful" ("Economimesis," 3).[16] Moreover, Derrida quite explicitly argues that aesthetic disinterest operates as its own economy, distinguishing the purely human from lower orders: "A divine teleology secures the political economy of the Fine-Arts, the hierarchical opposition of free art and mercenary art. *Economimesis* puts everything in its place, starting with the instinctual work of animals without language and ending with God, passing by the way of the mechanical arts, mercenary art, liberal arts, aesthetic arts and the Fine-Arts" ("Economimesis," 9). Bourdieu might object here that the themes are classically philosophical rather than political, but he would do so at the cost of his own insight that the seemingly abstractly classical takes on its political effect by offering a structure of distinctions for the class system to use, which is essentially Derrida's point here. On the issue of disgust, if Derrida's discussion is more complex in its itinerary and abstract in its formulations, again its point is precisely and manifestly Bourdieu's and indeed one might argue that Derrida's more formal discussion adds considerable force to Bourdieu's political claims. Indeed, if the end of the essay had not turned so explicitly to Derrida, one might have expected complimentary citational references to "Economimesis" earlier in the book, so much does Derrida offer extended arguments for Bourdieu's points about Kant.

I register these objections to Bourdieu's handling of Derrida largely to argue that his own treatment might have been much more positive, indeed sympathetic, without imperiling his own case. In the main, though, in its largest point, I think Bourdieu's reservation about Derrida is in fact accurate in important ways, not merely for Derrida's but for my own perhaps overly formal analysis here—and finally for Bourdieu as well. But let's start with Derrida. For Bourdieu, the problem with avoiding social breaks, with treating Kant's text on aesthetics as if it were an aesthetic object to be analyzed, is that it reproduces the philosophical forms and beliefs it seeks to deconstruct:

But Derrida's supremely intellectual game presupposes lucidity in commitment to the game. . . . Thus Derrida tells us the truth of his text and his reading (a particular case of the experience of pure pleasure), that is, that it implies the epoche of any thesis of existence or, more simply, indifference to the existence of the object in question, but he does so in a text which itself implies that epoche and that indifference. . . . Because he never withdraws from the philosophical game, whose conventions he respects, even in the ritual transgressions at which only traditionalists could be shocked, he can only philosophically tell the truth about the philosophical text and its philosophical reading. (*Distinction*, 495)

Posed in this way, this accusation is common enough in relation to Derrida. Indeed, he asks for it, since he regularly asserts that his departure from traditional philosophy takes its strength from its initial respect for philosophy's protocols and from its retracing of traditional readings and definitions.[17] And with the charge left in this condition, ignoring the details of any specific argument, the answer is equally expectable. Derrida argues precisely that one cannot show the limits of philosophical discourse from outside its boundaries because it is a discourse that claims to be without boundaries. Only an analysis from within those boundaries can delineate them despite philosophy's claims; hence, only a recuperation of the boundaries will enable the sociological questionings Bourdieu undertakes. Thus, according to Derrida, rather than failing to be material, his presentation of the departures his argument shares with Bourdieu in a pointedly traditional mode of analysis actually enables Bourdieu's subsequent departures from Derrida's stylistic traditionalism. At this level of generality, this argument over whose analysis represents the originating and effective break from tradition can go on forever: each position bases its case on an equally logical, purely abstract, and formal position.

To give Bourdieu's accusation a more specific defense—though one I well recognize he would not accept in all its implications—I want to look somewhat more closely at Derrida's use of the topic of disgust to deconstruct the concept of pure taste. Derrida begins with the opposition Bourdieu notes between pure taste and the barbarism of physical pleasure, mere eating and drinking, which pure taste would raise and expel: "What is already announced here is a certain allergy in the mouth between pure taste and actual tasting [*dégustation*]. We still have before us the question of where to inscribe disgust. Would not disgust, by turning itself back against actual tasting, also be the origin of pure taste, in the wake of a sort of catastrophe?" ("Economimesis," 16). By making disgust, in all of its physicality, the origin of pure taste's expulsion of orality, Derrida, even more than Bourdieu, inscribes in the very workings of the theory the class judgments the latter finds implicit in Kant. And Derrida's analysis of disgust goes further still, since he argues a necessary vicariousness inscribed in its involuntariness that makes it simultaneously an expelled negative of taste and a negative reflection of the distance that defines pure taste. Indeed, even more than in the case of pure taste, because neither its orality nor its vicariousness can be escaped, disgust forces on us the structure of pure taste in both a highly physical and a highly negative form: "The word *vomit* arrests the vicariousness of disgust; it puts the thing in the mouth; it substitutes, but only for example, oral for anal. It is determined by the system of the beautiful, 'the symbol of morality,' as *its* other; it is then for philosophy, still, an elixir, even in the very quintessence of bad taste" ("Economimesis," 25).

Rather than laying out in any detail the steps by which Derrida reaches such a conclusion, I ask that its accuracy as a deconstruction of Kant's use of aesthetics for making a certain kind of moral judgment be at least for the moment assumed, if only within brackets (the moral interest Derrida notes is one we have in the very existence of aesthetic judgments being possible, not an interest in any specific judgment). Those concerned to support Bourdieu's analysis of disgust, at least, should have no trouble in accepting Derrida's conclusion, since this deconstruction gives a much deeper analytic content to Bourdieu's claim that class disgust works within Kant's aesthetic theory, necessarily rather than just in its specific contemporary upper-class embodiment.

But does Derrida effectively deconstruct disinterest as Kant defines it, as opposed to questioning its moral ties? And does his analysis expel disinterest or, as Bourdieu claims, enact it? To answer these questions, we must return to the Kantian discussion that both Bourdieu and Derrida treat, the one that culminates with a declaration of the barbarism of the pleasure of mere eating and drinking, and restore some elisions that they make. In establishing a moral interest in aesthetic taste, Kant originally distinguished not between pure taste and physical enjoyment but between a taste for the beautiful in nature and a taste for the beautiful in art. In a passage constructed out of very explicit contradiction, he asserts that we have a moral interest in the ability to take pleasure in the beauty of nature, but not in the ability to take pleasure in the beauty of art, because only the former can be truly disinterested:

> It is easy to explain why the satisfaction in the pure aesthetical judgment in the case of beautiful art is not combined with an immediate interest, as it is in the case of beautiful nature. For the former is either such an imitation of the latter that it reaches the point of deception and then produces the same effect as natural beauty (for which it is taken), or it is an art obviously directed designedly to our satisfaction. In the latter case the satisfaction in the product would, it is true, be brought about immediately by taste, but it would be only a mediate interest in the cause lying at its root, viz. an art that can only interest by means of its purpose and never in itself. (*Judgment,* 144)

Kant follows this claim with his assertion, now only too familiar to us, that the song of a bird in nature is beautiful because in hearing it we interpret it as nature proclaiming "gladsomeness and contentment with existence"

(*Judgment,* 144), and that that interpretation gives us pleasure whether nature "have this design or not" (*Judgment,* 145). If we found the song were a human imitation, though, it would cease to have this beauty because we could no longer construe it as a beauty given to us without intention but only as an effect of an intended skill. It is the inability to feel this special unintended beauty, one perhaps founded on an inaccurate interpretation of nature, that Kant finds morally wanting. Furthermore, he does not compare disinterested pleasure with the pleasures of eating and drinking, but compares the inability to feel any pleasure in nature but only pleasure in art with the inability to experience any pleasure but eating and drinking: "We regard as coarse and ignoble the mental attitude of those persons who have no *feeling* for beautiful nature (for thus we describe a susceptibility to interest in its contemplation) and who confine themselves to eating and drinking" (*Judgment,* 145). Both Bourdieu and Derrida quote this passage but forget that in context a pure taste for beautiful art that would not also be extendable to a taste for beautiful nature is precisely as "coarse and ignoble." The disinterest that even an interest in the contemplation of nature evidently has, and the moral interest we feel in the ability to have that disinterested interest, accrue as little to a pure taste for art as to a physical pleasure in eating and drinking. Indeed, the distinction between a moral interest consequent on the appreciation of natural beauty and not consequent on that of fine art is the explicit theme of section 42.

But since the taste for an object of fine art can be non-physical, and indeed, by Kant's own admission, can, in its immediate experience, be a "pure aesthetical judgment," why would one who could experience this taste, as well as the physical gratification of eating and drinking, but not the taste for beautiful nature, also be "coarse and ignoble"? To answer this question, we must first restore Kant's claim that aesthetic satisfaction is disinterested in the sense that it is "indifferent as regards the existence of an object" (*Judgment,* 43–44). If one considers disinterest as occurring if one desires neither gratification nor moral benefit from the object, but rather seeks only that aesthetic pleasure that Derrida describes as "arid," then the claim that one needs to be indifferent as to whether the object even exists, as we saw earlier, goes too far. We might value an object—for instance a beautiful painting—that gave us only that arid pleasure precisely because it gave us that pleasure, and thus take measures to preserve it (if it were a painting by putting it in a museum; if it were a poem by preserving it and disseminating knowledge of it through education and canonization). But for us reasonably to undertake such an act of preservation, we would have to know that our pleasure came in fact from the object of our perception as an effect of that object's existence. In the case of an aesthetic apprehension whose result is pleasure, as we have seen, that is exactly what we cannot know. Since the pleasure occurs as a result of apprehending the object as being purposive, as having the form of an object made, so to speak, on purpose, while in fact knowing that that purposiveness is without purpose, the purposiveness we experience does not necessarily correspond to a purpose whose achievement the object was designed to enact (*Judgment*, 55). So, again, our interpretation of the significance of a bird's song may not correspond to any real design in nature. We care about our apprehension of the bird's song, but not about the song itself as an object in nature. Preserving the song, to the extent that that was possible, might not therefore preserve the aesthetic apprehension that occurs with it at certain times. Would a tape of the song necessarily be any better than a perfect human imitation of it?

Once we recognize that the judgment of beauty can be completely disinterested in the way Kant means—without interest in the object's existence, its causes or the intentions behind it, as well as disinterested in gratification—only in the face of an object that may well not reliably give the pleasure afforded by the beautiful and that was not designed to give that pleasure, we can see the distinction he wants to draw between the beautiful in nature and in fine art, and why a moral interest accrues only to the ability to experience the former. Unlike an object in nature, a work of art, even a work of free, non-mercenary, fine art, has been designed to give us an experience of the beautiful. It is "directed designedly to our satisfaction" (*Judgment*, 144). Not only is art, therefore, not the primary example of objects judged as beautiful, as we have seen, but while we can in a certain sense make a pure aesthetical judgment of an artwork, independent its ability of the object to gratify a desire or to fulfill a moral interest, ultimately we do have an interest in the artwork's existence as one designed to fulfill the purpose of giving us the pure aesthetic pleasure. Thus Kant claims that our satisfaction in such an object "would, it is true, be brought about immediately by taste" (*Judgment*, 144). The immediate judgment of it is purely aesthetic. But "it would be only a mediate interest in the cause lying at its root, viz. an art that can only interest by means of its purpose and never in itself" (*Judgment*, 144). Since the object was designed to give us an immediate satisfaction, its design becomes a purpose in excess of that satisfaction and leading up to it, thus creating a mediate interest in the object's existence. Only by eliding this distinction between a disinterest in an object of fine art and the disinterest in the beautiful in nature, which extends even to an indifference to the object's existence, can Derrida get to the opposition between a physical and an abstract pleasure on which his deconstruction of disgust is based.

That Kantian disinterest goes beyond mere disinterest in physical gratification does not imply that the distinction between a desire for physical gratification and a more disinterested, "arid" pleasure does not also exist. It clearly does and it carries with it in Kant all the moral weight and sociological bias that Derrida deconstructs and that Bourdieu objects to in their discussions of disgust and coarse, physical pleasures. Within the terms of Derrida's deconstruction of the disinterest merely in physical gratification, his elision, in the above passage, of Kant's opposition into one between aesthetic taste and physical pleasure may be taken as a convenient compression. But Bourdieu's accusation is that Derrida's "supremely intellectual game," his deconstructing philosophy on its own terms, "presupposes lucidity in commitment to the game" (*Distinction*, 495), and that therefore even a successful deconstruction will merely repeat not only the game of philosophy, but to the extent that lucidity is, as Bourdieu claims, the most refined of Kantian aesthetic pleasures (*Distinction*, 485), also the game of aesthetics. And in support of this charge, the Kantian disinterest that is indifferent even to the existence of the object it judges, the disinterest both Derrida and Bourdieu mention but elide into the category of disinterest in gratification, does have a role to play. That indifference arises, as we have seen, from Kant's separation of a purposiveness that the judgment imputes to the object from any claim that that purposiveness matches up with a purpose, design, or intent that produced the object. Given that separation, the judgment has no reason to attend to the existence of any particular object, as opposed to the perception of formal purposiveness, which is the subject of aesthetic judgment.

But this handling of an object to find forms and effects that exceed its own ends applies as well to deconstructive analysis as it does to the aesthetic judgment. Derrida frequently discusses his mode of using the terms of philosophy to arrive at effects of its structure that exceed and undercut its explicit ends, but on which those ends depend. In discussing his treatment of Kant in *Truth in Painting*, he makes the comparison explicit in a passage Bourdieu quotes:

Starting out from pleasure, it was for pleasure that the third *Critique* was written, for pleasure that it should be read. . . . In letting myself be guided by pleasure I recognize and simultaneously put astray an injunction. *I follow it* [*je le suis*]: the enigma of pleasure puts the whole book in movement. *I seduce it* [*je le séduis*]: in treating the third *Critique* as a work of art or a beautiful object, which it was not simply designed to be, I act as if the existence of the book were indifferent to me (which, as Kant explains, is a requirement of any aesthetic experience) and could be considered with an imperturbable detachment. (*Truth in Painting*, 43)

Few who follow Derrida's reading of Kant would actually confuse it with a judgment of an aesthetic object (even assuming that such a judgment could be extended into an analytical method with more critical content than the only kind of judgment that Kant actually proposes: "This is beautiful"). But Derrida does mean seriously to treat the work with indifference to its own ends in order to show those elements of its own functioning that it cannot recognize. But although he is explicit, in a deceptively playful tone, about the ground he shares with Kant here, he rarely allows Kant the full force of his own definition. Following Kant's formulation, he calls this disinterest an "indifference" to the object's existence, which suggests not quite detachment but an absolute lack of caring or attention. But following Heidegger's critique of Nietzsche, he immediately withdraws this definition, restoring the "disinterest" he will proceed to deconstruct (*Truth in Painting*, 44). Or perhaps it would be more accurate to say that he does not allow Kant to claim the disinterest that he himself deploys. Of Kant's project, he says, "Now you have to know what you're talking about, what *intrinsically* concerns the value 'beauty' and what remains external to your immanent sense of beauty. This permanent requirement—to distinguish between the internal or proper sense and the circumstance of the object being talked about—organizes all philosophical discourses on art" (*Truth in Painting*, 45). Perhaps to write a philosophy of art, one has to know what one is talking about. But to have a disinterested judgment—or at least a judgment indifferent to its object's existence—that is exactly what one does not have to know. The distinction between internal sense and circumstance is just what that judgment brackets by separating purposiveness from purpose. The deconstruction of ornament and essence that follows this establishment of boundaries, then, is already there in the concept of aesthetic indifference. So, in judging the *Critique* as a work of art, Derrida does reproduce a part of the philosophy he deconstructs in somewhat the way that Bourdieu describes.

I say "somewhat" because my point is somewhat but significantly different from Bourdieu's. Bourdieu suggests that Derrida participates willingly in the game he deconstructs. He quotes Derrida on following Kant's aesthetic disinterest without making clear that Derrida sees this procedure as his version of a refusal to participate in Kant's game. In contrast, by arguing that both Bourdieu and Derrida suppress part of Kant's game, and that Derrida's deconstruction draws on the part they both suppress, I am suggesting not that Derrida is just disguised traditionalism, but that Kant's seemingly "traditional" aesthetics functions centrally in precisely the most corrosive aspect of Derrida's analysis. Perhaps Derrida avoids tracing out this aspect of Kant's theory as part of its design rather than applying it explicitly as part of his deconstruction because such a tracing would occlude the analytical departure he wants to claim for deconstruction. And if, moreover, Derrida captures, even in overly abstract terms, the main elements of Bourdieu's critique of Kant, and if the Kantian element of his deconstruction does not really undercut that critique, but allows it, where does that leave Bourdieu's own critique?

At this point, one may turn upon Bourdieu the rather tattered question of the problem of his own discourse without, I hope, risking, much less settling for, the glib dismissal of contradiction that usually follows upon such a question. Certainly, the contradictions between the grounds for Bourdieu's condemnation of Derrida and his own description of his practices are so obvious that they could only be our starting point. Without the example of deconstructing Kant directly in front of him, Bourdieu openly employs the justifications he condemns in Derrida:

> The style of the book [*Distinction*], whose long, complex sentences may offend—constructed as they are with a view to reconstituting the complexity of the social world in a language capable of holding together the most diverse things while setting them in rigorous perspective—stems partly from the endeavour to mobilize all the resources of the traditional modes of expression, literary, philosophical or scientific, so as to say things that were de facto or de jure excluded from them, and to prevent the reading from slipping back into the simplicities of the smart essay or the political polemic. (*Distinction*, xiii)

This passage from the preface to the English-language edition will, of course, have been written some years after the book's concluding pages on Derrida. Still, Bourdieu's claim to use the resources of academic expression against themselves is striking in view of his criticizing Derrida for the same modus operandi. For the moment let us set aside the question of why he criticizes Derrida for his own practice and ask it in reverse: assuming his suspicion that academic language re-creates the class biases of traditional philosophy is genuine—as I do—why would he use this suspicious style and method? One may put the question in an even more self-referentially specific form. Bourdieu extends his suspicions of academic discourse fairly enough to the discourses of sociology itself: "The existence of a scientific sociology is as improbable as ever in times when the position of sociologist is one of the refuges for those intent on escaping classification" (*Distinction*, 587). But, of course, either Bourdieu's discourse escapes his own classifications or it reenacts one of the class biases those classifications reveal. Either he has the inauthentic desire or he capitulates to being caught within the class system.

Above, I said that Bourdieu's desire to separate his own discourse from the academic one that it means to critique, but in which it so clearly participates, would reveal its contradictions in his turn on Derrida. But surely this is the kind of contradiction that my last chapter argued was purely formal: it might be true that academic discourse has the shape it does from the class distinctions it supports and still be the best discourse for unveiling that cause (this is the reverse of the traditional defense of reason and disinterest, which notes that the discourse may have the effect of supporting class distinctions and still have all the qualities of reason and disinterest usually claimed for it). For one academic to persuade another (and Bourdieu's audience is academic) of the class bias of that discourse, he or she will still have to employ it. And this will be true even if academic discourse has only a much more local value than Enlightenment reason, even if there is some clearer manifestation of that reason that would trump it. To the extent that we academics identify our discourse with reason, we will always identify any discourse that persuades us of its reason with our own. Thus an effective trumping of academic discourse immediately participates in that discourse. And this is why the finding of contradiction can be glib. If Bourdieu's position about academic discourse is true, and also he can only formulate it in that discourse's own terms, then the contradiction would be a formal necessity, but it wouldn't have much ontological force. Like other postmoderns, Bourdieu's position about Enlightenment reason and value can be articulated, but it cannot be proven within the terms of the Enlightenment that it uses. Its strength will be in the force of its articulation—but only in that.

The glibness of wanting to catch postmodernism in the net of its own discourse thus lies in the cheapness of the victory it offers. In the face of the massiveness and detail of Bourdieu's sociological analysis, the self-contradiction here seems cheap and small indeed. But the accusation has a particular force for Bourdieu because, unlike Foucault, he will not accept the means of extricating himself from it, the recognition of the aesthetic resources of his position. Kant's indifference as to the existence of the object, the willingness to analyze circumstance without regard to propriety or essence, serves him as well as it does Derrida, and in the same way. Both Bourdieu and Derrida engage in an academic or philosophic analysis as Kant would judge aesthetically, mixing circumstance and essence, accident and intent, to delineate a structure whose significance stands apart from its origin and even the problem of its own internal integrity. Once one has become indifferent to existence, in the mode of Kant's aesthetic apprehension, one's capture in one's own analysis is equally a matter of indifference. The only question is the status of the purposiveness one judges, the sociological system one outlines, the philosophical system one traces and deconstructs. The problem of the status of one's own discourse becomes a trivial, psychological matter once one simply accepts one's own entrapment within it. Even if Bourdieu were the most disingenuous of sociologists, trying to evade his own classifications, the accuracy or inaccuracy of those classifications would remain unchanged. Even if Derrida were the most mystified of standard philosophers, reproducing in his discourse the limits he hopes to question, the accuracy or inaccuracy of his analysis would also remain unchanged. In effect, the status of the writer becomes as indifferent to the existence of the discourse as the existence of its content was to the writer.

So we return to the question addressed at the outset: "Why Derrida?" Why does Bourdieu proceed from attacking Kant to attacking Derrida for committing transgressions that are his own as well? Given Bourdieu's use of the Kantian aesthetics he so unrelentingly combats, one might guess that Derrida was the screen image for the Kantian elements he will not recognize. Like Derrida, Bourdieu can at moments see the Kantian nature of his project, but he cannot allow himself to hold on to that perception. Thus he ends his English-language preface with an explicit recognition of the aesthetic quality of his sociological analysis:

At all events, there is nothing more universal than the project of objectifying the mental structures associated with the particularity of a social structure. Because it presupposes an epistemological break which is also a social break, a sort of estrangement from the familiar, domestic, native world, the critique (in the Kantian sense) of culture invites each reader, through the "making strange" beloved of the Russian formalists, to reproduce on his or her own behalf the critical break of which it is the product. For this reason it is perhaps the only rational basis for a truly universal culture. (*Distinction*, xiv)

Derrida's critique of Kant's aesthetics coexists only too notoriously with his recognition that his deconstruction lives within the Western philosophy it deconstructs. There may be, so to speak, an anxiety of influence in the enthusiastic deconstruction of aesthetics that deconstructive literary critics have engaged in, almost in direct response to the accusation that deconstruction is all too formalist. But this anxiety has its mirror in Bourdieu's fear of being trapped in the merely academic, an entrapment Derrida clearly represents for him. Derrida's problem, for Bourdieu, is too great an abstraction of the issues whose basic analysis they both share. But Derrida's style, as we have seen, fails to make a social break (*Distinction*, 496). In a sense, this is a version of refusing to recognize one's own Kantianism, but it is extended to a refusal to recognize one's own participation in a project virtually descriptive of the academic culture one also seeks to analyze. Thus Bourdieu finds himself caught between two nauseas. He wants to avoid "the smart essay or the political polemic," surely his versions of Kant's coarse and ignoble indulgences, which a higher, more rigorous analysis disdains. But, not wanting to participate in an academic discourse whose class markers also turn his stomach, by vomiting out Derridean style, perhaps he may also expel the academicism resulting from his own desire to avoid "slipping back" into being merely "smart."

But if Kantian indifference toward the existence of the object of judgment enables the achievements of Foucault's, Bourdieu's, and Derrida's cultural and philosophical analyses, it may also allow us to take advantage of those achievements without the particular anxieties that accompany at least some of them at times. After all, indifference is in excess of Kant's disgust with the physical and thus may also go beyond Bourdieu's repulsion from the traditional and the lucid. At the opening of this section, I asked rhetorically why one would subject Bourdieu to an aesthetic analysis: by analyzing his reading of Derrida's reading of Kant as a conclusion of a discussion of his detailed sociology, has this chapter not risked a reduction into aesthetic ornament? One might almost say I was risking an indifference to the real political issues at stake. The accusation is of course both Bourdieu's and Foucault's of Derrida in the first instance. Nor is the motivation behind it trivial since it motivates Derrida as well: if one is to escape irrelevant academic discourse that continues the status quo, it would seem that one ought to worry over what would recapture one within that discourse. I have been arguing here, however, first the common ground among Bourdieu, Derrida, and even one aspect of Kant in producing the skeptical analysis at least the first two want. And second, I have been suggesting that the answer to the Bourdieuvian and Foucaultian worry is a certain Kantian indifference. We are regularly told that it leads to quietism or even a positive defense of the status quo. But it may lead as directly to the kind of corrosive questioning that only a complete indifference can enable. The case of Foucault exhibits what a consciously accepted aestheticism does to give coherence to his critique of Enlightenment reason and value. The greater strength of that case is that only acceptance gives Bourdieu's critique of aesthetics its coherence as well.

Notes

INTRODUCTION

1. I will discuss and cite the works in which these attacks have been mounted in the body of this work as each becomes relevant.

2. The most important of these have been Wendy Steiner's *The Scandal of Pleasure: Art in the Age of Fundamentalism*, Elaine Scarry's *On Beauty and Being Just*, Peter de Bolla's *Art Matters*, and Isobel Armstrong's *The Radical Aesthetic*.

3. As with all generalizations in this chapter, this one simplifies greatly. Bourdieu, throughout his works as we shall see, both distinguishes cultural capital from economic capital and also shows them as part of the same larger system of class distinction. Guillory, in a work influenced by Bourdieu, *Cultural Capital*, also sees aesthetic and economic value as convertible, though he does not think that this means that one reduces to the other (327; also see Armstrong's discussion of this issue, *Radical Aesthetic*, 156). See also Mary Poovey's "Aesthetics and Political Economy in the Eighteenth Century: The Place of Gender in the Social Constitution of Knowledge." Peter Bürger's *Theory of the Avant-Garde*, although it does not use the issue of economic exchange, also discusses the rise of aesthetic autonomy in terms of a conscious attempt by artists to separate art off from surrounding capitalist values.

4. The features this aesthetic sensibility valued were, as we will see, certainly class based; if, for instance, Shaftesbury's point had been to prove that these features were part of the objective value of art, this would be a problem for his theory. But, in fact, he more or less took the features as a given in order to establish the internal moral sensibility of human beings. While this does not make his theory any more tenable either as an aesthetics or as an ethics, it does affect how we need to construe his thinking about aesthetics.

5. I will cite numerous sources for this critique in Chapter 2. Paul de Man has made the most famous versions of both of its claims, the first in his essay, reprinted in *Blindness and Insight*, "The Rhetoric of Temporality" (187–228), and the second in "Kant and Schiller," in *The Aesthetic Ideology* (129–162).

6. Artworks are, of course, intended to be perceived as such, so when we apprehend their aesthetic beauty we in fact apprehend them according to the pur-

poses for which they were created. When he spoke of apprehending purposiveness without purpose, Kant had in mind apprehending beauty in natural objects. Duchamp's *Fountain* forces extending Kantian apprehension to artworks—and thus shows why this apprehension is necessary to an aesthetic theory that will account for it as an artwork—because, as we shall see, in order to interpret even what it was intended to mean, paradoxically, we must interpret it as having significances that were beyond what Duchamp could have intended.

7. Marc Redfield has noted the identification of deconstruction with theory in both *Phantom Formations* and *Politics of Aesthetics*, noting in the second work: "When debates about theory grow heated, as sooner or later they generally do, theory sooner or later turns out to mean deconstruction. Deconstruction is 'high theory,' the theoretical essence of theory" (5).

8. In *Aestheticism and Deconstruction*, I discussed at length the charge that deconstruction is a form of aesthetics and hence politically conservative or quietist.

9. Marc Redfield makes a particularly clear statement claiming a connection between aesthetics and the deconstructive identification of the Enlightenment's foundational delusion: "As a philosophic field, aesthetics forms part—a crucial, though . . . almost always subordinate part—of modern philosophy's effort to ground itself in the subject and its perceptions" (*Politics of Aesthetics*, 10–11). The inaugural claim of the connection between aesthetics and totalitarian ideology is de Man's in "Kant and Schiller" (*Aesthetic Ideology*, 129–162), although, as I argued in "Materialism and Aesthetics," I think de Man does see a strand of aesthetics in Kantian materialism that he thinks of as an aesthetic critique of ideology rather than an aesthetic embodiment of it. The most important contemporary exponent of this critique of aesthetics has been Marc Redfield, in the two books cited above. Michael Sprinker, in "Art and Ideology: Althusser and de Man" (Cohen et al., *Material Events*, 32–48), has seen aesthetics as both manifesting and critiquing ideology.

CHAPTER 1: AESTHETICS AND THE ARGUMENT FROM DESIGN

1. M. H. Abrams discusses in one paragraph the connection between the argument from design and seventeenth-century mechanistic theories of the physical universe (*Mirror and the Lamp*, 164).

2. A footnote annotating recent critical works that have taken aesthetics as an ideologically-driven mystification could well turn into a bibliography of its own. Linda Dowling, in *The Vulgarization of Art: The Victorians and Aesthetic Democracy*, sums up the tendency this way: "We have been reluctant to take [aesthetic claims] seriously, I think, because of a certain tendency in contemporary criticism to regard the very idea of the aesthetic as mystification, to see all talk of art or beauty as no more than one of the ruses or stratagems through which societies perpetuate themselves as orders of domination" (x). She goes on to note as examples of this Peter Bürger's *Theory of the Avant-Garde*, which devotes its first two chapters to the links between the rise of aesthetics and the rise of bourgeois society and

the ideological effects of the concept of autonomy; Pierre Bourdieu's *Distinctions*, the burden of which is the class-distinguishing effects of a disinterested appreciation of art; and Martha Woodmansee's *The Author, Art, and the Market*, in which, in Dowling's words, "the study of the aesthetic is dismissed at the outset . . . to proceed with the more pressing business at hand: uncovering 'the underlying motives' of writers or artists as revealed by their 'professional and economic interests'" (x). Perhaps more noticeably because George Levine's collection of essays *Aesthetics and Ideology* is devoted to questioning this position, nevertheless two of its most powerful essays, Mary Poovey's "Aesthetics and Political Economy in the Eighteenth Century: The Place of Gender in the Social Constitution of Knowledge" (79–105), and Geoffrey Galt Harpham's "Aesthetics and the Fundamentals of Modernity" (124–149), reproduce it. The position has also been extremely influential in practical criticism of Romantic poetry, probably as a way of disentangling itself from the importance various Romantic concepts of the aesthetic have had to contemporary literary theories, particularly the New Criticism and de Manian–influenced deconstruction. As an example, every one of the five essays on Wordsworth in Karl Kroeber's and Gene Ruoff's collection, *Romantic Poetry: Recent Revisionary Criticism*, articulates a politics or an economics behind lyrics such as "Tintern Abbey" or "The Ruined Cottage," as well as behind *The Prelude* (123–188). This collection is exemplary, since the authors of several of its essays—Alan Liu, Marjorie Levinson, and Jerome McGann, among others—have been models in defining the role of historicism in the analysis of Romanticism as historically locating the role of the aesthetic. This location then supports an ideological explanation of that aesthetic.

3. One should note that the problem here is not with Richards's definition of poetry itself, but with the consequences of that definition for practical criticism. No necessary logic ties art to a responsibility to provide a way for an objective criticism of it to occur. If this is a problem, it is a problem of criticism, not of art or poetry. This distinction is important here because Richards's position, while a minority viewpoint in the twentieth century, was central, as we will see, in the eighteenth century, and its complexity has been considerably reduced by the tendency to write affective theories off as part of a moribund associational psychology. The consequent lack of curiosity about eighteenth-century aesthetic theories has been so general that when affective criticism became current some years back, few reader-response critics looked back to Kames or Burke for a discussion of the emotive workings of literature and art—perhaps because those earlier writers did not presume, as both Brooks and affective critics do, that emotive effect equals unshareable subjectivity.

4. I specify "evaluate" because although some New Critics have in fact argued that a poem's meaning may be interpreted without reference to a poet's intention, Wimsatt's and Beardsley's notorious essay "The Intentional Fallacy" never makes such an argument. Its opening statement of aim is clear enough: "The design or intention of the author is neither available nor desirable as a standard for judging

the success of a work of literary art" (Wimsatt, *Verbal Icon*, 3). And this insistence on the topic of evaluation is maintained consistently throughout the essay. Wimsatt and Beardsley never deny that the words of a poem mean what the author intended them to mean. The one part of the essay that explicitly engages intention and meaning, the interpretation of Donne's image of the trepidation of the spheres, does not argue that their textually extrapolated meaning is the right one because more complex, or aesthetically better than the one they oppose, which is derived from a knowledge of Donne's interest in the new cosmology. They argue that the text simply will not bear that ostensibly historically more informed argument, that it provides better evidence for an alternative meaning, one actually intended by Donne (Wimsatt, *Verbal Icon*, 13–14).

5. Perhaps unfairly, but not unsurprisingly, Wimsatt and Beardsley have been criticized for the mechanism in the first of the sentences by an aesthetician concerned with defending non-mechanistic ideas of order, and who consequently does not quote the sentences that follow (Sobol, "Arguing, Accepting," 288). A more purely non-intentional, but analogous sense of formalism obtained in the art criticism coincident with the New Criticism. Because paintings do not clearly have meanings, these critics were able to discuss formal techniques and solutions rather than painters' beliefs and philosophies (see Ingrid Stadler's "The Idea of Art and of Its Criticism," 196). This form of non-intentionalism did not appeal to a special concept of organic unity to explain its order, perhaps since the status of a technique is inherently somewhat mechanistic but also split enough from intended meaning to keep critical attention fixed on form.

6. One should perhaps note that the concept of immanentalism, regardless of Chytry's defense of Winckelmann, has since the nineteenth century been found conservative, not because it is repressive but because it tends always to defend the status quo. Mill noted this about Coleridge in his generally admiring essay "Coleridge" (*Essays on Ethics*, 120, 146), and Raymond Williams followed suit in *Culture and Society*.

7. Partially, this passage may be quoted so frequently because much of it is a word-for-word translation of a passage in Schlegel's *Course of Lectures on Dramatic Art and Literature* (340). Those wishing to see a parallel matching of the two texts, combined with a harsh criticism of Coleridge for plagiarism, should consult Norman Fruman's *Coleridge, the Damaged Archangel*, 160–162. For a display of the texts in parallel that treats the issue as one of literary influence, see G. M. Orsini's "Coleridge and Schlegel Reconsidered." Managing to depart from both views, Thomas McFarland, in *Coleridge and the Pantheist Tradition*, insists on the situation as one of formal plagiarism coupled with the argument of much of the book as a whole that Coleridge plagiarized passages but not ideas, frequently espousing views in contradiction to the passages he borrows (256–261). The real issue here, of course, which I will consider below, is not one of scholarly ethics but of intellectual history, of determining the relation between Coleridge's concept and the various sources from which it came.

8. Raimondo Modiano (*Coleridge and the Concept of Nature*, 66–86) has an extensive discussion of the connections between Coleridge's ideas about the symbol and his conceptions of nature. De Man, of course, uses Coleridge's contrast of symbol and allegory to question the coherence of Coleridge's linking of symbolic immanence with organicism, and of the history of Romanticism that derives from this linking (*Blindness and Insight*, 191–193). Since de Man's article "The Rhetoric of Temporality," my cursory reading of Coleridge here has become more than a bit old-fashioned. Jerome Christensen's *Coleridge and the Blessed Machine of Language* has shown that a more nuanced reading of the structure, logical and narrative, of Coleridge's prose shows its imbedding of the elements in it that others might use to deconstruct organicism from the outside. And more recently, David Ferris, in *Theory and the Evasion of History*, 37–134, while faulting Christensen for assuming that a single text could offer a privileged version within it of the deconstructive insight, still uses the various problems that Coleridge's texts raise, both thematically and structurally, to exemplify current interpretive problems. My justification here for returning to an older reading of Coleridge is not to create a straw man for yet another deconstruction but to restore a literary history that will both buttress and comprehend that deconstruction, as well as the attacks of other recent theories on aesthetics that Coleridge's formulations veil as well as convey into the Anglo-American tradition.

9. The issue of Coleridge's relationship to his German sources has of course been much discussed. Rene Wellek, in *Immanuel Kant in England* (65–135), discusses in detail Coleridge's departures from Kant and generally sees him as misunderstanding what he doesn't knowingly misuse for his own reasons. Orsini's *Coleridge and German Idealism* argues for Coleridge's total comprehension of and influence by German idealism in general and Kant, Fichte, and Schelling in particular, summing up: "At this time Coleridge was an absolute or transcendental idealist. Historically, this is more than remarkable. It is a unique phenomenon in early nineteenth-century England, which has not yet been completely recognized even by historians of philosophy" (219–220). Modiano sees Coleridge refining his understanding of German idealism into an even more complex philosophy (100). Fruman manages to agree with both opposed positions, his whole book tracing every passage he can find that Coleridge has plagiarized from German sources even as his chapter on Coleridge's aesthetics generally argues that Coleridge misapplied and misunderstood the ideas he stole (176–218). McFarland's intervention into this debate has been quite influential. Recognizing the extent of Coleridge's plagiarism, he nevertheless noted that Coleridge frequently lifted passages whose ideas he pointedly did not follow. He thus contests Wellek directly, as he points out (13), arguing that Coleridge meant to oppose what McFarland sees as the Spinozism and pantheism of later German idealism. More recently, Jerome Christensen, in *Coleridge's Blessed Machine of Language*, has analyzed much of Coleridge's struggles with ostensible idealist ideas of freedom and necessity, as well as textual consistency and form, in terms of his struggle with English empiricism and

particularly with David Hartley's associationism (58 117). David Ferris, although contesting Christensen's analysis because using deconstruction it privileges Coleridge as a founding example of deconstructive textuality (*Theory and the Evasion of History*, 258), also ties Coleridge's concerns in with the problems of New Critical theory, and does so in terms of a resistance to Kant and Schelling (37–134). Although my analysis here has been informed by parts of all of these arguments, I have no particular stake in whether or not Coleridge did or did not understand or use or misuse his German sources generally. On the issue that does concern me, however—his articulation of the idea of organic form as it has been received by Anglo-American criticism—my argument has most in common with Christensen's. Coleridge certainly did use German sources but his ideas came out oddly empiricized.

10. The most extensive comparison of Coleridge with Kant is G. N. G. Orsini's *Coleridge and German Idealism*. Both Abrams, 174, and Orsini, 171, compare Coleridge's definition of organic form specifically with Kant's discussion of a teleological order in nature in the second half of *The Critique of Judgment*.

11. See, for example, Schelling's *Philosophy of Art*, 17, which defines art in terms of its presentation of archetypes as objects, and Schiller's *On the Sublime*, 195, which marks the aesthetic tendency in human beings as one which learns to see the moral and the idealistic in terms of sensible objects. In this, of course, both Schelling and Schiller follow the main German idealist tradition after Kant of seeing art as the mode of seeing the idea sensuously embodied, a tradition that culminates in Hegel's definition of the highest art: "In the highest art are Idea and presentation truly in conformity with one another, in the sense that the shape given to the Idea is in itself the absolutely true shape" (*Aesthetics*, I, 74–75). Symbolic embodiment will be a matter of direct concern in the next chapter.

12. Thus Winckelmann argues that Greek artists could model their sculptures of Gods after human examples because they had "in view a more beauteous and more perfect Nature" (*Reflections*, 14).

13. Fichte objects to Kant's claim that one could only know appearances and not their real causes (their noumena) because Kant claims that the existence of the noumena could only be known as necessary causes, but since causality, in Kant, is a pure concept of the understanding, one cannot properly use it to explain anything supersensible without being guilty of the paralogism of Pure Reason as it is later explained. To solve the problem, both Fichte and Schelling contend that the organizing principles of the mind are identical with the realities they organize and not, as Kant argues, merely necessary to our comprehension. This problem is explained in numbers of secondary philosophical texts, but the one most readily available to non-specialists is Orsini's *Coleridge and German Idealism*, 173. My doubts about Orsini's more general claim for the closeness with which Coleridge follows Kant's views of nature and art should be sufficiently clear in the body of my argument.

14. At least by eighteenth- and nineteenth-century definition. Virtually every

writer on aesthetics distinguishes more or less carefully between beauty in nature and artistic beauty precisely in terms of the intended and made quality of the latter. To different ends, both Kant and Hegel insist on the distinction—Kant, as we will see, to rate natural beauty more highly (Kant, *Judgment*, 144–147); Hegel, to rate aesthetic beauty as the only one that has real significance to the mind (Hegel, *Aesthetics*, I, 152). Only contemporary anti-intentionalism leads to the concept of found art-objects. And of course, intentionalists counter that even they are not art objects but merely objects until an intending mind chooses to apprehend them as art.

15. John Stuart Mill uses precisely this argument later in the century to show that the argument from design tends to disprove a Christian God, though it might allow for a higher power of a limited nature *(Essays on Ethics, Religion and Society,* 451).

16. The logical trap here became historically manifest later in the nineteenth century, when Herbert Gosse tried to make divine creation consistent with geological and biological evidence of gradual development, arguing that, of necessity, God had created the world along with the "evidences" of a history it did not have. Without those evidences, he argued, the world could not have existed in logically consistent terms. His book, *Omphalos*, while logically sound in theological terms, was notoriously ineffective, according to his son, Edmund, because it made divine creation seem a giant shell game, so to speak. Edmund Gosse has one reader summing up the argument as one in which God created fossils to tempt geologists into infidelity (Gosse, *Father and Son*, 87).

17. Cassirer argued that "the great systems of English psychology contributed practically nothing towards the real foundation of aesthetics" and that "aesthetics is not a product of the general trend of English empiricism, but of English Platonism" (*Platonic Renaissance,* 196, 197). More recently, Linda Dowling has shown that Shaftesbury's resistance to the political implications of Lockean empiricism, and his discussion of ethics and aesthetics in terms of the idealism he learned from the Cambridge Platonists, led to the enduring contradictory tendency in English aesthetics to see art as both democratic and elitist (2–17). And Oscar Kenshur, in "'The Tumour of Their Own Hearts': Relativism, Aesthetics, and the Rhetoric of Demystification," has argued much more closely for the influence of Ralph Cudworth's response to Hobbes on Shaftesbury's definition of art as the basis for ethical response (Levine, ed., *Aesthetics and Ideology,* 57–78).

18. Cassirer, again, marked this tendency to see nature as plastic rather than mechanical (50). And McFarland, who generally is skeptical of attempts to see Coleridge's influence by and liftings from German idealist writers as actually ideas he had absorbed from Cambridge Platonists, nevertheless marks Cudworth's definition of "plastick nature" in *The True Intellectual System of the Universe* as an early definition of an organic view of nature (261). McFarland also quotes some of the formulations about plastick nature cited below that seem most strikingly to predict the concept of organic form.

19. The other form is Stratonic atheism, which holds nature to be animated by an internal, but artificial and unconscious, force to the exclusion of any external deity. One of the underrated pleasures of reading Cudworth is the mad proliferation of strange names for strange unbeliefs. One would never have thought that atheism had, among its other virtues, such a wild profusion of arcane variants.

20. The appeal to the eye as evidence of design is constant, almost no matter what the status of the rest of the argument. Cudworth instances it (685). So does Clarke, who, as we will see, does not appeal to design to prove the existence of God (Clarke, *Discourse*, 68–69). And it is Paley's first extended analogue after the notorious watch (*Natural Theology*, 13). So unanswerable seemed this example that Darwin explicitly confronted it at length in *The Origin of Species* in order to show how the eye's complexity could be accounted for in terms of variation and natural selection (186–189). And Huxley declared the success of Darwin's theory precisely in terms of how it undoes natural theology's appeals to the eye as evidence of a designing intelligence: "The Teleology which supposes that the eye such as we see it in man or one of the higher *Vertebrata*, was made with the precise structure which it exhibits, for the purpose of enabling the animal which possesses it to see, has undoubtedly received its death-blow" (110). Despite Huxley and Darwin, the power of the eye as an example of design did not die easily, as witness Mill's modified and cautious acceptance of it as at least indicating a strong possibility of design (*Essays on Ethics*, 448).

21. Thus Terry Eagleton, in his discussion of Baumgarten in *Ideology of the Aesthetic*, starts with "aesthetics is born as a discourse of the body" (13) and soon winds up describing it as a "prosthesis to reason" (16).

22. The standard histories of aesthetics tend like Bosanquet to classify Shaftesbury as a Neoplatonist, but Burke, Kames, Hogarth, and Reynolds as empirical (*A History of Aesthetic*, 177, 202–210). From the perspective of the Continent, Croce classes everybody from Shaftesbury through Hutcheson, to the Scottish school of Smith and Reid, as followers of Locke (*Aesthetic as Science*, 206). A more recent history, connecting Shaftesbury through Hutcheson to the writers that followed, argues that the empiricism of those writers did not obstruct a constant turn to seventeenth-century classicism (Gilbert and Kuhn, *History of Esthetics*, 233–234).

23. The term *poetical justice* was coined in the late seventeenth century by Thomas Rymer and referred to the proper distribution of rewards and punishments within a drama (*Critical Works*, 22).

24. This is Addison's objection (Bond, *The Spectator*, IV, 465). Although Rymer speaks of the allotment of rewards and punishments, he in fact was writing about tragedy. He surely did not intend to disallow the suffering of the sympathetic that is necessary to the genre, and really only insisted on the visible and appropriate punishment of "Malefaction" (26). But the problem of why we enjoy tragedy, which exercised eighteenth-century critics, did rest on its infliction of pain on characters with whom we might feel sympathy. On the issue of what kind of pleasure we take in tragedy, see Hume's "Of Tragedy" (*Of a Standard*, 29–38) and

Burke's *Philosophical Enquiry into the Origin of Our Ideas of the Sublime and Beautiful* (45–48).

25. Positions in this debate pretty much cover the range of logical possibilities. In two essays—"Style as Philosophical Structure: The Contexts of Shaftesbury's *Characteristics*" and "Sentimentality as Performance: Shaftesbury, Sterne, and the Theatrics of Virtue"—Robert Markeley has argued for the class-based nature of Shaftesbury's arguments for taste as a code of conduct. Lawrence Klein's *Shaftesbury and the Culture of Politeness* (9) sees Shaftesbury as genuinely trying to define universal moral values, albeit out of the material of his own class and personal experience. Linda Dowling's *Vulgarization of Art* (3–17) sees both forces at work.

26. Kenshur quotes another critic who claims that neither Cudworth's *The True Intellectual System of the Universe* nor his *Discourse Concerning Eternal and Immutable Morality* would have been written but for Hobbes's *Leviathan* (Levine, 76).

27. Earlier I noted that Shaftesbury was predicted by natural theologians in using art as a model for adducing the moral governance of the world. Although there is no particular evidence that he followed Clarke particularly in this, Clarke, Ray, Cudworth, and others all preceded Shaftesbury and set up the outlines of the analogy. Cudworth's influence on Shaftesbury is, of course, well known, and Shaftesbury follows him in comparing the contriving artist both with "plastick nature" and with "that Sovereign Artist" (*Characteristics*, I, 207).

28. This narrator does not seem generally to represent Hume's position since he judges Cleanthes's natural theology to have carried the dispute. But since Philo later testifies to his own sense of the weakness of his argument here, I think we may take this description of his embarrassment as accurate.

29. In this context, Hume's contention in "Of the Standard of Taste" (*Of the Standard*, 3–25) that regardless of the difficulties of proving it, there is a standard of taste shared by the educated that has objective reality must be taken more than a little ironically as an assertion in a category with Cleanthes's insistence upon the sensational reality of design, and Barbara Hernnstein Smith's objections against Hume's aesthetic position as "axiological" (*Contingencies of Value*, 55–64) oddly refuses to see the devastating effect of the limitations he places on his ostensibly axiological assertions.

30. Gilbert and Kuhn note the frequent opinion that Kant "added little to former writings except 'systematic form'" (323). They argue that this systematic form was no little addition, as it gave aesthetics philosophic seriousness. But this hardly goes far enough. Virtually no central idea that Kant imports from earlier critics goes untransformed by his notorious Copernican shift in philosophy. For instance, Kant's "harmony of the faculties," which will be discussed in some detail below, surely has similarities to Shaftesbury's concept of harmonious systems reflecting each other. And Shaftesbury did recognize that the perception of harmony was the core of aesthetic pleasure and its moral import rather than the actual harmony in the object. Nevertheless, as I will argue, if we see Kant's concept about how we

perceive in terms of Shaftesbury's concept of what we perceive, we will miss the point of his argument.

31. Elsewhere, in his articulation of the pure concepts of the understanding (*Pure Reason*, 127), Kant does mean to refute or at least analyze the limits of Hume's debunking of causality and more generally he restores the claims of reason to function intelligibly (606–612).

32. Since I will later be contesting some of Derrida's deconstructions of Kant's aesthetic theories, I think it right to note here that Derrida's claim that the assertion of an abyss between two realms presupposes as an analogy an existence of a bridge (*Truth in Painting*, 36), and that thus Kant's way of proposing the problem about the relation of understanding's cognition and reason's moral dictates already presupposes the solution whose existence is in question. More generally, while I think Kant's direct aesthetic formulations already comprehend Derrida's objections to them, I think those objections take on their full force when one considers them in relation to Kant's claimed transition to the teleological judgment.

33. The most important example, here, is Paul Guyer in *Kant and the Claims of Taste*. Guyer opens with his argument that Kant claims that aesthetic judgments are "intersubjectively valid." In other words, the aesthetic judgment is not universal with regard to objects but with regard to a certain kind of response to them. Starting from this principle, Guyer, giving up as much baggage as he thinks necessary, nevertheless wants to establish the validity of this basic principle. As a result, he early on throws overboard the whole discussion of the teleological judgment on the grounds that the discussion seems too close to making judgments about objects, the avoidance of which he sees as the whole strength of Kant's argument (33–34). It follows that when Guyer finds problems with Kant's discussion of the principle of purposiveness as necessary to the reflective judgment, he proceeds to unlink reflective judgment and taste (66–67). Guyer quite rightly denies that Kant is concerned with what most literary critics want from an aesthetic theory—either a method of making objective evaluative judgments of specific works of art or an argument showing why that cannot be done (thus Smith's final dismissal of Kant as demanding too much purity to be relevant to any actual judgment—*Contingencies*, 64–72). But once he has also denied the purposes Kant gives aesthetics, the work of grounding the reflective judgment, he makes it less and less pointed. Guyer's analyses of every detail of the first half of *The Aesthetic of Judgment* is indispensable, and yet probably has not had the effect on the reading of the work that it ought to have had on literary critics, as opposed to philosophers, because it already seems to evade what for literary critics, at least, are the largest concerns of the work in favor of analyzing its details. Regardless of my disagreements with it over this issue, it has shaped much of my reading here.

34. This is James Creed Meredith's translation of the terms. Guyer follows Meredith, knowing that it elides the obvious connection between *zweck* and *zweckmässigkeit*, but arguing that "purposiveness" may connote more of connections with purpose than Kant wanted, and that "finality" and "end" may function

as technical terms allowing Kant's definitions to function in isolation from our own connotations (*Kant and the Claims of Taste*, 405).

35. If one substituted "finality" and "end" for "purposiveness" and "purpose," but maintained Kant's definitions, the phrase would actually lose none of its contradictory character, since "end" would have to be "intended end" and "finality" would apply to the kind of form we perceive when we say of a literary work that it has closure. Indeed "finality without end" merely adds other contradictory resonances, which may or may not be relevant. Thus Derrida (*Truth in Painting*, 84–88) rings various changes on the phrase "finality without end," but only to reproduce the contradiction only too apparent in the phrase "purposiveness without purpose." If philosophers such as Guyer and Pluhar try to explain the difficulties of the phrase, though, at least they are aware of it. When aesthetic and literary theorists invoke the phrase, it comes to mean almost unproblematically something like an internal, organic form. Thus Monroe Beardsley tries to explain away the contradictoriness, arguing that "we can say that the object doesn't have a purpose, but its harmony and wholeness make it *look* as though it were purposefully made" (*Aesthetics From Classical Greece to the Present*, 216). And Gilbert and Kuhn offer much the same explanation (337). But what does it mean to say that a thing looks as if it were purposefully made while also saying that it was not so made? This is the key issue in Kant that formalism evades rather than confronts.

36. More recently, a number of commentators, by eliding the difference between the teleological and the aesthetic judgment, argue that Kant intends the aesthetic judgment to offer a kind of knowledge of unknown natural phenomena. Thus, Rodolphe Gasché argues that the aesthetic judgment offers a "para-epistemological" cognition of wild nature (*The Idea of Form*, 6). And Samuel Weber argues that "faced with the bewildering multiplicity of natural phenomena," the judgment projects a cognizable form on them (*Mass Mediauras*, 18). Part of this claim, explicit in Gasché and in Derrida (*Truth in Painting*, 85), is that the aesthetic judgment is applied primarily to wild nature. First, if the question is one of mere apprehension, it is simply untrue that there is any part of nature, wild or tame, that the understanding cannot cognize through the concepts of the pure understanding. There is no such thing as an object of experience for which "no concepts are available" (Gasché, 93). Second, as we will see, it is also untrue that Kant limits aesthetic apprehension to any sort of object. It is true that by applying the principle of unity under the concept of purposiveness, the teleological judgment gives us something in nature in addition to what the understanding gives us, and in that sense it may be para-epistemological (and subject to the deconstructions Derrida and Weber apply to the aesthetic judgement), but the teleological judgment's realm is not limited to wild nature. Nor does Kant think it operates on a perceptual realm simply unavailable to the understanding. Gasché's theory, however, whatever my disagreements with it, does recognize that the aesthetic judgment is about judgment and not about art objects. And although I am disputing its central contention, the book reads Kant meticulously and well on numbers of issues and needs to be dealt with, even, if not especially, in disagreement.

37. One should note also Gilles Deleuze's insistence that the aesthetic judgment can never legislate its conclusions but can only legislate over itself (*Kant's Critical Philosophy*, 47–48).

38. See Guyer's discussion of these issues (*Kant and the Claims of Taste*, 99–119).

39. Thus John Sallis (*Spacings*, 94–96), rightly in my view, insists on the free play intrinsic in the experience of the harmony of the faculties. Not only must we recognize that the purposiveness in question is ours rather than the object's, but, moreover, we must experience a contingency within any specific object's connection to it. It is always possible that a given object might or might not be the occasion for an aesthetic pleasure within the judgment of taste, and that possibility adds to its lack of purpose with regard to that end and is thus part of our experience of the pleasure in purposiveness without purpose.

40. Thus Makreel (*Imagination*, 88–107) talks about Kant's viewing nature as a symbol of a living mind, and Henrich outlines Kant's "moral image" of the world.

41. Meerbote ("Reflections of Beauty," 81), Makreel (60–63), and Henrich (*Aesthetic Judgment*, 43–44) all note and discuss this problem.

42. Guyer finds this view surprising (*Kant and the Claims of Taste*, 240) and argues against it at some length in "Interest, Nature, and Art." Frances Ferguson finds as positive Kant's specification that beautiful objects cannot be intentionally created, though not perhaps for the same reasons that Kant gives (*Solitude and the Sublime*, 82–84).

43. Bernard translates *schöne Kunst* literally as "beautiful art." This phrase in English has more the connotation of an evaluation than a category, however. Pluhar's translation of "fine art" seems more accurate and is how the phrase is generally translated elsewhere. Since I have been consistently using Bernard's translation as the one most available, though, I will stay with his text here.

44. Bernard uses the word "delineation" rather than "design" (61), a translation which would do no particular harm to my argument but possibly obscures Derrida's and is surely wrong in the larger context in which the aesthetic judgment responds to purposiveness, which whatever it is, is a form and not an outline.

45. The Meredith translation of Kant, which Derrida's translator uses to translate the citations of Kant in *Truth in Painting*, has a definite article, "the genuine beauty." But since that article does not refer to any particular object's genuine beauty, it is just a more awkward translation, which does not change the central point. Pluhar also translates without a definite article (72).

46. As only one example of such a positive deployment of deconstruction, consider Jameson's argument, in *The Political Unconscious*, that while history may not be seen directly, from formal contradictions within texts that cannot be formally resolved, one may see the absent cause that is its mark (35). Examples of such interpretive modes, informed by post-structural methods that articulate cultural constructs without claiming direct apprehension of natural realities, could of course be considerably multiplied.

CHAPTER 2: INDIFFERENT EMBODIMENT

1. In the course of this chapter, I will discuss the history of disinterest and indifference, and symbolic embodiment, as concepts. These concepts are still widely
defended among writers on aesthetics. But the critiques of disinterest and indifference now have a history only slightly shorter than the history of the development of those concepts. They date at least to Nietzsche, who in *The Genealogy of
Morals* (103–106) attacked both Kantian disinterest and Schopenhauerian indifference. Heidegger, in *Nietzsche*, agreed with Nietzsche's attack on indifference but
tried to recuperate Kantian disinterest in terms of a pure encounter with the beautiful object (108–109). More recently and famously, Derrida has also critiqued the
concept of disinterest as concerned with "a somewhat arid pleasure" (*Truth in
Painting*, 43). Pierre Bourdieu has devoted his book *Distinction* to an undercutting
of the concept through a sociological analysis of it (Bourdieu's and Derrida's arguments will be discussed in detail in Chapter 4). And of course disinterest is also a
continuing object of attack in Barbara Hernnstein Smith's *Contingencies of Value*.
This is a much abbreviated list, but it gives some impression of how many distinguished philosophers and theorists are on record as opposed to the concepts. The
attack upon the concept of symbolic embodiment has been mostly a matter of theory since the late-twentieth-century and the common ground has been that it
forms the basis of totalitarian thinking of various kinds. The most distinguished
and extensive version of this argument is in Phillipe Lacoue-Labarthe's and Jean-
Luc Nancy's *The Literary Absolute: The Theory of Literature in German Romanticism*, but see more recently Marc Redfield ("De Man, Schiller, and the Politics of
Reception" and "Humanizing de Man") and Cynthia Chase (*Decomposing Figures*,
82–112, and "Trappings of an Education"). The most recent and thoroughgoing
critique is Jean-Marie Schaeffer's *Art of the Modern Age*. Schaeffer undertakes the
dismantling of the entire tradition of aesthetics, which seeks to define an essence
of art that is also an interpretation of art, as an expression of essence in general. He
discusses all of the philosophers addressed in this chapter—Kant, Hegel, Schopenhauer, and Nietzsche. And while he does not discuss symbolic embodiment per se
at any length, his critique of art as essence applies to embodiment since embodiment always operates as a manifestation of at least some essence or other. For a
contemporary defense of symbolic embodiment as an aesthetic concept, see Paul
Crowther. Crowther's connection of embodiment with Heidegger's notion of the
uncovering of truth (*Art and Embodiment*, 41) in particular outlines a view of embodiment that has been the target of the kinds of objections cited above.

2. This critique of symbolic embodiment as aesthetic ideology is so widespread that it brings into agreement such unlikely allies as Terry Eagleton and Paul
de Man. In *The Ideology of the Aesthetic*, referencing an essay that became part of
de Man's *Aesthetic Ideology*, Eagleton records his assent to de Man's "demystification" of the "aesthetic ideology" which "involves a phenomenalist reduction of the
linguistic to the sensuously empirical, a confusing of mind and world, sign and

thing, cognition and percept, which is consecrated in the Hegelian symbol" (Eagleton, 10).

3. Although, as we saw in Chapter 1, Coleridge famously developed the idea of the symbol in Anglo-American discourse, he also justified poetry in terms of pleasure deriving from its formal arrangement (*Biographia*, II, 13). Ruskin also valued art, in the first instance, because of the pleasure it gives us, although he insists that this pleasure is as much intellectual as sensual (Ruskin, IV, 47). In the twentieth century, I. A. Richards, in the opening chapters of *Principles of Literary Criticism*, justified poetry in terms of the psychic state it leads to, and he has been followed by Monroe Beardsley (*Aesthetics*, 573–576) as well as Clement Greenberg, who insists that aesthetic intuition is "a psychic shift" in which "you become relieved of, distanced from, your cares and concerns as a particular individual coping with your particular existence" (*Homemade Esthetics*, 4–5).

4. In note 36 of Chapter 1, I disputed Gasché's argument that Kant meant the aesthetic judgment to define a "para-epistemological" knowledge of wild nature. Nevertheless, my argument in this chapter does follow his background claim that the aesthetic judgment was about an apprehension that was "para-epistemological."

5. According to Danto (*After the End of Art*, 50–51), the narrative of art history, created by Vasari, "is a system of learned strategies for making more and more adequate representations, judged by unchanged perceptual criteria." This he takes to be a more or less adequate history (although it is a history that he thinks contemporary art both ends and shows the artifice of) until a period of modernist self-consciousness in artists (66), which he dates to various points in the nineteenth century.

6. This claim needs considerable refining. Both Derrida and Foucault have had things to say about Magritte, for instance, and his "Ceci n'est pas une pipe." But the problems of signifying that they have discussed are only roughly analogous to the problem raised by readymades or other artworks indistinguishable from non-art objects. The problem has also been the focus of some influential twentieth-century literature, most obviously William Gaddis's *The Recognitions*, and so literary criticism of that work, for instance, have had to discuss the issue. But those interpretations have not played much of a role in literary theory, nor is that work often referred to in literary theoretical discussions. Most noticeably, George Dickie's institutional theory of art, discussed below, has obvious analogies to the theory of interpretive communities outlined by Stanley Fish in *Is There a Text in This Class?* and his work since. More pointedly, Fish's argument that we cannot tell the difference between literary and non-literary language in terms of the features of the language, but decide in advance what texts to call literary and then find the appropriate features of language there (98–111, 332–337), has clear similarities to Dickie's position. Because in literary debates the problem of meaning has always seemed primary, however, there has been little of the kind of consideration of what it means to argue that institutions determine not what texts mean but what kinds of things artworks are without there being any prior basis independent of those in-

stitutions to determine those declarations. For that, one still has to look to the responses to Dickie and others arguing in the wake of Duchamp.

7. This history is told in rich detail in three sources: Thierry de Duve's *Kant After Duchamp* (89–143), which has considerable theoretical and narrative interpolation, all of it quite sharp, William Camfield's "Marcel Duchamp's *Fountain*: Its History and Aesthetics in the Context of 1917" and his "Marcel Duchamp's *Fountain*: Aesthetic Object, Icon, or Anti-Art?"

8. The J. L. Mott Ironworks had produced the urinal. Duchamp signed as Mutt, he later claimed, because he felt the name Mott was too close and he wanted to recall the cartoon, *Mutt and Jeff* (Camfield, "History and Aesthetics," 68).

9. Thus, Peter Bürger's argument (*Theory of the Avant-Garde*, 51–52) that Duchamp was negating the idea of the artist as creator of the artwork needs some refinement. He was certainly testing its limits, but, in an odd way, the commonness of the object displayed seems to necessitate signed authorization even more than might a work that bears its individuality on its face, so to speak.

10. Indeed not until some years after. *Fountain* went unmentioned in the 1920s and 1930s and extended debate did not occur until the 1960s (Camfield, "Aesthetic Object," 155), when, of course, the example of Duchamp's readymades became important to a variety of artists working with the same ideas (see the series of interviews in Buskirk and Nixon, *The Duchamp Effect*).

11. Once the example of the urinal is in place, multiplying the examples in even more problematic ways becomes all too easy: in a dizzying first paragraph to *The Transfiguration of the Commonplace*, Arthur Danto imagines eight identical square rectangles, six of which are entirely different paintings—one for instance represents the Red Sea after the Israelites had crossed and the Egyptians had drowned, while the other is a still life of a red table cloth—and two of which are not artworks at all—one a canvas grounded in red but on which the painting has not been executed, another simply a rectangle painted red (1–2).

12. Thierry de Duve attempts to distinguish between Kant's indifferent judgment and the judgment about *Fountain*, on the basis that the Kantian judgment is evaluative while the judgment that *Fountain* is art is merely identificatory: "With the readymade, however, the shift from the classical to the modern aesthetic judgment is brought into the open, as the substitution of the sentence 'this is art' for the sentence 'this is beautiful'" (302). But this isn't precisely true. Although the beautiful elicits a form of pleasure in Kant and thus the judgment declares itself pleased, it does not first go through a stage in which it identifies the object in question as a candidate for aesthetic judgment and then decides whether it is a successful object or not. In declaring beauty, the judgment in fact identifies the object in question as having elicited an aesthetic response and not another kind (the distinction between artworks and objects in nature, in any case, is not itself an aesthetic one in Kant but a standard judgment of the understanding about how to categorize an intuited set of sensations).

13. I choose Greenberg rather than the New Critics to discuss mid-century for-

malism not merely because Duchamp's sculptures more obviously challenge his theories of art than they do the New Critics' theory of literature, but also because both Greenberg's art criticism and the dissents from it more openly accept its participation in aesthetic theory, while New Criticism, to articulate a method of interpretation, generally underplayed and sometimes denied the pertinence of aesthetics. The logical result has been that the reaction among literary theorists to New Criticism has been concerned with the epistemological problems of making interpretive claims, while sharing its skepticism and antipathy to aesthetics, and the reaction to Greenberg and the interest in Duchamp has entailed a more direct response to aesthetic issues. One should not, however, miss the common ground between Greenberg and the New Critics. Greenberg thought that the analogous movement in literature to abstraction in painting would involve the eschewing of meaning: "To deliver poetry from the subject and give full play to its true affective power it is necessary to free words from logic. . . . Poetry subsists no longer in the relations between words as meaning, but in the relations between words as personalities composed of sound, history and possibilities of meanings" (*Collected Essays*, I, 33). In this state, this claim certainly would not be borne out by most modern poetry. But Cleanth Brooks's idea in *The Well Wrought Urn*, that the essence of literature was literary meaning, in the form of paradox, ambiguity, irony, and generally the doubleness of metaphor, and that this concentration on metaphor created a particular form of experience that contrasted with scientific logic (3–21, 192–214), has obvious affinities with Greenberg's ideas about concentrating a painting on the shape of its own plane.

14. Much of what I say in this paragraph has been worked out in detail for me by two extended and careful critiques of Greenberg, Thierry de Duve's (200–279), which works out the connection between Duchamp and the hypothetical blank canvas and Arthur Danto (*After the End of Art*, 61–99) as well as Danto's earlier discussion of "Aesthetics and the Work of Art" (*Transfigurations*, 90–114).

15. One possible response to the problem Duchamp represents for formalism, of course, would be to deny that the readymades are in fact art. This was Beardsley's response (see the discussion of the issue in Davies, *Definitions of Art*, 70–72). Given Duchamp's influence in art since the 1960s, though, this denial maintains consistency at the cost of disabling narrowness. It leaves unexplained too much of what too many people have for too long called art.

16. In justice to the formalist defense, though, one should note that while Steiner and I may find it unsatisfying, it did play its part in persuading the jury to find the photographs not to be obscene. Although I take Duchamp, among other directions in modern art, to make formalism ultimately unviable, I do not want to suggest that the theory is either trivial or wrongheaded. Its endurance in Anglo-American aesthetics demonstrates that it seems to offer one of the best explanations of what at least most artworks do, if not precisely what they are.

17. Danto's formulations throughout *Transfigurations of the Commonplace*, *The Philosophical Disenfranchisement of Art*, and *After the End of Art* relieve us of the

necessity of imagining very hard. His books are so filled with works of art that look just like Brillo boxes but are not (and this has as a consequence that now everyday Brillo boxes will look just like a famous work of art, even though they are not, in fact, artworks), that we need only imagine objects looking just like Mapplethorpe's photos but that would be, say, evidence of certain events having taken place—hardly a leap, given Danto's imagining of a book being very nearly identical with *Silas Marner* but in fact having described real events and thus not having the particular aesthetic significance of the novel, which could still exist as the same novel it is now (*Philosophical Disenfranchisement*, 176).

18. Duchamp famously objected to this interpretation in a letter to Hans Richter: "I threw the bottle rack and the urinal into their faces as a challenge and now they admire them for their aesthetic beauty" (Richter, *Dada*, 208, quoted in Camfield, "History and Aesthetics," 80, and Danto, *After the End of Art*, 84). But one must note that these remarks were made in 1961, after Duchamp had been picked up by those who precisely want to stress this aspect of his achievement. Camfield proposes as counter-evidence the weight of all his work in the decade that produced *Fountain*.

19. I say "arguably" because one could hold that Duchamp's decision to present the urinal as art immediately transformed it into art. This claim may seem to avoid a subjectivism that appears to make the status of an object depend on its reception. But it will be, paradoxically, even more relativist than one that suggests that at least some objects can only become art when they are so construed (as opposed to usual paintings and sculptures), since it would entail accepting that anything is art that anyone says is art. More importantly, such an argument really does not accommodate what the urinal Duchamp presented was when it was not widely accepted as *Fountain*. For instance, it might have been so easily lost precisely because as yet the object did not have the value of art.

20. Although anyone can be a member of the artworld, in Dickie's sense, membership, though not limited, is not without definition. He recognizes that the most obvious manifestation of the artworld is in social institutions but finally says, "The core personnel of the artworld is a loosely organized, but nevertheless related set of persons including artists (understood to refer to painters, writers, composers), producers, museum directors, museum-goers, theater-goers, reporters for newspapers, critics for publications of all sorts, art historians, art theorists, philosophers of art, and others" (35–36). There is some question as to whether anyone can elect himself or herself to any category in this list. Dickie does say that if a plumbing salesman submitted the urinal to an art exhibition, meaning to have it be considered a work of art, he could do so, but "such a thing probably would not occur to him" (38), leaving the question somewhat open. One value of this open definition is that it would enable Dickie to claim that *Fountain* was an artwork at the moment of submission, thus giving it at least a short physical existence as an artwork (a claim I find at least questionable). It does so, however, at the cost of making the concept of institution start to evaporate into the kind of individuality the

subjectivism of which Dickie wants to avoid. This problem is not that serious to the theory, however, since it could survive if Dickie tightened the rules for inclusion in the artworld, even at the cost of making it somewhat more politically constraining (a cost other theorists of art would be all too glad to pay).

21. On the other hand, critiques of Danto's position can be equally circular. Davies, for instance, takes Danto to be making two unrelated criticisms: first that Dickie does not explain what makes something a work of art prior to having that status conferred upon it by the artworld, and second, how being an artwork affects an object such that, even though it looks like non-artworks, it assumes certain aesthetic properties (82–83). Davies's distinction, while logically possible, misses Danto's point in a significant way. Danto's whole point is that *Fountain* is not a work of art because of some features it has, since it in fact does not, as an object, have aesthetic features. That it is a work of art reveals something about the definition of art, and we need to know that definitional "something," why it is an artwork, in order to understand how it is an artwork. In effect, Danto faults Dickie for not defining the essence of what an artwork is, something one would think it is the point of an institutional theory to avoid. But Davies then faults Danto with confusing what the essence of an artwork is with what its aesthetic properties are, a conjoining of which it is equally the point of an essentialist theory to claim.

22. One should note that this objection need not be logically fatal if one stipulates that understanding objectively why a given object is or is not an artwork is in principle impossible because such questions will always be answered differently by different artworlds, or, in Stanley Fish's terms, different interpretive communities. That Dickie seems to have no desire to go this far (as we will see, he insists on a real difference between aesthetic and non-aesthetic objects) also indicates the way in which *Fountain* and its role as a sculpture indicates a weakness in Fish's theories that their literary context has not. In an obvious way, even if Fish's theory is right, as a response to *Fountain* it is completely uninteresting since it denies in principle the ability to answer any question the work raises that makes it of value. This irrelevance of institutional theories to understanding the artwork may be why Duve (94) fairly scornfully dismisses Dickie even as his own ostensibly Foucaultian definition of under what conditions the statement "this is art" can be made successfully (389–390) could be easily translated into an institutional theory. Fish's theory has not seemed as irrelevant in a literary context, perhaps, because the question of how to distinguish a literary from a non-literary work has largely not been taken as theoretically interesting or answerable, given the long existence of works of ambiguous identity. Identifying a work as literary may always have been a matter of interpretation, but accurate interpretation could in principle solve the issue of identification along with that of meaning. In that context, Fish's denial of univalent meaning and his tying of that denial to accounts of the vagaries of interpretive claims in the history of interpretations of given literary works has rightly seemed quite pointed.

23. Danto's discussion of Barnett Newman's series of abstract paintings, *The*

Stations of the Cross, in its attention to the implications of the title and the poverty of its discussion of what the paintings actually look like, demonstrates the bent of his criticism (*Philosophic Disenfranchisement*, 73–74).

24. As has perhaps been evident already, my consideration of Duchamp's work owes a considerable debt to Arthur Danto's writing about artworks that appear exactly like non-artworks, particularly in *Transfigurations of the Commonplace* but also in *After the End of Art*. I should also list Thierry de Duve's *Kant After Duchamp*, particularly in that the history he writes of the original submission of the work offers considerable matter for what follows.

25. Whether or not Duchamp has disproved Kant's claim, *Fountain* is a strong enough contestation of it that various critics have tried to follow the original exhibition board in refusing the submission. As we have seen, Beardsley denied that *Fountain* was art. And Ted Cohen, in contesting Dickie's claim that any object can be aesthetically appreciated, claimed it impossible to appreciate some objects: "ordinary thumbtacks, cheap white envelopes, the plastic forks given at some drive-in restaurants" and of course, urinals ("The Possibility of Art," 78). Cohen claims that the artistic element in *Fountain* is entirely in the gesture of exhibiting it (or trying to). If Cohen takes the gesture to have been successful, though, it remains true that one cannot appreciate it without appreciating the fact that the thing exhibited was a urinal, and thus appreciating this urinal, if not any other.

26. Although Duve does not address the question of whether *Fountain* could have been an artwork if it had been successfully rejected, he does sharply discuss the ways in which Duchamp's maneuverings of it from its rejection by the Exhibit through its exhibit by Steiglitz in particular, whose taste in art was formalist, "elitist and purist," and who thus could bestow the full aura of art on the object (Duve, 119), indicate Duchamp's awareness of how showing the work successfully was vital to its significance (Duve, 116–120).

27. I choose Van Gogh as the example here precisely because his anonymity while alive eliminates any element of his reputation in verifying a hypothesized lost painting as a painting. If the object had the usual properties by which we recognize a painting, then its disappearance no more challenges its identity as a painting than the disappearance of a chair challenges that object's identity as a chair. Obviously, a skeptical epistemology that argued that our ignorance of an object's existence would entail its non-existence would doom a lost Van Gogh painting to non-identity. But it would do so only in a way that did not differentiate between artworks, chairs, baseballs, and so on. The difference between the conceptual status of a lost Van Gogh painting and a lost urinal whose status as an artwork was lost with it would remain the same.

28. I follow Pluhar's translation here, rather than Bernard's (43–44), because his rendering of *Vorstellung* as "presentation," though unidiosyncratic in English, captures Kant's use of the term to refer to that of which we are directly aware, even before the organizing activities of concepts.

29. De Man attacks the Schillerian ideology of the aesthetic state and its de-

pendence on asserting the material embodiment of significance in "Aesthetic Formalization: Kleist's *Uber das Marionettentheater*" (*Blindness and Insight*, 262–290) and "Kant and Schiller" (*Aesthetic Ideology*, 119–128). Although I part with other sympathetic analysts of de Man, who think his critique of this Idealist notion of symbolism extends to a general position on aesthetic theory and particularly to versions of it in Kant, Hegel, and Nietzsche, in fact my reading of Kant in particular is indebted to his argument, or at least my understanding of it (see my article, "Materialism and Aesthetics: Paul de Man's *Aesthetic Ideology*." In the reverse, though my argument about embodiment disputes Marc Redfield's identification of that as grounding a conservative or totalitarian ideology of aesthetics, I would agree with his arguments in *The Politics of Aesthetics* about the way the Schillerian view underwrites certain conservative and totalitarian notions of gender and nationalism. I would only add that the concepts of embodiment and indifference as I outline them in this chapter are the best responses to the views Redfield attacks.

30. Ian Balfour argues that Coleridge's concept of the symbol should not be translated into aesthetics and literary theory precisely because it was non-linguistic and about the meaningfulness of certain religious objects such as the Incarnation of Christ in the Eucharist (*Rhetoric of Romantic Prophecy*, 282–283). And Hegel likewise, as we will see, distinguished quite clearly between symbolism, which he saw as a form of language and sensuousness embodiment, which was not language at all. The question, however, is not whether the critique of symbolic embodiment applies only to linguistic symbols. The claim of that critique is that embodiment, to the extent that it succeeds in embodying a meaning at all, must be linguistic and that quality of linguistic reference will always undercut its claims of non-linguistic, numinous embodiment.

31. Derrida first articulates his ideas about iteration in "Signature Event Concept" (*Margins*, 307–330). He repeats them in a register particularly significant here when, in "Typewriter Ribbon: Limited Ink (2) ('within such limits')," he talks about the idea that for an event to be an event, it must be both absolutely singular and also mechanically repeatable (Cohen et al., *Material Events*, 277–279).

32. On May 13, 2002, the 1964 *Fountain*, along with the other readymades Duchamp re-readymade for Arturo Schwartz, was auctioned. A Web site describing the auction refers to these objects both as Duchamp readymades and as remakings of originals (www.thecityreview.com/s02pco1.html).

33. Oddly, Dickie has essentially the same complaint about what he calls aesthetic attitude. He imagines the spectator of a play not knowing to what he should apply his aesthetic attitude: "The operation of aesthetic attitude alone cannot exclude anything perceivable from a theater seat (the backs of spectators' heads, the stage curtains, etc.), since the aesthetic attitude allegedly can be taken toward anything" (88). This objection is odd in Dickie's case because, although he is correct that the attitude has no selection process built in, since he also argues that anything can be appreciated aesthetically, without regard to its material features, it is hard to see why this aspect of institutional openness cannot extend to stage curtains or the backs of spectators' heads.

34. Danto also raises the familiar objection that there are times when taking an aesthetic perspective would be immoral: "to see a riot, for instance, in which police are clubbing demonstrators, as a kind of ballet, or to see the bombs exploding like mystical chrysanthemums from the plane they have been dropped from" (*Transfiguration*, 22). First, although it would be immoral to espouse the clubbing of demonstrators or the dropping of bombs because of whatever aesthetic features may be perceived in them, if the mere fact of perceiving them aesthetically is immoral, then too many works of art both depicting and disturbed by such beauty would have to be declared immoral. More importantly, it would be immoral in exactly the same way to regard the rioters being clubbed or the bombs being dropped as merely examples of certain physical laws. The moral problem arises not because they can't be such examples, and certainly not because applying physical laws to events in the world is immoral. But at certain times thinking like a physicist or evaluating like an aesthetic percipient evades the central issue being raised. That perspectives or fields of knowledge can be misapplied doesn't prove that there is something wrong with them, only that, at the moment, one should be concerned with something else.

35. The most influential statement of this connection is Jerome Stolnitz's "On the Origins of 'Aesthetic Disinterestedness.'" Paulson, trying to recuperate the concept, distinguishes strong disinterestedness from weak disinterestedness by characterizing the better, weaker (in the sense of less extreme) claim much as Stolnitz would and contrasting it with extreme distinctions between aesthetics and religion, ethics and rhetoric. Still, if in the weak form, as Paulson explains it, "aesthetics is independent . . . of personal or private interest or advantage," it is hard to see how it will escape the criticisms of it as "a disguise for bourgeois mystification," since that criticism precisely entails the claim to transcend private interest or advantage (*Beautiful, Novel and Strange,* 23). In order to recuperate the concept, we must separate it entirely from the standard ideas of both interest and disinterest. Caygill also discusses the way in which aesthetic pleasure in Shaftesbury and Hutcheson was disinterested (*Art of Judgment,* 62). Guyer (*Kant and the Experience of Freedom,* 48–93) gives an extended rereading of this history, making interesting distinctions among Shaftesbury, Hutcheson, Burke, and others, finding, for instance, Hutcheson's position to have been more radical than either Shaftesbury or that of later writers in the century, and finding Kant to have followed and extended it. Nevertheless, he follows Stolnitz and the others in seeing disinterestedness as predicating something about the separateness of aesthetic pleasure.

36. Kant, after all, was also influenced by Wolff and Baumgarten, who, following Leibniz, saw aesthetic experience in terms of a form of cognition, although what was cognized were the rules for creating beauty's type of perceptual pleasure (see Pluhar's introduction, l–li).

37. It will have been noticed, by now, that if certain modern treatments of Kant's aesthetics concentrate on the sublime at the expense of the beautiful, my discussion has concentrated on the beautiful almost at the complete expense of the

sublime. And this analogizing of a bit of the discussion of the sublime to the discussion of the beautiful both questions my reasons for doing so and outlines them. To speak strictly, to see the ocean as sublime, one does not see it as having a threatening significance but rather is threatened by its appearance of violating purpose (*Judgment*, 83), which violation leads to our recognition that human destiny is in reason's freedom and not understanding's limits—hence the acceptance of a subjective purposiveness that we completely detach even from our apprehension of the appearance of the object. Despite this difference, the main feature of reading the object as a matter open to perspectival choice, without any concern for its phenomenal existence, remains the same. Such a reading is not literal cognition but an artificed choice. See also de Man's discussion of this moment in "Phenomenality and Materiality in Kant" (*Aesthetic Ideology*, 80–82), and Warminzki's reading in "'As the Poets Do It': On the Material Sublime" (Cohen et al., *Material Events*, 20–22). In other words, whatever elements his theory of the sublime adds to Kant's aesthetics, on the matters of purposiveness and perspectival indifference, it follows those concepts in the ways that matter to what I am arguing.

38. A deconstruction of Kant's epistemology, such as Paul de Man's in *Aesthetic Ideology* (46–49) might well want to question the reliability of schemata, but since Kant does not mean to extend that reliability to the symbol, the problems in claiming schematic reliability need not concern us here.

39. Actually, Hegel no more believes in perfect *symbolic* embodiment than does Kant, but that is because he thinks that symbols are still a form of sign. When the embodiment is perfect in Hegel, it is no longer even a symbol. As we will see, though, this distinction will turn out to be merely one of terms.

40. I choose Pluhar here because Bernard's translation renders "preceding section" as "preceding paragraph," a reference that makes no sense. Kant fairly clearly has in mind section 57, as we will see.

41. The most significant version of this position is probably Crawford's (*Kant's Aesthetic Theory*, 145–150). Crawford takes Kant to be saying that we have a moral duty to have a taste for the beautiful and that this moral duty gives aesthetic taste its universal validity. Guyer (*Kant and the Claims of Taste*, 373–389) gives an extended critique of this position, which, in *Kant and the Experience of Freedom*, 12–19, he updates and reaffirms.

42. Critics who actually read *The Critique of Judgment* closely do largely recognize this (for example, Guyer, *Kant and the Claims of Taste*, 167, and Kemal, *Kant's Aesthetic Theory: an Introduction*, 34–35). The standard misreading that Kant is posing an aesthetic version of objective neutrality occurs mostly in critics concerned with larger ideological issues, though Heidegger certainly seems to share this view when he claims that "in order to find something beautiful, we must let what encounters us, purely as it is itself, come before us in its own stature and worth. We may not take it into account in advance with a view to something else, our goals and intentions, our possible enjoyment and advantage" (Heidegger, *Nietzsche*, 109).

43. De Man describes this view of the human body as in deliberate opposition to organicism: "We must, in short, consider our limbs, hands, toes, breasts, or what Montaigne so cheerfully referred to as 'Monsieur ma partie,' in themselves, severed from the organic unity of the body" (*Aesthetic Ideology*, 88). De Man calls this view Kant's materialism, and it is that materialism that I mean to argue is more fundamental to aesthetics than its phenomenalism, its drive to embody, and indeed as more primary to it.

44. Philip Barnard and Cheryl Lester, in their introduction to Lacoue-Labarthe and Nancy (*Literary Absolute*, ix), claim that Kant's insistence that symbols could not embody the ideas of Pure Reason was "radical," and that his successors did not follow him. And Schaeffer separates what he describes as Kant's meta-aesthetics from the speculative theory of Art, which he finds so flawed (17–64). I hope to show in the course of this chapter that the power of Kant's definition shows itself in the fact that one cannot fail to follow it, regardless of one's own ideological stakes. I think Hegel and Nietzsche constructed their deepenings of Kant's positions knowingly. But, as the chapter will go on to argue, even in the case of philosophers such as Schopenhauer, who want to claim that aesthetics does embody essence, the force of the concept of embodiment has a tendency to undo the claims for revealing essence.

45. This dual claim of perfect aesthetic objectification and philosophical transcendence of it leads to two kinds of complaints. In an explicit and often instructive comparison of Kant with Hegel, Guyer concentrates on a recognition of contingency within Kant's aesthetics that Hegel must deny in the service of his insistence on a final "harmonious relation between the will and the world" (*Kant and the Experience of Freedom*, 181). Luc Ferry, in contrast, argues that embodiment must always be, from an epistemological perspective, an imperfect form of communicating an idea and so "In Hegel's eyes, art remains . . . by definition inferior to that which takes place within philosophy" (*Homo-Aestheticus,* 29), a position with which Bowie (*Aesthetics and Objectivity,* 106–107) essentially agrees.

46. Schiller, objecting to Kant's split between reason's ethics and the nature perceived by understanding, as well as the split between ethics and interest, famously proposed art as the mediation of "reason and sense, between inclination and duty." Although Schiller claimed this mediation as art's embodiment to the senses of ethical ends, and this claim has been the subject of objections to his theory and thus to the theory of symbolism (see de Man's "Kant and Schiller" in *Aesthetic Ideology*, as well as Redfield's *Phantom Formations*, 20–21), Hegel effectively deconstructs the Schillerian claim of mediation not as a claim of embodiment but as by necessity not embodiment enough, as always caught in the separations of mediation.

47. This seems the appropriate place to answer one important objection to this definition of art as embodied thought, a definition that insists that pleasure is incidental to rather than definitive to art. The objection concerns forms of at least seeming artworks whose sole purpose is to provide some form of entertainment—

light fiction, popular music, even pornographic photos. Although one can capture high art that means to be nothing but beautiful within a Hegelian definition by stating that it proclaims its own formal self-sufficiency as both its meaning and its effect, such a justification does not carry forward to a work that means to provide pleasure as an effect and means merely to do that. The problem with denying that such works are art is not elitism but incoherent ontology: if light fiction isn't fiction, exactly what is it? We may solve this problem by positing the fairly minimal proposition that any work that has the formal features of fiction is in fact fiction (and so on for music, photography, etc.). And one of the features of all these art forms is in fact concentration on mere appearance—either in sensuousness of painting, music, and so on, or, to the extent that literary art rests on the representation of that which is not, on the self-justifying quality of its representations. Even the forms of entertainment most concerned with the most ostensibly un-Kantian pleasures, then, would depend on the aesthetic presentation of appearance in the way that Hegel connects with a special form of knowledge rather than a special form of pleasure. Take as an example a form of representation almost universally scorned as art, pornography. Even the Supreme Court distinguishes the two by claiming that a work with artistic value cannot be pornography. But pornography will always be art because only art can be pornographic. Two people having sex is obviously not pornography. Only a representation of the spectacle can be pornographic and it will simultaneously, in however an uninteresting way, be an aesthetic representation, as one can tell by considering the role of the audience: observing people having sex surreptitiously is an infringement on their privacy that does not depend on their actually having sex. In other words, a Peeping Tom would be a Peeping Tom even if he were watching actors engaged in simulating sex rather than partners actually engaged in sex, as long as he were watching the actors surreptitiously, without their knowledge. Observing a representation of their having sex or even the spectacle of their having sex with their consent is only a crime—if it is one—to the extent that one outlaws representations of sexual content as opposed to spectacles or representations of other kinds of content. The form of representation, photo, film, or spectacle is undistinguishable from other examples of like aesthetic representations of different contents. And no one tries to distinguish aesthetic representation from other forms as a result of its represented content. From the perspective of an aesthetic theory that does not try inappropriately to turn its ontologies into evaluations, all forms of pornography are art because they cannot be anything else.

    48. Cleanth Brooks offers a particularly extreme form of trying to avoid the implication in the act of interpretation that an artwork is not self-explanatory by arguing that all explanation of a poem's meaning is basically paraphrase and a departure from rather than an approach to a poem's meaning, which is actually, like an experience, something that can only be sensed completely (*The Well-Wrought Urn*, 192–214). There are two obvious problems to this claim. The first relates to it as a theory of *poetry* since that which functions as irreducible experience in Brooks

is poetic language, generally metaphor. But, as Stanley Cavell has argued, metaphor precisely is that in language which *can be* paraphrased (*Must We Mean What We Say?* 74–82). If one asks what a flat, referential sentence means ("Juliet is fourteen years old") one is likely to get definitions of terms. But if one asks what a metaphor means ("Romeo is the sun"), one is precisely looking for an interpretive paraphrase. But since this limitation to interpretation may be a function of poetry's being language, Brooks's theory might hold more generally, in the manner of Susan Sontag's famous "Against Interpretation," which also claimed that all interpretation tainted the artwork. But the mere fact that we engage in interpretation, and indeed, rightly or wrongly, look to have works interpreted for us, creates a problem for this claim. We do not generally feel the need to have our sensations explained to us. We may look for scientific explanations of their causes, psychological explanations of their origins or implications. But the actual feelings are notoriously not only not in need of explanation, but not even fully shareable through language. If art were actually like that, one would think its audience would no more seek interpretation than it seeks interpretation of feeling hot or cold.

49. Geuss ("A Response to Paul de Man," 380) complains about de Man's interpretation here. I have discussed this dispute in terms of de Man's larger claims about the connections between Hegel's aesthetic theory and other elements in his philosophy in *Aestheticism and Deconstruction*, 150–151.

50. Ferry dismisses as insipid Schopenhauer's view of art as a tranquilizer (*Homo-Aestheticus*, 178). Bowie describes his aesthetics as simply a Neoplatonic derivation from Kant (*Aesthetics and Objectivity*, 208). Eagleton (*Ideology of the Aesthetic*, 158–162), although finding Schopenhauer's physiological interests comic, gives a more interesting than usual reading of the working of the will in his philosophy. But his reading of the aesthetic as "a temporary escape from this prison-house of subjectivity" (162–163) ends up dismissing it as a form of the quietist aesthetics that his book means to critique. Schaeffer takes Schopenhauer's thought completely seriously as a significant example of the speculative theory of Art, but he finds in him the contradictions and flaws he finds in that theory generally, if anything in a more exaggerated fashion (186–208).

51. Cortazar's novel, though, does not interpolate what he calls "expendable chapters" in the order in which they are printed in the book, thus suggesting other novels that could be created out of separable parts, while Schopenhauer certainly does not envisage other valid philosophies created by rearranging the parts of his work.

52. Heidegger would certainly object to my identifying Schopenhauer's passional indifference with disinterest. He wanted to recuperate what he took to be Kantian disinterest by differentiating it from Schopenhauer's resignation. But his definition of a disinterested judgment, quoted above, strikingly recalls Schopenhauer here: "Whatever exacts of us the judgment 'This is beautiful' can never be an interest. That is to say, in order to find something beautiful, we must let what encounters us, purely as it is in itself, come before us in its own stature and worth"

(*Nietzsche*, 109). Indeed, Heidegger's view of art as unveiling essence, in "The Origin of the Work of Art," and of will as the Being of beings, in "What are Poets For?" (*Poetry, Language, Thought*, 71, 111), all make his aesthetics, at least taken in isolation from the rest of his thinking on Being, far more Schopenhauerian than is commonly recognized.

53. See also Tracy Strong's claim that in *The Birth of Tragedy*, Nietzsche argues that the "attempt to ground the world in 'truth, in a philosophical argument, destroys the world's reality" ("Nietzsche's Political Misappropriation," 141), an argument that assumes that *The Birth of Tragedy* posits an apprehensible reality.

54. Although, as Nicholas Martin claims throughout *Nietzsche and Schiller*, Nietzsche's references to Schiller are virtually never negative, he does in effect contradict his and Hegel's claim that the sense of "the oneness of man with nature" is a lost origin. For Nietzsche, it is "the highest effect of Apollinian culture" (*Birth of Tragedy*, 43), a hard-won wisdom rather than an innocence.

55. For Nietzsche's valuing of the artist's perspective, see *Will to Power*, sections 795–798 (419–420). See also Heidegger's commentary on these sections under the heading, "Art must be grasped in terms of the artist" (*Nietzsche*, 71–72).

56. In Nehamas's words, his perspectivism shows "that his positions are expressions of his particular point of view besides which there may be many others" (*Nietzsche*, 41).

57. Denying the difference between doer and deed has the odd, seemingly contradictory effect of justifying Nietzsche's tendency toward ad hominem attack, since if doer and deed are versions of the same, then there is an "essential connection between the thought and the thinker" (Solomon, *Nietzsche Ad Hominem*, 193).

58. This is the same basic fallacy as argument ad hominem, as we can see by Solomon's claim cited above, and so the justification given above of that form of argument in Nietzsche will also rest on the justification of this genealogical gesture.

CHAPTER 3: FOUCAULT'S AESTHETICS

1. As only a particularly significant example, Edward Said, in the short article he wrote in response to Foucault's death, stated that "the old demarcations between criticism and creation do not apply to what Foucault wrote" ("Michel Foucault, 1926–1984," 3).

2. Derrida comments on the "dense beauty" of Foucault's style in his famous critique of *Histoire de la folie*, but only in passing and in reference to a passage that is at least partially a citation from the poet René Char (Derrida, *Writing and Difference*, 37). Gary Gutting, in a generally sympathetic analysis of Foucault's works through *The Archaeology of Knowledge*, nevertheless blames the "self-important tone" and "fuliginous pronouncements" of *The Order of Things* for the difficulties of its reception (Gutting, *Michel Foucault's Archaeology*, 175).

3. The formative version of this argument is probably Frank Lentriccia's claim,

in *After the New Criticism*, to finding common ground between Derrida and Foucault as staking out a politics in criticism, while separating both of them from Yale critics in general and Paul de Man in particular. The opposition between Derrida and/or de Man and Foucault as a metonymy for an opposition between formalist and politically pointed criticism was endemic in the discussions that surrounded the New Historicism.

4. I certainly do not mean to limit the term only to the Parisian intellectual movements of the last forty years, though that would have its conveniences. The effect of not only Foucault and Derrida, but Kristeva, Irigiray, Bourdieu, and Macherey, among others, on American and British literary critics, philosophers, political scientists, and feminists in all those disciplines, who have been willing to take those thinkers on their own terms rather than translate them into a more readily comprehensible empirical skepticism, has been broad well beyond the capabilities of a note to register. The definition in this paragraph gives a focus to the term so that it can be meaningfully applied first to Foucault and then in the next chapter to Bourdieu. But I do mean it to be sufficiently and vaguely capacious to identify a large intellectual movement with various individual differences and refinements.

5. At the risk of stating the obvious, well before postmodernism, Marx and Lenin argued that law and justice in the bourgeois state merely legalized the dominance of the capitalist class, and much of their argumentation has carried over particularly in the work of postmodern Marxian and non-Marxian thinkers. But Marx and Lenin both had concepts of a classless, unalienated society that operated as a ground against which to make their critiques, and hence, to that extent, partook of the Enlightenment project of defining a just state in terms of universalist standards. Habermas (*Philosophical Discourse*, 282–283) makes essentially this distinction.

6. The most fully worked out version of this position is in Allan Megill's *Prophets of Extremity*, which discusses Nietzsche, Heidegger, Derrida, and Foucault as articulating an aestheticism from which to analyze and critique modern philosophy. This kind of aestheticism, which is supposed to reduce truth to the "merely" aesthetic, and which is usually attributed to these postmodern thinkers, has little to do, as we will see, with the concepts of indifference, autonomous form, and symbolic embodiment that play such an important role in eighteenth-century and nineteenth-century aesthetics and that I will be claiming play central roles in Foucault and Bourdieu.

7. The most recent analysis of the special place of art in German Romantic philosophy is Jean-Marie Schaeffer's *Art of the Modern Age*.

8. Schaeffer (135) notes that Schiller, Schelling, and Hegel all struggle to distinguish philosophy from art as a result of their exalted view of art.

9. As to the redundancy, Derrida, in "The Double Session," quite pointedly uses literary language, at least, to call into question straightforward reference as the grounding form of language (*Dissemination*, "The Double Session"). And Fou-

cault, at least in his early work, had a quite similar view of literary language as a way to contest the limits between reason and unreason, which he was then investigating. In a discussion on poetry sponsored by *Tel Quel* in 1964, for instance, he stated, "It is, actually . . . in the area of language that the game of limits, of contestation and transgression appears most vividly. We now find the problem reason-unreason [*déraison* would more usually be insanity, but when he uses the word, Foucault almost always wants to designate the opposite of reason]—or in any case, the violence of the problem reason-unreason—in the interior of language" (*Dits*, I, 426, my translation). As a general rule, I will cite all of Foucault's books from their English translations, noting when I emend the translation. The exception is *Histoire de la folie*. Since *Madness and Civilization* comprises less than half the original text, rather than go back and forth between two editions, citations will be my translations from the 1972 French edition. For the same reason, as a matter of economy, all citations from essays and interviews will be my translations of *Dits et ecrits*, which collects all his writing other than published books.

10. I will go into detail about this accusation in my discussions of Foucault's ideas about power. Here, one may cite, as a positive statement, Gutting's claim that "we can accordingly characterize his fundamental intellectual project as a philosophical critique of the human sciences, carried out by a history of thought in the service of human liberation" (*Michel Foucault's Archaeology of Scientific Reason*, 4). The most famous example of the accusation that Foucault is contradictory in refusing to ground any values when he quite clearly values some sort of freedom is of course Habermas (*Philosophical Discourse*, 276). But that charge is echoed by Taylor, Rorty ("Foucault and Epistemology"), Norris, Fraser, and Said ("Foucault and the Imagination of Power"), among any number of others.

11. Nehamas's *The Art of Living* argues that certain philosophers both argue for and embody a certain sense of what makes a good life. He analyzes the unsurprising cases of Socrates and Montaigne and the more surprising ones of Nietzsche and Foucault. He limits his discussion of Foucault explicitly to the late turn toward arguing for a life constructed as a work of art, seeing, as many readers of Foucault do, a turn toward more humanist values in his last years. I will be arguing against seeing these ideas as representing a change in Foucault's thinking precisely because one can see this view of the value of constructing one's works and one's career (that which Nehamas means by "life") throughout his writings.

12. Foucault's declaration of the death of man, long before he started to theorize about power, inaugurated the debate about how he could consistently have values. Thus a sympathetic Italian interviewer in 1967 complains about the "antihumanism" of Foucault's declaration of man's death: "But aren't you proposing yourself a humanism? . . . What does one find as the basis of economics if not man, not only as a force of labor but as an end? How can you not, at least on this point, retract, at least in part, the nihilist affirmation of the death of man? In short, I don't believe that you would give an absolute value to these affirmations" (*Dits*, I, 645).

13. The definition of a late turn in Foucault is held by almost all critics who write on the last two volumes of *History of Sexuality* and on the late lectures and interviews. It includes those who welcome the change, such as Nehamas (*Art of Living*, 170–175) and Bernauer ("Michel Foucault's Ecstatic Thinking"), and those who oppose it, such as Mark Poster, who asserts that *Le Souci du soi* "manifests a loosening of the grip Foucault has on his theoretical strategy" ("Foucault and the Tyranny of Greece," 216).

14. See Dreyfus and Rabinow (*Michel Foucault*, 20), and Gutting (*Michel Foucault's Archaeology*, 199).

15. I have changed the translation of *acceder* from "leads to" to "gives way to," since I think Foucault means both opens onto and yields to.

16. Much of what Foucault says in this section would be both less gender marked and I think clearer if "Man" were replaced by "human being," a term that more clearly insists on questions of human existence and essence.

17. He does, in the 1960s and 1970s, regularly deny that he is a philosopher. And his distinction in this interview between the death of philosophy and the death of philosophers really doesn't get him out of contradiction. When Deleuze defines Foucault's interviews as "diagnostics," in the context of which we may better understand his books, he makes a useful suggestion on how to read various texts ("What Is a *Dispositif*," 166). But one must read through a lot of statements that Foucault makes for effect. I think it remains the case, though, that Foucault regularly spoke positively of a thinker who would, as he says here, "diagnose the present of a culture." He only changed what he was willing to call that thinker.

18. In *The Art of Living*, Nehamas discusses Nietzsche's interpretation of Socrates' dying words (136, 150–151) and Foucault's (157–162). In the course of these pages, he addresses critical attempts to interpret the words so as not to bear the meaning that Socrates thinks life is a disease, but he finally thinks that this is the only meaning that they will really bear.

19. Those who criticize Foucault in some form or other for dandyism or an irresponsible aestheticism include Wolin, Rochlitz, and Hadot. Critics who defend him from the charge include Osborne ("Critical Spirituality," 44), Bernauer in both "Beyond Life and Death" and "Michel Foucault's Ecstatic Thinking," though in the second article he does so by articulating an explicitly transcendental, ecstatic element that seems at odds with any Foucault, early, middle, or late.

20. Sheridan Smith's translation of the last sentences enhances the sense that demanding a stable identity from the writer is the function of policing by translating *état-civil* as "bureaucrats and police," and stresses Foucault's impatience with this by translating *Qu'elle nous laisse libres* as "At least spare us their morality." This translation is obviously more idiomatically apt then mine and in no way inaccurate. Since my reading of these lines also depends on these implications, I thought it was more proper to use a literal translation that doesn't make that interpretation a given.

21. This claim had its moment in American deconstructive criticism in the ar-

gument that literature was a privileged discourse in that it at least was aware of its ungroundedness, was self-deconstructive. One sees this argument in de Man's (*Blindness and Insight*, 139) and J. Hillis Miller's argument that great literary works are ahead of their critics ("Deconstructing the Deconstructors," 31). Whatever its problems or values as a literary critical claim, as with any relativist claim to relativist self-awareness, it runs into logical contradictions. But that relativism is still an ontologically possible situation, whatever the linguistic problems of describing it. Serious contradictions would follow only from any specific knowledge claims one might make about history or politics. One can coherently claim an inherent limit to human knowledge, but one cannot then make that claim say anything specific about any particular area of human knowledge.

22. There are, in effect, five variations of Foucault's first work. The first edition, which appeared in 1961, bore the title *Folie et déraison: Histoire de la folie à l'âge Classique*. Foucault abridged this version by more than half for a different French edition. This abridgement, with some additions from the first edition, is the basis of the English translation, *Madness and Civilization*, which still represents less than half the original text. In 1972, a second French edition came out, now entitled *Histoire de la folie à l'âge Classique*, with the original preface, in which he made many of the claims Derrida criticized, eliminated, and a new one added. This edition also had a new preface and two appendixes, one of them, "Mon Corps, ce papier, ce feu," Foucault's reply to Derrida's review. Finally, this second edition was reprinted, but without the two appendixes, a few years later. With the exception of the prefaces and appendixes removed and added, the body of the text remains the same through all versions but the abridgement. The changes amount to new ways of framing how to take the text.

23. Both Gordon ("*Histoire de la Folie*," 19–20) and Deleuze (*Foucault*, 12–13) suggest that Foucault may not mean this claim seriously, despite the fact that he withdraws it in *Archaeology of Knowledge*, with no indication that he was joking (16).

24. Derrida delivered "Cogito and the History of Madness" as a lecture in 1963, at which Foucault was present, and to which he did not seem at the time to take offense. Derrida published the paper a few months later and then again in book form in 1967, both times with no response from Foucault. Foucault's biographer, Eribon, from whom I take this account (*Michel Foucault*, 119–121), speculates that Foucault's belated response in 1972 may have had more to do with a collateral issue: "Both Foucault and Derrida were on the editorial board of the review *Critique*. An article by Gérard Granel arrived in the review's office, full of praise for Derrida's collection and equally full of venom toward Foucault, who took offense and asked Derrida to prevent the article's publication. Derrida refused to intervene. . . . And Foucault shortly afterward wrote an extremely violent response to Derrida's 1963 lecture" (121). I include this account as much for the gossipy pleasure it affords as for the skeptical light it sheds on the actual content of the Foucault-Derrida debate. It remains the case that, having withdrawn the claim to de-

lineate an experience of madness, Foucault could only have been complaining about Derrida's reading of Descartes and its status to his critique of that claim, a critique Foucault had silently granted.

25. In effect, Foucault certainly does articulate and attack the hyperbolic claim of reason to ground itself in a moment outside of the difference between reason and madness or even its opposite, unreason. In this sense, regardless of the reading of Descartes, when Derrida describes Descartes' claim as hyperbolic (*Writing and Difference*, 56), he describes rather than attacks Foucault's overall position. The difference between them may come down to the mode in which they want to capture and give limits to that hyperbolic claim. Derrida insists on staying within the limits of a formal analysis of philosophical texts, since he thinks that the hyperbole establishes itself there, and Foucault charges this method with being "a historically well-determined little pedagogy" (*Dits*, I, 1135). He wants to give a historical picture in which the claims of philosophy play a part. Derrida wants to claim that one can create this picture through a philosophical critique of philosophical hyperbole. Thus Foucault argues that Descartes represents an "event" that Derrida's analysis obscures (*Dits*, I, 1163). If one wants neither to create from Foucault an exit out of that pedagogy into the bright day of historical reality (a claim a full reading of Foucault would have to abandon), nor to argue that Derrida's deconstruction is the one privileged form for interrogating Enlightenment reason (surely a claim to privilege a Derridean would have to abandon fairly quickly), the disputes between Derrida's critique and Foucault's response, after thirty years, seem, as Foucault says about the differences between Ricardo and Marx, "no more than storms in a children's paddling pool" (*Order of Things*, 262). They merit the attention I give them here, though, because the desire to establish Foucault's important difference as a postmodernist is part of the elision of the aesthetic elements of his work and the mistaken antagonism of postmodernists to aesthetics.

26. One finds full accounts of the historical critiques of *Histoire* in Gordon, Megill, "The Reception of Foucault by Historians," and Gutting, "Foucault and the History of Madness." These three articles also represent the modes of recuperating the text, Megill arguing that Foucault's work isn't history at all, Gordon that one can see that it is good history when one recognizes its actual claims, and Gutting arguing that, whatever its historical flaws, it is a good "illumination" of the claims of modern psychiatry.

27. This opposition may appear to follow the one set up by Dreyfus and Rabinow in *Michel Foucault: Beyond Structuralism and Hermeneutics*. But they want ultimately to set up a mode of ontological explanation that escapes the problems of those two systems, whereas I will be describing here modes of accounting for the relationship between the facts or items one puts forth and the design one adduces.

28. He removed the word *structural* from later editions, which made numbers of other emendations. The English translation is of the first edition.

29. Foucault's statements, in *The Order of Things*, about the formations he de-

scribes sometimes do go much further than his redescription of them in *Archaeol-ogy of Knowledge* toward arguing for them as saturating their periods to the extent of calling into question whether any science generated within them could survive their passing. And Canguilhem, in a very positive review of the book, did criticize it on the grounds that it called into question the possibility of their being a norm that would ground scientific knowledge (84–85). Still, whether the positions in *Ar-chaeology* are taken as clarifications or revisions, they do not undercut any central claim in *Order of Things* and do make better sense of its positions. I do not, then, think that this is a matter of choosing one Foucault over another but of choosing the most comprehensive position.

30. I have emended the translation here. The English edition translates *par un pur anachronisme?* as "Why? Simply because I am interested in the past?" which seems somewhat figurative and obscures the meaning of the next sentence. The translation seems an example of not wanting to take Foucault at his word when he expresses a fairly relaxed view of the historicity of his arguments.

31. I have changed the translation of *résorbée* from "reabsorbed" to "absorbed." Both are possible translations of the French, but signification didn't exist in the Re-naissance and it couldn't have been "reabsorbed" without having been there in the first place.

32. Foucault ceases to mention the formations of similitude and representation much after *The Order of Things*. But one need only look at the way he talks about how the classical age taxonomized by confining the mad with the unemployed and the criminal in *Histoire de la folie* and the description of an eighteenth-century idea of punishment in which each punishment represented the crime it punished (*Discipline*, 104–114) to see that they silently structure his view of historical periods both before and after the book.

33. All of these histories also depict moments prior to the rise of new knowl-edges to show how one could live without them, without asylums, the idea of man, prisons. This has often led to a reaction that Foucault thought those earlier states were superior, even though he regularly denied that he wanted to depict in them anything other than an alternative. Because the last two volumes of the *His-tory of Sexuality*—*The Use of Pleasure* and *The Care of the Self*—never proceeded to the period at which a fall into confining knowledge is defined as a rise into freeing science, those books have seemed to mark a shift in Foucault's concerns. This shift has been defined as seeing a golden age in Greece and as Foucault's having a more positive sense of human freedom. The first claim, at least, is an error: he describes the Greek morality as tied to a virile society that oppressed women and was "not attractive" (*Dits*, II, 1431, 1433). And, on the whole, the last two books do not, it seems to me, mark a shift in his major themes or in his most basic historical method. They do lack the hard irony of the earlier works' view of the modern pe-riod, though his introduction to the second volume and the interviews surround-ing the works are amply provided with that.

34. Dreyfus and Rabinow argue that the archaeology was a methodological

failure (79–103) and that genealogy replaces it (104–122). Said is the only critic I have read who sees this period as a falling off from the more subtle archaeology ("Foucault and the Imagination of Power," 152–153), but then Said in *Beginnings* and *Orientalism* was the critic most influenced by Foucaultian archaeology and felt his influence before his move toward a more primary concern with power.

35. This would be true whether one follows the older reading of the will to power as a will to domination (though it creates problems with how to construe domination so that it does not raise elemental ethical problems), or one follows a reading such as Deleuze's, which sees the will to power as something like the power to be able to will (*Nietzsche and Philosophy*, 49–52).

36. Perhaps because the term *cryptonormativism* seems to recall the old charge of "cryptofascism," and because Habermas sometimes seems at least to imply that Foucault was in effect if not in intention a conservative (his description of Foucault's position in *The New Conservatism*, 176–177, effectively aligns Foucault with the neoconservatism he describes elsewhere in the book)—an almost willfully bad argument about his position—Foucault's defenders have too frequently argued essentially that even to answer this charge amounts to granting its premises (see, for instance, Dean, "Normalising Democracy," 168). Although I think Habermas wrong about Foucault because Foucault does not view power in the way I am describing here, he is not wrong about a theory of power that looks like this one and which is commonly ascribed to Foucault.

37. One can see an attempt to use the essay from which I am quoting to align Foucault with a more usual postmodern critique of liberalism in Dean (173–175). I think even the passage Dean quotes fairly clearly does not support the positions he extrapolates from it.

38. I think a distinction can be made, though. Although the final chapter of the book on "The Carceral" sees it as ultimately everywhere, it describes it in terms of institutions of confinement, particularly, in addition to prisons, reform schools, military barracks, hospitals, and so on. One might say that capture in the carceral archipelago (297) befalls those who do not sufficiently give themselves to discipline without the aid of those institutions.

39. I have changed the translation of *féerique* from "elfin-like" to "fairy-like." Foucault summarizes the plot of *Les Bijoux indiscrets* a couple of pages later, but *les sexes* is again translated as "the sexes," thus obscuring the comedy of a ring that makes the genitals one encounters speak (79).

40. I have changed the translation of *dispositif* from "deployment" to "apparatus," both because that is a more nearly literal rendering and because it more fits the image of the middle classes trying a contraption out on themselves.

41. Said ("Foucault and the Imagination of Power," 152) has quite sharply noted that "Foucault's imagination of power is largely *with* rather than *against* it." Because he identifies power with domination, he construes this as a weakness of the work after *Archaeology of Knowledge*. But Foucault identifies with power as that which gives the ability to change and transform. Oddly, without the ostensibly

anti-humanist power of *Discipline and Punish* and *History of Sexuality*, the interest
in an aesthetic sculpting of the self of his ostensibly more humanist period would
have been incoherent.

42. Foucault's famous late, positive essay on Kant's "What Is Enlightenment,"
actually withdraws nothing of his earlier attack on Kant's construction of an empirico-transcendental doublet. It lauds the act of a philosophical reflection on one's
own present that Foucault has always meant to construct with his histories (*Dits*,
II, 1382), while explicitly refusing what he calls the "blackmail" of the Enlightenment, the demand that one be for it or against it (*Dits*, II, 1390–1391). This double
attitude, I think, carries through virtually all of Foucault's work, which might be
more accurately taken as a projected alternative to Enlightenment liberalism than
a simple attack on it.

43. Kant did, of course, say numbers of interesting things about artworks, but,
again, he construed artworks as things intending to be beautiful, to embody purposiveness without purpose. They were therefore not the primary example of
beauty, and the things he said about them take as their starting point the way an
artwork might best fit the intentional concept that gives it form, which is appearing to be something that has purposiveness without purpose. He thus judged artworks according to their actual aims and intents.

44. The word I am translating as "produces" is *fabrique*. Although this word
does not mean "fabricate," it can mean "invent," and that meaning has to be kept
in mind given the context of fiction here.

45. These kinds of statements are not without problems, as witness the extended discussion in analytic philosophy of how it makes sense to say that the sentence "Sherlock Holmes lives at 221B Baker Street" is true. I do not know of an
analogous discussion of how it makes sense to say that a sentence in *War and Peace*
describing something Napoleon actually said or did is fictive, though the problem
seems to me of the same order. But the problems the statements raise do not make
them less accurate or make Foucault's claims problematic in themselves as opposed
to making problematic the status of the sentences that describe them.

46. The fact that artworks by Warhol and fiction by Borges are both designated, at times, as postmodern has no particular relevance for my argument here.
As I argued in the prior chapter, the status of such artworks is entirely explicable
with the resources of Enlightenment aesthetics. And their relation to mid-century
modernism in art and literature has no connection I can see to the postmodern
critique of Enlightenment philosophic and political foundationalism discussed
here.

47. Since this reading is an account and not a deconstruction, one would have
to call it what Derrida would label a "doubling commentary" of the kind with
which deconstruction could not be content (*Grammatology*, 158). But given what
the implications are of claiming that Foucault recognizes the need to pose his histories as aesthetic presentations, it would amount to a doubling commentary of
someone already in essential accord with the Derridean use of literary language to

question philosophic language, and through that, philosophic foundationalism. From this perspective, what Guillory calls the "spontaneous philosophy" of American literary studies, in which Derrida and Foucault hold a common position, may be as philosophical as it is spontaneous ("The Sokal Affair," 476).

1. To discuss this project, I will use most extensively Bourdieu's *The Logic of Practice*, a translation of *Le Sens pratique*, which came out in France in 1980. This book postdates much of Bourdieu's writing on culture and aesthetics but also returns to some of his earliest anthropological studies. To make chronological matters more complex, it is also explicitly a revision of the theories worked out in *Outline of a Theory of Practice*, which revises as much as it translates the original French version, *Esquisse d'une théorie de la pratique*, which came out in France in 1972, well before much of the writing on culture and aesthetics.

2. This book translates most of *Ce que parler veut dire*, published in France in 1982. But it adds articles published as recently as 1984 and includes articles from the original book that were first published as far back as 1975. Because Bourdieu not only revises books for translation, but fairly constantly revisits old books and articles in more recent books offering newer theoretical articulations, proposing chronological distinctions in his writing is always a fairly arbitrary task. Whether all his topics are as related to each other as he claims, he has effectively made them so in his work by his methods of revision, reinclusion, and cross-referencing.

3. I have elided Bourdieu's early and late versions of his critique here, as well as simplified it. For a more extensive account as well as an explanation of the evolution from *Outline of a Theory of Practice* to *The Logic of Practice*, see Robbins, *Work of Pierre Bourdieu*, chapters 5 and 9.

4. To take a parallel from an entirely different field of criticism, for instance, Louis Renza has argued that autobiographies must be fictive, cannot even accurately assert a connection between the writing self and the self being written about, because the text written cannot communicate the most vital aspect of the events described, their pastness, their having been experienced by a past self ("The Veto of Autobiography," 280). One can easily imagine further extensions of such a critique of a text's or description's inability to carry the experience of subjectivity within it.

5. Despite my preference for the term *indifference* as more nearly expressing what Kant had in mind, in this chapter, I will follow Bourdieu and Derrida in using the term *disinterest*, since it more clearly corresponds to what they object to in the concept. In the second section of this chapter, the differences between those two meanings will become significant.

6. In a review article on *Distinction*, Elizabeth Wilson centralizes that concept in her opening sentence: "In *Distinction: A Social Critique of the Judgement of Taste*, Pierre Bourdieu elaborates a model of symbolic power describing the role of culture in the reproduction of social relations in contemporary France" ("Picasso and

Paté de Foie Gras," 47). This description of the book, while certainly not inaccurate, focuses on the social functioning of cultural capital rather than on Bourdieu's attempt to redescribe what aesthetics and taste are and how we can see that. Wilson's description thus indicates the primary interest of the book for the literary theoretical discussion that will follow.

7. The problem here entails taking an aesthetic apprehension as a complete description of an object: it mistakes the articulation of a purposiveness with the finding of an intended purpose. Foucault, better aesthetic theorist that he is, avoids this problem by refusing to take either his discursive formations or his idea of power as more than structures of organization. This has meant that he has been attacked far more than Bourdieu for denying agency or for holding norms while denying the possibility of norms, but that is another issue.

8. Critics who want to give Bourdieu a political power of resistance to the domination of the bourgeoisie through the unmasking of their aesthetic pretensions have particular problems with this aspect of the book. Toril Moi quotes a particularly sniffy attack on the egregiously sniffy *Nouvel Observateur* ("Appropriating Bourdieu," 1026) as an example of Bourdieu's political critique, justifying the obvious self-contradiction of the moment, unpersuasively, by arguing that Bourdieu's lack of power with regard to the *Nouvel Observateur* removes the contradiction (1045). It of course does not, if one wants to take as seriously comprehensive Bourdieu's analysis of elitist aesthetic rhetoric. Thus, in reverse, Elizabeth Wilson concludes that Bourdieu's theories lack the ability to effect political intervention precisely because they don't offer modes of judging that are free from his critique of culture and aesthetics (58–60).

9. The emphasis here is on the word *straightforward*. One feels an obvious political significance to Bourdieu's project. Bourdieu, however, quite pointedly resists drawing direct political implications. In an interview, his translator Richard Nice has said that "he situates himself outside conventional politics" and that "he's not very political in everyday life" (Mahar, "Pierre Bourdieu," 53). This reticence, not just in "everyday life" (what would Bourdieu make of that category?), no doubt leads to the frustration of some of his critics discussed in calibrating the critique in *Distinction*.

10. Bourdieu offers an essentially similar position in the more abstractly posed article "The Historical Genesis of a Pure Aesthetic," 208.

11. Given its concern with the inability of philosophy to define metaphor without recourse to metaphor and its concern with the exchanges between metaphoric transfer and economic exchange, Derrida's "White Mythology" (*Margins*, 207–271) becomes an inescapable, if by this time somewhat stereotypical, reference.

12. We have seen Bourdieu connect philosophic and academic discourse as politically motivated in his discussion of Heidegger in *Language and Symbolic Power*, 157–158.

13. One would think that Bourdieu would have as little sympathy for Stanley

Fish's attacks on objective aesthetic values in *Is There a Text in This Class?* or Barbara Hernnstein Smith's defense in *Contingencies of Value* of an aesthetics that accommodates relative value and interested gratification, as he does for Derrida's deconstructions of Kant. In fact, Bourdieu has written a complimentary sentence printed on the back of Smith's book. But then so has Richard Rorty, and one assumes he does not agree with Smith's criticisms of him. Smith discusses Kant's theory from the viewpoint of an abstract relativism (64–72). She also has a brief discussion of *Distinction* that proposes it as offering evidence for her position. In effect this coincidence will only be as good as the coincidence I will work out in the case of Derrida, since her argument would certainly run afoul of his skeptical analysis of traditional academic discourse.

14. Thus Eve Shaper introduces Kant's project in this way: "In much eighteenth-century usage, to be a person of taste was to be a person of independent judgment based on individual conviction, not on slavishly following rules. Kant is aware of this usage, and it is part of the aim of his analysis to secure a grounding of the judgment of taste in something that, as the personal, namely individual feeling, can carry the weight of an implied claim to autonomy" ("Taste, Sublimity, and Genius," 372). One may doubt whether eighteenth-century attitudes toward taste generally contrasted individual judgment with following rules, since most writers on aesthetics preceding Kant, like him, tried to articulate universal principles of taste. Still the contrast between the slavishness of those without taste and the autonomy of those with it marks at least a contemporary attitude toward Kant's theory.

15. Bourdieu connects Kant with "'high' aesthetics" and "legitimate aesthetics" (*Distinction*, 485), while Derrida identifies the elements he discusses in Kant as those that have dominated the philosophy of art since Kant (*Truth in Painting*, 73).

16. Although "Parergon" is rarely as explicit in its political themes and therefore more open to Bourdieu's criticism, a more sympathetic reading might note that Derrida at least thinks that it too has more than formal significance: "It is because deconstruction interferes with solid structures, 'material' institutions, and not only with discourses or signifying representations, that it is always distinct from an analysis or a 'critique'" (*Truth in Painting*, 19).

17. Derrida has stated this many times, but the best statement of his procedure and its relation to traditional reading remains "The Exorbitant. Question of Method," *Of Grammatology*, 157–164.

Bibliography

Abrams, M. H. *The Mirror and the Lamp: Romantic Theory and the Critical Tradition.* New York: Oxford University Press, 1953.

Appleyard, J. A. *Coleridge's Philosophy of Literature.* Cambridge, MA: Harvard University Press, 1965.

Arac, Jonathan, ed. *After Foucault: Humanistic Knowledge, Postmodern Challenges.* New Brunswick, NJ: Rutgers University Press, 1988.

Armstrong, Isobel. *The Radical Aesthetic.* Oxford: Basil Blackwell, 2000.

Balfour, Ian. *The Rhetoric of Romantic Prophecy.* Stanford, CA: Stanford University Press, 2002.

Baumgarten, Alexander. *Reflections on Poetry.* Tr. Karl Aschenbrenner and William B. Holther. Berkeley: University of California Press, 1954.

Beardsley, Monroe C. *Aesthetics from Classical Greece to the Present.* University: University of Alabama Press, 1966.

———. *Aesthetics: Problems in the Theory of Criticism.* New York: Harcourt, Brace, 1958.

Bernauer, James. "Beyond Life and Death: On Foucault's Post-Auschwitz Ethic." *Michel Foucault: Philosopher.* Ed. and tr. Timothy J. Armstrong. NY: Routledge, 1992. 260–279.

———. "Michel Foucault's Ecstatic Thinking." *The Final Foucault.* Ed. James Bernauer and David Rasmussen. Cambridge, MA: MIT Press, 1988. 45–82.

Bond, Donald, F., ed. *The Spectator.* 5 vols. Oxford: Oxford University Press, 1965.

Bosanquet, Bernard. *A History of Aesthetic.* London: Allen and Unwin, 1966. First published, 1892.

Bourdieu, Pierre. *Distinction: A Social Critique of the Judgment of Taste.* Tr. Richard Nice. Cambridge, MA: Harvard University Press, 1984.

———. "Flaubert's Point of View." *Critical Inquiry* 14 (1988): 539–562.

———. "The Historical Genesis of a Pure Aesthetic." *Journal of Aesthetics and Art Criticism* 46 (1987): 201–210.

———. *Language and Symbolic Power.* Tr. Gino Raymond and Matthew Adamson. Ed. John B. Thompson. Cambridge, MA: Harvard University Press, 1991.

———. *The Logic of Practice.* Tr. Richard Nice. Stanford, CA: Stanford University Press, 1990.

———. *Outline of a Theory of Practice.* Tr. Richard Nice. New York: Cambridge University Press, 1977.

Bourdieu, Pierre, and Jean-Claude Passeron. *The Inheritors: French Students and Their Relation to Culture.* Tr. Richard Nice. Chicago: University of Chicago Press, 1979.

Bowie, Andrew. *Aesthetics and Subjectivity: From Kant to Nietzsche.* New York: St. Martin's Press, 1990.

Brooks, Cleanth. "Implications of an Organic Theory of Poetry." *Literature and Belief.* Ed. M. H. Abrams. New York: Columbia University Press, 1958. 53–79.

———. *The Well Wrought Urn.* New York: Harcourt, Brace, 1947.

Brown, Marshall. *The Shape of German Romanticism.* Ithaca, NY: Cornell University Press, 1979.

Bürger, Peter. *The Theory of the Avant-Garde.* Tr. Michael Shaw. Minneapolis: University of Minnesota Press, 1984.

Burke, Edmund. *A Philosophical Enquiry into the Origin of Our Ideas of the Sublime and Beautiful.* Ed. J. T. Boulton. Notre Dame: University of Notre Dame Press, 1968.

Buskirk, Martha, and Mignon Nixon. *The Duchamp Effect.* Cambridge, MA: MIT Press, 1996.

Butler, Joseph. *The Analogy of Religion, Natural and Revealed, to the Constitution and Course of Nature.* Cincinnati: L. Swormstedt and J. H. Power, 1848.

Camfield, William. "Marcel Duchamp's *Fountain*: Aesthetic Object, Icon, or Anti-Art?" *The Definitively Unfinished Marcel Duchamp.* Ed. Thierry de Duve. Cambridge, MA: MIT Press, 1991. 133–178.

———. "Marcel Duchamp's *Fountain*: Its history and Aesthetics in the Context of 1917." *Marcel Duchamp: Artist of the Century.* Ed. Rudolf Kuenzli and Francis M. Naumann. Cambridge, MA: MIT Press, 1989. 64–94.

Canguilhem, Georges. "The Death of Man, or Exhaustion of the Cogito." Tr. Catherine Porter. *The Cambridge Companion to Foucault.* Ed. Gary Gutting. Cambridge: Cambridge University Press. 71–91.

Cassirer, Ernst. *The Platonic Renaissance in England.* Tr. James P. Pettegrove. New York: Gordian Press, 1970. Originally published 1953, by University of Texas Press.

Cavell, Stanley. *Must We Mean What We Say?* Cambridge: Cambridge University Press, 1969.

Caygill, Howard. *The Art of Judgment*. New York: Blackwell, 1989.

Chase, Cynthia. *Decomposing Figures: Rhetorical Readings in the Romantic Tradition*. Baltimore: Johns Hopkins University Press, 1986.

———. "Trappings of an Education." *Responses: On Paul de Man's Wartime Journalism*. Eds. Werner Hamacher, Neil Hertz, and Thomas Keenan. Lincoln: University of Nebraska Press, 1989. 44–79.

Crawford, Donald W. *Kant's Aesthetic Theory*. Madison, WI: University of Wisconsin Press, 1974.

Christensen, Jerome. *Coleridge's Blessed Machine of Language*. Ithaca, NY: Cornell University Press, 1981.

Chytry, Josef. *The Aesthetic State: A Quest in Modern German Thought*. Berkeley: University of California Press, 1989.

Clarke, Samuel. *A Discourse Concerning the Being and Attributes of God*. 9th ed. London: 1738.

Codd, John. "Making Distinctions: The Eye of the Beholder." *An Introduction to the Work of Pierre Bourdieu: The Practice of Theory*. Eds. Richard Harker, Cheleen Mahar, and Chris Wilkes. New York: St. Martin's Press, 1990. 132–159.

Cohen, Ted. "The Possibility of Art: Remarks on a Proposal by Dickie." *Philosophical Review*. 82 (January, 1973): 69–82.

Cohen, Tom, Barbara Cohen, J. Hillis Miller, and Andrzej Warminski, eds. *Material Events: Paul de Man and the Afterlife of Theory*. Minneapolis: University of Minnesota Press, 2001.

Coleridge, Samuel Taylor. *Biographia Literaria*. 2 vols. Ed. James Engell and W. Jackson Bate. Princeton, NJ: Princeton University Press, 1983.

———. *Lay Sermons*. Ed. R. J. White. Princeton, NJ: Princeton University Press, 1972.

———. *Lectures, 1808–1819, On Literature*. Ed. R. A. Foakes. Princeton, NJ: Princeton University Press, 1987.

Croce, Benedetto. *Aesthetic as Science of Expression and General Linguistic*. Tr. Douglas Ainslie. New York: Farrar, Straus, and Giroux, 1970. First published in 1901.

Crowther, Paul. *Art and Embodiment: From Aesthetics to Self-consciousness*. New York: Oxford University Press, 1993.

Cudworth, Ralph. *The True Intellectual System of the Universe*. Stuttgart: Friedrich Frommann Verlag, 1964. Reprint of original edition of 1678.

Danto, Arthur, C. *After the End of Art: Contemporary Art and the Pale of History*. Princeton, NJ: Princeton University Press, 1997.

———. "The Artworld." *Journal of Philosophy* 61 (1964): 571–584.

———. *The Philosophical Disenfranchisement of Art*. New York: Columbia University Press, 1986.

———. *The Transfiguration of the Commonplace: A Philosophy of Art*. Cambridge, MA: Harvard University Press, 1981.

Darwin, Charles. *On the Origin of Species: A Facsimile of the First Edition*. Cambridge: Harvard University Press, 1964.

Davies, Stephen. *Definitions of Art*. Ithaca, NY: Cornell University Press, 1991.

Dean, Mitchell. "Normalising Democracy: Foucault and Habermas on Democracy, Liberalism, and Law." *Foucault Contra Habermas: Recasting the Dialogue Between Genealogy and Critical Theory*. Ed. Samatha Ashenden and David Owen. London: Sage Publications, 1999. 166–194.

de Bolla, Peter. *Art Matters*. Cambridge, MA: Harvard University Press, 2001.

Deleuze, Gilles. *Kant's Critical Philosophy: The Doctrine of the Faculties*. Tr. Hugh Tomlinson and Barbara Habberjam. London: Athlone Press, 1984.

———. *Foucault*. Tr. and ed. Sean Hand. Minneapolis: University of Minnesota Press, 1988.

———. *Nietzsche and Philosophy*. Tr. Hugh Tomlinson. NY: Columbia University Press, 1983.

———. "What is a *Dispositif*." *Michel Foucault: Philosopher*. Ed. and tr. Timothy J. Armstrong. New York: Routledge, 1992. 159–168.

de Man, Paul. *Aesthetic Ideology*. Minneapolis: University of Minnesota Press, 1996.

———. *Blindness and Insight: Essays in the Rhetoric of Contemporary Criticism*. 2nd rev. ed. Minneapolis: University of Minnesota Press, 1983.

Derrida, Jacques. *Dissemination*. Tr. Barbara Johnson. Chicago: University of Chicago Press, 1981.

———. "Economimesis." Tr. Richard Klein. *Diacritics* 11 (1981): 3–25.

———. *Margins of Philosophy*. Tr. Alan Bass. Chicago: University of Chicago Press, 1982.

———. *Of Grammatology*. Tr. Gayatri Chakravorty Spivak. Baltimore: Johns Hopkins University Press, 1976.

———. *Positions*. Tr. Alan Bass. Chicago: University of Chicago Press, 1981.

———. *The Truth in Painting*. Tr. Geoff Bennington and Ian McLeod. Chicago: University of Chicago Press, 1987.

———. *Writing and Difference*. Tr. Alan Bass. Chicago: University of Chicago Press, 1978.

Dickie, George. *Art and the Aesthetic: An Institutional Analysis*. Ithaca, NY: Cornell University Press, 1974.

Dowling, Linda. *The Vulgarization of Art: The Victorians and Aesthetic Democracy*. Charlottesville: University of Virginia Press, 1996.

Dreyfus, Hubert, and Paul Rabinow. *Michel Foucault: Beyond Structuralism and Hermeneutics.* Chicago: University of Chicago Press, 1982.

Duve, Thierry de. *Kant After Duchamp.* Cambridge, MA: MIT Press, 1998.

Eagleton, Terry. *The Ideology of the Aesthetic.* London: Basil Blackwell, 1990.

Eribon, Didier. *Michel Foucault.* Tr. Betsy Wing. Cambridge, MA: Harvard University Press, 1991.

Ferguson, Frances. *Solitude and the Sublime: Romanticism and the Aesthetics of Individuation.* New York and London: Routledge, 1992.

Ferris, David. *Theory and the Evasion of History.* Baltimore: Johns Hopkins University Press, 1993.

Ferry, Luc. *Homo-Aestheticus: The Invention of Taste and the Democratic Age.* Tr. Robert Loaiza. Chicago: University of Chicago Press, 1993.

Fish, Stanley. *Is There a Text in This Class?* Baltimore: Johns Hopkins University Press, 1980.

Fogle, Richard Harter. *The Idea of Coleridge's Criticism.* Berkeley: University of California Press, 1962.

Foucault, Michel. *The Archaeology of Knowledge and The Discourse on Language.* Tr. A. M. Sheridan Smith. New York: Random House, 1972.

———. *The Birth of the Clinic.* Tr. A. M. Sheridan Smith. NY: Random House, 1973.

———. *The Care of the Self: Volume 3 of the History of Sexuality.* Tr. Robert Hurly. New York: Pantheon Books, 1986.

———. *Discipline and Punish: The Birth of the Prison.* Tr. Alan Sheridan. New York: Random House, 1977.

———. *Dits et ecrits.* 2 vols. Paris: Gallimard, 2001.

———. *Histoire de la folie à l'âge Classique.* Paris: Gallimard, 1972.

———. *History of Sexuality: An Introduction.* Tr. Robert Hurley. New York: Random House, 1978.

———. *The Order of Things: An Archaeology of the Human Sciences.* No tr. New York: Random House, 1970.

———. *The Use of Pleasure: Volume 2 of the History of Sexuality.* Tr. Robert Hurley. New York: Pantheon Books, 1985.

Fraser, Nancy. *Unruly Practices: Power, Discourse, and Gender in Contemporary Social Theory.* Minneapolis: University of Minnesota Press, 1989.

Fruman, Norman. *Coleridge, the Damaged Archangel.* New York: George Braziller, 1971.

Gasché, Rodolphe. *The Idea of Form: Rethinking Kant's Aesthetics.* Stanford, CA: Stanford University Press, 2003.

Geuss, Raymond. "A Response to Paul de Man." *Critical Inquiry* 10 (1983): 375–381.

Giddens, Anthony. "The Politics of Taste." *Partisan Review* 53 (1986): 300–305.

Gilbert, Katherine Everett, and Helmut Kuhn. *A History of Esthetics: Revised and Enlarged.* Bloomington: Indiana University Press, 1954.

Gordon, Colin. "*Histoire de la folie*: An Unknown Book by Michel Foucault." *History of the Human Sciences* 3 (1990): 3–26.

Gosse, Edmund. *Father and Son: A Study of Two Temperaments.* New York: Norton, 1963.

Greenberg, Clement. *The Collected Essays and Criticism.* 4 vols. Ed. John H. O'Brian. Chicago: University of Chicago Press, 1986–1993.

———. *Homemade Esthetics: Observations on Art and Taste.* New York: Oxford University Press, 1999.

Guillory, John. *Cultural Capital: The Problem of Literary Canon Formation.* Chicago: University of Chicago Press, 1993.

———. "The Sokal Affair and the History of Criticism." *Critical Inquiry* 28 (Winter 2002): 476.

Gutting, Gary. "Foucault and the History of Madness." *The Cambridge Companion to Foucault.* Ed. Gary Gutting. Cambridge: Cambridge University Press, 1994. 47–70.

———. *Michel Foucault's Archaeology of Scientific Reason.* Cambridge: Cambridge University Press, 1989.

Guyer, Paul. *Kant and the Claims of Taste.* Cambridge, MA: Harvard University Press, 1979.

———. *Kant and the Experience of Freedom: Essays on Aesthetics and Morality.* Cambridge: Cambridge University Press, 1996.

———. "Interest, Nature, and Art: A Problem in Kant's Aesthetics." *Journal of Aesthetics and Art Criticism* 36 (1978): 449–460.

Habermas, Jürgen. *The New Conservatism: Cultural Criticism and the Historian's Debate.* Ed. and tr. Shierry Weber Nicholssen. Cambridge, MA: MIT Press, 1989.

———. *The Philosophical Discourse of Modernity: Twelve Lectures.* Tr. Frederick Lawrence. Cambridge, MA: MIT Press, 1987.

Hadot, Pierre. "Reflections on the Notion of 'the Cultivation of the Self.'" *Michel Foucault: Philosopher.* Ed. and tr. Timothy J. Armstrong. New York: Routledge, 1992. 225–232.

Hegel, G. F. W. *Aesthetics: Lectures on Fine Art.* Tr. T. M. Knox. 2 Vols. Oxford: Oxford University Press, 1975.

Heidegger, Martin. *Nietzsche.* Vols. 1 and 2. Tr. David Krell. New York: HarperCollins, 1991.

———. *Poetry, Language, Thought.* Tr. Alfred Hofstadter. New York: Harper & Row, 1975.

Henrich, Dieter. *Aesthetic Judgment and the Moral Image of the World: Studies in Kant.* Stanford, CA: Stanford University Press, 1992.

Hume, David. *Dialogues Concerning Natural Religion.* Ed. Norman Kemp Smith. Indiana: Bobbs-Merrill, 1947.

――――. *Of the Standard of Taste and Other Essays.* Ed. John W. Lenz. Indiana: Bobbs-Merrill, 1965.

Hutcheson, Francis. *An Inquiry Concerning Beauty, Order, Harmony, Design.* Ed. Peter Kivy. The Hague: Martinus Nijhoff, 1973.

Huxley, T. H. *Darwinia: Essays.* Vol. 2. New York: Appleton, 1892.

Jameson, Fredric. *The Political Unconscious.* Ithaca, NY: Cornell University Press, 1981.

Johnson, Samuel. *Rasselas: Poems and Selected Prose.* 3rd ed. Ed. Bertrand H. Bronson. San Francisco: Rinehart Press, 1971.

Kames, Henry Home, Lord. *Elements of Criticism.* New York: Huntington and Savage, 1845.

Kant, Immanuel. *Critique of Pure Reason.* Tr. Norman Kemp Smith. New York: St. Martin's Press, 1965.

――――. *Critique of Judgment.* Tr. J. H. Bernard. New York: Hafner, 1951.

Kemal, Salim. *Kant's Aesthetic Theory: An Introduction.* New York: St. Martin's Press, 1992.

Klein, Lawrence. *Shaftesbury and the Culture of Politeness: Moral Discourse and Cultural Politics in Early Eighteenth-Century England.* Cambridge: Cambridge University Press, 1994.

Krieger, Murray. *A Reopening of Closure: Organicism Against Itself.* New York: Columbia University Press, 1989.

Kroeber, Karl, and Gene Ruoff, eds. *Romantic Poetry: Recent Revisionary Criticism.* New Brunswick, NJ: Rutgers University Press, 1993.

Lacoue-Labarthe, Phillipe, and Jean-Luc Nancy. *The Literary Absolute: The Theory of Literature in German Romanticism.* Tr. Philip Barnard and Cheryl Lester. Albany: SUNY Press, 1988.

Lentriccia, Frank. *After the New Criticism.* Chicago: Chicago University Press, 1980.

Levine, George, ed. *Aesthetics and Ideology.* New Brunswick, NJ: Rutgers University Press, 1994.

Loesberg, Jonathan. *Aestheticsim and Deconstruction: Pater, Derrida, and de Man.* Princeton, NJ: Princeton University Press, 1991.

――――. "Materialism and Aesthetics: Paul de Man's *Aesthetic Ideology*," *Diacritics* 27 (Winter 1998): 87–108.

McFarland, Thomas. *Coleridge and the Pantheist Tradition.* Oxford: Oxford University Press, 1969.

Mahar, Cheleen. "Pierre Bourdieu: The Intellectual Project." *An Introduction to the Work of Pierre Bourdieu: The Practice of Theory.* Ed. Richard Harker,

Cheleen Mahar, and Chris Wilkes. New York: St. Martin's Press, 1990. 26–57.

Mahar, Cheleen, Richard Harker, and Chris Wilkes. "The Basic Theoretical Position." *An Introduction to the Work of Pierre Bourdieu: The Practice of Theory.* Ed. Richard Harker, Cheleen Mahar, and Chris Wilkes. New York: St. Martin's Press, 1990. 1–25.

Makreel, Rudolf A. *Imagination and Interpretation in Kant.* Chicago: University of Chicago Press, 1990.

Markeley, Robert. "Sentimentality as Performance: Shaftesbury, Sterne, and the Theatrics of Virtue." *The New Eighteenth Century.* Ed. Felicity Nussbaum and Laura Brown. New York: Methuen, 1987. 210–230.

———. "Style as Philosophic Structure: The Contexts of Shaftesbury's *Characteristics.*" *The Philosopher as Writer: The Eighteenth Century.* Ed. Robert Ginsberg. Selinsgrove: Susquehanna University Press, 1987. 140–154.

Martin, Nicholas. *Nietzsche and Schiller: Untimely Aesthetics.* New York: Oxford University Press, 1996.

Meerbote, Ralf. "Reflections of Beauty." *Essays in Kant's Aesthetics.* Ed. Ted Cohen and Paul Guyer. Chicago: University of Chicago Press, 1982. 55–86.

Megill, Allan. *Prophets of Extremity: Nietzsche, Heidegger, Foucault, Derrida.* Berkeley: University of California Press, 1985.

———. "The Reception of Foucault by Historians." *Journal of the History of Ideas* 48 (1987): 117–141.

Mill, John Stuart. *Essays on Ethics, Religion, and Society.* Vol. 10 of *Collected Works of John Stuart Mill.* Ed. J. M. Robson. Toronto: University of Toronto Press, 1969.

Miller, J. Hillis. "Deconstructing the Deconstructors." *Diacritics* 5 (Summer 1975): 24–31.

Modiano, Raimondo. *Coleridge and the Concept of Nature.* London: Macmillan Press, 1985.

Moi, Toril. "Appropriating Bourdieu." *New Literary History* 22 (1991): 1017–1049.

Nehamas, Alexander. *The Art of Living: Socratic Reflections from Plato to Foucault.* Berkeley: University of California Press, 1998.

———. *Nietzsche: Life as Literature.* Cambridge, MA: Harvard University Press, 1985.

Nietzsche, Friedrich. *The Birth of Tragedy and The Case of Wagner.* Tr. Walter Kaufmann. New York: Random House, 1967.

———. *The Gay Science With a Prelude in Rhymes and an Appendix of Songs.* Tr. Walter Kaufmann. New York: Random House, 1974.

———. *On the Genealogy of Morals and Ecce Homo.* Tr. Walter Kaufman and R. J. Hollingdale. New York: Vintage Books, 1967.

———. *The Will to Power.* Tr. Walter Kaufmann and R. J. Hollingdale. New York: Random House, 1967.

Norris, Christopher. "What Is Enlightenment": Kant and Foucault." *The Cambridge Companion to Foucault.* Ed. Gary Gutting. Cambridge: Cambridge University Press, 1994. 159–196.

Orsini, G. N. G. *Coleridge and German Idealism.* Carbondale: Southern Illinois University Press, 1969.

———. "Coleridge and Schlegel Reconsidered." *Comparative Literature* 16 (1964): 99–118.

Osborne, Thomas. "Critical Spirituality: On Ethics and Politics in the Later Foucault." *Foucault Contra Habermas: Recasting the Dialogue Between Genealogy and Critical Theory.* Ed. Samantha Ashenden and David Owen. London: Sage Publications, 1999. 45–59.

Paley, William. *Natural Theology; or, Evidences of the Existence and Attributes of the Deity Collected from the Appearances of Nature.* Boston: Gould Kendall and Lincoln, 1850.

Paulson, Ronald. *The Beautiful, Novel and Strange.* Baltimore: Johns Hopkins University Press, 1996.

Plato. *The Collected Dialogues.* Ed. Edith Hamilton and Huntington Cairns. Princeton, NJ: Princeton University Press, 1961.

Pluhar, Werner S., tr. *Critique of Judgment,* by Immanuel Kant. Indianopolis: Hackett, 1987.

Poovey, Mary. "Aesthetics and Political Economy in the Eighteenth Century: The Place of Gender in the Social Constitution of Knowledge." *Aesthetics and Ideology.* Ed. George Levine. New Brunswick, NJ: Rutgers University Press, 1994. 79–105.

Poster, Mark. "Foucault and the Tyranny of Greece." *Foucault: A Critical Reader.* Ed. David Couzens Hoy. New York: Basil Blackwell, 1986. 205–220.

Ray, John. *The Wisdom of God Manifested in the Works of Creation.* 3rd ed. London: Smith and Walford, 1701.

Redfield, Marc. "De Man, Schiller, and the Politics of Reception." *Diacritics* 20 (1990): 50–70.

———. "Humanizing de Man." *Diacritics* 19 (1989): 35–53.

———. *Phantom Formations: Aesthetic Ideology and the Bildungsroman.* Ithaca, NY: Cornell University Press, 1996.

———. *The Politics of Aesthetics: Nationalism, Gender, Romanticism.* Stanford, CA: Stanford University Press, 2003.

Renza, Louis. "The Veto of Autobiography." *Autobiography: Essays Theoretical and Critical.* Ed. James Olney. Princeton, NJ: Princeton University Press, 1980.

Richards, I. A. *Principles of Literary Criticism.* New York: Harcourt, Brace, 1925.

Richardson, Samuel. *Clarissa.* Everyman ed. 4 vols. London: Dent, 1968.

Richter, Hans. *Dada: Art and Anti-Art.* New York: McGraw Hill, 1965.

Robbins, Derek. *The Work of Pierre Bourdieu.* Boulder, CO: Westview Press, 1991.

Rochlitz, Rainier. "The Aesthetics of Existence: Post-Conventional Morality and the Theory of Power in Michel Foucault." *Michel Foucault: Philosopher.* Ed. and tr. Timothy J. Armstrong. New York: Routledge, 1992. 248–259.

Rorty, Richard. "Foucault and Epistemology." *Foucault: A Critical Reader.* Ed. David Couzens Hoy. New York: Basil Blackwell, 1986. 41–50.

Ruskin, John. *Works.* 39 vols. Ed. E. T. Cook and Alexander Wedderburn. London: George Allen, 1903–1912.

Rymer, Thomas. *The Critical Works of Thomas Rymer.* Ed. Curt A. Zimansky. New Haven, CT: Yale University Press, 1956.

Said, Edward. *Beginnings: Intention and Method.* New York: Basic Books, 1975.

———. "Foucault and the Imagination of Power." *Foucault: A Critical Reader.* Ed. David Couzens Hoy. New York: Basil Blackwell, 1986. 149–156.

———. "Michel Foucault, 1926–1984." *After Foucault: Humanistic Knowledge, Postmodern Challenges.* Ed. Jonathan Arac. New Brunswick, NJ: Rutgers University Press, 1988. 1–11.

———. *Orientalism.* New York: Vintage Books, 1978.

Sallis, John. *Spacings—of Reason and Imagination in Texts of Kant, Fichte, Hegel.* Chicago: University of Chicago Press, 1987.

Scarry, Elaine. *On Beauty and Being Just.* Princeton, NJ: Princeton University Press, 1999.

Schaeffer, Jean-Marie. *Art in the Modern Age: Philosophy of Art from Kant to Heidegger.* Tr. Steven Rendall. Princeton, NJ: Princeton University Press, 2000.

Schelling, F. W. J. *The Philosophy of Art.* Ed. Douglass W. Stott. Minneapolis: University of Minnesota Press, 1989.

———. *System of Transcendental Idealism (1800).* Tr. Peter Heath. Charlottesville: University Press of Virginia, 1978.

Schiller, Friedrich. *Naive and Sentimental Poetry and On the Sublime.* Tr. Julias A. Elias. New York: Frederick Ungar, 1966.

Schlegel, Augustus William. *Course of Lectures on Dramatic Art and Literature.* Tr. John Black. New York: AMS Press, 1965. Reprints London ed.: Henry G. Bohn, 1846.

Schopenhauer, Arthur. *The World as Will and Representation.* 2 vols. Tr. E. F. J. Payne. New York: Dover, 1966.

Shaftesbury, Third Earl of, Anthony Ashley Cooper. *Characteristics of Men, Manners, Opinions, Times.* London: 1732. Fifth ed.

Shaper, Eva. "Taste, Sublimity, and Genius: The Aesthetics of Nature and Art."

The Cambridge Companion to Kant. Ed. Paul Guyer. Cambridge: Cambridge University Press, 1992. 367–393.

Smith, Barbara Hernnstein. *Contingencies of Value.* Cambridge, MA: Harvard University Press, 1988.

Sobol, Jerry E. "Arguing, Accepting, and Preserving Design in Heidegger, Hume, and Kant." *Essays in Kant's Aesthetics.* Ed. Ted Cohen and Paul Guyer. Chicago: University of Chicago Press, 1982. 271–305.

Solomon, Robert. "Nietzsche Ad Hominem: Perspectivism, Personality, and *Ressentiment.*" *Cambridge Companion to Nietzsche.* Eds. Bernd Magnuson and Kathleen M. Higgins. New York: Cambridge University Press, 1996. 180–222.

Sontag, Susan. *Against Interpretation and Other Essays.* New York: Farrar, Straus, and Giroux, 1966.

Stadler, Ingrid. "The Idea of Art and of Its Criticism: A Rational Reconstruction of a Kantian Doctrine." *Essays in Kant's Aesthetics.* Ed. Ted Cohen and Paul Guyer. Chicago: University of Chicago Press, 1982. 195–218.

Steiner, Wendy. *The Scandal of Pleasure: Art in the Age of Fundamentalism.* Chicago: University of Chicago Press, 1995.

Stolnitz, Jerome. "On the Origin of 'Aesthetic Distinterestedness.' *Journal of Aesthetics and Art Criticism* 20 (1961): 131–143.

Strong, Tracy B. "Nietzsche's Political Misappropriation." *Cambridge Companion to Nietzsche.* Eds. Bernd Magnuson and Kathleen M. Higgins. New York: Cambridge University Press, 1996. 119–150.

Taylor, Charles. "Foucault on Freedom and Truth." *Foucault: A Critical Reader.* Ed. David Couzens Hoy. New York: Basil Blackwell, 1986. 69–102.

Weber, Samuel. *Mass Mediauras: Form, Technics, Media.* Stanford, CA: Stanford University Press, 1996.

Wellek, Rene. *Immanuel Kant in England.* Princeton, NJ: Princeton University Press, 1931.

Williams, Raymond. *Culture and Society.* New York: Harper and Row, 1966.

Wilson, Elizabeth. "Picasso and Paté de Foie Gras: Pierre Bourdieu's Sociology of Culture." *Diacritics* 18 (1988): 47–60.

Wimsatt, W. K. *The Verbal Icon: Studies in the Meaning of Poetry.* Lexington: University Press of Kentucky, 1954.

Winckelmann, J. J. *Reflections on the Poetry and Sculpture of the Greeks, with Intructions for the Connoisseur and an Essay on Grace in Works of Art.* Tr. Henry Fusseli. London, 1765.

Wolin, Sheldon. "Foucault's Aesthetic Decisionism." *Telos* 67 (Spring 1986): 71–86.

Woodmansee, Martha. *The Author, Art, and the Market: Rereading the History of Aesthetics.* New York: Columbia University Press, 1994.

Index